# Jurisprudence

IN AN

## AFRICAN
## CONTEXT

# Jurisprudence

IN AN
## AFRICAN
## CONTEXT

JURISPRUDENCE

DAVID BILCHITZ
THADDEUS METZ
ORITSEGBUBEMI OYOWE

**OXFORD**
**UNIVERSITY PRESS**
SOUTH AFRICA

# OXFORD
## UNIVERSITY PRESS

Oxford University Press is a department of the University of Oxford.
It furthers the University's objective of excellence in research, scholarship,
and education by publishing worldwide. Oxford is a registered trade mark of
Oxford University Press in the UK and in certain other countries.

Published in South Africa by
Oxford University Press Southern Africa (Pty) Limited

Vasco Boulevard, Goodwood, N1 City, Cape Town, South Africa, 7460
P O Box 12119, N1 City, Cape Town, South Africa, 7463

**Jurisprudence in an African Context**

ISBN 978 0 19 904849 6

Typeset in Utopia Std Regular 9.5pt on 12pt
Printed on 70 gsm woodfree paper

**Acknowledgements**
Publisher: Penny Lane
Project manager: Lindsay-Jane Lücks
Copy editor: Allison Lamb
Proofreader: Lee-Ann Ashcroft
Indexer: Clifford Perusset
Typesetter: Barbara Hirsch
Cover designer: Judith Cross
Designer: Oswald Kurten
Printed and bound by ABC Press, Cape Town
129784

# Contents in brief

# Contents

Law and philosophy (particularly ethics, political philosophy and jurisprudence) are disciplines that are deeply intertwined. Laws are often understood as rules that govern our societies. Yet, immediately, when stated this way, a number of questions arise: which rules should govern our societies? How do we identify those rules, and what makes them distinctive from the rules of a game such as soccer? Are legal rules always in some sense connected to morality?

Philosophy is a discipline usually concerned with trying to answer a number of foundational questions by reasoning. Practitioners of any practical area, such as law, may become occupied with the day-to-day activities of arguing in courts and, if they are judges, of delivering judgments. Yet, underlying what they do are always deeper questions about how laws are made, and whether those laws are in fact decent or just. On the African continent in particular, there has been much experience with law that has been unjust.

Jurisprudence is a discipline that is taught in most LLB curricula and is designed to enable students to think about some of these deeper questions. That, in turn, hopefully enables them to be better lawyers and also perhaps to influence how they go about practising and adjudicating the law.

This book was borne out of the experience of teaching Jurisprudence in South African law schools. Many students struggled with the subject, as well as its relevance for their lives. The dominant approach in South African law schools has involved teaching material mostly drawn from Europe and North America. There has tended to be limited engagement with the work of African philosophers or the relationship of the material to the African and South African context, in particular. Furthermore, lecturers have not been prescribing original material due to the difficulty of some of the sources for students.

Oxford University Press approached one of the authors with the idea of a new textbook in Jurisprudence. The initial idea was simply to adapt an excellent existing textbook for South African law schools. As we gave more thought to what was needed in this subject, we realised that a quite different book would be needed to address some of the above issues surrounding the teaching of Jurisprudence currently.

We decided to put in a proposal for a book that would situate the jurisprudential theories firmly in the African context. This would be reflected strongly in the issues that were addressed, such as engaging with the nature of law in traditional African societies and dealing with historical injustice. We put forward the idea of a textbook in which there would be extracts from primary sources, thus enabling students to engage with philosophers in their own words. This became particularly important as we also sought to ensure that, for the first time in this discipline, the thought of African philosophers would be engaged for each topic. We would not exclusively focus on African thought but seek to show the richness of placing these texts into critical dialogue with those from Europe and North America. We would, of course, seek to assist students by providing a range of questions (which could be used to test their knowledge) as well as a narrative explanation with examples of the particular thought in question.

Our proposal was accepted and the result is this textbook, which we hope will be a contribution towards the teaching and learning of Jurisprudence within law schools in South Africa and the wider African continent. Indeed, we see no reason why open-minded teachers of Jurisprudence in the law schools of the Global North and other continents of the Global

South should not utilise it as well to enrich their students' understanding of the subject as well as features of African philosophical thought.

The authors are most grateful to Oxford University Press and, particularly, Penny Lane – our wonderful publisher – for the encouragement and, indeed, persistence in convincing us to embark upon this project over several years. We are also grateful for her enthusiasm for the changes we thought were necessary to produce a textbook that would be of particular relevance to the present South African and African context. We hope you are satisfied with the result.

We would also like to thank the production team at Oxford University Press, who worked extremely hard to ensure the book was out in time for the 2018 academic year. Lindsay-Jane Lücks oversaw the process and gently nudged us when this was necessary. Allison Lamb's expert eye took over at the copy-editing phase and ensured that any language and formatting errors were ironed out. Patricia Rademeyer had the difficult task of engaging with various publishing houses to gain copyright permission, and we are grateful for her excellent and speedy work in ensuring that this occurred on time. We are also grateful to Oxford University Press for enabling us to meet twice in the course of the project (as the authors live in both Johannesburg and Cape Town). These face-to-face engagements were invaluable and allowed us to plan the structure of the book as well as, later on, to engage with each other's work.

David Bilchitz would like to thank the University of Johannesburg Faculty of Law as well as all the staff at the institute he directs (the South African Institute for Advanced Constitutional, Public, Human Rights and International Law) for creating the conducive environment in which this book was created. In particular, he would like to thank Dr Emile Zitzke for research help and commenting on one of the chapters and Raisa Cachalia for research help. He would also like to thank his fellow editors for the constructive and rigorous engagement that led to this book unfolding in the smooth and efficient manner in which it did. He is also grateful to his parents Ruven and Cynthia Bilchitz for their unending support and caring, as well as the love and support of Lennie, Lara, Gavi and Shalev as well as his extended family and friends. He hopes that his nephews will grow up to develop an interest and love of the deep philosophical questions around law and justice and develop the commitment to enable ideas around justice to reach fruition.

Thaddeus Metz hopes that David Lyons, his postgraduate mentor in the field of the philosophy of law, will appreciate his influence on this project, even if it was delayed by more than 20 years. Much of the foundation for Metz's understanding of, and approach to, jurisprudence was laid by Lyons' textbook *Ethics and the Rule of Law* and his teaching of legal theory in the light of American racial history. In addition to thanking his Jurisprudence teacher, Metz would like to thank his Jurisprudence students, mostly those in courses instructed at the Departments of Philosophy at the Universities of Nebraska-Lincoln and of Missouri-St Louis, but also those in guest lectures given at the Faculty of Law at the University of Johannesburg. Metz's theoretical understanding of law in the South African context has also benefited from engagements over the years with David Bilchitz, Drucilla Cornell, Adila Hassim, Patrick Lenta, and Stu Woolman. Finally, he is grateful to David Bilchitz and Oritsegbubemi Anthony Oyowe for their input on this project.

Oritsegbubemi Anthony Oyowe would like to acknowledge Simon Beck, Bernard Matolino, Olga Yurkivska and Thad Metz, all of whom have been extremely influential in his development over the last few years. He would also like to thank his fellow editors, David and Thad, for their support and encouragement, which made the experience of contributing to this project immensely rewarding. He is grateful to Jacques de Ville of the University of the Western Cape Department of Law for the invitation to be guest lecturer in the

Jurisprudence course during the early stages of this project – an experience that enabled him to test, modify and hopefully improve some of the materials in the present book. Thanks also go to Johnbosco Nwogbo and Uchenna Okeja for their research assistance. He would like to acknowledge his mum, Mabel Oyowe, and his siblings – Comy, Tonia, Dora and Helen, and is especially grateful to his wife, Khanyisa Oyowe, for her support and encouragement during the course of the project.

We hope that this book will ignite an interest in Jurisprudence amongst the students that study it and thus develop the depth of their engagement with law. We also hope that it will provide a small entry into the world of African philosophical thinking and situate it in relation to other schools of thought in the discipline. Through broadening our horizons, we also hope that the approach adopted in this text can be built upon and perhaps help provide compelling responses to some of the most difficult challenges of justice facing the African continent.

**David Bilchitz**
**Thaddeus Metz**
**Oritsegbubemi Anthony Oyowe**
Johannesburg and Cape Town, June 2017

# Foreword

Jurisprudence is the philosophy or theory of law. It is the outcome of systematic questions posed by legal thinkers and jurists about what the law is or ought to be, about its underlying purpose and doctrine, about legal systems, legal reasoning and the adjudication function.

The word 'jurisprudence' conjures the idea of theoretical aloofness unrelated to the practical or forensic search for just legal outcomes in actual or live disputes. The perception of the remoteness of jurisprudence is also fuelled by a history that says the grand theories of law, society and justice that sprung from the Global North since the sixteenth century did nothing to shield the Global South from the abiding injustice and scorn of coloniality together with its social constructs, theories, practices, hierarchies and violence.

However, that limited perception of jurisprudence, as this outstanding publication, *Jurisprudence in an African Context*, rightly argues, is neither always useful nor an adequate response to the question whether law students and scholars within an African context or other post-colonial paradigm should wrestle with Eurocentric theories of law, society and justice. In other words, is a study of jurisprudence that originates from the Global North likely to be useful to the decoloniality project?

Walter Mignolo, in *The Darker Side of Western Modernity: Global Futures, Decolonial Options*[1] reminds us that decoloniality is synonymous with decolonial 'thinking and doing', and it questions or problematises the histories of power emerging from Europe. These histories underlie the logic of Western civilisation. This means that decoloniality refers to analytic approaches and socioeconomic and political practices that question the pillars of Western civilisation: coloniality and modernity. This makes decoloniality both a political and epistemic project – a form of epistemic or philosophical disobedience. Mignolo adds that decoloniality is in effect, a continuing confrontation of, and delinking from, Eurocentrism.

Ironic as it may seem, one cannot mount a proper or fruitful philosophical 'delinking' without, at a bare minimum, engaging critically with the primary texts of legal theorists from the Global North. One cannot formulate a far-reaching, decolonising and liberating philosophy of law without appreciating the essential theoretical divergences from Eurocentrism and in turn re-purposing the theory of law to fit decolonised notions of power, society and justice. That intellectual weight-lifting to craft a progressive theory of legal knowledge must surely start with an insight into the work of preceding law philosophers, whatever their ilk or breed.

When I went to law school nearly 45 years ago, Jurisprudence was taught. The offering unashamedly privileged theories of law that emanated from the Global North, starting with Plato, immediately followed by Aristotle and then Thomas Aquinas and his ruminations over eternal law, divine law and natural law. To pass a post-graduate law degree, one had to display a reasonable mastery of legal positivism in its historical variants starting with Thomas Hobbes' social contract theory and as it was later annotated by John Locke. One had to contend with John Austin's early, 'command' formulation of legal positivism and its later versions through the prism of utilitarianism of Jeremy Bentham as well as the 'rule theory' of HLA Hart and his emphatic rejection of the necessary connection between law and morality.

I digress to remind myself that our current jurisprudence parts ways with Hart's austere disdain for the role of morality. It makes an open preference for and election of the normative grid or value system that underpins and informs the constitutional project and its envisaged

---

1   Mignolo 2011 *The Darker Side of Western Modernity: Global Futures, Decolonial Options* at 122–123.

just society. In our jurisprudence, there is a legitimate concern over not only what the law is but also what it ought to be in light of the overarching transformative purpose of the constitutional scheme.

I return to my law school days. Law students had to grapple with legal realism as propounded principally by American realists like Oliver Wendell Holmes Jr, Jerome Franklin and Roscoe Pound. They reduced law to the activity of courts and other state officials who brought to the adjudication and administration their potential subjectivity derived from their 'inarticulate premise'.

At the time, law schools could not escape the continued competition for the higher place between English law and Roman-Dutch law – perhaps a relic of the Anglo-Boer colonial contestation. For us students of Jurisprudence, this meant a compulsory study of continental thinkers like Immanuel Kant who taught the doctrine of a state based upon the law – a *Rechtstaat*. In Kantian terms 'a regime can be judged by no other criteria, nor be assigned any other functions, than those proper to the lawful order as such.'[2] For much the same reason we were compelled to study Hans Kelsen's 'pure theory of law' including the hierarchy of norms that owed their 'bindingness' to the basic norm, the grundnorm of a state or nation.

African indigenous or customary law and the underlying notion of personhood – *ubuntu* – and kinship and the related communitarian value system did not feature in the Jurisprudence offering. It was an optional course which was taught as an adjunct to a course known as Native Administration. The underlying normative scheme of indigenous law or its claim to the status of law was irrelevant and at best unimportant. Indigenous law was not 'the law of the land'. Its force did not run across the length and breadth of the country nor did it bind all citizens. It applied variedly and only at the election of the parties or litigants with the right to opt out. In time, indigenous law was 'codified'. It atrophied and virtually succumbed until it was partially resuscitated by the start of the democratic Constitution. That constitutional space allowed judges to write effusively about the place of *ubuntu* – that seminal bedrock of indigenous social organisation and law.

To this extent, *Jurisprudence in an African Context* is a remarkably valuable and necessary contribution to the ever-growing discourse around a de-linked or decolonised notion of power, justice and society in a present-day African setting. The enquiry into the philosophical underpinning of a just and progressive post-colonial society remains vital because, first, most features of coloniality persist in post-colonial societies and, second, the post-colonial ruling elite have dismally failed to ensure the alteration of the material conditions of their citizens in their so-called 'free democracies'. The power relations within the post-colonial state have altered only marginally. Third, modern African constitutional democracies have opened valuable philosophical spaces to forge new frontiers better suited to their generational mission.

Jurists, other social scholars and activists must continue to put out critical indigenous thought on truly decolonised and more just legal orders and social constructs in Africa. Even in the face of faltering regimes we must continue to initiate students of law to hard philosophical questions as thoughtfully posed in *Jurisprudence in an African Context*.

Unlike my days at law school, this groundbreaking work displays actual texts of philosophers, not only from the Global North but also from Africa. The contrasting approaches are self-evident, instructive and likely to help debunk undue Eurocentrism and to privilege and elevate African thought to where it rightly belongs – in the mainstream of

---

2  Strauss & Cropsey 1987 *History of Political Philosophy* at 581–582, 603.

jurisprudential decoloniality. Much of that task is well underway when one looks at some of the remarkably ground-breaking, transformative and value-drenched jurisprudence of our Constitutional Court.

In my fifteen-year stay on the bench I have talked often about the value of constant conversation between the law academy and the judiciary – between philosophy and forensic adjudication. The judicial function imposes a closeted and casuistic adjudication conditioned by the factual matrix of each dispute. The academy has the helpful facility of a superior taxonomy and systematic theoretical thinking. The happy medium between the judicial function and the academy sits somewhere in between. A work such as the present should facilitate the kind of conversation I have always yearned for. After all, a systematic theory of law helps light up the path for an inspired and valuable judicial function.

We ought to be indeed grateful to the authors – Prof. David Bilchitz, Prof. Thaddeus Metz and Dr. Oritsegbubemi Oyowe – for what will prove to be a tremendous and valuable contribution to the teaching and understanding of contextual jurisprudence on our continent and elsewhere.

**Dikgang Moseneke**
Retired Deputy Chief Justice
Tshwane, August 2017

# About the authors

**David Bilchitz**
BA (Hons) LLB (University of the Witwatersrand) MPhil PhD (University of Cambridge)
David Bilchitz is a Professor of Fundamental Rights and Constitutional Law at the University of Johannesburg and Director of the South African Institute for Advanced Constitutional, Public, Human Rights and International Law, a centre of the University of Johannesburg. He is also Secretary-General of the International Association of Constitutional Law. He has been recognised as an internationally acclaimed researcher by the National Research Foundation and is a member of the South African Young Academy of Science. He has taught Jurisprudence for many years at an undergraduate level and also teaches the philosophical underpinnings of fundamental rights in the LLM on human rights, offered by the University of Johannesburg. He is an admitted Attorney of the High Court of South Africa and serves on the board of several journals. His writing often involves an engagement at the intersection of philosophy and law.

**Thaddeus Metz**
BA (Iowa) MA PhD (Cornell University)
Thaddeus Metz is Distinguished Professor and Research Professor at the University of Johannesburg, where he is affiliated with the Department of Philosophy. Author of about 200 books, articles, and chapters, he is particularly known for having analytically articulated an African moral theory, applied it to a variety of ethical, legal and political controversies, compared it to East Asian and Western moral perspectives, and defended it as preferable to them. His book, *A Relational Moral Theory: African Contributions to Global Ethics,* is expected to appear with Oxford University Press in 2018.

**Oritsegbubemi Anthony Oyowe**
BA (Hons) MA PhD (University of KwaZulu-Natal)
Oritsegbubemi Oyowe is a lecturer in the Department of Philosophy at the University of the Western Cape where he teaches African Philosophy and Political Philosophy. He was a lecturer at the University of KwaZulu-Natal and a Postdoctoral Fellow in the African Humanities Programme of the American Council of Learned Societies. He is currently the Secretary of the Philosophical Society of Southern Africa. His research interests straddle the Western and African philosophical traditions and lie at the points of intersection between metaphysics and value theory, with a specific focus on ethical, political and legal issues. He has researched and published in both local and international journals on questions related to personhood, justice and human rights.

# Permissions and acknowledgements

## Chapter 1

Ch 1 Segments of the first section of the introduction are drawn from Bilchitz, 2007. Source: Bilchitz, D. 2007. Book Review: 'Understanding Jurisprudence' *South African Law Journal* 124:900–908. Reprinted by kind permission of Juta & Company Ltd.

Ch 1 Text 1: The question of African philosophy. Source: Bodunrin, P.O. (1981), 'The Question of African Philosophy' in *Philosophy* vol. 56, no. 216, Cambridge University Press, pp. 161–179. Reprinted by permission of Copyright Clearance Center on behalf of Cambridge University Press.

## Chapter 2

Ch 2 Text 1: Selections from Mbiti, JS. 1969. *African Religions and Philosophy*. London: Heinemann. Reprinted by kind permission of Dr John Mbiti.

Ch 2 Text 2: Selection from Austin, 1954:9–10. Source: Austin, J. 1954. *The Province of Jurisprudence Determined Etc.* Berlin, I, Hampshire, S & Wollheim, R. (Eds) Series: Library of Ideas. London: The Curwen Press. [Originally published in Austin, 1832: 1 Austin, John, 1832. *The Province of Jurisprudence Determined*. London, John Murray.]

Ch 2 Text 3: Ramose, MB. 2001. 'An African Perspective on Justice and Race.' Source: polylog: *Forum for Intercultural Philosophy* 3 (2001). Online: https://them.polylog.org/3/frm-en.htm. Reprinted by permission of Prof MB Ramose and the editor, *Forum for Intercultural Philosophy*.

Ch 2 Text 4: Herbert Hart's *The Concept of Law*. Source: *The Concept of Law* 2E by H.L.A. Hart, edited with a postscript by Joseph Raz & Penelope Bulloch (1994): 1,385 words (pp. 91–93, 94–95 & 96–98) © Oxford University Press 1961, 1994, reprinted by permission of Oxford University Press.

## Chapter 3

Ch 3 Text 1: Selection from John Dugard, 'The Jurisprudential Foundations of the Apartheid Legal Order', *The Philosophical Forum*, 1986–87, vol. 18, nos. 2–3, pp. 115–23. © John Wiley & Sons, Inc. Reprinted by permission of the publisher.

Ch 3 Text 2: Selection from Lon Fuller, 'Positivism and Fidelity to Law', *Harvard Law Review*, February 1958, vol. 71, no. 4, pp. 630–72. Reprinted by permission of *Harvard Law Review*.

Ch 3 Text 3: Selection from Martin Luther King Jr., 'Letter from Birmingham Jail'. Originally published as 'The Negro Is Your Brother', *The Atlantic Monthly*, August 1963, vol. 212, no. 2, pp. 78–88. Reprinted by arrangement with The Heirs to the Estate of Martin Luther King Jr., c/o Writers House as agent for the proprietor New York, NY.

Ch 3 Text 4: From William Idowu, 'African Jurisprudence and the Reconciliation Theory of Law', *Cambrian Law Review*, 2006, vol. 37, pp. 1–16. Reprinted by kind permission of the editor, *Cambrian Law Review*.

## Chapter 4

Ch 4 Text 1: HLA Hart's core and penumbra theory. Hart, HLA. 1958. ISSN: 0017-811X 'Positivism and the Separation of Law and Moral'. *Harvard Law Review* 71:593–629. Reprinted by permission of *Harvard Law Review*.

Ch 4 Text 2: Fuller's critique of Hart. Fuller, 1958: 662–663. Fuller, L. 1958. 'Positivism and Fidelity to Law – a Reply to Professor Hart'. *Harvard Law Review* 71:630–672. Reprinted by permission of *Harvard Law Review*.

Ch 4 Text 3: Dworkin's chain novel. Dworkin, 1986:255–257. Source: Law's Empire by Ronald Dworkin, Cambridge, Mass.: The Belknap Press of Harvard University Press for United States and its territories and dependencies and Canada, and by permission of Harts Publishing, an imprint of Bloomsbury Publishing Plc for the rest of the world. Copyright © 1986 by Ronald Dworkin.

Ch 4 Text 4: Dworkin's chain model of adjudication. Dworkin, 1986:255–257. Source: Law's Empire by Ronald Dworkin, Cambridge, Mass.: The Belknap Press of Harvard University Press for United States and its territories and dependencies and Canada, and by permission of Harts Publishing, an imprint of Bloomsbury Publishing Plc for the rest of the world. Copyright © 1986 by Ronald Dworkin.

Ch 4 Text 5: Langa CJ's transformative constititionalism. Langa, 2006:357–358. Source: Langa, P. 2006. 'Transformative Constitutionalism'. *Stellenbosch Law Review* 17:351. Reprinted by kind permission of Juta & Company Ltd.

Ch 4 Text 6: Moseneke DCJ's transformative adjudication. Moseneke, 2002: 315–316. Source: Mosencke, D. 2002. 'Transformative Adjudication'. *South African Journal on Human Rights* 18:309. Reprinted by kind permission of Juta & Company Ltd.

## Chapter 5

Ch 5 Text 1: Patrick Lenta on postmodern jurisprudence. From Patrick Lenta (2001) 'Just Gaming? The Case for Postmodernism in South African Legal Theory'. *South African Journal on Human Rights* 17:2, 173–209 (specifically with passages taken from pp. 181, 182–183, 184–185, 186, 187, 191, 192, 196). Reprinted by kind permission of Juta & Company Ltd.

Ch 5 Text 2: Selection from Ronald Dworkin, *Justice for Hedgehogs*, Harvard University Press, 2011. Source: *Justice for Hedgehogs* by Ronald Dworkin, Cambridge, Mass.: The Belknap Press of Harvard University Press, Copyright © 2011 by Ronald Dworkin.

Ch 5 Text 3: Selection from Akinola Akintayo, 'The Pliability of Legal Texts under a Transformative Constitution in Perspective', *Southern African Public Law* 27 (2012):639–651. Reprinted by permission of the editor, *SAPL*.

Ch 5 Text 4: Selection from Joel Modiri, 'Race as/and the Trace of the Ghost', *Potchefstroom Electronic Law Journal* 16 (2013):582–614. Reprinted under the Creative Commons Attribution-ShareAlike 4.0 International (CC BY-SA 4.0) See: https://creativecommons.org/licenses/by-sa/4.0/

Ch 5 Text 5: Selection from Karin van Marle, 'The Capabilities Approach', 'The Imaginary Domain', and 'Asymmetrical Reciprocity: Feminist Perspectives on Equality and Justice'. *Feminist Legal Studies* 11 (2003):255–278, from 255, 256, 266–268, 272 © 2003 Kluwer Academic Publishers. Printed in the Netherlands.

## Chapter 6

Ch 6 Text 1: Mill: Utilitarianism and justice. The first two extracts are from JS Mill *Utilitarianism* (1863) Chapter two Mill, J.S. *Utilitarianism*. Parker, Son, and Bourn: London, 1863. Available at https://www.utilitarianism.com/mill5.htm

Ch 6 Text 2: John Rawls: The original position. Source: *Justice as Fairness: A Restatement* by John Rawls, Cambridge, Mass.: The Belknap Press of Harvard University Press, Copyright © 2001 by the President and Fellows of Harvard College.

Ch 6 Text 3: John Rawls: Two principles of justice. Source: *Justice as Fairness: A Restatement* by John Rawls, Cambridge, Mass.: The Belknap Press of Harvard University Press, Copyright © 2001 by the President and Fellows of Harvard College.

Ch 6 Text 4: Yvonne Mokgoro on the idea of *ubuntu*. Source: Makwanyane, 1995: paras 306–7. *S v Makwanyane* 1995(3) SA 391 (CC), available at http://www.saflii.org/za/cases/ZACC/1995/3.html

Ch 6 Text 5: Oritsegbubemi Anthony Oyowe on the priority of the collective in some African philosophy and a critique thereof. Oyowe, OA. 2014. 'An African Conception of Human Rights? Comments on the Challenges of Relativism'. *Human Rights Review* 15:329–347. Reprinted by permission of Copyright Clearance Center on behalf of Springer International Publishing AG.

Ch 6 Text 6: Kwame Gyekye on African socialism. Source: *Tradition and Modernity: Philosophical Reflections on the African Experience* by Kwame Gyekye (1997): Extract of 652 words (pp. 160 & 162) © 1997 by Kwame Gyekye. By permission of Oxford University Press, USA.

## Chapter 7

Ch 7 Text 1: Robert Nozick's entitlement notion of justice, 1974, pp. 171–172. Source: Robert Nozick, *Anarchy, State and Utopia* (1974), pp. 149–182, New York: Basic Books, [1974], Reprint edition (November 12, 2013). Reprinted by permission of Copyright Clearance Center on behalf of Perseus Books Group (for World excluding UK and British Commonwealth), and by John Wiley & Sons, Inc. for UK and Commonwealth usage).

Ch 7 Text 2: Peter Singer on famine, affluence, and morality. Republished with permission of John Wiley and Sons Inc, from *Philosophy and Public Affairs*, Peter Singer, vol. 1, no. 3 (Spring, 1972): 229-243. Permission conveyed through Copyright Clearance Center.

Ch 7 Text 3: Kwame Gyekye's communitarianism and supererogation extract. Source: Kwame Gyekye, 1997, *Tradition and Modernity: Philosophical Reflections on the African Experience*, pp. 66–68, 71–73. Oxford University Press, 1997. By permission of Oxford University Press, USA.

Ch 7 Text 4: David Bilchitz, 'Do corporations have fundamental rights obligations?' This article was originally published as Bilchitz, D. 2010. 'Do Corporations Have Positive Fundamental Rights Obligations?' in *Theoria: A Journal of Social and Political Philosophy*, 57(125):1–35.

## Chapter 8

Ch 8 Text 1: Kant: Dignity and rationality. Kant, I. 1785. *Groundwork of the Metaphysics of Morals* in MJ Gregor (Ed). Kant, I. 1996. *Immanuel Kant: Practical Philosophy* (trans. MJ Gregor). Cambridge: Cambridge University Press. pp. 79–80, 84.

Ch 8 Text 2: Singer: Sentience and the argument against categorical thinking. Singer, 2004:79–80. Singer, P. 2004. 'Ethics Beyond Species and Beyond Instincts' in C Sunstein and M Nussbaum (Eds). 2004. *Animal Rights: Current Debates and New Directions*. Oxford: Oxford University Press. Reprinted by permission of OUP (http://www.oup.com).

Ch 8 Text 3: Sen: Functionings and capabilities. Sen, A. 1995. *Inequality Re-Examined*. OUP (pp. 39–40). Reprinted by permission of Oxford University Press (http:// www.oup.com).

Ch 8 Text 4: Nussbaum: Dignity beyond rationality. Source: *Frontiers of Justice: Disability, Nationality Species Membership* by Martha C. Nussbaum, Cambridge, Mass.: The Belknap Press of Harvard University Press, Copyright © 2006 by the President and Fellows of Harvard College.

Ch 8 Text 5: Thabo Mbeki: Being an African and the environment. Mbeki, T. 1996. Source: Mbeki, T. 1996. 'I Am an African' Statement on Behalf of the ANC on the Occasion of the Adoption by the Constitutional Assembly of 'The Republic of South Africa Constitution Bill

1996', Cape Town, 1996/05/08, available at: http://www.mbeki.org/2016/06/06/statement-on-behalf-of-the-anc-on-the-occasion-of-the-adoption-by-the-constitutional-assembly-of-the-republic-of-south-africa-constitution-bill-1996-cape-town-19960508/
Ch 8 Text 6: DT Chibvongodze: *Ubuntu* is not only about the human. Chibvongodze, D. 2016. 'Ubuntu is Not Only about the Human! An Analysis of the Role of African Philosophy and Ethics in Environment Management' Author: D.T. Chibvongodze, School of Built Environment and Development Studies, University of KwaZulu-Natal, South Africa), Guest Editor: Dr. Mayashree Chinsamy (Research Manager, DST-NRF Centre in Indigenous Knowledge Systems, Westville Campus, University of KwaZulu-Natal, South Africa) Source: www.krepublishers.com *Journal of Human Ecology* 53(2):157–166. 2016 © KAMLA-RAJ ENTERPRISES, DELHI, INDIA (JHE-SV-53-2-157-16-2960).
Ch 8 Text 7: MB Ramose: Ecology through *Ubuntu.* Ramose, 2009: 309. Source: Ramose, MB. 2009. 'Ecology through *Ubuntu*' in MF Murove (Ed). *African Ethics: An Anthology of Comparative and Applied Ethics.* Scottsville: University of Kwazulu-Natal Press. The extract was used with the permission of the publisher, UKZN Press.

### Chapter 9
Ch 9 Text 1: Judith Thomson on preferential hiring and compensation, 1973, pp. 380–384 Source: Thomson, JJ. 1973. 'Preferential Hiring.' *Philosophy & Public Affairs* 2(4):364–384. Reprinted by permission of Clearance Center on behalf of John Wiley and Sons Inc.
Ch 9 Text 2: Vincent Maphai on affirmative action, preferential hiring and black advancement. Source: Maphai, VT. 1989. Affirmative Action in South Africa – A Genuine Option? *Social Dynamics* 15(2): pp. 9, 10–12, 13–15, 16–17. Reprinted by permission of Copyright Clearance Center on behalf of Taylor & Francis.
Ch 9 Text 3: Thaddeus Metz's *ubuntu* as a moral theory and human rights in South Africa, pp. 537, 538, 539, 551–554. Source: Metz T (2011). 'Ubuntu as a Moral Theory and Human Rights in South Africa.' *African Human Rights Law Journal* 11:532–559. This work is licensed under a Creative Commons Attribution 4.0 International License https://creativecommons.org/licenses/by/4.0/
Ch 9 Text 4: Lungisile Ntsebeza's 'Land redistribution in South Africa: the property clause revisited', pp. 119, 120–121 Ntsebeza, L. 2007. Source: 'Land Redistribution in South Africa and the Property Clause Revisited,' in Ntsebeza, L & Hal, R. (Eds). *The Land Question in South Africa: The Challenge of Transformation and Redistribution.* Cape Town: HSRC Press, pp. 107–131. Reprinted by permission of HSRC Press.
Ch 9 Text 5: Emily Mawhinney on restorative justice in post-genocide Rwanda, pp. 22, 23–25, and 42. Mawhinney, Emily B. (2015) 'Restoring Justice: Lessons from Truth and Reconciliation in South Africa and Rwanda', *Hamline University's School of Law's Journal of Public Law and Policy.* Vol. 36: Iss. 2, Article 2, available at: http://digitalcommons.hamline.edu/jplp/vol36/iss2/2 This article is brought to you for free and open access by DigitalCommons@Hamline. It has been accepted for inclusion in *Hamline University's School of Law's Journal of Public Law and Policy* by an authorized administrator of DigitalCommons@Hamline. For more information, please contact jneilson01@hamline.edu

### Chapter 10
Ch 10 Text 1: Jeremy Bentham on incapacitation, reform, and deterrence. Source: Bentham, Jeremy, *Principles of Penal Law.* Publisher: W. Tait, 1843. Available at: https://ebooks.adelaide.edu.au/b/bentham/jeremy/principles_of_penal_law/complete.html

# Chapter 1

# Jurisprudence in an African context: An introduction

*David Bilchitz, Oritsegbubemi Oyowe and Thaddeus Metz*

## 1.1   Why Jurisprudence?

Jurisprudence is a compulsory subject for law students in most South African universities. The discipline is usually taken to involve the study of two key sets of questions and their relationships:

1.   What is the nature and distinctive features of law as a discipline?
2.   What should the law be? What is the content and meaning of justice? What is its relationship with law?

These questions involve taking a step back from the concrete rules of law to ask philosophical questions about the very characteristics of the discipline itself. The questions have universal relevance, yet the focus of most Jurisprudence textbooks has been on the answers provided by theory developed in Europe and North America. When African states became independent in the late 1950s and 1960s, a number of debates surfaced about decolonising the curriculum and knowledge systems in African universities. Those debates often involved attempting to integrate and develop curricula that reflected the thought that has emerged from Africa on deep philosophical questions. Many of these debates have been resuscitated recently within South African universities, where students have strongly pressed for the decolonisation of the curriculum. These external pressures are to be welcomed, as they encourage serious reflection on the place of a course like Jurisprudence in the legal curriculum, as well as the content and manner in which it is taught. Does Jurisprudence then deserve to remain a core part of the curriculum, and, if so, how do our justifications in that regard affect the content of the course and our pedagogical approach?

In making the case for Jurisprudence, it is useful to canvass a number of the objections teachers of Jurisprudence are privy to when they engage students concerning the subject.[1]

---

1   Segments of the first section of this introduction are drawn from Bilchitz 2007 *South African Law Journal* at 900–908.

First, some charge that the subject has no practical benefit for those who wish to be practitioners, who constitute the vast majority of the students. Second, others contend that it is too abstract and conceptual and removed from day-to-day policy issues and concerns of the law. Finally, others claim – in light of the recent impetus discussed above to reflect on the content of curricula – that Jurisprudence has often required students to become familiar with the currents of thought in Europe and North America concerning its central questions, without considering the contributions to thought in this arena by African philosophers and jurists. The theories from the 'Global North' have also been taught often without considering their applicability and implications for the African context. What then can be said in response to these criticisms, and what are the implications of these answers for how it should be taught?

In our view, the very charges against Jurisprudence, as a subject, provide some cogent arguments for its retention as a compulsory and important component of the LLB degree. The 'lack of practical benefit' charge can be challenged on several counts. First, it may be denied that Jurisprudence lacks all practical benefit. In fact, studying theories of adjudication, for instance, may well be of importance to a practitioner in seeking to develop a successful approach to cases that arise. It may also help practitioners to predict the potential outcome of cases, and thus assist them in advising clients.

Another response, however, challenges the assumption that only those subjects should be taught that have usefulness in some practical sense. Sadly, given funding limitations, many African universities have, out of necessity, often been faced with making very pragmatic decisions concerning what can be studied, and practical utility often has won out. Nevertheless, this focus can lead to an instrumentalisation of knowledge, whereby the development of human understanding becomes purely contingent upon practical outcomes. Our society becomes one so focused on the practical that there is no outlet for intellectual curiosity, no space to step back and consider the deeper questions of existence, ultimately impoverishing us all as we become simply units in a productive machine.

The second 'abstract' charge against the subject suggests a disjunction between theory and practice, the abstract and the concrete, that is simply, we would argue, not true of the law. Practical questions often require one to have reference to considerations that are more abstract. Without understanding the theoretical positions that are available, practical decisions may be taken that cannot adequately be justified. Moreover, such decisions may well be ultimately based on a background theory that even the decision-maker regards as unacceptable, if the assumptions underlying the decision remain unexpressed. Thus, in deciding whether to enforce a restraint of trade clause, or whether a person who is drunk can have criminal capacity, the court inevitably must engage a range of theoretical issues that enable it to arrive at a conclusion on these practical matters. Through making these theoretical matters explicit and drawing our students' attention to them, Jurisprudence can enable lawyers to have a level of theoretical sophistication that may indeed broaden and deepen their approach to more concrete issues. We here indicate that Jurisprudence may be taken not simply to be the overarching study of the two main questions mentioned above. It involves also deeper philosophical reflection about what concrete laws should contain and thus is a necessity when engaging with any branch of the law. Indeed, this point is illustrated by extracts we have chosen in this book from practising judges who, themselves, display the need to reflect on these questions in a theoretically complex manner.

Concrete implications may thus flow from a deeper theoretical consideration of legal doctrine or political philosophy. What then about such abstract questions as the connection between law and morality? In fact, one's approach towards a particular case may well also be connected with one's self-awareness as to the particular jurisprudential theory one adopts. If a matter falls for a Hartian positivist within the core meaning of a statute, then the outcome will be determined by the 'plain meaning' of the law; if it is in the penumbra, the decision may be reached through the exercise of a discretion by the judge (see Chapter 4 for this discussion). If law and morality are separable, one may be compelled as a judge, for instance, to make decisions that are legal but not just or possibly the converse. If law and morality are intimately connected on the other hand, one may be duty bound to find a construction of the law consistent with morality. Even in connection with such an abstruse matter as this, then, concrete consequences may follow.

The 'seemingly' abstract and conceptual nature of Jurisprudence may also assist and enhance the critical skills that students require for the law. Reading and understanding philosophical texts require close attention to the argumentation of the philosophers, and compel students to work out how to extract difficult arguments from the text. The complexity of the arguments often requires students to develop their logical skills, and the critical engagement with the material requires students to spot errors in reasoning. The very difficulty of Jurisprudence provides much of its value to the student: stretching students to expand their reading and critical skills that are of such great importance in the law. Universities should not be afraid to stretch students intellectually, so as to gain the skills necessary to confront difficult arguments and texts.

Different teaching methods will develop these skills to a greater or lesser extent. It has become common practice, in several universities, as a result of the difficulty of philosophical writing, to teach Jurisprudence virtually wholly through secondary texts. In our view, one of the central benefits of Jurisprudence as a subject, is to enable students to read and re-construct the arguments of the philosophers for themselves. The reading and critical skills developed by the students in this process is of use to them in developing the analytical rigour required to deal with difficult areas of the law. Access to original texts thus is empowering. It enables students to interpret these texts themselves and to come up with their own insights in relation to this work. Lectures and secondary material can then help students determine whether or not they have an adequate grasp of the material, but, in themselves, they do not enable the student to have unmediated access to these arguments. Moreover, particularly in the African context, students have often never had much exposure directly to the thought of African thinkers. It is thus of specific importance in this context to provide students with direct access to the thought of prominent African philosophers and judges.

In light of our views in this regard, this book attempts to select segments of the primary material from influential texts on the key questions of Jurisprudence outlined above. These provide an invitation to students to engage directly with the primary texts and attempt to re-construct the arguments of the philosophers therein. A series of questions follows the text, which can help guide the students in this process, and should be able to be answered through engagement with the text itself or at least independent thought about it. After each text, there is an exposition of the key arguments therein, a linkage with other theories and themes in Jurisprudence, as well as some critical discussion. To assist in the development of critical skills, students should attempt first to work out what the text means and the key arguments therein. Our engagement thereafter can be a means of checking whether the core arguments have been extracted. A process of critical reflection on these texts is also encouraged. To assist in the latter process, at the end of the chapter, we have placed a number of questions designed to stimulate critical reflection by the students on the material covered in each chapter.

## 1.2  Jurisprudence in an African context

Beyond the desirability of having students read primary texts, the third objection outlined above concerning the 'Global North'[2] orientation of existing Jurisprudence courses also provided the impetus for a new textbook on Jurisprudence. As we have mentioned, universities across South Africa have been faced recently with a strong charge to decolonise the curriculum. As we understand it, this notion requires academics to address the fact that there has been a historic privileging of 'Global North' knowledge and worldviews with a concomitant under-valuation and marginalisation of thought from Africa (and the Global South more generally). In particular, we focus on two specific problems which are of relevance to the discipline of Jurisprudence.

First, the Global North is often thought of as being the source and creator of theory whilst countries in the South simply apply what has been developed in the North to their contexts. Bonilla explicates this idea in the legal context as follows:

> [w]hile legal academia from the North is seen as creating original academic products, legal academia from the South is considered solely a weak reproduction of the knowledge generated in the North – a form of diffusion or local application of the same.[3]

The colonial context in South Africa exacerbated these dynamics where local ways of interpreting the world were not respected and replaced by colonial modalities of thought. This has led some theorists such as Catherine Odora Hoppers to speak of 'the manner in which colonialism engaged in "cultural violence"[4] and "symbolic castration".'

The second problem relates to the fact that authors in the Global North often make claims about the global validity of their theories, but fail to reflect on the manner in which their theories might be particular to the North.[5] As Parvati Raghuram and Clare Madge write, 'the often unstated claim to universality is one of the key problems of how many northern academics currently theorize'.[6] Southern theorists do not have this luxury and usually circumscribe their claims to a particular location; thus, instead of theorists in Africa doing 'philosophy', they instead are seen as merely doing 'African philosophy'.

The identification of these problems cannot automatically achieve a resolution thereof but suggests lines of approach to address them. In relation to the first problem, the wiping out of certain indigenous cultures and their erasure, in many cases, is an historic injustice which remains difficult to correct. The fact that much of the knowledge in these systems was transmitted orally renders it even more difficult to retrieve. Nevertheless, whilst a complete recovery of what was lost is not possible, there is clearly an importance to engage with theorists and theories that have emerged from the Global South and their contributions to knowledge. Since our focus is on the African context, we attempt in this book to provide

---

2   The terminology of Global North and Global South is not geographical in nature but, in the words of Meekosha 2011 *Disability and Society* at 669:

> shorthand for a complex of inequalities and dependencies: industrialised versus raw material producing countries, rich versus poor, those with military power versus those without, high technology versus low technology, and so on.

3   Bonilla 2013 *Yale Human Rights and Development Law Journal* at 176.

4   Odora Hoppers 2000 *African Voices in Education* at 5.

5   Connell 2007 *Southern Theory*.

6   Raghuram & Madge 2006 *Singapore Journal of Tropical Geography* at 280. See also, Matolino 2015 *South African Journal of Philosophy*.

students with some of the key thinking that has emerged from this continent on the key questions of the discipline of Jurisprudence, namely, what is law and what is justice. In doing so, it is hoped that these African texts gain a wider readership and more influence on the legal communities on the continent and beyond.

In addressing the first problem, there are two approaches that could be adopted. The 'exclusive' approach would suggest that, in light of the historical devaluation of African knowledge systems, our courses should focus exclusively on modes of thought that emanate from Africa. Only such a radical shift would correct the imbalances that have taken place in the past. Such an approach in our view is undesirable for a number of reasons. First, it is based on an assumption that it is entirely possible to divorce currents of thought in Africa from those elsewhere. Yet, if we recognise a common humanity between peoples and ongoing exchanges between them, there is a strong likelihood that modes of thought are not entirely distinct from one another. Moreover, the records we have of African philosophers often demonstrate that they have engaged with other thought systems elsewhere. To comprehend their thought, we need to have a wider approach.

Apart from these points, the study of ideas, in some sense, is not concerned so much with their origin but their truth. If there are good ideas that emerge in other places, these are worthy of consideration for their own sake. Creating silos in the world of thought whereby only certain thinkers are studied in particular geographical locations would be to impoverish our ability to benefit from the brilliance of thinkers in different cultures beyond our own. There are also pragmatic reasons that count against this approach. Knowledge today is not simply a local matter, but involves global discussions and conversations that impact upon one another. To be an individual who can engage on the world stage requires an understanding and knowledge of the main currents of thought across the world. Avoiding the currents of thought from elsewhere would also exacerbate the problem of Global North influence. Countries that are outward-looking would have their theories influence others, whereas those that are inward-looking would simply avoid extending their influence beyond their borders. Maintaining an exclusive focus on the Global South or Africa, in particular, would thus 'score an own goal' in failing to change the global power dynamics of knowledge production and dissemination.

A preferable approach therefore, in our view, is an 'inclusive' one. This involves gaining an understanding of the key currents of thought that have influence in the global discussion of Jurisprudence, whilst attempting to ensure that African thought is well represented in the discussion. In this regard, one African philosopher, Kwasi Wiredu, has argued persuasively, in our view, that this sort of comparative approach to knowledge is indeed possible and worth pursuing. This is because the biological similarity of human beings quite generally makes cross-cultural communication a real possibility.[7] As such, the impulse towards understanding ideas from beyond one's own immediate setting is not something human beings should seek to overcome, but instead should embrace. Wiredu's insistence on a cross-cultural approach coincides with the 'inclusive' one we have adopted. Even so, it is recognised that global knowledge inequalities will play a role in what is considered an 'influential theory'. Yet, being open to ideas entails that there is no reason why students should not gain an understanding of the currents of thought that exist elsewhere and benefit from them. African theories will deliberately be included in each chapter and be placed in conversation with theories from outside its borders. In this way, students will gain a

---

7   Wiredu 1996 *Cultural universals and particulars* at 22–23, 60.

wide-ranging knowledge of a particular topic, and for the first time be offered in a Jurisprudence textbook the opportunity to study the approach of African theorists on a wide variety of topics. We hope this will also stimulate further development of philosophy from Africa that can, in turn, influence and shape global discussions about law.

In relation to the second problem mentioned above, the proper range of a theory, it is important that theories developed in the Global North (and elsewhere in the Global South too) are not simply applied without thinking about the African context. The bare fact that a theory was created somewhere else does not necessarily mean it is inapplicable here. However, an important prior question that should always be asked by students concerns whether a given theory is in fact applicable in that context. This will require an understanding of the particularities thereof. Africa is a diverse continent and the conditions and contexts vary. It thus offers the opportunity for rich reflection on the applicability of particular theories. Given that the authors are located in South Africa, our examples are often drawn from that context. We encourage seeing South Africa as part of the wider African continent and students will need to consider how the South African context may differ from the circumstances in other African countries. A number of the thinkers we engage also often emerge from all over the African continent and thus it is necessary to consider their applicability in other parts of the continent. We have sought to provide examples and practical problems that can enable students to test their understanding of what the implications of a particular theory would be in that context and whether it would be desirable. Lecturers and students should naturally feel free to think of additional examples and contexts that provide tests of the applicability of various theories.

We recognise the particularities of our approach to teaching Jurisprudence in the African context. As academics who have taught Jurisprudence and philosophy more generally, we offer our contribution in part as an attempt to meet a responsibility we feel to the African context in which we live and work. We also do so humbly, in the knowledge that other approaches are possible and, indeed, we hope the advent of this textbook will help catalyse a much-needed discussion around how to teach this subject in a manner that connects with students and their context, as well as helps address some of the historical imbalances discussed above.

In addressing the question of the marginalisation of African theory, we need to outline what it is that qualifies a theorist or theory as 'African'. Apart from being an important debate, which can be discussed in any such course, we attempt – in addressing this question – to outline the methodology we have adopted throughout this book. First, we include a key text by a leading African theorist, which is followed by a number of questions that focus on the text. We then seek to explicate the key features of the text, provide a brief critical engagement with it and provide our preferred approach. In the rest of the book, we usually do not provide an indication of a preferred approach and allow students to make their own decisions in this regard. In this instance, since it is of importance to the scheme of the book, we do provide an indication of our thinking.

## 1.3   What is African philosophy?

The text we have selected is from a classic essay by the philosopher Peter Bodunrin titled 'The Question of African Philosophy'.

| PRIMARY TEXTS | **Text 1  The question of African philosophy**[8] |
|---|---|

Bodunrin was a Nigerian Professor of Philosophy, who taught and researched both African philosophy as well as the Western analytic tradition of philosophy. He held academic positions in Nigeria and then later in the United States, in the Department of Philosophy of Ohio University.

> The African philosopher cannot *deliberately* ignore the study of the traditional belief systems of his people. Philosophical problems arise out of real life situations. In Africa, more than in many other parts of the modern world, traditional culture and beliefs still exercise a great influence on the thinking and actions of men. At a time when many people in the West believe that philosophy has become impoverished and needs redirection, a philosophical study of traditional societies may be the answer. The point, however, is that the philosopher's approach to this study must be one of criticism, by which one does not mean 'negative appraisal, but rational, impartial, and articulate appraisal whether positive or negative. To be "critical" of received ideas is accordingly not the same thing as rejecting them: it consists rather in seriously asking oneself whether the ideas in question should be reformed, modified or conserved, and in applying one's entire intellectual and imaginative intelligence to the search for an answer'.

> What seems to me clear is that the philosopher cannot embark on a study of African traditional thought wholesale. He would have to proceed piece-meal. He may have to begin by an examination of philosophical issues and concepts that have loomed largely in the history of world philosophy, and he must not be charged for being unoriginal or being irrelevant as an African philosopher simply because he is discussing in the African context issues that have also received attention elsewhere. If a problem is philosophical, it must have a universal relevance to all men. Philosophical systems are built up by systematic examination of specific features of the world and out of the relationships that are perceived to obtain between them ...

> ... The remaining point is this: what does an expression like "British Philosophy" mean? It does not mean the philosophy of the average Englishman, nor a philosophy generally known among the British people. The average Briton is not aware of much of *Principia Mathematica* [by Bertrand Russell–ed.] or of the contents of the *Tractatus* [by Ludwig Wittgenstein–ed.]. British philosophy is not a monolithic tradition. At this point in time empiricism and logical analysis seem to be the predominating features of that tradition but by no means can all present philosophers in the British tradition be described as empiricists or analysts. Towards the close of the last century, the dominant figure was Bradley, a Hegelian

---

8   Bodunrin 1981 *Philosophy* at 173.

idealist. British philosophy is not a body of thoughts that had its origins in the British Isles. Greek thought (itself informed by early Egyptian thought), continental idealism, and scientific philosophy (the philosophy of the Vienna Circle) have all had influences on British thought. Some of the most influential figures in British philosophy have not even been British by birth – e.g. Wittgenstein and Popper. Similarly, Alfred North Whitehead was born in England and began his philosophical career in England, but his later philosophical work belongs to the history of American philosophy. The thoughts of the ancient Greeks belong to the history of western philosophy but the ancient Greeks and ancient Britons were mutually ignorant of each other. Caesar described the Britons as barbarians when he first went there.

The point I am trying to make is that the philosophy of a country or region of the world is not definable in terms of the thought-content of the tradition nor in terms of the national origins of the thinkers. As Wiredu [an influential Ghanaian African philosopher–ed.] puts it, "for a set of ideas to be a genuine possession of a people, they need not have originated them, they need only appropriate them, make use of them, develop them, if the spirit so moves them, and thrive on them. The intellectual history of mankind is a series of mutual borrowings and adaptations among races, nations, tribes and even smaller sub-groups". And "the work of a philosopher is part of a given tradition if and only if it is either produced within the context of that tradition or taken up and used in it". If these points are realized, the philosopher should be allowed the intellectual liberties allowed his colleagues in other disciplines. He may be asked to apply his training to the study of his culture and this would be an understandable request, but it would have to be understood that his reaction will be guided by his own philosophical interests.[9]

## Questions

1. Does African philosophy, according to Bodunrin, involve the study of traditional belief systems in Africa?
2. What is central to adopting a philosophical approach for Bodunrin as opposed to simply doing anthropology (the empirical study of particular cultures and groups)?
3. Is there a way, according to Bodunrin, to say whether a philosophical system is African by referring to the content thereof alone?
4. For Bodunrin, does African philosophy necessarily emerge from thinkers who have their origin on the African content? What do you think about his view?
5. According to Wiredu, what is necessary for a philosophy to be described as African? Is Christianity according to his account African?
6. What, ultimately, in your view would render a philosophical approach African?

One possible answer as to what constitutes African philosophy may well be that it is the study of the traditional, that is, long-standing and especially pre-colonial systems of thought of people who live in the geographical area of Africa. Thus, if we, for instance, study what groups in Africa thought about ethics or the nature of reality (metaphysics), we are then engaging in African philosophy. One particular problem for this view involves the difficulty that

9   Bodunrin 1981 at 177–178.

African systems of belief were often held by communities and transmitted orally. With the advent of connections between particular communities and particularly the influence of systems of belief brought by colonial powers, it is not always possible to reconstruct what exactly 'pure' African thought involved.

Bodunrin, however, does not focus on this problem as he does not consider such a study of traditional belief systems as sufficient to constitute 'philosophy'. The discipline of anthropology is concerned with understanding the belief systems and thoughts of people in particular groups. It simply describes and seeks accurately to capture what people thought. Philosophy, on the other hand, according to Bodunrin as a discipline, must involve a critical component. This involves engaging with received ideas and thinking about whether they can rationally be justified. If they can be, philosophy seeks to strengthen our understanding of why those ideas are persuasive and should command our attention; if their justification is lacking, philosophy requires us to think of whether to reject them or modify these ideas in a suitable way. If one is doing African philosophy then, according to Bodunrin, one is not simply engaged in studying the thought systems that emerge from a particular place. Rather, one must attempt to understand them in the best light possible, to examine the justifications for these systems of thought, to modify them where necessary to render them more persuasive, and to reject what cannot be defended.

Bodunrin also rejects the idea that somehow African philosophy must be focused on a set of concerns that are particular to Africa. He rather emphasises the continuity of African thought with the concerns of philosophy in other parts of the world. Indeed, he sees a defining feature of philosophical problems as having universal relevance for understanding the world around us. Bodunrin can thus be seen to reject the 'exclusive' approach above that suggests a focus only on thought that emerges from Africa alone. The study of philosophy for Bodunrin must of necessity involve openness to ideas and solutions to difficult problems that emerge from across the spectrum of human thought. Philosophy involves for him an attention to universal problems and, hence, part of its beauty is the capacity of everyone in every place to contribute towards their resolution. It is worth indicating that Bodunrin's take on African philosophy is similar to the views of other well-known African philosophers. In particular, the Cameroonian philosopher Marcien Towa argued that if the concept of 'philosophy' in African philosophy was not at all related to the concept of philosophy in other parts of the world, then the insistence on African philosophy would amount 'to a fight for a word' merely.[10] So, while recognising what might be particular about African philosophy, we should not lose sight of its universal character.

Bodunrin also here essentially recognises the challenge that modern African philosophical discussions have, in general, been conducted by African philosophers whose training involves an engagement with 'Global North' philosophical traditions. This might lead to a situation in which much of what goes by the name of African philosophy is simply a duplication of the themes and methods of Western philosophy. Like Bodunrin, it is important to acknowledge the potential risks. However, it is also possible that one can approach this situation as an opportunity rather than one about which to despair. Indeed African philosophers who also have a training in Western philosophy are able to occupy two epistemological orders at once. Not only have they acquired the knowledge of the methods and themes of a non-African mode of philosophising, they are also deeply familiar with the cultural thought worlds of Africa. As such, these methods can be used where necessary in the service of knowledge production in Africa. In other words, they have a responsibility to

---

10   Marcien Towa 1971 at 26–33, cited in Appiah 1992 *In My Father's House: Africa in the Philosophy of Culture* at 103.

determine which of those methods are applicable to the African situation and to reject those that are not beneficial. Ultimately, this involves for African philosophers with Western philosophical training a demand to do philosophy with an African conscience. In Wiredu's words, 'the test', is whether 'a contemporary African philosopher's conception of African philosophy ... enables him to engage fruitfully in the activity of modern philosophising with an African conscience'.[11]

Bodunrin makes a number of other important points about how we define a philosophy as 'African' and, to do so, he explores what could analogously be meant by 'British philosophy'. He rejects three answers to the question. The first position states that what constitutes 'African' philosophy or 'British philosophy' is a *particular set of ideas* which define the thought of that place or region. There may well be a current of thought that tends to be predominant in a certain place. Yet, that school of thinking, in contexts as diverse as Africa (or even a smaller place such as Britain), does not define all the philosophy that emerges from that place. Bodunrin thus resists the idea that somehow African thought can be reduced to one set of doctrines to which all would subscribe. It is also not the thoughts or beliefs of the average person in that particular place or location. Philosophy seems to imply the 'considered' thoughts and beliefs of individuals that often emerge from those who are the intellectual leaders of their societies.

A second answer to the question of what African philosophy is would say that it is the *thought that emerges from Africa uniquely*, a particular place. Bodunrin, however, rejects this idea as he does not see thoughts as sealed in regional compartments. He points out in relation to 'British philosophy' that it is heavily influenced by the thoughts that emerged from ancient Greece. As such, the distinctive currents of thought in British philosophy do not emerge uniquely from a particular geographical place. The same would be true of Africa, which has a long history of engagement with those who are not African and which would have had an influence on ideas on this continent.

A third position would be that African philosophy *emerges from philosophers who are born in or live in the continent of Africa*. Yet, as Bodunrin points out, some of the most famous 'British philosophers' were not born in Britain. Others who were born in Britain became the founders or leaders in what is considered distinctive of American philosophy. The same would be true of Africa. Fanon, for instance, was born in the Caribbean, spent much of his life in Algeria, and is commonly considered to be an African philosopher. There are also many individuals born in Africa who live and teach philosophy overseas and whose ideas seem unconnected with their African origins. For example, Anton Wilhelm Amo was born in what is now Ghana, and taken (forcibly) as a child to Germany by the Dutch West Indian Company. He was presented as a 'gift' to Anthony Ulrich, Duke of a region in Germany (Brunswick-Wolfenbuttel). He was treated as a member of the Duke's family and sent to university. He gained his PhD in 1734 and reputedly became the first Professor of Philosophy of African descent in 1736, writing a number of books of philosophy. Much of Amo's philosophical work, however, belongs to the German (and wider European) tradition rather than to what is today regarded as African philosophy.[12] Consequently, the birth origins or place of residence of philosophers does not seem capable of giving us an adequate criterion of what constitutes African philosophy.

---

11  Wiredu 1980 *Philosophy and an African Culture* at x.
12  Sadly, his university environment at the time was far from accepting of a black philosopher and, after the liberal-minded Duke, who had brought him up, died, he was subject to harassment and racism, which led him to leave Germany and return to Ghana.

Bodunrin quotes another philosopher, Kwasi Wiredu, for the proposition that what makes thought characteristic of a place is its *reception* in that place: the fact that it is appropriated in a space, made use of, and enables people to flourish in that space. The thought of Fanon, for instance, which has found resonance with many in Africa, may thus be thought of as part of African philosophy. Christianity would, therefore, in some sense be African despite the fact that it did not originate here. A key aspect for determining whether something is African philosophy is whether there is a concern to work in the context of ideas that have currency within Africa or ideas that are drawn from elsewhere but made sense of therein. Part of what makes a philosophy African then, for Bodunrin, is to engage ideas from all over but have a strong sense of one's locatedness within a particular context. Indeed, there is an importance of thinking and re-thinking ideas of relevance to the context.

Of course, in some sense, this position can also be challenged. If ideas have become dominant in Africa because of the power relations that emerged from colonialism, can we really see those ideas as African in nature? It seems to be the case that the reception of ideas cannot be definitive of the place in question if it is simply a result of wholesale replacement of existing doctrines through imposition by those who wield power. We can imagine a challenge to the notion that Christianity is essentially African given that its adoption in Africa was often accompanied by economic inducements to believe in it (through missionary schools offering education, for instance), drumming up fear in people and coercion.

Bodunrin provides us with much food for thought in relation to how to define African philosophy, and the problems with various answers to this question. Indeed, this question has generated a lot of writing and there are a diversity of views in this regard. We encourage students to read more widely around these. We see this book as partly attempting to give expression to some of the main dimensions of thought that emerge from thinkers like Bodunrin.

How do we engage with the notion of what constitutes African philosophy in the context of this book and the study of the philosophy of law? First, we take Bodunrin's point that we must not obscure the complexity and diverse characteristics of traditional African societies.[13] Traditional cultures of pre-colonial Africa were not uniform and unanimous with respect to the beliefs and practices relating to law, and not all traditional African peoples held the same concept of law. It does not follow that because certain groups of people happen to occupy the same geographical areas they are also unanimous about the meaning of concepts. Yet, we can reasonably expect the term 'African' to refer meaningfully to the cluster of beliefs, norms, values and practices that have predominated over a long span of time and wide array of peoples who have inhabited this continent.[14] Concepts of law (and justice) that will be attributed to traditional African societies will be based on these dominant ideas, while leaving ample room for other potentially conflicting views. Following Bodunrin's lead, we will not be content simply to describe the views that emerge but seek to provide justifications and critical analysis thereof.

It might be suggested that trying to define an African conception of law or justice commits us to a provincial understanding of such concepts, that is, one that belongs to a particular jurisdiction – traditional Africa. So constrained by geography and culture, one might doubt its philosophical appeal. Why should we care at all about some people's concept of law or justice, and not a universal one?[15] Moreover, a theory of law or justice should give an account

---

13   Taiwo 1985 *International Philosophical Quarterly* at 198.
14   Nwakeze 1987 *International Philosophical Quarterly* at 101.
15   Leiter 2007 *Naturalizing Jurisprudence: Essays on American Legal Realism and Naturalism in Legal Philosophy* at 177–179.

of the essence of law or justice itself and not what some people think it is, in the same way as an investigation into the nature of water should examine its molecular structure, $H_2O$, and not merely what some people think water is.[16] Nevertheless, law and justice are also social and political phenomena. As such, they are partly informed by people's beliefs and attitudes, which vary across place and time. Furthermore, since any long-standing tradition probably has some insight into the way things are, understanding how they are conceived in some parts of the world, for instance, in traditional African societies, might illuminate our general and universal understanding of these ideas. Indeed, we hope to show in this book that ideas which have been salient in African traditions offer plausible alternatives to those that emerge particularly in 'Global North' contexts. The failure to give adequate attention to these views – which has reflected universal global inequalities in the production of knowledge – might well have impoverished scholarship more generally and, so, this methodology can help with addressing the epistemic injustices we articulated above.[17]

## 1.4   Theories of law and theories of justice

The book, as has been mentioned, is structured around the two central questions that make up the study of Jurisprudence. The first half of the book explores the concept of law, its nature and its relationship to morality and politics. An important sub-component of this section of the book considers how judges are to decide cases in the law, namely, the question of adjudication. The second half of the book deals more with questions of justice and political philosophy: what *should* our laws be? How should our laws distribute benefits and burdens between individuals, and how should legal infractions be handled?

Many African universities focus much of their Jurisprudence teaching the first issue concerning the nature of law. Theories of justice are often dealt with cursorily and without exposing students to the range of philosophical thinking around the question of justice. In our view, theories of justice are equally important to theories of law. In order to enable students to have some form of normative framework to understand and engage with the type of laws the legislature should seek to pass (or judges should develop, or police should enforce), it is of great importance to engage with questions of justice.

This is of particular significance in an African context, where, as is discussed, there is often no strict separation in general between questions of justice and questions of law. It is also of particular importance in a country like South Africa, where the Constitution[18] is central to the legal system. To engage with the Constitution, and to be able to ensure that the vision contained therein is realised, involves having an understanding of what it entails for South African society. There are different ways of capturing the vision of the South African Constitution that have concrete implications. Theories of justice enable individuals to develop a deep understanding of some of the main issues involved in the relationship between the individual and the state, the obligations of individuals more generally, and the distribution of benefits and burdens within the state. They also enable individuals to engage with some of the difficult tensions involved in the recognition of rights, and to develop a deeper understanding of these features of the political system.

The Jurisprudence course often involves a relatively unique opportunity for students in the LLB curriculum to examine issues that go beyond the law in particular areas. It thus

---

16   Raz 2004 *The Blackwell Guide to the Philosophy of Law and Legal Theory* at 10.
17   See Metz 2017 *Knowledge and Change in African Universities*.
18   Constitution of the Republic of South Africa, 1996.

offers an opportunity for an engagement with thinking that is outside the domain of traditional legal sources and encourages a wider reflection on the legal system and the content of particular laws. Our approach encourages students to take this opportunity to learn about important currents of thought that have important implications for shaping the way in which law develops in African countries.

Our approach in addressing these problems is the following. We usually seek to outline an example of a practical issue that emerges from the African context and sets the scene for a particular philosophical discussion. We then provide extracts from a number of key primary sources that explicate the main currents of thought in the area under focus. Questions are provided that can help students to work out the main lines of thinking in these primary texts. We then provide an explication of the central ideas and arguments in these texts, situating them within the context of the theory more generally, and providing additional information and explication. Some of the main lines of critique are often included, though, sometimes, the choice of texts helps to provide an understanding of the different responses to a particular question. African philosophical texts are included, as mentioned, as part of these schools of thinking and may involve continuities with approaches in other places or, alternately, radical departures. The texts that emerge from traditions outside Africa also raise important questions. If they are relevant and convincing, how are they to be applied in the African context? Is it necessary to transform these theories in the process of such application? These are important questions for students to consider.

Each chapter traverses a number of theories and, thus, it is not envisaged that it will always be possible to cover one chapter per lecture. In several cases, it will be necessary to allocate several lectures (depending on the length thereof) to a particular chapter. Lecturers may of course want to go into issues and detail that are not covered in particular chapters. We believe, however, that overall the scheme of the book and its contents offers a well-designed curriculum that will enable students to understand the key currents of thought in the field of Jurisprudence. We briefly now outline the structure and logic of the book and how each chapter fits into it.

The first half of the book focuses on the key questions relating to the first question of Jurisprudence, namely, the nature of law. Chapter 2 asks the provocative question as to whether there was law in traditional African societies. In order to answer this question, it considers first the features of such societies. Having done so, it focuses on positivist theories of law. This is the view that law and morality are conceptually distinct and not necessarily connected in any way. The criteria for the identification of a legal system involve certain formal features, on this view. Different theorists focus on different components and the context of traditional African societies provides a rich opportunity to test their implications. This positivist view of law will be juxtaposed with a view of law ostensibly germane to traditional African societies.

Chapter 3 then considers the main alternative view on the nature of law, namely, natural law theory. It does so in the context of the question as to whether there is in fact law in wicked political systems. The practical focus of this chapter is on apartheid South Africa. Some of the main natural law approaches will be outlined and their plausibility examined.

One of the questions that arises in the positivism/natural law debate concerns whether law can be identified without recourse to moral thinking. This raises squarely the question as to how law is adjudicated by judges, which is the subject matter of the fourth and fifth chapters. The practical question at the heart of these chapters is how judges are to adjudicate within the context of a constitutional order that seeks to transform society in the direction of greater social justice – an imperative that has emerged in South Africa in the wake of apartheid, but also in other African countries in response not only to colonialism but also the rule of authoritarian and corrupt leadership. Chapter 4 focuses upon theorists who are of the view that judges must seek to achieve some kind of objective approach to adjudication, whether that be through utilising the plain language of statutes or through utilising the objective morality that flows from the texts. Chapter 5, on the other hand, mainly examines the approach of those who are sceptical that objectivity in this area is forthcoming. These views sometimes see law as fundamentally indeterminate and only being capable of entrenching the biases of those who are most powerful. The chapter looks at theories that both offer general critiques of the law in this vein – legal realism, postmodern critiques and critical legal studies – as well as schools of thought that focus on exposing the biases of law from a particular perspective – critical race theory and feminism.

The second half of the book focuses on questions about the nature of justice (and thus, what law *should* be as opposed to what it is or how to interpret it). The questions that are addressed seek to provide students with a broad knowledge of this area and some of the leading theorists and thinkers both from Africa and elsewhere, but also link to issues of particular importance within the African context. Chapter 6 focuses on questions of how resources should be distributed in society (distributive justice) and takes a particular example of an individual living in extreme poverty. Does the state have any obligations towards her and her family? This question offers the opportunity to explore some of the leading approaches in this area towards justice and to compare and contrast how they would answer this question. In so doing, they offer an opportunity for students to think about economic injustice and what a defensible position would be for the state to adopt. This is, of course, of importance in understanding and applying socio-economic rights that have been included in various constitutions on the African continent – such as those in South Africa and Kenya.

Whilst Chapter 6 focuses largely on the state's obligations (or those of the political community as a whole), Chapter 7 raises the important issue of the duties of individuals towards others in their society. If an individual falls on hard times, do others have a duty to assist? Does their distance from the individual matter? This chapter also seeks to engage the topical question of new forms of agents such as corporations and their obligations towards society.

Whereas Chapter 7 focuses on who has to perform obligations flowing from justice, Chapter 8 seeks to address who is rightly entitled to be considered within the domain of justice and thus to be able to claim rights. It focuses on two key examples of great relevance in the African context. Primarily, it engages with our duties to the rich diversity of animals that share the continent with human beings, but it also traverses the question of our duties to human beings who are not citizens but who come into a state such as South Africa as refugees or economic migrants. The chapter thus offers the opportunity to become acquainted with the key lines of thought as to who is entitled to duties of justice.

Chapter 9 turns to the question of compensatory justice. What must be done in response to wrongs and injustices that are committed? Chapter 9 seeks to focus on broad historical wrongs such as the confiscation of land from black people that took place through actions of the South African government over a long period of time, and the genocide in Rwanda. The question for this chapter is how are we to correct for such harms? The chapter traverses a range of theories and new approaches that have been suggested in this regard. Chapter 10 then addresses the problem of responding punitively to crimes that are committed against individuals. What is the justification that can be given for punishing an individual for wrongs done to another individual? In this area, students will be able to see the relevance of these theories to the discipline of criminal law and its development, thus showing the practical relevance of the study of Jurisprudence to the practice of law.

As can be seen from this outline, this book attempts to engage with live debates on the African continent and thus render the material relevant and exciting to teach. It does so by offering an opportunity to discover some of the best thinking that has emerged in Jurisprudence from around the world on these topics, with a particular goal of ensuring African contributions to these debates are considered and critically discussed. We also hope that this textbook will provide a pedagogical approach to teaching Jurisprudence which helps to develop the critical faculties and skills of students. The content of the subject matter is vitally important for encouraging creative thinking about law and justice within Africa and South Africa, in particular. We thus also hope that it will not only be a platform for teaching, but also stimulate further writing in Jurisprudence on the continent that can then be included in future editions.

# Chapter 2

# What is law? I: Positivism and traditional African societies

ORITSEGBUBEMI OYOWE

## 2.1 Introduction

Law is a fundamental aspect of human society and an attractive object of enquiry. We can distinguish two ways of enquiring into law. One might enquire into what the law is on a particular issue. So, one might ask what the law is in relation to the constitutional duties of a public official, say the president of South Africa. That enquiry would be mostly empirical and descriptive, however, requiring one to identify what pieces of legislation there are and are in fact applicable to that specific issue. Whereas lawyers are typically interested in such an undertaking, philosophers of law routinely seek to understand what makes all such pieces of legislation instances of law, or otherwise what all laws have in common. This alternative enquiry generalises about law. It assumes that there are core features that all instances of law share and that these can be systematically elucidated. To do this requires stepping outside the practice of law of itself, so as to delineate its conceptual limits.

One reason why it is important to clarify the meaning of law concerns the fact that law is only one of many systems of norms purporting to regulate human behaviour. For example, like law, the conventional rules of table etiquette: 'sit properly on your chair during meals', 'do not reach across the table to get the food', 'do not talk about gross things', and so on, also aim to regulate human behaviour. Are table manners instances of law, then? If not, why and in what way does law differ? Ultimately, philosophical interest in law also involves specifying what, if anything, is distinctive about law. That is, whether and in what way law as a system of norms differs from other normative systems, for example the norms that govern table manners.

In this chapter, we will engage with the question of what law essentially is, with an overarching focus on whether there was law in traditional African societies. The point is not to compare traditional societies with their modern counterparts. Instead, it is both to critically examine the implications of some of the prominent theories of law in mainstream English-speaking jurisprudence, including especially the positivist theories of John Austin, Hans Kelsen and Herbert Hart for the existence of law in traditional African societies and to learn about what, if any, notion of law was operative in them. As we shall see, these standard forms of positivism seem to imply, for differing reasons, that these societies lacked a system of law. Part of our aim, then, will be to evaluate the plausibility of these judgements. Specifically, we will be asking whether these positivist theories fully encapsulate the essence of law or whether there are aspects of legal phenomena exhibited in traditional African societies that these positivist theories simply fail to capture. On the latter, as we shall see, traditional African societies seem to have conceived law in a way not obviously compatible with the positivist theories we will be considering.

We will begin with a brief anthropology of traditional African societies, in particular, John Mbiti's description of a kinship society (section 2.2). We will then investigate whether these societies had a system of law. To guide us through that investigation, we will discuss and assess the implication of John Austin's theory of law as command (section 2.3). This will be followed (section 3.4) by a conception of law, specifically Mogobe Ramose's *ubuntu* conception of law, presumably compatible with the structures of traditional African societies. This conception of law will then be tested against both Hans Kelsen's view of law as a hierarchical system of autonomous norms and Herbert Hart's view of law as a union of primary and secondary rules. The implication of these two positivist theories will be assessed (section 2.5). We will then explore the possibility that there was law, in Hart's sense of law, in traditional societies by briefly considering an alternative characterisation of traditional African societies.

Throughout, the African approach to law will be brought into conversation with these positivist theories. The comparative approach will afford us the context not only to learn about these well-known European theories, and about a traditional African notion of law, but more importantly to determine whether the response to the question of the nature of law in traditional African societies raises problems for these positivist theories.

More clearly, the chapter will aim to provide answers to the following questions:
- What essentially is law in traditional African thought? Is there something distinctive about it?
- What is legal positivism?
- Is the notion of law in traditional African thought at all compatible with theories of law in mainstream, English-speaking jurisprudence?
- Do mainstream positivist theories of law capture all there is about legal phenomena?

## 2.2   The nature of traditional African societies

PRIMARY
TEXTS

**Text 1   John Mbiti on traditional kinship societies**

John Mbiti (1931) is a Kenyan philosopher and theologian. He has taught at the University of Makerere, in Uganda and later of Bern, in Switzerland, where he still lives. We will be looking at an extract from John Mbiti's classic *African Religions and Philosophy* (1969). The extract lays out what Mbiti deems to be the central aspect of the social organisation of traditional African societies.

> One finds many cultural similarities which cut across ethnic and linguistic differences, while at the same time some peoples who for generations have existed side by side, exhibit cultural traits that are remarkably different from those of their neighbours.[1] ... The deep sense of kinship, with all it implies, has been one of the strongest forces in traditional African life. Kinship is reckoned through blood and betrothal (engagement and marriage). It is kinship which controls social relationships between people in a given community: it governs marital customs and regulations, it determines the behaviour of one individual towards another. ... Almost all the concepts connected with human relationship can be understood and interpreted through the kinship system. This it is which largely governs the behaviour, thinking and whole life of the individual in the society of which he is a member.
>
> ... The kinship system is like a vast network stretching laterally (horizontally) in every direction, to embrace everybody in any given local group. This means that each individual is a brother or sister, father or mother, grandmother or grandfather, or cousin, or brother-in-law, uncle or aunt, or something else, to everybody else. That means that everybody is related to everybody else, and there are many kinship terms to express the precise kind of relationship pertaining between two individuals. When two strangers meet in a village, one of the first duties is to sort out how they may be related to each other, and having discovered how the kinship system applies to them, they behave to each other according to the accepted behaviour set down by society.[2]
>
> ... Apart from localizing the sense of kinship, clan systems provide closer human co-operation, especially in times of need. In case of internal conflicts, clan members joined one another to fight their aggressive neighbours, in former years. If a person finds himself in difficulties, it is not unusual for him to call for help from his clan members and other relatives, e.g. in paying fines caused by an accident (such as accidental wounding or killing of another person or damage to property); in finding enough goods to exchange for a wife; or today in giving financial support to students studying in institutes of higher education both at home and abroad.[3]
>
> In traditional society, the family includes children, parents, grandparents, uncles, aunts, brothers and sisters who may have their own children, and other immediate relatives. In many areas there are what anthropologists call extended families ... The family also includes the departed relatives, whom we have designated as the

---

1   Mbiti 1969 *African Religions and Philosophy* at 103.
2   Mbiti 1969 at 104.
3   Mbiti 1969 at 106.

living-dead. ... African concept of the family also includes the unborn members who are still in the loins of the living. They are the buds of hope and expectation, and each family makes sure that its own existence is not extinguished.[4]

... We have so far spoken about the life and existence of the community. What then is the individual and where is his place in the community? In traditional life, the individual does not and cannot exist alone except corporately. He owes his existence to other people, including those of past generations and his contemporaries. He is simply part of the whole. The community must therefore make, create or produce the individual; for the individual depends on the corporate group. ... Only in terms of other people does the individual become conscious of his own being, his own duties, his privileges and responsibilities towards himself and towards other people. ... Whatever happens to the individual happens to the whole group, and whatever happens to the whole group happens to the individual. The individual can only say: 'I am, because we are; and since we are, therefore I am'. This is a cardinal point in the understanding of the African view of man.[5]

**Questions**
1. How does Mbiti characterise the kinship system?
2. According to Mbiti, what are the benefits of the kinship system?
3. What, according to Mbiti, is the nature of the individual's relationship to the community in a kinship society?
4. In Mbiti's view, what is the cardinal principle in traditional African thought?

## 2.2.1. Social organisation and the kinship system

Human societies are usually organised in some recognisable way. According to Mbiti, traditional African societies were organised on the basis of the kinship system. So, in order to understand these societies, we will need to understand what the kinship system entails and how it was able to actuate social life. Mbiti develops the idea of the kinship system in two steps. The first step is mostly descriptive. That is, it involves describing the kinds of relationships that constitute the kinship system, as opposed to evaluating whether they are good, valuable, and so on. As Mbiti describes it, individual members of traditional societies were, as a matter of fact, related in some way to each other, starting from the most basic biological sort of relationships characterising the (extended) family through those forged by the union of families, by way of marriage, and spiraling outward to the clan and the wider community.

So, first, the (extended) family is the most basic unit of kinship societies. Individuals did not exist in isolation, or at least were not seen as existing in isolation, instead each individual was first and foremost a member of this or that family, and then related in particular ways to other members of the community. Second, the kinship system entails that *relationship* is an indispensable feature of social organisation in traditional Africa. It is worth highlighting that Mbiti includes, as part of the relationships that define the kinship system, those between members of the living human community, on the one hand, and departed family members, specifically ancestors, and those yet to be born, on the other.[6] Indeed, many contemporary Africans still maintain strong ties with ancestors. The importance of relationships between

---
4  Mbiti 1969 at 106–107.
5  Mbiti 1969 at 108–109.
6  Mbiti 1969 at 105.

living and non-living members of the community is seen as intelligible in the context of a well-defined worldview, according to which everything there is in reality is related and mutually interdependent. Nothing exists in isolation.[7] The kinship system, as Mbiti conceives it, mirrors this cosmic relationality and interdependence.

The second step in Mbiti's articulation of the kinship system is evaluative. In other words, he makes judgements about the relative significance and value of the kinship system, beyond merely describing what it consists in. Initially, Mbiti notes that it is *instrumentally* valuable. That is, it is valuable as a means to some other end. More clearly, the kinship system, with its focus on relationship, is valuable because it enables people to achieve certain desirable ends, for example protection of the group against outside aggression; co-operation and welfare in times of need, and so on. But he also suggests that it has *intrinsic* value. In other words, it is significant in itself, quite apart from it being a valuable means to achieving some further end. Its intrinsic value lies in it being the basis for relationships that are neither optional nor dispensable to human flourishing. This is why Mbiti affirms the fundamental dependence of each individual on the community in the statement: 'The individual can only say "I am, because we are; and since we are, therefore I am".' This saying will be familiar to speakers of *Nguni* languages, as its meaning coincides with the popular and oft used maxim namely, *umuntu ngumuntu ngabantu*, which translates as 'a person is a person through other people'. According to Mbiti, this is a cardinal principle in African thought.

### 2.2.2   Kinship as a system of norms

Essentially, then, a society modelled on the kinship system entails ordinary relationships between people, typically in the context of the (extended) family, and a social life organised in terms of relationships deemed to have some worth. Mbiti gives some indication of how the kinship system actually works, but it would help to slightly modify his example. Suppose that Sipho encounters Xolani at the market square and soon after exchanging pleasantries, Sipho realises that Xolani is an uncle on his mother's side of the family. In line with what is expected in that society, Sipho shows some form of respect towards Xolani. Perhaps, he refers to Xolani as *uMalume*, rather than by his first name. Otherwise, Sipho is naughty and does not give Xolani the required respect. In such case, Xolani may be expected to report Sipho to senior members of the family who may then take appropriate measures. In both cases – of showing and failing to show respect – it seems clear that there are norms that regulate how people in a kinship society should relate and behave. Other encounters between people in a kinship society may be more complex, involving families rather than individual members of families. For example, two families might regularly co-operate during farming seasons; one family supports another in planting and the other then reciprocates. Again, there are likely to be norms that regulate how groups of people co-operate towards shared ends.

There are two key lessons we can glean from these illustrations. The first is that the kinship system is normative, in that it is characterised by a set of norms that regulate how people behave. This is, in part, what Mbiti means when he says that the kinship system regulates social relationships, as well as institutions in traditional African societies. In order to regulate people's behaviours and relationships, it would have to entail norms that guide conduct in some way and that people regularly adhere to. Some of these may specify duties that people have, for example the duty that Sipho has towards Xolani, to not, as the latter's nephew, address him by his first name. Others may aid co-operation between families.

---

7   See Ramose 2003 *The African Philosophy Reader*.

Mbiti notes that some of these norms directly impact certain practices and institutions. His example of marriage signals that appropriate norms regulate how two families may be joined together in marriage. Still other norms may enjoin wealthy members of that society to contribute towards improving the welfare of the needy, and perhaps, also, specify duties to oneself, which may include improving one's human nature or seeking to become a better member of the community.[8] The second relates to the criterion for determining which norms are valid for a kinship-based society. There is an implicit suggestion in Mbiti that the validity of these norms depends on the rationale offered in favour of them, in particular that they forge and reinforce the kinship system. For example, a norm that requires Sipho to exhibit respect towards his uncle, Xolani, would be a valid norm for this society to the extent that it helps to honour, as opposed to harming, the relationship between them. Similarly, norms that require the wealthy to support the poor, and those that regulate the unions of families in the context of marriage are seen as acceptable in this society because they enable and improve relationships between people. On the contrary, those norms that tend to undermine relationships, and therefore the kinship system, may be deemed unacceptable.

Let us call the norms that regulate social life in a traditional kinship society, *customs*. The question we want to now investigate is whether there was law in a kinship society. Alternatively, are the customs of such a society equivalent to legal norms? Obviously, customs, like legal norms, also purport to regulate human behaviour, so the question is whether, and in what way, law, as a system of legal norms, differs from custom, as a system of kinship norms? In what follows, we will consider one positivist theory of law that seems to predict that Mbiti-type kinship societies were without law.

## 2.3 Legal positivism and conditions of legal validity I

Legal positivism is the view according to which law can be analysed solely in terms of more basic social facts about the conduct, beliefs and attitudes of human persons and particularly relationships of power and authority. It construes a legal system as a collection of these social facts, which are intelligible without appeal to valid moral principles. This is often referred to as the social thesis. Moreover, positivist theories are committed to the *separation* thesis. That is, the claim that law and morality are not essentially connected. More clearly, legal positivism is the view that whether some norm counts as law depends solely on the way it was enacted, or otherwise, the source of the norm, and not on whether it is morally sound. Naturalism, explored in Chapter 3, denies at least one of these two theses.

| PRIMARY TEXTS | Text 2 John Austin's *The Province of Jurisprudence Determined* |
|---|---|
| | John Austin (1790–1859) was an English jurist whose theory of law has been influential. Some of the lectures from a course he offered were published into a book, *The Province of Jurisprudence Determined*, in 1831. The selection below is taken from that book. |
| | The matter of jurisprudence is positive law: law, simply and strictly so called: or law set by political superiors to political inferiors. … A law, in the most general and comprehensive acceptation in which the term, in its literal meaning, is employed, may be said to be a rule laid down for the guidance of an intelligent |

8  Ramose 1999 *African Philosophy through Ubuntu* at 52.

being by an intelligent being having power over him. Under this definition are concluded, and without impropriety, several species.[9] ... Every law or rule (taken with the largest signification which can be given to the term properly) is a command. Or, rather, laws or rules, properly so called are a species of commands. Now, since the term command comprises the term law, the first is the simpler as well as the larger of the two. But, simple as it is, it admits of explanation. And, since it is the key to the sciences of jurisprudence and morals, its meaning should be analysed with precision. Accordingly, I shall endeavour, in the first instance, to analyse the meaning of 'command.'

... If you express or intimate a wish that I shall do or forbear from some act, and if you will visit me with an evil in case I shall comply not with your wish, the expression or intimation of your wish is a command. A command is distinguished from other significations of desire, not by the style in which the desire is signified, but by the power and the purpose of the party commanding to inflict an evil or pain in case the desire be disregarded. ... Being liable to evil from you if I comply not with a wish which you signify, I am bound or obliged by your command, or I lie under a duty to obey ... your command or to violate the duty which it imposes. Command and duty are, therefore correlative terms: the meaning denoted by each being implied or supposed by the other. ... Concisely expressed, the meaning of the correlative expressions is this. He who will inflict an evil in case his desire be disregarded, utters a command by expressing or intimating his desire: He who is liable to the evil in case he disregard the desire, is bound or obliged by the command. The evil which will probably be incurred in case a command be disobeyed or (to use an equivalent expression) in case a duty be broken, is frequently called a sanction, or an enforcement of obedience. Or (varying the phrase) the command or the duty is said to be sanctioned or enforced by the chance of incurring the evil. Considered as thus abstracted from the command and the duty which it enforces, the evil to be incurred by disobedience is frequently styled a punishment.[10]

... Command, duty, and sanction are inseparably connected terms: that each embraces the same ideas as the others though each denotes those ideas in a peculiar order or series. 'A wish conceived by one, and expressed or intimated to another, with an evil to be inflicted and incurred in case the wish be disregarded,' are signified directly and indirectly by each of the three expressions. Each is the name of the same complex notion.[11] ... It appears, from what has been premised, that a law properly so called, may be defined in the following manner. A law is a command which obliges a person or persons. But, as contradistinguished or opposed to an occasional or particular command, a law is a command which obliges a person or persons, and obliges generally to acts or forbearances of a class. In language more popular but less distinct and precise, a law is a command which obliges a person or persons to a course of conduct. Laws and other commands are said to proceed from superiors, and to bind or oblige inferiors.[12]

---

9   Austin 1954 *The Province of Jurisprudence Determined Etc* at 9–10.
10   Austin 1954 at 13–15.
11   Austin 1954 at 17–18.
12   Austin 1954 at 24.

**Questions**

1. What precisely does Austin mean by the proposition that law is essentially command?
2. In what way does Austin distinguish between law and other kinds of commands that are not law?
3. How does Austin connect the key concepts of command, sanction and sovereign in his analysis of law? What do these concepts mean?
4. In Austin's view, could there be law without sanction? What other feature besides sanction does he deem necessary for law?

## 2.3.1   The command theory of law

Austin analyses law in terms of other more basic concepts, in particular command, sanction and sovereign. In order to determine what he takes to be the essence of law, then, we need to grasp what these concepts mean. Austin proposes that law is essentially command. So, what does it mean to command? As a first approximation, he says to command is to express some wish. Ordinary cases of giving commands are expressions of some wish. For example, an army officer who commands troops to hold their fire expresses his or her wish that they refrain from shooting. A judge who directs a correctional service official to keep a suspected criminal in custody also expresses his or her wish that the suspect not be released.

Austin recognises, however, that not all expressed wishes are commands in the sense relevant to law. Some commands merely express a wish, while others, in addition to expressing a wish, are also backed by sanction. To sanction, as Austin uses it, is to be able to enforce obedience or to coerce others to obey the expressed wish by the threat of harm or punishment. It is the fact of sanction that distinguishes those commands that are law from those that are not. For example, our suspected criminal might express the wish that the sitting judge acquits him or her of every charge and order his or her release. But that is all it is – a wish! The judge, however, does not just merely express a wish that the suspect remain in custody; he or she is also able to coerce the suspect to comply by way of threatening punishment, perhaps a harsher sentence. Likewise, the army officer is able to coercively enforce the obedience of the troops by threatening punishment. The point is that Austin held that law is the sort of command that is backed by sanction or that can be coercively enforced.

Even so, anyone may give a command and back it up with a threat of punishment. But law is not the sort of command everyone may give. For Austin, law is command backed by sanction and issued by a political superior, rather than just anyone. By political superior, Austin has in mind a sovereign. So, law is the command of a sovereign backed by sanction. He defines a sovereign as a determinate person or body of persons who most people in society habitually obey and is not itself habitually obedient to any other person. Austin believed that all independent political societies have a sovereign. Moreover, the commands issued by a sovereign are usually general in character. They are not like the particular or occasional commands that ordinary people, like parents and employers, might sometimes issue to children and employees respectively (for example, study for your test; you must meet the deadline, and so on). Instead, they apply quite generally, and not merely in particular circumstances or only occasionally.

Let us focus a little on the idea of a sovereign. As we have seen, a sovereign is an entity that is able to demand the obedience of others but is not itself obedient to anyone else. God may be a sovereign in this sense. But Austin's interest is in positive law, that is, those laws made by humans or otherwise created by a political entity, like a state, as opposed to divine law. This is why Austin points out at the outset of the extract that law in this strict sense refers to something operative in the context of the relationship between political superiors and inferiors. Thus, a system of law exists if most people within a political society, typically political inferiors, habitually obey desires to perform or refrain from performing certain kinds of actions, where these are specified by a person or a group of persons – that is, political superiors who do not normally obey another and are able to sanction disobedience.

Additionally, the idea that the sovereign is a person or a body of persons who is able to compel the obedience of others, while not obeying anyone, suggests that the sovereign has absolute political power. In other words, whether or not something is law, according to Austin, is a matter of who has been able to exercise political power to compel the obedience of others, and not about morality, that is, whether in exercising political power one has acted morally right or wrong. Crucially, it is the awareness of the power of the sovereign to sanction disobedience that ultimately compels the political inferior to obey the sovereign. Put differently, the fear of punishment that might be imposed on him or her makes the political inferior feel duty-bound to comply with the commands of the sovereign.

### 2.3.2   Assessing Austin's command theory

We have so far linked three distinct concepts – command, sanction and sovereign – in analysing the essence of law. For Austin, law is essentially a species of command. That is, the sanctionable command of a sovereign. It entails some criteria for determining law, namely, for something to count as law, it must be a command issued by a sovereign and backed by sanction.

Austin's theory captures a lot of what law is. Much of what we regard as law is command of some kind backed up by sanctions. Legal injunctions often take the form of command: 'do $Y$', are typically categorical and often attached to penalties in the event of noncompliance. A law prohibiting murder, for example, is a categorical command to citizens: 'do *not kill*', Also, it is enforceable (there are usually special agencies of state tasked with enforcing law) or typically aims to be punitive (violations may be punishable with a life sentence, or the death penalty in some countries). Importantly, we do not normally regard the command of a school teacher, employer or a parent as law; instead, we regard law as issuing from some politically constituted authority, for example parliament, as is the case in contemporary South Africa. By identifying the source of law as a political superior, Austin's command theory is able to explain that aspect of legal phenomena.

Even so, the theory seems to yield the judgement that there was no law in traditional African kinship societies, insofar as they lack a sovereign who issues commands backed up by sanctions. Let us now critically assess the implication of Austin's theory. First off, if law is essentially *command* then a traditional kinship society like Mbiti's was without law. Unlike Austin's commands, which need not be justified in some way, kinship norms, as we saw, were taken to be valid only insofar as there was some rationale for them namely, that they support and reinforce the relationships that define the kinship system. Also, commands in Austin's sense do not bind the one (that is, the sovereign) who makes them, whereas kinship norms apply to everyone in the society. Finally, kinship norms do not necessarily command, instead they enable harmonious co-existence. Unlike commands that take the categorical form of 'do $Y$', kinship norms typically take the hypothetical form: 'if you want $X$, do $Y$'. For example, kinship norms that require one family to assist another in a planting season do not command, but merely enjoins the family to assist if they want to be assisted. Thus, not being commands, kinship norms could not be law.

But perhaps there are some laws that are not commands. If there are, then law is not essentially command, and kinship norms could be law. And indeed it appears there are some laws that are not commands. Consider reflexive rules. These are rules that bind those who make them, rather than merely binding others. If there are reflexive rules and if some of these are laws, then it seems that Austin's command theory is not able to account for the self-binding character of law. For example, a law enacted by the South African parliament prohibiting corrupt practices is a reflexive rule in that it also binds the parliamentarians who made the rule. But it is not a command since the idea of commanding oneself makes little sense. The table below clearly summarises the argument.

> **Proposition 1:** Some laws are reflexive rules.
> **Proposition 2:** Reflexive rules are not commands.
> Therefore,
> **Conclusion:** Some laws are not commands.

So, if we accept the command theory of law, we will be unable to account for those laws that are not commands. Perhaps kinship norms are laws of this type.

A friend of Austin might contend that the idea of commanding oneself can be made intelligible. Austin himself appears to envisage this possibility by appealing to differential capacities in those who make laws.[13] For example, the people who make law act in a public capacity (as officials) but are bound to that law in a private capacity (as citizens). So, perhaps it can make sense to conceive of commanding *others* in a way that includes *oneself in a private capacity*. This revision, however, does not quite convince since laws do actually bind those who make them in their public capacity as officials.

Similar difficulties arise in relation to facilitative or power-conferring rules. These rules enable or confer on people the power to carry out certain tasks or give effect to certain institutions, for instance the rules that facilitate marriage or the signing of contracts. Like kinship norms, facilitative rules are not commands in that they take the hypothetical form: 'if you want X, do Y'. For example, 'if you want to make a will, get two witnesses'. If there are such rules, and if some of them are laws, then such laws do not command. So, either we reject the view that the essential character of law is that laws command or we deny that facilitative rules, including kinship norms, have legal validity. The core of the argument is summarised below.

> **Proposition 1:** Some laws are facilitative rules.
> **Proposition 2:** Facilitative rules are not commands.
> Therefore,
> **Conclusion:** Some laws are not commands.

Again, a friend of Austin might insist instead that so-called facilitative rules can ultimately be viewed as commands directed towards *officials*, not towards citizens.[14] For example, perhaps the law governing wills is a command to a judge as follows: 'if two witnesses attest that a competent person has signed a will, then consider the will valid'. Ultimately, then, Austin's command theory would be able to accommodate facilitative rules only if they are

---

13   Austin 1954 at 29–30; see also Hart 1994 at 42.
14   See Hart 1994 at 45, 64.

construed as commands directed to officials. However, these rules are not usually understood in this way in contemporary political societies that exhibit a legal system.[15] In these societies, facilitative rules are understood to confer powers on public officials as opposed to commanding them.

The point of the two arguments above is to demonstrate that the proposition that law is essentially command does not fully capture the entire gamut of legal phenomena. To the extent that some laws are reflexive or facilitative (and so not commands), the idea that law is command excludes these laws. As such, we might doubt the implication of Austin's command theory that there was no law in traditional kinship society.

Further, if law requires sanction then it would seem that kinship societies in traditional Africa were without law. Not only did kinship societies not typically develop established machinery (for example, a police force) for the enforcement of norms, in part because emphasis was placed on developing good character and the value of the kinship system in people such that enforcement was less urgent, it also appears that the norms that govern these societies did not aim to be punitive at all.[16] Indeed, social sanction was sometimes applied, for example, community members who were found guilty of grave crimes, perhaps murder, were ostracised or banished, and collective action could be mobilised to do so. However, punishment, and especially severe punishment, was not characteristic of these societies. Instead, the primary aim was always to restore the broken relationships and rehabilitate offenders.[17] In other words, although punishment or coercive enforcement was applied sometimes, it was not seen as essential to the system of norms. If this was the case, then these societies could not have had law, since, on Austin's view, sanction is necessary to law.

Is sanction or punishment really essential to law? Perhaps a legal system can exist without any punishment. Such a system might comprise public rules but, instead of being punished for breaking them, offenders are rehabilitated and broken relationships restored. Perhaps the traditional society described by Mbiti had a system of law that did not aim to be punitive. This is not at all improbable. As we saw above, facilitative rules are laws in contemporary legal systems that are not punitive. For example, the failure of the legislature to conform to the rules that facilitate the passing of a law does not result in punishment, but only in invalidity. So, if some rule that does not aim to be punitive counts as law, then Austin's theory is doubtful. The table below summarises the core of the argument:

> **Proposition 1:** There can be laws that are not punitive or coercively enforced.
> **Proposition 2:** If there can be laws that are not punitive or coercively
> enforced, then some laws are not backed up by sanctions.
> Therefore,
> **Conclusion:** Some laws are not backed up by sanctions.

Notice that a friend of Austin may still insist that a rule that is not backed up with sanctions is not law.[18] Perhaps a system of public rules without punishment is not a legal system in the truest sense, though it is something similar. If this is the case, then perhaps the norms that regulate social life in a kinship society are not truly legal norms, though they may be something similar.

---

15   Hart 1994 at 41.
16   Okafor 1984 *International Philosophical Quarterly* at 161.
17   Okafor 1984 at 161.
18   Austin 1954 at 26–28, 30.

Assuming, then, that sanction is essential to law, perhaps traditional kinship societies did have law insofar as they employed social sanctions. However, this move is undercut by the fact that in Austin's account it would seem that the sanctions relevant to law require a *sovereign*. To fully address this question we will need to examine the plausibility of this implication of Austin's theory namely, that law requires a *sovereign*. The point here is that even if it is granted that the kinship norms that regulate social life in traditional societies were backed up by (social) sanction, such societies nonetheless seem to lack Austin's sovereign, that is, a person or group of persons who is habitually obeyed but not habitually obedient to anyone. What is at issue is the suggestion that the sovereign has no limits at all. It is quite hard to determine who or what might fit this characterisation in the kinship society Mbiti portrays. Because the accepted norms in those societies were justified independently of any particular person or group of persons uttering them, and in terms of their usefulness in supporting and reinforcing the kinship system, it would seem that everyone in a kinship society was bound by kinship norms. So, no one person or group of persons in a kinship society was sovereign. If a sovereign is necessary for law, then there was no law in kinship societies.

But perhaps there can be law without a sovereign. Modern constitutional democracies, like South Africa and Kenya, appear to lack a sovereign in Austin's sense, although they have law. If societies without a sovereign have law, then law does not require a sovereign. So, law is not just what a sovereign commands. The table below clearly outlines the core of the argument:

> **Proposition 1:** There is no sovereign in modern, constitutional democracies such as South Africa.
>
> **Proposition 2:** Modern, constitutional democracies such as South Africa have law.
>
> Therefore,
>
> **Conclusion:** Law is not just what a sovereign commands.

The possibility that law could exist without a sovereign leaves open the possibility that traditional kinship societies did have law, even though they lacked a sovereign in Austin's sense. Of course, it is open to a friend of Austin to consider various suggestions about which persons might be the sovereign in a democratic society.[19] Or, perhaps, who or what might be a sovereign in traditional kinship societies. He or she might identify the chiefs in kinship societies as sovereigns. This seems unlikely, however, since, as noted, the validity of kinship norms depended on the rationale in favour of them, and were not simply what traditional chiefs decreed. Also, Mbiti is quite explicit that kinship norms regulated everyone and all aspects of social life.[20] He or she might instead identify the community or society itself as sovereign. Although not a person, it seems to fit the description of an entity that is habitually obeyed but not obedient to others. After all, Mbiti himself says that that it is 'the community' that must 'make, create or produce the individual'. Perhaps, the 'community' also creates norms that people abide by, even though the community itself does not obey these norms. It is unlikely, however, that traditional peoples conceived of the community this way, as some independently existing entity capable of issuing commands that regulate kinship societies. More accurately, the 'community' does not *do* anything; it is simply the context in which individuals can develop and flourish as human beings.

---

19   Austin 1954 at 24–25, see also Hart 1994 at 73.
20   Mbiti 1969 at 104.

One final difficulty for Austin's theory is that it does not seem to explain in a satisfactory manner why citizens have a sense of legal obligation. People who live under a system of law often have a sense that they are bound by those laws. A plausible theory of law should be able to explain this fact satisfactorily. Austin's theory does not seem able to. To see this, imagine that you are accosted by a gunman who demands: 'your money or your life'. You hand over your money to the gunman in order to preserve your life. The gunman coerced you to obey by threatening to kill you – that is, by backing up his command with sanction. If fear of harm leads you to obey the gunman, then you were not duty-bound to obey, even if you actually did, since the gunman had no authority to coerce you in the first place.

The state may be said to be the gunman writ large, with the exceptions that laws are general, obeyed over time and issue from a sovereign.[21] Now, suppose that a representative of the state, the taxman, orders you to pay your tax or otherwise face jail time. Suppose further that you comply because of the fear of punishment that would be brought upon you had you not. But if fear of punishment does not justify obedience to the gunman, even if you actually obeyed, neither should fear of punishment justify obedience to the state, in the person of the taxman. That is, just as the gunman may have power to force you to obey, but not the authority to do so, so also the taxman. What we need is a way of explaining the difference between the two, that is, some explanation of why the state has *authority* or is *justified* to compel citizens to comply, but the gunman does not. Crucially, since Austin's theory relies on the fear of punishment to account for why citizens ought to obey the law, it cannot neatly distinguish between obedience to a gunman and obedience to the state. This seems inadequate. It seems that law, and especially obligation to obey law, requires more than just command, sanction and a sovereign.

All these difficulties call into question the plausibility of Austin's theory of law as essentially command. As a result, its implication that traditional kinship societies, as envisaged by Mbiti, were without law is hard to believe. However, if there was law in these societies, what would a theory of it look like? In the next section, we turn attention to a notion of law presumably germane to traditional African societies.

## 2.4   Customary law and legal validity

Some African scholars hold that the customs of a society constitutes a system of law. Below, we will be reading a selection from philosopher Mogobe Ramose that approximates that view. Ramose has taught Philosophy of Law at the University of Tilburg, in the Netherlands and was Professor of Philosophy at the University of South Africa.

| PRIMARY TEXTS | Text 3  Mogobe Ramose's African conception of law |
|---|---|
| | ... Orientation towards the supernatural forces is the abstract dimension of *ubuntu* law. Its quest for justice is not focused in the world of the supernatural forces. Instead, it is directed immediately towards the world of the living in the first place and, the yet-to-be-born in the second place. Thus with regard to the application of justice it accords primacy to the concrete, the world of the living. In this sense it is different from Western legal thought which apparently stresses the abstract. |

---

21   The example is discussed in Hart 1994 at 23–24.

... Another feature of *ubuntu* law is that it is flexible, unformalised, reasonable and linked to morality. The flexibility of *ubuntu* law speaks to the idea that it is law without a center. This is because *ubuntu* philosophy holds that being is one continuous wholeness rather than a finite whole. On this reasoning, the legal subject cannot be the center of the law. This does not deny the importance of the legal subject in law. Thus conceived the legal subject is the active negation of a false abstract necessity and finality claiming to be the truth about law. This means that law consists of rules of behaviour contained in the flow of life. The idea that life is a constant flow and flux means that it cannot be decided in advance that certain legal rules have an irreversible claim to exist permanently. This speaks to the reasonableness of *ubuntu* law even though it might be unformalised. In this sense *ubuntu* law is a dynamology in search of justice as the restoration of equilibrium. ... Both the justice and the validity of law are judged by the criterion of *ubuntu* (*botho*). *Umuntu* a human being in the biological sense, is enjoined to become a human being proper by embracing *ubuntu*. *Umuntu* must be the embodiment of *ubuntu* because the fundamental ethical, social and legal judgement of human dignity and conduct is based upon *ubuntu*. *Ubuntu* is the principle that we act humanely and with respect towards others as a way of demanding the same from them. Similarly, law to be worth its name and to command respect must evince *ubuntu*.

### 2.4.1   An *ubuntu* conception of law

Ramose sets out what he terms *ubuntu* conception of law in opposition to what he sees as characteristic of Western legal thought, namely, that it conceives law in abstract terms. Ramose is suggesting that in Western thought, law is formalised, codified and abstracted from the concrete experiences of people in society. On the contrary, his *ubuntu* conception of law tends to focus on concrete social reality. It begins with and is rooted in the actual experience of people in society. And since social reality is dynamic, flexible, adaptable and never static, a corresponding conception of law is not likely to be formalised in the way theories in Western legal thought, like Austin's, are. Instead, it is flexible and adaptable to the changing circumstances of social reality.

There is, in Ramose's initial submission, an implicit criticism of the methodology of mainstream positivism and of Austin's command theory, in particular, which ostensibly specifies rigid and unchanging criteria for identifying law. According to Ramose, to take the conditions of legal validity, or the criteria for identifying law, as fixed and unchanging and to further require that only those norms that conform to these rigid conditions are law, is to render law by definition inflexible and incapable of adaptation to different circumstances. Put differently, Austin's rather rigid criteria that law is essentially the sanctionable command of a sovereign makes it unlikely that there could be law under substantially different conditions in which perhaps there is no sovereign and no sanction. Ramose's *ubuntu* conception of law appears to avoid that outcome, since it takes law to be essentially 'flexible' and 'unformalised', in the sense of being both unofficial, that is, not consisting of codified rules issuing from some politically constituted source, and adaptable to the constant changes and transformations typical of the social life and experience of any given community. Thus, in his view, 'law consists of rules of behaviour contained in the flow of life' and is basically 'unformalised'. As such, it 'cannot be decided in advance that certain legal rules have an irreversible claim to exist permanently' because life itself 'is a constant flow and flux'.

The idea that law comprises 'the rules of behaviour contained in the flow of life' seems to suggest that it is the customs of a community that constitutes its law. After all, customs emerge from everyday experiences and practices, that is, from 'the flow of life' and are readily adaptable to changing circumstances, thus exhibiting the kind of flexibility that Ramose sees as essential to law. Moreover, it is an *ubuntu* conception insofar as the norms that characterise that flow of life are based on the *ubuntu* principle, which requires people to exhibit humane qualities and respect towards each other. If this is right, then, Ramose's *ubuntu* conception of law is an account of law as customary law. Customary law proponents define it is 'a body of customs and traditions which regulates the various kinds of relationships between members of the community'.[22] Yet, the customs of a society could be codified. If so, it would lack the features Ramose deems defining, namely, flexibility and lack of formality. In response, two forms of customary law may be distinguished, one 'official', the other 'living'. Whereas official customary law refers to a people's documented, codified customs, in that they are contained in legal texts, Acts, court judgments and so on, the idea of a living customary law refers to a people's undocumented and uncodified customs, typically emerging from the actual conditions and experience of social life. Ramose's *ubuntu* conception of law appears to align with living customary law, seeing that he seeks to preserve its unofficial character and to locate it in the actual 'flow of life'.

It is worth pointing out that the notion of a living customary law, in the mold of Ramose's conception of law, recognised in contemporary South African law. For instance, in *Shilubana v Nwamitwa*,[23] the Constitutional Court of South Africa noted the 'adaptive' character of living customary law. Specifically, it noted that 'customary law is an independent and original source of law' and 'adaptive by its very nature'. Moreover, it noted that '... change is intrinsic to and can be invigorating of customary law'.[24] Moreover, Constitutional Court judges have implicitly affirmed living customary law over the official type. In *Bhe v Magistrate, Khayelitsha*[25] they argued that 'because of the dynamic nature of society, official customary law as it exists in the textbooks and in the Act is generally a poor reflection, if not a distortion of the true customary law ... which recognises and acknowledges the changes which continually take place'.[26]

## 2.4.2   Customs and social acceptance

In general, an account of law should be able to explain what makes some norm law. Typically, this involves determining whether the source, that is, the manner in which the norm is adopted, is sufficient to make it law (positivism) or whether in addition to, or perhaps instead of its source, the content of the norm, that is, what the norm directs us to do, is a condition of legal validity (naturalism). Although always evolving, the notion of living customary law entails certain conditions of legal validity.

Obviously, the source of customary law is custom. The key question is what makes some custom law. The validity of customary law depends also on social acceptance. This is entailed by the very notion of customs; they are precisely the sort of rules that a community have come to accept as regulative of their behaviour and practices. Ramose's reference to the fact that custom is a feature of the concrete social reality of people and the 'flow of life', implicitly

---

22   Jobodwana 2000 *Southern African Public Law* at 30.
23   2009 2 SA 66 (CC).
24   At para 54.
25   *Bhe v Magistrate, Khayelitsha (Commission for Gender Equality as Amicus Curiae); Shibi v Sithole; South African Human Rights Commission v President of the Republic of South Africa* 2005 (1) SA 580 (CC).
26   At para 86.

suggests that these customs have authority for members of a given community to the extent that they accept them as binding and regulative of behaviour. It would seem, then, that it is social acceptance that gives legal validity to customs. In addition to social acceptance, however, Ramose seems to indicate facts regarding the content of customs, that is, what they direct us to do, play some role in determining their status as law. For him, customary law is able to 'command respect' precisely because its injunctions, and 'its validity', are based on the principle of *ubuntu*, in that it enjoins people to be humane and respectful towards others. Roughly, then, customary law exists just in case members of a community routinely abide by customs they deem authoritatively binding because these customs are socially acceptable, which customs are always adapting to the changing circumstances of social existence.

So defined, customary law does not include any of the requirements, that is, command, sanction, sovereign, that Austin's command theory takes to be necessary. Moreover, the customary law view entails that traditional kinship societies had laws insofar as they had customs. Again, this implication clearly separates it from Austin's theory. One other respect in which customary law differs from Austin's command theory relates to the question of legal obligation. In order to see this, recall the comparison between the gunman and the taxman. On Austin's theory, fear of punishment justifies obedience in both cases. As such, we are unable to prise law and unjustified coercion apart. A customary law approach differs in this regard. On this view, the customs that regulate social life are based on social acceptance, and in Ramose's view, on *ubuntu*, and so are seen by members of the community as constituting adequate standard for assessing behaviour. In other words, the reasons for adhering to them are internal to the customs, rather than merely imposed from the outside by some powerful sovereign, as in Austin's account. In this sense, customary law captures the internal aspect of law, that is, its ability to generate in its adherents a sense of justified rather than forced obligation. Customary law, specifically the internal aspect of customs, thus allows us to explain why the action of the gunman may not be law and that of the taxman might be law. Whereas the rule applied by the gunman is unlikely to be based on social acceptance or correspond to the community's moral belief, in this case the principle of *ubuntu*, it is reasonable to expect that the rule upon which the taxman bases his action could be, if, for example, the proceeds of taxation are directed towards uplifting the needy and providing welfare to members of the community.

It is significant that although Ramose sees some relationship between law and morality, specifically *ubuntu* moral principle, he does not clearly specify the nature of this relationship. If, on the one hand, he is concerned merely with law as related to people's beliefs about morality, then this notion of customary law might as well as count as a form of positivism. This is because, for positivists, people's beliefs about morality might be one of the social facts upon which law is based. If, on the other hand, Ramose is gesturing towards *ubuntu* as a *valid* moral principle, and not merely people's beliefs about it, then his view of law comes very close to naturalism, which we discuss in detail in Chapter 3.

## 2.5   Legal positivism and conditions of legal validity II

The advantage of customary law over the command model of law notwithstanding, it seems that we could reasonably distinguish between law *proper* and customs. Perhaps, there are customs in kinship societies, like Mbiti's, but these are not legal norms. If so, on what basis could the distinction be made? In this section, we consider two attempts in the legal positivist tradition to distinguish law from customs.

## 2.5.1   Hans Kelsen's law as a hierarchical system of autonomous norms

Hans Kelsen (1881–1973) was an Austrian jurist and legal philosopher. He was born in Prague in what is now known as the Czech Republic. Following the rise of Nazism, Kelsen left his university post in Austria. He would later become a professor at the University of California, Berkeley in the United States. He is well known for his formulation of a positivist theory of law, the 'pure theory' of law.

Kelsen's 'pure theory' of law is 'pure', precisely because it distinguishes law clearly from what he deemed to be extraneous elements, including moral factors. He held that whereas law is an objective matter and can be subjected to scientific enquiry, moral claims are determined subjectively and in general value judgements, that is, judgements that state how things ought to be, cannot be objectively verified as they are based on emotional factors. For Kelsen, law is the object of objective, scientific enquiry. It would be a misguided venture to identify something objective as law by subjecting it to some subjective, moral test. Therefore, morality is not required to determine what the law is.

Moreover, for Kelsen, law and morality rely on two logically separate sets of statements. On the one hand, law relies on descriptive statements, that is, statements that describe some state of affairs in the world. For example, 'the presiding judge has arrived' describes some fact about the world. It is empirically and objectively verified. You could go out there and ascertain whether the proposition corresponds to the fact. Statements that constitute the natural sciences, for example the proposition, 'water is $H_2O$', are of this sort. Unlike descriptive statements, moral claims are normative, in that they state what ought to be the case. For example, the moral claim, 'one ought not to kill an innocent person', is not objectively and empirically verifiable. Even so, Kelsen held that law is not purely descriptive. Although sociological and psychological accounts of law describe how people *actually* behave and so are purely descriptive, Kelsen insists that laws describe how people *ought* to behave, and so law is partly normative. For example, laws state that people *ought* not to kill, rape, steal and so forth. So, although law statements are descriptive, law is also a system of norms, that is, law description of '*ought*-statements'.

Since laws describe *ought*-statements, and morality also concerns *ought*-statements, Kelsen goes on to distinguish between legal *ought* and moral *ought*, or otherwise, legal norms and moral norms. Kelsen defines a legal system as comprising those norms that prescribe some sanction. That is, a norm not prescribing a sanction and not connected to one prescribing a sanction is not law according to Kelsen. In other words, like Austin, Kelsen holds that what distinguishes law from morality is that it is coercive and can be backed up by sanctions. Kelsen thinks that laws are directed at appropriate legal officials who can impose sanctions for violating them. For example, prohibition on murder is an instruction to a judge: 'if anyone commits murder, you *ought* to impose a sanction on that person'. Kelsen believes that we can translate all law statements into statements of the above kind. But whether such sanctions are moral or applied justly is not relevant for the identification of law. In this sense, law is autonomous, that is, independent of morality. Legal science is the study of sanction – prescribing norms as they are contained in law reports, statutes, acts and so on, and not a study of whether they are moral or just.

Although Kelsen's and Austin's accounts of law require sanction, they are different in important ways. One such difference relates to the question of legal validity. For Austin, a sanctionable command of a sovereign has legal validity. However, for Kelsen, the validity of a sanction-prescribing norm depends on its place within a hierarchical system of norms. Each norm depends for its validity on a higher norm in the hierarchy.

The idea that norms acquire legal validity from higher norms that authorise them illustrates how Kelsen's account diverges from Austin's. To see this, consider again the example of the gunman and the taxman. Both make demands that are ought-statements and that prescribe some sanction. The difference, on Kelsen's system, is that the taxman's demands are authorised by a higher norm, namely tax law, and the tax law is validated by another higher norm, for example a constitution. More clearly, in South Africa, for instance, it is the Constitution that confers authority on the legislature to make tax laws, which gives legitimacy to the taxman's demands. In other words, whereas the norm 'you should pay your tax', which the taxman relies on, derives its legal validity within a hierarchical system of norms, no such validity exists in the case of the gunman. So, you are not obligated to fulfil his demand, even if you are forced to do so. In this way, Kelsen's hierarchical system of law, unlike Austin's command theory, competently deals with the question of legal obligation.

But if legal norms depend on higher norms for their validity, what does the higher norm depend on for its validity? That is, if the taxman's demand depends on tax laws, and tax laws depend on the South African Constitution, which authorises it, what makes the South African Constitution valid? According to Kelsen the hierarchy terminates in a basic norm or 'grundnorm'. The grundnorm is the foundation of a legal system and it is posited as the source of validity of all norms in the hierarchy. Its validity is not dependent on a higher norm. Part of Kelsen's motivation for positing the grundnorm is that without it, the series of norms in the hierarchy and chain of authorisation or validation will continue *ad infinitum*. By positing the grundnorm, he is able to terminate the series. The grundnorm is thus a necessary end point of justification of a hierarchical system of law. It exists just when a legal order is effective. And a legal system is effective when its legal norms are generally applied and obeyed.

Notice, however, that the grundnorm is not itself a legal norm. It has to be outside a legal system in order to account for legal validity. If it is part of the legal system, we would have to account for its validity in terms of a more fundamental norm. Kelsen construes it as a norm presupposed by a legal system. In the case of South Africa, the presupposition would be something like: 'we ought to obey the Constitution'. This presupposition is what gives the South African Constitution its validity, in that without it the South African system of law would not be possible at all. An analogy may be helpful at this point. Scientists are able to make valid statements about the natural world, like 'the bonding of a carbon atom and two oxygen atoms results in the gas carbon dioxide $(CO_2)$'. But these statements are valid because of the presupposition that 'scientific observations correspond to reality'. For Kelsen, just as this assumption about the natural world is necessary for scientific statements to be valid, so also is a grundnorm necessary for a legal system.

### 2.5.2   Assessing Kelsen's 'pure' theory of law

For our present purposes, it seems that Kelsen's view of law as a hierarchical system of norms would rule out law for traditional kinship societies, not only because kinship norms or customs are not necessarily seen as occupying different positions in a hierarchy system, but also because they are not autonomous in the sense that Kelsen envisages for law. As we saw, customs also encapsulate the moral norms of a community. If Kelsen is correct, then the notion of customary law is problematic. A useful way to proceed then would be to critically examine whether Kelsen's account is independently plausible, otherwise we are not rationally compelled to take seriously its implications for traditional kinship societies.

One difficulty with Kelsen's position relates to the role of sanction. Although, he introduces the notion of a norm into the analysis of law, his view is strikingly similar to Austin's, in that he sees sanction as a distinctive feature of law. However, as we observed, in relation to Austin's theory, the attempt to reduce something as complex as law to one element, that is, sanction, runs the risk of distorting it. It seems that different laws serve a variety of functions. For example, some laws are facilitative (such as the option of disposing of property on death). With regards to laws that confer powers on officials, Kelsen claims that we can interpret them as directives to the relevant official to enforce a certain order. As we saw, this suggestion is not entirely persuasive. If we are to fully understand the nature of power-conferring rules, we have to consider them from the point of view of those who exercise these powers. This is because quite apart from instructing some official to enforce some order, they transform a private citizen into a legislator. They add an 'additional element introduced by law into social life over and above that of coercive control'.[27] Kelsen, like Austin, fails to capture this feature of law.

More worrying for Kelsen's theory of law is the notion of the grundnorm. On his view, it is the basis of validity for a constitution that is effective, that is, generally applied and obeyed. Now, suppose that revolutionary leaders took over power. They are in effective control and generally obeyed. On Kelsen's view, since they are generally obeyed we would have to postulate a new grundnorm as the basis of validity of the new legal order. However, this seems to allow an armed group of individuals to take over by a coup d'état and enforce their will, as has been the case in some African states with a history of dictatorial regimes, and for us to have to presuppose the legal validity of their behaviour. In short, it appears we have returned to the situation of the gunman. The difficulty here is that Kelsen's view that we presuppose legal validity when a legal order is effective seems to dress gunmen in a cloak of legal decency. It appears that something other than the presupposition of a grundnorm when there is effective control and general obedience will be needed to adequately account for legal validity.

## 2.5.3   Law as a union of primary and secondary rules

**PRIMARY TEXTS**

**Text 4  Herbert Hart's *The Concept of Law***

Herbert Lionel Adolphus Hart (1907–1992) was a British legal philosopher and a Professor of Jurisprudence at Oxford University. He worked as a barrister prior to World War II, preferring to take up a teaching position in Oxford after the war. Hart's book, *The Concept of Law* (1961), is widely considered an important contribution to legal philosophy. The following selection is drawn from that book.

It is, of course, possible to imagine a society without a legislature, courts, or officials of any kind. Indeed, there are many studies of primitive communities which not only claim that this possibility is realized but depict in detail the life of a society where the only means of social control is that general attitude of the group towards its own standard modes of behaviour in terms of which we have characterized rules of obligation. A social structure of this kind is often referred to as one of 'custom'; but we shall not use this term, because it often implies that the customary rules are very old and supported with less social pressure than other rules. To avoid these implications we shall refer to such a social structure as one of primary rules of obligation. If a society is to live by such primary rules alone, there are certain conditions which, granted a few of the most obvious truisms about human nature and the world we live in, must clearly be satisfied.

---

27   Hart 1994 at 41.

The first of these conditions is that the rules must contain in some form restrictions on the free use of violence, theft, and deception to which human beings are tempted but which they must, in general, repress, if they are to coexist in close proximity to each other. Such rules are in fact always found in the primitive societies of which we have knowledge, together with a variety of others imposing on individuals various positive duties to perform services or make contributions to the common life.

... More important for our present purpose is the following consideration. It is plain that only a small community closely knit by ties of kinship, common sentiment, and belief, and placed in a stable environment, could live successfully by such a regime of unofficial rules. In any other conditions such a simple form of social control must prove defective and will require supplementation in different ways. In the first place, the rules by which the group lives will not form a system, but will simply be a set of separate standards, without any identifying or common mark, except of course that they are the rules which a particular group of human beings accepts. They will in this respect resemble our own rules of etiquette. Hence if doubts arise as to what the rules are or as to the precise scope of some given rule, there will be no procedure for settling this doubt, either by reference to an authoritative text or to an official whose declarations on this point are authoritative. For, plainly, such a procedure and the acknowledgement of either authoritative text or persons involve the existence of rules of a type different from the rules of obligation or duty which *ex hypothesi* are all that the group has. This defect in the simple social structure of primary rules we may call its uncertainty.

A second defect is the static character of the rules. The only mode of change in the rules known to such a society will be the slow process of growth, whereby courses of conduct once thought optional become first habitual or usual, and then obligatory, and the converse process of decay, when deviations, once severely dealt with, are first tolerated and then pass unnoticed. There will be no means, in such a society, of deliberately adapting the rules to changing circumstances, either by eliminating old rules or introducing new ones: for, again, the possibility of doing this presupposes the existence of rules of a different type from the primary rules of obligation by which alone the society lives.

... The third defect of this simple form of social life is the inefficiency of the diffuse social pressure by which the rules are maintained. Disputes as to whether an admitted rule has or has not been violated will always occur and will, in any but the smallest societies, continue interminably, if there is no agency specially empowered to ascertain finally, and authoritatively, the fact of violation. Lack of such final and authoritative determinations is to be distinguished from another weakness associated with it. This is the fact that punishments for violations of the rules, and other forms of social pressure involving physical effort or the use of force, are not administered by a special agency but are left to the individuals affected or to the group at large.[28]

---

28   Hart 1994 at 91–93.

... The remedy for each of these three main defects in this simplest form of social structure consists in supplementing the primary rules of obligation with secondary rules which are rules of a different kind. The introduction of the remedy for each defect might, in itself, be considered a step from the prelegal into the legal world; since each remedy brings with it many elements that permeate law: certainly all three remedies together are enough to convert the regime of primary rules into what is indisputably a legal system.

... The simplest form of remedy for the uncertainty of the regime of primary rules is the introduction of what we shall call a 'rule of recognition'. This will specify some feature or features possession of which by a suggested rule is taken as a conclusive affirmative indication that it is a rule of the group to be supported by the social pressure it exerts.

The remedy for the static quality of the regime of primary rules consists in the introduction of what we shall call 'rules of change'. The simplest form of such a rule is that which empowers an individual or body of persons to introduce new primary rules for the conduct of the life of the group, or of some class within it, and to eliminate old rules.[29] ... The third supplement to the simple regime of primary rules, intended to remedy the inefficiency of its diffused social pressure, consists of secondary rules empowering individuals to make authoritative determinations of the question whether, on a particular occasion, a primary rule has been broken. The minimal form of adjudication consists in such determinations, and we shall call the secondary rules which confer the power to make them 'rules of adjudication'.

... If we stand back and consider the structure which has resulted from the combination of primary rules of obligation with the secondary rules of recognition, change and adjudication, it is plain that we have here not only the heart of a legal system, but a most powerful tool for the analysis of much that has puzzled both the jurist and the political theorist.

### Questions

1. What does Hart mean by primary rules and why does he think a society with only primary rules cannot constitute a legal system?
2. What are secondary rules and what role do they play in Hart's concept of law?
3. According to Hart, in what essentially does a legal system consist?
4. What does Hart mean by the 'internal point of view' of law and what is its role in his concept of law?

Hart sought to provide a general theory of the institution of law in a municipal system. He did this by imagining a small, homogeneous community with shared beliefs and the most rudimentary set of rules, or rather customs. These customs restrict violence, theft, deception and so forth. Most of the people in such a society accept these rules, although it is conceivable that a minority of them are dissenting. A society so constituted will have what Hart describes as primary rules. Some rule is a primary rule if it imposes some duty, that is,

---

29   Hart 1994 at 94–98.

tells us what we must do. For example, rules like 'do not murder', 'pay your taxes', 'honour your contracts' and so on, are primary rules. Notice that Hart's picture of a small, homogenous community evokes Mbiti's traditional kinship society, comprising what Hart here calls primary rules. For Hart, a community constituted by primary rules only cannot have law. In order for a society to have law, it must have, in addition to primary rules, secondary rules. These are rules about primary rules. Whereas primary rules regulate what people should do or how they should behave, secondary rules are concerned with primary rules. Specifically, they enable us to recognise primary rules, determine when they change and settle disputes about how to apply them.

In order to justify why secondary rules must supplement primary rules so as to have a system of law, Hart considers a number of problems likely to confront a society comprising only primary rules. Secondary rules are then proposed as remedies to these problems. The first is the problem of uncertainty. At some point, it may become unclear, in a community with only primary rules, which rules actually exist or how to determine the nature of these rules. Since there are no authoritative texts or decision-making structure to consult, what might follow is widespread uncertainty as to which rules actually exist or what the rules really are. To remedy this problem, that community would have to adopt some secondary rule, namely, 'rules of recognition', that is, rules that specify how people in that society identify which primary rules are properly rules of the group and so can be supported by social pressure. Rules of recognition will also specify the procedure to follow where there is uncertainty as to primary rules. If some primary rule meets the criteria prescribed by rules of recognition, then it is legally valid. Moreover, Hart held that rules of recognition are purely conventional rules, that is, they depend entirely on whether, as a matter of social fact, they have been accepted in a particular society, and not on the reasons in favour of them. In contemporary South Africa, an example of a rule of recognition would be something like this: 'if a primary rule is passed by a legislature by a simple majority, it is valid and binding'. Such a rule permits easy recognition of primary rules, thus avoiding the problem of uncertainty. Moreover, its validity is based on it being socially accepted in virtue of people living together in a democratic society.

The second problem for a community of only primary rules is determining whether and how primary rules change. With only a set of primary rules in force, there will be no way of adapting the existing rules to changing circumstances. There will be no clear way of getting rid of old and perhaps outdated rules, and replacing them with new ones. Existing primary rules will thus be static and never adapt to changing circumstances. An alternative way to think of this point is to consider that although Ramose says that customary law is always evolving, it is not quite clear how it evolves or what kind of change might justify adapting the rules to new circumstances. The remedy, then, is to adopt what Hart calls, 'rules of change'. These will specify how and the conditions under which the change must occur to warrant adapting the rules. For example, in twenty-first century South Africa, a rule of change might specify that primary rules may be changed after broad consultation with citizens and once a referendum on the rule to be changed has been held. This ensures that primary rules are not static and provides the means for adapting them to changing circumstances.

Lastly, a community comprising only primary rules would be unable to settle disputes concerning the application of primary rules, since it lacks authoritative ways to resolve such disputes. Consider, for example, that in modern, constitutional democracies, the task of adjudication is done by the courts. A society, like Mbiti's kinship one, for example, lacking such established authoritative structures, would be unable to resolve disputes. These disputes will go on endlessly and lead to widespread inefficiency. To resolve this problem, 'rules of adjudication' will have to be adopted to give a person or a body of persons the authority to make determinations and impose penalties. This would also mean that the use of force is not left at the hands of any random person or group of persons, but on some authoritative body.

For Hart, then, supplementing primary rules with secondary rules creates a system of law. Secondary rules give an account of the sources and legal validity of primary rules. That is, they enable us to determine which primary rules are law. For example, the primary rule: 'pay your tax', can be said to be legally valid when combined with a secondary rule of recognition, namely, 'if a primary rule is passed by a legislature by a simple majority, it is legally valid and binding'. It is the combination of both that creates a legal system. This is why Hart says law is 'most illuminatingly characterized as a union of primary rules of obligation with secondary rules'.[30] Alternatively, a legal system exists where members of a community generally follow valid rules facilitating and restricting behaviour, where these valid rules are those that pass the test specified by generally accepted secondary rules, including especially a rule of recognition.

### 2.5.4   Assessing Hart's concept of law

As we saw, one of the attractions of the customary law approach is that it is able to explain satisfactorily the difference between coercion and legal obligation, or otherwise, between the gunman and the taxman. Hart's account also has similar explanatory advantage. It entails that the authority of the taxman derives from secondary rules that validate tax laws. Specifically, citizens have a justified sense of legal obligation not simply because of the fear of sanctions associated with tax laws, but because they and especially political officials have accepted a range of secondary rules, including modes of making law, including tax laws, in society, by virtue of accepting something like the Constitution and the principles of democracy. In this way, Hart's concept of law captures the internal point of view of law. That is, the ability of legal rules to generate an attitude of endorsement in those to whom they are addressed and the expectation that these rules constitute valid reasons in light of which their behaviour may be appraised.

Nevertheless, Hart's concept of law seems to entail that traditional kinship societies were without law, since they were composed of only primary rules, or customs, whereas law is essentially the combination of primary and secondary rules. This is not surprising at all. After all, Hart's portrayal of a small, homogenous community with only primary rules roughly coincides with Mbiti's representation of kinship societies in traditional Africa. So, either there was law in traditional societies, or law is not a combination of primary and secondary rules.

Is a society comprising only primary rules really without law? Perhaps, a society with only primary rules has law. After all, it appears that on Hart's account it is the fact of social acceptance and not secondary rules per se that ultimately confers legal validity. Sure, secondary rules occupy an important place in Hart's account in that they make possible easy recognition, for example, of primary legal rules. Even so, secondary rules acquire legal validity on the basis of social acceptance. But if social acceptance confers legal validity, and the primary rules or customs of a society are also based on social acceptance, then it seems that they can acquire legal validity. Thus, a system of primary rules based on social acceptance might be legally valid. If this is correct, then not only is it the case that traditional kinship societies had law (and perhaps Hart's theory is able to account for the view that custom counts as law), but also law is not just the combination of primary and secondary rules.

---

30   Hart 1994 at 94.

A friend of Hart might insist that without secondary rules such a system would be lacking the key features of a legal system. Indeed, Hart argued that the introduction of secondary rules not only transforms what was prelegal into a legal system, it also makes it possible to understand fully much of what was previously puzzling about law.[31] In response, however, perhaps the absence of secondary rules is evidence that the system of norms in question is not a sophisticated legal system. If that is so, secondary rules may then be said to be sufficient but not necessary for law at all.

Now consider the proposition that law is essentially a union of primary and secondary rules. If this is the case, then it should provide a reliable way of distinguishing law from related social phenomena. However, the proposition that law is a union of primary and secondary rules does not sufficiently distinguish law from other social institutions that are also a union of primary and secondary rules, but not law. A university, for example, is constituted by a union of primary and secondary rules. It has primary rules that specify how people should behave, for example 'do not cheat during exams', and secondary rules, for example a rule of recognition, namely, 'a valid university primary rule is a rule that is passed by the University Senate'. If this is the case, it is hard to see how a legal system differs from other similar institutions. The core of the argument is represented in the table below.

> **Proposition 1:** A university forms a union of primary and secondary rules.
> **Proposition 2:** If a university forms a union of primary and secondary rules, then Hart's theory is not an adequate account of the way law differs from other institutions.
> Therefore,
> **Conclusion:** Hart's theory is not an adequate account of the way law differs from other institutions.

## 2.5.5    Secondary rules and traditional political societies

Much of our analysis of traditional Africa focused on Mbiti's kinship societies. However, traditional societies were not structured uniformly. As would be expected, some of them evolved social and political systems that differed from what was characteristic of kinship societies. Elias has proposed a taxonomy of types of societies in traditional Africa as an important first step to understanding the nature of African societies. Moreover, he pays special attention to the political, and not just the social, organisation of these societies. The reason for this is that 'law and politics', Elias contends, 'are closely allied sciences', such that a description of 'African political organizations' is 'a necessary preliminary to the subsequent enquiries into the nature of African laws and customs'.[32] In other words, to grasp the nature of law in traditional societies, it is not enough to focus only on its social organisation. The political organisation of traditional societies also evince key features of legal phenomena.

According to Elias, 'indigenous African societies can be classified into two groups'. As it turns out, the basis of his classification of African societies into two types is essentially a function of the degree of complexity and sophistication they exhibited. So, one type of society, *Group B* societies, were neither characterised by a 'centralized authority', able to exercise political power over members of the community, nor did they evolve judicial and/or

---

31    Hart 1994 at 98.
32    Elias 1956 *The Nature of African Customary Law* at 8.

administrative systems to facilitate social and political existence. Some of his examples are the Logoli, Tallensi and Neur traditional societies.[33] For the most part, these type of societies converge strikingly with the Mbiti-type traditional kinship societies: exhibiting a distinctive social structure, often culturally homogenous, but tending to be less politically organised.

However, *Group B* societies are unlike the other type of societies Elias identifies. Notably, societies of this other type, *Group A* societies, were culturally heterogeneous, typically an amalgamation of peoples from diverse ethnic origins with a well-defined territory over which some central authority exercised effective legitimate control. They were not strictly-speaking kinship societies. Rather than having been modelled fundamentally on blood and marital ties, Elias points out that *Group A* societies each comprised 'units bound together by common interests and loyalty to a political superior, usually the Paramount Chief or the King-in-Council'.[34] Elias held that the Zulu, Ngwato, Bemba and so on, are examples of *Group A* societies, in that they evolved complex political structures. They evolved administrative machineries to mobilise collective action, for example the collection of tax, payment of tribute and so on, and judicial institutions for purposes of adjudicating disputes, the administration of justice, the management of basic rights and duties, and the promotion of appropriate values and standards. Moreover, in these societies, the central authority had the power to sanction, where necessary. As Elias states, 'in Group A societies there is the incidence of organized force which is the principal sanction in a society based upon cultural and economic heterogeneity'.[35] Lastly, the emergence of these complex and relatively sophisticated political societies is, according to Elias, partly motivated by 'factors of necessity and security', including but not limited to the practical need for co-operation, settlement of disputes, administration of justice among diverse peoples, in the event of internal conflict, and to ensure protection against external aggression.

If Elias is right, then perhaps *Group A* societies were composed not just of primary rules, but also secondary rules. After all, the complex political organisation and the practical necessity of regulating political life may have allowed societies of this type to evolve remedies to the problems that Hart believed would confront a society with only primary rules. If so, then *Group A* societies likely developed secondary rules and so had law in Hart's sense. And this would be so even if other types of traditional African societies, specifically kinship ones, did not have secondary rules and so did not really have law in Hart's sense. Moreover, it is worth pointing out that although *Group A* societies might have exhibited law in Hart's sense, this is no guarantee that they also exhibited law in Austin's and Kelsen's conceptions of it. In particular, Elias is keen to point out that political societies in traditional Africa evolved forms of government that were democratic in character since there were important checks and balances that constrained the exercise of political power.[36] As such, there would be no equivalent of a sovereign in Austin's sense and so it is not likely that, for him, there was law in them. And although it is possible that law in *Group A* societies is hierarchical in the sense required by Kelsen, it seems unlikely that they are also autonomous norms in his sense of law.

---

33  Elias 1956 at 8, 11.
34  Elias 1956 at 11.
35  Elias 1956 at 11.
36  Elias 1956 at 18–21. See also, Wiredu 1997 *Postcolonial African Philosophy: A Critical Reader* and Wamala 2004 *A Companion to African Philosophy*.

## 2.6 Conclusion

In this chapter, we have examined four theories of law, each one offering some criteria for determining what law is essentially and entailing particular judgements regarding whether there was law in traditional African societies. By way of concluding, let us summarise the main positions.

In Austin's model, law is essentially the command of a sovereign backed up by sanctions. Thus, a system of law requires a sovereign who issues sanctionable commands. As we saw, to the extent that traditional African societies lacked something like Austin's sovereign, they did not have law. Moreover, if it was the case that the norms that regulated these societies were not strictly commands and did not aim to be punitive, in part because these societies tended to focus on restorative and rehabilitative processes, then again Austin's theory implies that they lack a system of law. We discussed several problems with Austin's theory of law, thus eliciting doubt as to the plausibility of its inference that there was no law in traditional societies. We then followed that with a discussion of customary law, specifically Ramose's *ubuntu* law, on which law is just the living customs of a community. This view, we noted, implies that there was law in traditional African societies, in that these societies were characterised by customs. As such, the notion of customary law is a challenge to Austin's positivist account of law, since it seems to suggest that not all of the conditions specified by Austin are necessary for law.

Further, we considered other positivist views of law with a view to investigating whether law could be distinguished clearly from custom. Kelsen's pure theory construes law as a system of autonomous norms culminating in a grundnorm, which gives the system its legal validity. Because it characterises law as a hierarchical system of autonomous norms, Kelsen's view, we observed, seems to imply that law is not just custom, since custom is neither autonomous, in the sense of being independent of morality, nor is it explicable in terms of a hierarchy of norms. Again, we questioned the independent plausibility of Kelsen's theory and by extension its implication for traditional African societies. We then turned to Hart, according to whom law is a combination of primary and secondary rules. Again, this view of law seems to imply that traditional societies did not have law. Initially, we noted that this implication is questionable seeing that even if traditional societies were composed of only primary rules; these rules might still acquire legal validity on the basis of social acceptance, since so-called secondary rules get their validity from social acceptance. We also showed that what Hart takes to be sufficient for law, that is, the combination of primary and secondary rules, does not adequately distinguish law.

Finally, we moved away from the initial description by Mbiti of simple kinship societies to the more complex traditional African political societies of Elias. We then acknowledged that the proposal that traditional African societies varied in terms of complexity leaves open the possibility that some traditional African societies did not have law, but that others did have law, in Hart's positivist sense of law. This proposal is not surprising at all. Although positivism distinguishes between law and morality, and the idea of customary law does not quite, a notion of customary law might still count as positivist if it merely relates law to people's *beliefs* about morality, as opposed to valid moral principles. Also, it is worth pointing out that some contemporary African philosophers of law have leaned towards positivism and urged the rejection of the integration of moral principles in the identification of law.[37] The next chapter investigates in detail the relationship between law and morality.

---

37  See Oladosu 2001 *West Africa Review.*

## POINTS TO CONSIDER

1. In your view, who might be a sovereign, in Austin's sense, in modern constitutional democracies?
2. Do you think that a purely restorative and rehabilitative system of law, as envisaged in traditional societies, is at all possible?
3. What, if any, in your view, is the difference between the custom of a society and the law of a society? Is the positivist separation thesis correct in this regard?
4. Let us assume that North Korea is a dictatorship, headed by someone who rules with absolute power and characterised by strong sanctions for disobedience. Is there law in North Korea? Can you work out the implication of each of the four theories of law we have examined on the question of whether North Korea exhibits a system of law?
5. Can you think of other possible features that might be relevant to the essence of law besides the ones we have discussed?

# Chapter 3

# What is law? II: Natural law theory and apartheid

THADDEUS METZ

## 3.1  Introduction

The previous chapter focused on legal positivism, one of the two major theories of the essential nature of law as something distinct from other norms such as the rules of etiquette or of a university. Legal positivism is the doctrine that whether a norm counts as law depends solely on the way it was enacted, not on whether it is morally sound. It analyses law in terms of a rule's pedigree, as having come from a sovereign or been a product of conformity to secondary rules, that can be adequately described in historical and sociological terms. Law is merely something that human beings *posit*, that is, construct. Applied to a legal system, as opposed to a particular law, positivism is the view that it is a collection of practices created by a given society that can be fully understood using the scientific method and without appealing to valid principles of justice.

Chapter 2 explored influential versions of positivism, especially those that had been developed by nineteenth- and twentieth-century British philosophers, and evaluated their implications for traditional African societies. If those forms of positivism are true, then it appears that some of these societies did not have law, an implication that the reader may or may not have found plausible.

The present, third chapter addresses the other major account of law's essence, naturalism or natural law theory. The word 'nature' is used to suggest that law is not simply a social creation; there are moral standards independent of a given human society that partly determine whether there is law or not. More specifically, according to naturalism, whether a norm or system counts as law depends at least in part on whether it is morally sound, not solely on the way rules were adopted. From the naturalist perspective, a legal system (in contrast to, say, a university) consists of certain practices that cannot be fully understood without appealing to valid principles of justice.

Notice that the naturalist's claim is not the weak point that law is a necessary function of what most people in a society *believe* to be morally right. Instead, it is the strong view that law is essentially constituted by what is *in fact* [1] morally right. Whereas for the positivist, it is a contingent matter whether law is morally sound or not, for the natural law theorist, law is necessarily just in some way.

This chapter distinguishes variations of this claim that morality is essential to law, critically discusses arguments for and against it, and considers its implications for apartheid South Africa. If naturalism is true, then it appears to follow that any seriously unjust political system such as apartheid did not have law. That implication is counterintuitive on the face of it – for most people would be inclined to say that the problem with apartheid was that many of its laws were seriously unjust! This chapter reconsiders this sort of gut reaction, critically exploring the idea that the parliamentary statutes that created apartheid either were not law or were outweighed by moral norms that had not been formally adopted by any legislator but that were law nonetheless during the apartheid era.

The next section sketches the basics of the apartheid order (section 3.2), in order to set the stage for an appraisal of whether the problem with it was that it had laws that were gravely wrongful, which the positivist would surely maintain, or whether its gravely wrongful norms meant that there was not genuine law, which some naturalists would contend. Then, the chapter considers whether a legal system has certain *procedures* intrinsic to it that are morally sound (section 3.3). From this standpoint, advanced by the famous jurist Lon Fuller against HLA Hart's view, insofar as a state's rules have not been laid down in a particular, just manner, they lack the character of law. The next two sections consider not the way in which rules are made, but rather their *content* or substance, and work to flesh out the naturalist slogan 'An unjust law is no law at all'. This maxim is invoked by Martin Luther King Jr, the famous African-American civil rights activist, when he contends that breaking racially discriminatory statutes is not a matter of violating the law (section 3.4). In addition, one strong current in sub-Saharan thought about law is that it consists of whichever norms tend towards the realisation of a moral goal, say, one of harmonious relationships (section 3.5). If laws are essentially rules that foster harmony, or if an unjust law is not really law, then it seems to follow that apartheid policies were lacking the character of law.

## 3.2　The nature of apartheid

Although slavery was formally ended in South Africa in the 1830s, various racially discriminatory government policies continued until the early 1990s. In particular, provincial pass laws, requiring black people to carry documents indicating where they 'belonged', were common in the nineteenth century, and in 1913 the national government passed the Natives

---

1　One may say that there are 'objective' moral norms, according to the natural law theorist. Whether such exist or not is taken up in Chapter 5.

Land Act,[2] which prohibited black people from owning land in white areas, permitting them to buy and transfer land in only about seven per cent (later expanded to about 13 per cent) of South Africa's territory.[3]

These racist policies were given ideological coherence and systematic implementation with the advent of apartheid in 1948. Then, the National Party was elected because of its platform that a primary function of the state should be to keep races separate. Some white people, particularly of Afrikaner descent, believed that God had commanded different races not to intermingle and that the state should enforce God's will. Although racial segregation was common before the adoption of apartheid, under apartheid it was then rigorously enforced across the country.

Political philosophers of pretty much any tradition would today agree that apartheid was responsible for at least four major forms of serious injustice. All four were ultimately facilitated by a statute that required everyone in South Africa to be registered by the state and classified by it into a particular racial grouping as either white, black (in the narrow sense of African), coloured or Indian.[4]

First, there was autocracy in the political sphere. Instead of an equal or otherwise fair distribution of political power in parliament, white people were granted much more of it than black (in the broader sense of non-white) people. Prior to 1983 virtually only white people had the right to vote, although coloured people, that is, those of both African and European heritage, retained some semblance of this right until 1956 when they were allowed to vote only for white candidates.[5] The 1983 Constitution[6] created a tricameral parliament, which allowed for coloured and Indian representatives to be elected by their respective races and to vote. However, no number of their votes could overrule the votes of white representatives in parliament. In addition, this system continued to exclude the African majority from having any voting rights or even citizenship at a national level, relegating them to political representation only within decentralised 'homelands' for their respective peoples.[7]

In addition to usurping black people's right to representation in political affairs, the apartheid government violated their rights to land, including any housing on top and natural resources underneath. Although the Natives Land Act had already forbidden black people from owning much of South Africa's land, additional statutes in the 1950s then forced them to move from where they had been living.[8] In particular, many thousands of black people were forced to leave urban and especially well-developed areas, deemed by the government to be properly white, and were relocated to far away townships designated for their particular race. In order to enter a white area, where there tended to be decent employment, black people had to travel long distances and carry pass books giving them permission to visit for a specific purpose.

A third major injustice of apartheid involved the restriction of a wide array of civil liberties, beyond hindering people's freedom of movement mentioned in the previous paragraph. For example, individuals lacked legal protections to engage in consensual

---

2   27 of 1913.
3   Collins & McDonald Burns 2007 *A History of Sub-Saharan Africa* at 346; Hall & Ntsebeza 2007 *The Land Question in South Africa* at 3.
4   Population Registration Act 30 of 1950.
5   See, for instance, the Separate Representation of Voters Act 46 of 1951 and the Separate Representation of Voters Amendment Act 30 of 1956.
6   Republic of South Africa Constitution Act 110 of 1983.
7   Promotion of Bantu Self-Government Act 46 of 1959, and Bantu Homelands Citizenship Act 26 of 1970.
8   For example, the Group Areas Act 41 of 1950 and the Natives Resettlement Act 19 of 1954.

romantic relationships with whom they wanted, and instead were required to wed[9] or to have sexual relations[10] with only those of their own race group. In addition, black people could not use public services such as restrooms, parks and beaches as they liked, with some being reserved for people of European descent and others reserved for non-Europeans.[11] In practice, the better facilities were allocated to the former, there being no policy requiring equal standards of cleanliness, quality, or the like. For a third example, consider that the apartheid government forbade political speech that advocated racial equality or was likely to foster feelings of hostility between the races,[12] outlawed multiracial political parties,[13] and censored so-called 'undesirable' books, movies, and radio and television programmes.[14]

Fourth, and finally for the sake of this chapter, the apartheid government violated people's right to equal opportunities to obtain education and employment. The government set up separate schools for the various race groups, funding those in white areas much better than those outside them. In addition, despite the ostensible 'self-government' enjoyed by the African homelands, the national government assigned the administration of education in them to the Minister of Native Affairs,[15] with his judgement having been that African people, then referred to as 'natives' or 'Bantus', should be taught to perform only physical and menial tasks:

> There is no place for [the Bantu] in the European community above the level of certain forms of labour ... What is the use of teaching the Bantu child mathematics when it cannot use it in practice? That is quite absurd. Education must train people in accordance with their opportunities in life, according to the sphere in which they live.[16]

Although Africans and other black people were allowed to attend universities, they were forbidden from attending white ones (without obtaining special permission).[17]

The main way that a principle of equal opportunity to obtain work was violated was a consequence of the principle of equal opportunity to obtain an education having been violated. That is, not having been able to obtain qualifications at school, black people naturally found it difficult to compete for jobs, giving an unfair advantage to white people who were disproportionately able to obtain qualifications. In addition, there were some statutes that functioned more directly to reserve certain kinds of jobs for white people. For instance, one act[18] established an industrial relations framework that:

> enabled trade unions and employers' organizations to negotiate industrial labor contracts that specified which jobs went to the different race groups. Furthermore, the Act required unions to be racially segregated and excluded Africans from formal trade union representation. The consequence of this trade union segregation was that white unions were able to negotiate the exclusion of Africans from occupations that attracted large numbers of whites.[19]

---

9   Prohibition of Mixed Marriages Act 55 of 1949.
10   Immorality Amendment Act 21 of 1950.
11   Reservation of Separate Amenities Act 49 of 1953.
12   Suppression of Communism Act 44 of 1950, and Internal Security Act 74 of 1982.
13   Prohibition of Political Interference Act 51 of 1968.
14   Publications and Entertainments Act 26 of 1963.
15   Bantu Education Act 47 of 1953.
16   Hendrik Verwoerd quoted in Boddy-Evans 2017 *Apartheid Quotes – Bantu Education*.
17   Extension of University Education Act 45 of 1959.
18   Industrial Conciliation Act 28 of 1956.
19   Mariotti 2009 *Working Papers in Economics & Econometrics* at 5.

There were also sometimes even cruder policies, such as an act that permitted Africans to perform skilled work on buildings only in townships, not in urban centres.[20]

Although the apartheid system was not genocidal, in the sense of seeking to kill off an entire group of people,[21] the injustice was great enough for the United Nations and the International Criminal Court to have deemed it to have been a crime against humanity.[22] Now, if apartheid was a crime, how could it have been law? In the following text, a South African academic and judge explains why many in control of the South African state believed that apartheid was the law of the land and so had to be enforced.

**PRIMARY TEXTS**

**Text 1  John Dugard on jurisprudential influence on apartheid[23]**

John Dugard was Director of the University of the Witwatersrand's Centre for Applied Legal Studies, a research unit committed to the promotion of human rights in South Africa from 1978–1990. He is currently an Honorary Professor of Law at the University of Pretoria's Centre for Human Rights and an ad hoc Judge at the International Court of Justice.

No coherent theory of law has been expounded by the ideologues of apartheid, unless one is prepared to dignify a policy of racial inequality and political repression with the title of 'legal theory.' On the other hand, a number of jurisprudential strains have greatly influenced the legislative and judicial strategies of apartheid ... The imperative theory of law, historical jurisprudence, and anti-humanism have ... operated silently and organically to produce a State premised on legislative supremacy and judicial subordination, in which the notion of legally protected individual rights plays no part.

Both legislator and lawyer have been deeply influenced by the imperative theory of law associated with the name John Austin. In the early days of National Party rule every effort was made by the legislature to establish the principle that the South African Parliament is the uncommanded commander of society and, after initial obstruction from the Appeal Court, judicial acquiescence in this principle was secured. Thereafter the *volkswil* (the will of the Afrikaner people) expressed in Parliament became the supreme law of the land with the result that the National Party Government was able to enact a discriminatory and repressive body of law without fear of judicial disapproval.

It would be incorrect to suggest that positivism as a theory of law is to blame for this state of affairs. At most one can claim that Austin's theory of command, which gives legitimacy to the notion of legislative supremacy, has provided a justification for parliamentary absolutism ... Both courts and legal profession, albeit unwittingly, became disciples of Austin. For them law became simply the command of the National Party-controlled Parliament, which they were obliged to follow, irrespective of its immoral content.

---

20  Native Building Workers Act 27 of 1951.
21  A commonly cited figure is approximately 7 000 politically motivated killings between 1948 and 1989. See, for example, Coleman 1998 *A Crime against Humanity: Analysing the Repression of the Apartheid State.*
22  General Assembly of the United Nations 1973 *International Convention on the Suppression and Punishment of the Crime of Apartheid*; International Criminal Court 1998 *Rome Statute* Art. 7, 1(j) and 2(h).
23  Extracted from Dugard 1986–1987 *The Philosophical Forum.*

That the command theory of law still inspires the legislator in South Africa is apparent from the controversial Constitution of 1983. Although this Constitution departs from the Westminster model, in constructing a Parliament with legislative chambers for whites, coloreds, and Indians ... it remains firmly committed to the principle of parliamentary supremacy in a Parliament controlled by the National Party. The colored House of Representatives and the Indian House of Delegates may not veto legislation approved by the National Party-controlled White House of Assembly.

In 1973 a prominent Afrikaans legal academic, Professor Venter, rejected the Rule of Law ... on the ground that it 'presupposes the notion of "fundamental rights" accruing to the individual against (State, Government) authority and thus reflects a humanist philosophy which is unacceptable in South Africa' ... He goes on to suggest that South African lawyers should ... embrace 'Christian Government.'

Venter's view received full backing from the constitutional committee of the President's Council charged with the task of considering the desirability of including a Bill of Rights in the 1983 Constitution. It advanced as one of the principal reasons for a 'negative attitude' towards the adoption of a Bill of Rights the humanist emphasis it placed on individual rights *vis-à-vis* the authority of the State ... In the light of this opposition, it was hardly surprising that the Constitution Bill presented to Parliament contained no guarantees for personal liberty.

**Questions**
1. Explain how widespread acceptance of Austin's account of the nature of law led to the view amongst many South African jurists that apartheid statutes were legal.
2. What does Dugard mean by 'parliamentary absolutism'?
3. Why did some apartheid advocates reject the idea of giving constitutional protection to individual rights?

The prior part of this section sketched the key apartheid-era statutes, indicating four distinct kinds of injustice, relating to a lack of political representation, inability to access natural resources such as land, restriction of civil liberties, and unequal opportunities to obtain positions. In the reading from Dugard, he focuses less on spelling these out, and more on the kind of thought about law (and values) that helped to make them possible or to legitimate them.

With regard to the nature of law, Dugard contends that a belief in Austinian positivism amongst legislators, lawyers and judges contributed to the acceptance of apartheid statutes as valid law. Recall from Chapter 2 that, for Austin, law is nothing more than the command of a sovereign, an agent or body that routinely commands others but is not itself routinely commanded by anyone else. It appeared during the apartheid era that parliament counted as a sovereign. It consistently forced others to obey it, while it did not habitually obey any other group in society, not even the judiciary. Although South Africa had had Constitutions (in 1910, 1961 and 1983), at least in the apartheid era the judiciary deemed parliament to have supreme authority and tended to defer to its understanding of them. Since many of parliament's commands took the form of statutes, the legal profession and the courts considered them to be the law.

Parliamentary statutes do straightforwardly seem to have counted as law under apartheid, from the standpoint of Austin's positivism. Since law is not inherently moral for any positivist, the injustice of the statutes does not provide any reason to doubt their status as law. However, just because the statutes were legal by positivism does not mean that they should have been enforced. It is important to note that positivism is a theory of what law is, not how to adjudicate in the light of it or whether to obey it. It is quite open to a positivist to contend that the apartheid-era parliamentary statutes were law but that judges, prosecutors, police officers and corrections officials should have disobeyed them much more often than they did.

What might be incorrect with this position? What, if anything, is mistaken about the view that unjust statutes normally count as law (either because they are a sovereign's commands or because they are primary rules enacted in accordance with secondary rules), but their status as law does not necessarily mean they should be enforced? Why take seriously the naturalist view that the injustice of apartheid meant that there was not truly a legal system or that the statutes were not really law? The remaining sections in this chapter critically explore answers to these questions.

## 3.3  The procedural morality of a legal system

It is tempting to say that positivism conceives of law in terms of a formal procedure, whereas naturalism does so (at least partially) in terms of its moral content. Although it is true that many forms of naturalism appeal to the moral content of a norm in order to determine its legality and that many forms of positivism consider the institutional process by which a norm was adopted, it would be a mistake to characterise the theories in these limited ways. On the one hand, there is a conceivable form of positivism according to which law is constituted by a society's strongly held customs (see Chapter 2). Although there is no essential reference to what is in fact morally right here, there is also no mention of a formal or institutional process by which norms have been enacted. On the other hand, there is a possible form of naturalism, explored in this section, according to which law's inherent morality is a function not of a norm's content, but rather the procedures by which it has been adopted, promulgated and enforced.

### 3.3.1  Expounding Fuller's procedural naturalism

Lon Fuller is the most prominent exponent of such a procedural instance of natural law theory. According to him, we cannot understand a legal system fully without using concepts of justice; a purely historical or sociological description would necessarily be inadequate, in his view.

An important question for the naturalist is where morality 'comes from'. In suggesting both that law is not merely the creation of a given human society and that a norm must have a morally sound dimension to count as law, the naturalist is committed to the universalist (or non-relativist) view that morality is not merely the creation of a particular human society. If it is not, how do objective moral facts come into being? What makes it the case that some judgements about morality are true or justified while others are not?

Traditionally, natural law theorists such as Thomas Aquinas, a thirteenth-century Catholic priest and philosopher from Italy, believed that morality is determined by something other than human beings, namely, by God's will. God, understood as an all-knowing, all-powerful and all-good spiritual person who was the source of the physical universe, was thought to have created human beings with certain purposes in mind. Human beings are meant, say, to glorify God, to love one another, or to put themselves in a position to unite with God in Heaven. Fulfilment of these ends assigned by God is morally right, while failure to fulfil them is morally wrong.

An appeal to God as the source of morality is one straightforward way of making sense of natural law theory. The eighteenth-century English jurist William Blackstone described naturalism this way:

> This law of nature, being co-eval with mankind and dictated by God himself, is of course superior in obligation to any other. It is binding over all the globe, in all countries, and at all times: no human laws are of any validity, if contrary to this; and such of them as are valid derive all their force, and all their authority, mediately or immediately, from this original.[24]

'Supernatural' might seem to be the best word for such a conception of how law necessarily overlaps with rightness.

However, the term 'natural' has more often been used, for two major reasons. For one, traditional naturalists often maintained that God had implanted in us a special rational faculty by which to distinguish right from wrong, an ability that could cut through the variability of upbringing and custom, and judge justice objectively in a way similar to how we biologically ('by our nature', one might say) can perceive shapes.

For another, not all naturalists believe that morality is a function of God's will or indeed anything about God. Some instead maintain that human reason in general (not a particular society's beliefs) constructs principles of morality.[25] Others contend that the essence of morality consists of whichever properties that human beings as a species characteristically refer to when they label something 'moral' or 'immoral', analogous to the way that the essence of what humans call 'water', we have learned over time, is $H_2O$.[26] Still others, such as the ancient Greek philosopher Aristotle,[27] contend that morality is a matter of what conduces to the realisation of human nature, an essence that all humans share.

Fuller is a natural law theorist who expounds a secular account of morality, meaning that his description of law's justice does not appeal to anything about God. Instead, there are procedural features of a genuine legal system that many readers would readily describe as 'fair'.

---

**PRIMARY TEXTS**

**Text 2  Lon Fuller on law's intrinsic moral order**[28]

Lon Fuller, an American philosopher of law who had been based at Harvard University, was one of the two most influential natural law theorists to have critically engaged with the positivist theory of HLA Hart (the other having been Ronald Dworkin).

> Hart emphatically rejects 'the command theory of law', according to which law is simply a command backed by force ... [because] such a command can be given by a man with a loaded gun, and 'law surely is not the gunman situation writ large' .... His conclusion is that the foundation of a legal system is not coercive power, but certain 'fundamental accepted rules specifying the essential law-making procedures' ... The question may now be raised ... as to the nature of these fundamental rules ... [T]hey seem to be rules, not of law, but morality. They derive

---

24  Blackstone, W 1765/1979 *Commentaries on the Law of England* at 41.
25  For example, Gewirth 1978 *Reason and Morality*; Beyleveld & Brownsword 1986 *Law as a Moral Judgement*.
26  For example, Brink 1988 *Philosophy and Public Affairs*.
27  See his *Nicomachean Ethics*.
28  Extracted from Fuller 1958 *Harvard Law Review*.

their efficacy from a general acceptance, which in turn rests ultimately on a perception that they are right ... On the other hand, in the daily functioning of the legal system they are often treated and applied much as ordinary rules of law are. Here, then ... there is ... a 'merger' of law and morality.

[S]uppose an absolute monarch, whose word is the only law known to his subjects. ... {F}urther suppose him to be ... selfish ... in his relations with his subjects .... This monarch issues commands, promising rewards for compliance and threatening punishments for disobedience. He is, however, a dissolute and forgetful fellow, who ... habitually punishes loyalty and rewards disobedience. It is apparent that this monarch will never achieve even his own selfish aims.

{N}ow suppose that our monarch ... becomes hopelessly slothful in the phrasing of his commands. His orders become so ambiguous and are uttered in so inaudible a tone that his subjects never have any clear idea what he wants them to do. Here, again, it is apparent that if our monarch for his own selfish advantage wants to create ... anything like a system of law he will have to pull himself together.

Law, considered merely as order, contains, then, its own implicit morality. This morality of order must be respected ... to create ... anything that can be called law, even bad law.

When we realize that order itself is something that must be worked for, it becomes apparent that the existence of a legal system, even a bad or evil legal system, is always a matter of degree. When we recognize this simple fact of everyday legal experience, it becomes impossible to dismiss the problems presented by the Nazi regime with a simple assertion: 'Under the Nazis there was law, even if it was bad law'. We have instead to inquire how much of a legal system survived the general debasement and perversion of all forms of social order.

### Questions

1. Fuller suggests that some of Hart's secondary rules are adopted by officials because 'of a perception that they are right'. Suggest one secondary rule that plausibly meets this description. Justify your answer.
2. Fuller maintains that a legal system necessarily contains a 'morality of order'. Sketch one of Fuller's examples in which a practice would not include such order. In what respect would there plausibly be *disorder* in such a practice?
3. Fuller says that there are degrees to which something can be a system of law. What do you think about that? Is a legal system more like pregnancy (where either one is pregnant or not, without gradation), or is it, with Fuller, more like intelligence (where one can be more or less intelligent)?

In the above reading, Fuller maintains that whether or not something counts as a legal system is a matter of a degree. An institution can be more or less legal; it is not an all or nothing matter. According to Fuller, an institution is less legal, the less it produces a 'morality of order'. By 'order' Fuller seems to mean a situation in which someone is able to achieve goals efficiently. Fuller provides two examples in which such order is lacking. In one case a king punishes obedience and rewards disobedience, while, in another case, a king does not publicise the rules that he wants his subjects to obey.

Elsewhere in his work, Fuller specifies an additional six 'ways to fail to make law' for a total of eight.[29] Some of these include formulating rules that: apply only to the past, not to the future; are incomprehensible; cannot be lived up to; and change constantly. These examples also suggest that by 'order' Fuller is pointing to a state of affairs in which ends are easily realised. Fuller probably has in mind the idea that a king would be most likely to achieve certain goals if he laid down law, suggested when Fuller remarks that the 'monarch will never achieve even his own selfish aims' if he fails to make law.

Having explained what Fuller probably means by a legal system's 'order', the next question is why he calls it a 'morality'. Intuitively, there would be something unjust about a state that punished people for breaking the kinds of non-legal rules that Fuller has in mind. It seems unfair to punish people for any of the following: obeying rules that people have been told to obey, or disobeying rules of which the state had not informed them, or performing actions that had not been forbidden ahead of time, or breaking rules that were impossible not to break, or failing to live up to rules that change every day.

Another way to see Fuller's point is in terms of the obligation to obey the law. In another place in his work Fuller remarks:

> Certainly there can be no rational ground for asserting that a man can have a moral obligation to obey a legal rule that does not exist, or is kept secret from him, or that came into existence only after he had acted, or was unintelligible, or was contradicted by another rule of the same system, or commanded the impossible, or changed every minute.[30]

Conversely, there is probably *some* (not necessarily conclusive or overriding) moral reason to obey a rule if it is publicised, is not retrospective, is intelligible, commands what is possible, does not change constantly, and so on. A system of such rules is more entitled to deference, and, for Fuller, is alone owed the dignified title of 'law'.

### 3.3.2 Evaluating Fuller's procedural naturalism

Having spelled out Fuller's account of how a system is more legal, the more it includes a morality of order within it, it is time to appraise it. One concern is that there does not seem to be anything essentially moral about order as Fuller conceives it. His example is one of a king who frustrates his own ability to achieve his selfish aims by making rules in certain ways. Why call 'moral' a selfish person's ability to get what he wants or 'immoral' his frustration of his own goals? Usually by 'moral' we mean acting in ways that are often expected to conflict with our self-interest.

In reply, Fuller would probably point to the considerations advanced above about why 'morality' is a suitable label for a system that includes rules that are consistent, clear, publicised, possible to live by, and the like. It would be unfair to punish people for breaking rules that lack these features, and rules that lack them do not morally deserve obedience.

Another way that Fuller could reply would be to suggest another sense of 'order'. What he might have in mind is the idea that, with the order that comes with law, a state's residents would be much more able to achieve their goals, insofar as they could much more easily avoid breaking the law and consequently being punished for it. A state that enables those subject to its rules to predict when it will punitively restrict their liberty thereby enables them to achieve their aims, which seems on the face of it to be morally desirable.

---

29  Fuller 1969 *The Morality of Law* at 33.
30  Fuller 1969 at 39.

A second objection to Fuller is grounded on different intuitions about when a body of rules counts as a legal system. It does not seem absurd to say of a state that its laws change frequently, or that it applies the law retrospectively, or that the state has not publicised the law, or that it is impossible to do what the law requires. If Fuller were right that 'order' is essential to a system of law, then these kinds of statements would probably be contradictions in terms, but they are not.

Fuller may reply by appealing to the idea that a legal system comes in degrees. He can accept that a legal system can include *some* rules that are retrospective, secret, impossible to live up to, and so on, but would contend, perhaps plausibly, that it is less of a legal system than one with no or fewer such rules.

Ultimately, even if Fuller's argument for naturalism were sound, note, for a third objection, that it would not ground a very 'thick' or 'robust' conception of how law is inherently moral. One can easily imagine a system that counts as fully legal in the light of Fuller's procedural criteria but that is terribly unjust. Indeed, the apartheid statutes (perhaps unlike the rules of Nazi Germany) did not generally fall afoul of Fuller's standards for what counts as a system of law; they were publicised, consistent, could be complied with, applied prospectively, and so on and therefore helped to constitute a legal system even by Fuller's lights. However, many in the natural law tradition want to be able to say that apartheid-era statutes did not truly count as law, something Fuller's approach cannot ground. The following sections explore approaches that are more promising in this regard.

## 3.4   The substantive morality of law I: An unjust law is not law

The previous section explored a procedural kind of naturalism, according to which the way a rule has been adopted, promulgated and enforced at least partly determines its status as law. In contrast, this section and the following one address a substantive naturalism, one according to which the content of a norm influences whether it is a law or not. In addition, whereas the argument for naturalism in the previous section focused on the extent to which a practice counts as a legal system, this section and the next one consider whether a particular norm counts as a valid law.

According to the form of naturalism presently under consideration, whether a norm counts as valid law depends at least in part on whether it is morally sound. Roughly, if a rule is in fact unjust, then it is not law, or at least not conclusive or overriding law, even if it has been formally adopted. Conversely, if a norm is just, it is (perhaps conclusive) law, even if it has not been formally adopted. From this perspective, apartheid statutes, although formally adopted, were not law, or at least were not the only, most weighty sources of law.

### 3.4.1   Natural law as the ground of punishing injustice

Why believe this understanding of the essence of law? There have been two major arguments in the literature. One is that it can be right to punish people for unjust ways they acted that were permitted by the formally adopted rules at the time.[31] The best explanation of why it is right to punish people now for acts that positivist rules had permitted in the past is that even then the law included some principles of justice that had not been formally adopted, so this argument goes.

Applied to apartheid, the idea would be that it has been permissible for the post-apartheid state of 1994 onwards to punish people for having engaged in political wrongdoing

---

31   Elsewhere in his work, Fuller (1958 at 652–657) makes this kind of argument.

during apartheid, that is, from 1948 to 1993, that statutes clearly allowed during that period. For example, many would say that it would be right for the post-apartheid state to punish those officials responsible for adopting and enforcing the statutes that forcibly removed black people from their houses and land in order to make way for white people. Now, if punishment is permissible only for having broken the law, then it follows that the law at the time of apartheid must have included certain principles of justice (not formally adopted by the state) that these officials violated.

Of course, one way for positivists to object to this argument is to deny that it is permissible to punish people for having done things that the formally adopted rules of the time allowed. However, this 'bite the bullet' approach is not the main way that positivists tend to object.

Instead, they more often suggest a broader form of positivism according to which an international or local community's customs count as law. By this approach, long-standing and widely held *beliefs* about justice are what partly determined South African law during the apartheid era, not *true* principles of justice *themselves*.

In addition, positivists sometimes suggest that even if it had been perfectly legal at the time for apartheid officials to forcibly remove black people to townships, it would on moral grounds be right to punish them now. Perhaps these officials should be punished not for having broken the law, but simply for having acted so unjustly. Similarly, if the law has changed (because a certain rule has been formally adopted) in post-apartheid South Africa, so that it is now illegal to facilitate forced removals, perhaps it is morally right to apply this law retrospectively.

### 3.4.2   Natural law as the ground of legal obligation

Whereas the first major argument for naturalism appeals to intuitions about who should be punished and why, the second one invokes purportedly uncontroversial ideas about when people have an obligation to obey the law. The basic idea is that we normally associate something being the law with having a certain kind of moral authority. Usually the fact that a norm is called 'law' carries with it some moral duty to respect and adhere to it. Naturalism makes much better sense of that association than does positivism; for only if laws are inherently just can it be reasonable to suppose that they invariably deserve to be obeyed. This kind of argument for natural law theory has been made by the famous civil rights activist Martin Luther King Jr.[32]

| PRIMARY | Text 3  Martin Luther King Jr on civil disobedience[33] |
|---------|----------------------------------------------------------|
| TEXTS   | Martin Luther King Jr is famous for having led non-violent protests against segregation during the 1950s and '60s in the United States, which earned him a Nobel Peace Prize in 1964. He was assassinated by a white supremacist in 1968. |

> I guess it is easy for those who have never felt the stinging darts of segregation to say 'wait.' But when ... you see the vast majority of your twenty million Negro brothers smothering in an airtight cage of poverty in the midst of an affluent society; when you suddenly find your tongue twisted and your speech stammering as you seek to explain to your six-year-old daughter why she cannot go to the public amusement park that has just been advertised on television, and see tears welling up in her little eyes when she is told that Funtown is closed to colored

---

32   See also Finnis 2011 *Natural Law and Natural Rights* at 354–362.
33   Extracted from King Jr 1963 *The Atlantic Monthly*.

children, and see the depressing clouds of inferiority begin to form in her little mental sky, and see her begin to distort her little personality by unconsciously developing a bitterness toward white people; when you have to concoct an answer for a five-year-old son asking in agonizing pathos, 'Daddy, why do white people treat colored people so mean?'; when you take a cross-country drive and find it necessary to sleep night after night in the uncomfortable corners of your automobile because no motel will accept you; when you are humiliated day in and day out by nagging signs reading 'white' and 'colored'; when your first name becomes 'nigger' and your middle name becomes 'boy' (however old you are) and your last name becomes 'John,' and when your wife and mother are never given the respected title 'Mrs.'; when you are harried by day and haunted by night by the fact that you are a Negro, living constantly at tiptoe stance, never quite knowing what to expect next, and plagued with inner fears and outer resentments; when you are forever fighting a degenerating sense of 'nobodyness' – then you will understand why we find it difficult to wait.

You express a great deal of anxiety over our willingness to break laws. This is certainly a legitimate concern. Since we so diligently urge people to obey the Supreme Court's decision of 1954 outlawing segregation in the public schools, it is rather strange and paradoxical to find us consciously breaking laws ... I would agree with St. Augustine that 'An unjust law is no law at all.'

Now, what is the difference between the two? How does one determine when a law is just or unjust? ... An unjust law is a code that is out of harmony with the moral law. To put it in the terms of St. Thomas Aquinas, an unjust law is a human law that is not rooted in eternal and natural law. Any law that uplifts human personality is just. Any law that degrades human personality is unjust. All segregation statutes are unjust because segregation distorts the soul and damages the personality. It gives the segregator a false sense of superiority and the segregated a false sense of inferiority ... So I can urge men to obey the 1954 decision of the Supreme Court because it is morally right, and I can urge them to disobey segregation ordinances because they are morally wrong.

### Questions

1. King advocates breaking segregation ordinances that, in some states in the US, had been chosen by majorities. Is King therefore being 'undemocratic' in some way? Why or why not?
2. King seems to believe that white people who benefited in some ways from segregation laws were also damaged by them and done an injustice. How so?
3. People disagree with one another about which laws are just. Consider the proposition that if people routinely disobeyed whichever laws they thought were unjust, there could be no just order at all, however defined. Do you think this a good argument for obeying laws one thinks are unjust? Why or why not?

This text is from a letter that King wrote during a time when he had been incarcerated for his resistance to segregation. In it he responds to published criticisms of his support for non-violent methods that nonetheless broke statutory rules, along the way outlining a naturalist approach to understanding law.

King appears to accept the proposition that one is always morally obligated to obey the law. This principle, however, does not require obedience to segregation statutes, for King. Why not? Because the law includes what is just. Insofar as law is just, one should obey the United States Supreme Court ruling that forbade segregation in schools (*Brown v Board of Education*).[34] However, one need not obey segregation statutes, since, being unjust, they are not really law or the most weighty aspects of it.

This position seems clear enough, but the terminology that King uses to express it is not. King invokes the famous maxim of St Augustine of Hippo, an early Christian theologian and philosopher from North Africa (354–430), which says that 'an unjust law is no law at all'. This statement appears to contradict itself. On the one hand, it speaks of an 'unjust law', but, on the other, it says that such a thing is 'no law at all'. If something is an unjust law, then *it is a law*, and hardly no law at all!

Here is a way to make sense of St Augustine's maxim.[35] The basic idea is that there can be degrees to which something counts as law, with a *genuine* law being one that is just (or that merits obedience).[36] Consider some analogies. One might say that a jalopy 'is not a *real* car', and it is common in the indigenous African tradition to contend that someone who is morally wicked is not a real person.[37] An old, broken down car is indeed a car, but it is not what one really wants from a car. Similarly, an immoral person is of course a person, but not the sort of person that is desirable; indeed, often in traditional sub-Saharan contexts an evildoer would be called a 'non-person' or 'zero-person'.[38] Similarly, an unjust law is technically a law, but it is not a *real* law, where only real laws merit obedience. Or so King is fairly read as saying.

This position is a robust form of naturalism insofar as it includes the claim that a legal system at any time includes real law, that is, true principles of justice, that outweigh any unjust statutes or other sources of law. It is of course a matter of some debate about how to identify the true principles of justice, with King offering one, Western and Christian analysis in terms of equality, and a different, more African one being proffered (in terms of harmony) in the following section. However plausibly specified, when applied to the South African context, the implication would be that apartheid statutes were technically law, but were not entitled to obedience since they were overridden by the morally sound law that had not been formally adopted by parliament.

How might the positivist criticise this position? He or she would likely opt for the following combination of views: law consists only of rules that human beings have formally adopted in a certain way, but one is not always morally obligated to obey the law. When it comes to segregation, most positivists would argue that the apartheid statutes were full-blown laws, and that the legal system did not include any further principles of justice that are purportedly sound or true. However, it does not follow from this claim that people were morally right to obey these laws. A view about the nature of law is one thing, while a view about what merits compliance is another. It is open to the positivist to maintain that the problem with apartheid was that its laws were seriously unjust and that much of the legal profession was wrong to comply with them too readily.

At this point, the debate in the literature has become about whether this distinction between what law is and how to respond to law is as rigid as the positivist maintains.

---

34  *Brown v Board of Education of Topeka*, 347 U.S. 483 (1954).

35  Drawing on Kretzmann 1988 *American Journal of Jurisprudence*; and Bix 1996 *A Companion to Philosophy of Law and Legal Theory* at 214.

36  Finnis 2011 at 363–365.

37  For both examples, see Gaie 2007 *The Concept of Botho and HIV/AIDS in Botswana* at 33.

38  Nkulu-N'Sengha 2009 *Encyclopedia of African Religion*.

Ronald Dworkin, an extremely influential critic of Hart, for instance, contends that it is not. He argues that any interesting issue when it comes to the philosophy of law is a matter of asking which interpretation of the law is best, where the best interpretation is (roughly) the one that renders law as morally sound and worthy of obedience as possible.[39] When a judge needs to make a pronouncement on what the law is, he or she cannot avoid appealing to moral principles to ground a sensible decision, so Dworkin contends.

Rather than pursue this line further, the rest of this chapter considers in more detail what it might mean to contend that law includes true principles of justice. Which principles are these? King provides a sketchy account of them in the above extract, while other recent natural law theorists in the West, such as Robert George,[40] John Finnis[41] and Mark Murphy[42] have provided intricate accounts. However, the following section explores a more detailed view of law's morality that is informed by traditional sub-Saharan values.

## 3.5    The substantive morality of law II: Law as harmonisation

African philosophers have taken a variety of positions on the nature of law. Some have been positivist, contending (as per Chapter 2) that many sub-Saharan peoples had law in the form of complex systems of authority (or perhaps in terms of customs that, while believed to be moral, may not have been). However, other African philosophers of law have been naturalist, the focus of this section.

What makes a natural law theorist African as opposed to Western is not the theorist's ethnicity, but rather the way he or she understands the content of morality (see Chapter 1). There are views about right and wrong that are salient in the sub-Saharan philosophical tradition in a way that makes them different from many other (not necessarily all) traditions, including the Western one. In particular, community, harmony and cohesion are relational values that have been routinely espoused by African philosophers[43] and that have not been as frequently advanced in the modern Western philosophical tradition, which has focused more (but not exclusively) on individualist goods such as autonomy, human life (soul), pleasure and desire satisfaction.

According to some traditional African philosophers, law includes the commands of God, albeit as expressed by ancestors, wise founders of a clan who have survived the deaths of their bodies, continue to reside on earth, and guide the clan by sending messages and inflicting punishments.[44] This is a natural law position and not positivism because, although these rules have been thought to have been laid down by an agent, it was not human beings who did the positing, and it is not essential that human beings enforce them for them to count as the law.

### 3.5.1    Expounding Idowu's view of law as harmonisation

A different strain of African natural law theory is not supernatural, or not explicitly. According to this view, espoused by the influential Nigerian legal theorist William Idowu, law consists of whichever norms tend towards the realisation of certain just ends, namely, those of

---

39   Dworkin 2004 *Acta Juridica*.
40   George 1999 *In Defense of Natural Law*.
41   Finnis 2011.
42   Murphy 2009 *Natural Law in Jurisprudence and Politics*.
43   These are not the only salient values in the African tradition. Many sub-Saharan philosophers instead fundamentally prize what is known as 'life-force', an imperceptible energy that has come from God. For examples, see Dzobo 1992 *Person and Community*; and Magesa 1997 *African Religion*.
44   See Okafor 1984 *International Philosophical Quarterly* and 1988 *Journal of Value Inquiry* for an articulation of this perspective.

harmony, cohesion, and reconciliation amongst (at least in the first instance) human beings. Such an approach naturally begs the question of what counts as the latter ways of relating. In the reading below, Idowu does not define what he means by these terms and similar ones such as 'social stability' and 'equilibrium'.

However, Idowu's ideas about what law is are similar to Desmond Tutu's ideas about what law ought to be, explored later in Chapter 10. Borrowing from there, one may suggest that African relational values are well captured by Tutu's phrase, 'I participate, I share'. One harmonises or coheres with others insofar as one participates with them on a co-operative basis and enjoys a sense of togetherness with them, on the one hand, and insofar as one shares one's attention, time, money and other resources to enable them to live well, on the other. When this way of relating is disrupted by a crime, then the goal should be to reconcile, that is, to repair the relationship so that harmony is restored. Some such as Tutu would call this aim 'restorative justice'.

If law consisted essentially of whichever norms tend to foster harmony or justice, so construed, then it would follow that apartheid-era statutes were not law, or at least were not conclusive law. Apartheid policies are well understood as having egregiously undermined harmony, that is, they forbade different races from participating with each other and enjoying a sense of togetherness, and prevented them from engaging in mutual aid, too. Instead, Idowu would suggest, there was real law at least with the advent of South Africa's Truth and Reconciliation Commission, which sought to overcome division and ill-will between racial groups.

| **PRIMARY** | **Text 4  William Idowu on the reconciliation theory of law**[45] |
| --- | --- |
| **TEXTS** | William Idowu is a leading African philosopher of law, and is known for having argued against positivism in several published articles. He lectures at the Obafemi Awolowo University in Nigeria. |

> The nature and element of African philosophy of law consists in the view that law is held to be a reconciliatory instrument for the restoration of social equilibrium ... [L]aw is not an end in itself but a means to an end. This much is latent in this Africanist definition or conception of law. If we accept the view that law is a reconciliatory instrument for the enhancement of social cohesion, it then follows that what law is used to achieve becomes of more importance than the very instrument itself ... What is of importance for African jurisprudence is not that law performs an instrumental function but in what this function ideally entails. It behoves one to state that African jurisprudence, in the primary sense, underscores the idea of law as a reconciliatory phenomenon. In other words, 'peace-keeping and the maintenance of social equilibrium' stands at the heart of African law.
>
> But then, how does this confer a sense of distinction for African law since we cannot rule out conciliation and reconciliation in other cultures? ...
>
> The point is that in these systems, the substance of jurisprudence is the essentially adversarial or winner-takes-all. The inquisitorial and accusatorial nature of law and judicial activity is remote in African jurisprudence ... We see in post-apartheid South Africa, the establishment of the Truth and Reconciliation Committee [sic] (TRC) ...

---

45   Extracted from Idowu 2006 *Cambrian Law Review.*

to deal with the violence and human rights abuses of the apartheid era on a morally accepted basis and to advance the cause of forgiveness and reconciliation. One of the central emphases and objectives of the Committee was the need to promote social stability which is considered a greater good than the individual right to obtain retributive justice ... Leading members of the African National Congress (ANC) contended that the 'retributive justice' was 'un-African'.

There are a number of immediate objections that this conceptualisation of African jurisprudence elicits. Does it then mean that the concept of punishment is alien to African legal philosophy? Are punitive measures lacking in African jurisprudence? ...

It is not the case that there are no elements of sanctions or punishments existing in African jurisprudence. When reconciliation is projected as the basis of law, it does not at all preclude the idea of punishment; it only establishes the ultimate target and aim of law.

What can be considered the most important critique of law-as-reconciliation is the view that reconciliation epitomizes a moral affair and not legal and to that extent that it conflates morality with legality ... [T]o set an agenda of reconciliation as the basis of law is to set not a legal but an essentially moral agenda ... One may reason that the idea of law-as-reconciliation is clearly in need of revision since it is only ascribing to law a moral goal. A moral goal is only incidentally important to a legal system.

[However], law and society are blended and harmonised with each other such that the history of law is the history of society as well. It is then the cultural and national spirit prevalent within that society that explains the substance and goal of laws within that society. It is in this sense that reconciliation is taken to be at the heart and substance of law in general in African societies. It is in this sense that the relationship between law and morality in African jurisprudence is held to exhibit a kind of epiphenomenal character since both law and morality in this kind of society are mutually defining. Thus, the reconciliatory nature of law endorses the view that law and morality are not antagonistic to each other since, by virtue of their inherent origin and development, they both exist to promote societal interests. In the case of African jurisprudence, this entails the enhancement and maintenance of social cohesion and equilibrium.

## Questions

1. According to Idowu, if one wants to understand law, one must appeal to its social purpose or function. Is there any reasonable way to disagree with this claim?
2. At one point Idowu seems to suggest that a concern for cohesion and reconciliation is more important than a concern for the individual right of retribution. Are these relational values incompatible with individual rights in general, or is there a way of understanding them that includes respect for individual rights?
3. Give an example of how a characteristically Western legal system is plausibly characterised as 'adversarial' or 'accusatorial'. How might someone argue that it is an attractive feature?

In the passage above, Idowu articulates the view that, from a characteristically African perspective, what law is must be understood in terms of what law ought to be, that is, which function social norms ought to perform. More specifically, the relevant function, according to Idowu, is to enhance cohesion, often by reconciling parties who are at odds with one another.

### 3.5.2   Evaluating Idowu's view of law as harmonisation

It is not entirely clear from the passage precisely what kind of claim Idowu is making when he says that 'African jurisprudence ... underscores the idea of law as a reconciliatory phenomenon'. It could be one of three ideas, each of which has apparent weaknesses.

One understanding of Idowu's point is a sociological interpretation of it. He could be read as making a claim about the nature of law as it was common to find in traditional African societies and only in them. There law is what tends to foster harmony, but that is not true for other, non-African societies.

Such an interpretation is 'weak' in the sense that it does not tell us anything yet about the essence of law, the philosophical enquiry of this chapter (and the previous one). A philosopher would be inclined to pose this question: even if law in African societies has differed from law in Western ones, what has been common to law in both societies such that it is law? Again, there is a species of African law and a species of Western law, but what is the genus of which they are both members? If Idowu were making a merely sociological point, he would not be answering these philosophical questions.

A second reading of Idowu is more philosophical for indeed being about the essence of law, that is, of law's nature wherever one may find it in the world. Perhaps Idowu is suggesting that law in any society consists of those norms expected to foster harmony and cohesion, as Africans have tended to understand these relationships. From this perspective, just as Western scientists discovered that the earth is round, and people from a non-Western society would be mistaken to think that it is flat, so African philosophers such as Idowu have discovered that law is what tends to promote harmonious relationships, and people from a non-African society would be mistaken to think that law is instead, say, the union of primary and secondary rules or a sovereign's command.

However, this does not appear to be Idowu's view, for he characterises law in some non-African (and implicitly Western) societies as *not* tending towards cohesion as he understands it. He is straightforwardly read as maintaining that in some societies law has been adversarial and competitive, not harmonising. And insofar as law in some societies has not served the function of advancing harmony, one cannot say that the essence of law is to do so.

Consider, therefore, a third way to read Idowu that seems faithful to his text while also being philosophically interesting. It is the claim that there is no essence of law, that is, that law varies so much from society to society that there is no core, common feature to be found in every circumstance that it exists. Such a reading is suggested by Idowu's remark that the 'history of law is the history of society as well. It is then the cultural and national spirit prevalent within that society that explains the substance and goal of laws within that society'.

From this perspective, the question that Chapters 2 and 3 of this book have sought to answer is misguided! These chapters have been supposing that legal systems all share certain core features (for example, being a sovereign's command, forming a union of primary and secondary rules, including true principles of justice), regardless of when and where they have existed. Instead, perhaps there is such a variety amongst legal systems that one cannot specify whether positivism or naturalism is universally true (a claim about complexity), or perhaps societies' widely divergent beliefs about what law is determine its nature (a claim of relativism). One theory of law might apply to some societies, but not to others.

An analogy to illustrate the (relativist) point might be the norms of etiquette. Whereas in American society it is usually rude to eat with one's hands rather than with cutlery, in many African (and Indian) societies it is not. There is no real *disagreement* between these societies about what is rude and what is not; there are instead merely *differences*. What is rude is constituted by whatever people believe to be rude, so that different standards apply to different contexts. Perhaps Idowu is suggesting that legal norms are similar to norms of etiquette. What counts as law in one society need not count as law in another one, depending on what a given society believes about law.

Another analogy to illustrate the (complexity) point might be with a game.[46] Is there something that all games have in common? Perhaps not. Some use a board and pieces or a computer, while some use no equipment at all. Some have inflexible rules, while others allow for changing rules in the course of the game. Some are played with other people, while some are played alone. Given all the variations in what we call 'games', perhaps there is no essence to them, nothing that they all have in common and must have in order to count as a game. Similarly, Idowu might be contending that law has taken such a variety of social forms over time and across space that it lacks an essence as either positivist or naturalist.

Idowu does not make these arguments, but they are in the spirit of his text, and they are important to consider. Reflecting with him on the African experience as distinct from the Western makes us question implicit assumptions that have guided much English-speaking philosophical enquiry into the nature of law for nearly 200 years. When we ask about the nature of law, is it a mistake to suppose that one can find an answer that applies to all societies?

Theorists seem to have come up with plausible universal accounts of other human behaviour; for instance it is reasonable to think that one can define what an economy in general is, even though there is a wide variety of particular economies. Might a universal account of a legal system be available as well?

## 3.6    Conclusion

This chapter and the previous one have sought to answer the question of what law essentially is, for instance what makes something a legal system as opposed to a university. As we have seen, positivists maintain that a legal system is merely what is sometimes called a 'social fact'; whether a norm is a law or not is merely a function of how certain human beings came to adopt it. In contrast, naturalists contend that law is not fully understood in merely social scientific terms, and that it is instead essentially tied to morality in some way. Either the procedures by which a rule is adopted must be objectively just to count as a genuine legal system, or the content of certain norms must be morally sound in order to be real, weighty laws.

Applied to South African apartheid, here is a bird's-eye view of the respective advantages of the theories. The advantage of positivism is that it grounds a powerful explanation of why apartheid was to be abhorred: statutes separating races, and degrading and harming black people, were the law of the land and seriously unjust. Naturalists need not deny that the apartheid statutes were law, but they would normally say that it was not conclusive, that is, that there were other kinds of law in South Africa that were weightier, even though they had not been formally adopted. And naturalists would contend that such an interpretation of

---

46   This famous example comes from Ludwig Wittgenstein's *Philosophical Investigations*.

the essence of law makes the best sense of the intuitions that it can be right to punish people for wrongful actions that were permitted by a positivist conception of law and that there is always some moral obligation to obey the law, but not to obey racist statutes. As with all other debates explored in this book, the reader is encouraged to decide for himself or herself which position is more attractive, or to read further with an eye to coming to a firm conclusion about that.

Unlike Chapters 2 and 3, the remaining chapters in Part 1 of the book play down the question of what law is and instead focus more on how judges tend to interpret it and how they should. There are philosophers who deny that there is any real distinction between these questions; according to them whenever a judge asks a live question about what the law is, he or she is making an interpretation that must include a moral enquiry into what should happen.[47] This book, however, supposes that these questions are distinct, or at least admit of a different emphasis.

## POINTS TO CONSIDER

1. Imagine you were a judge during apartheid having to decide whether to enforce a statute that forced black people to move out of a developed urban centre. How would you be inclined to rule, and on what basis? Be sure to include the positivism/naturalism distinction in your reasoning.
2. Imagine you are a judge after the end of apartheid having to decide whether to punish officials who had adopted and enforced a statute that forced black people to move out of a developed urban centre. How would you be inclined to rule, and on what basis? Be sure to include the positivism/naturalism distinction in your reasoning.
3. In your view, what distinguishes a legal system from a university's system of rules?

---

47   See Dworkin 2004.

# Chapter 4

# How should judges adjudicate in an African constitutional democracy?

DAVID BILCHITZ

## 4.1 African constitutions and questions of adjudication

> At the heart of a transformative Constitution is a commitment to *substantive* reasoning, to examine underlying principles that inform laws themselves and judicial reaction to those laws. Purely *formalist* reasoning tends to avoid that responsibility.[1] [own emphasis]

New constitutions are usually passed against a backdrop of a momentous event for a particular society. Most African countries received their independence in the late 1950s and early 1960s, in the wake of the Second World War and the new world order that emerged thereafter. The new constitutions that were adopted by these countries sought to establish the framework of governance for a newly formed state against the backdrop of a long period of colonial rule. In the case of South Africa, the Constitution was passed in response to a history of legalised discrimination and segregation – known as 'apartheid' and implemented

---

1 Langa 2006 *Stellenbosch Law Review* at 357.

intensively with the rise to power of the Nationalist Party in 1948. Apartheid privileged white people simply on the basis of the colour of their skin and maintained the subordination and inequality of black people.[2]

In such cases, the constitutions ushered in a new order. These constitutions did not seek to preserve the status quo. Instead, they were 'transformative' in the sense that they sought to utilise the law to change their societies in the direction of greater justice and equality.[3] Many of these constitutions confer the power of interpreting the constitution upon judges. Some of these constitutions also allow their judges to strike down the laws of parliament or actions of the executive if they do not conform to the substantive rights and processes enshrined in the new constitutional order.

Some constitutions, like that in South Africa, provide some guidance as to how judges should utilise their powers. Section 39(1)(*a*) of the South African Constitution, for example, provides that:

> [w]hen interpreting the bill of rights, a court, tribunal or forum must promote the values that underlie an open, and democratic society based on human dignity, equality and freedom.

This Constitution thus expressly directs judges to utilise values in interpreting it and provides an understanding of the central values that must be considered. The South African Constitution goes even further in section 39(2) and requires the 'spirit, purport and objects' of the Bill of Rights to be considered when interpreting any legislation or developing the common law or customary law. The Constitution thus is designed to have an influence on the entire legal system. Chief Justice Langa indicates in the quote at the beginning of this chapter that, in his view, the Constitution requires judges to approach the adjudication of the Constitution in a particular manner. Adjudication in the new constitutional era, for Chief Justice Langa, involves a deeper grappling with the substance of a dispute which involves, drawing on section 39 of the Constitution, an engagement with the values and principles underlying the new constitutional order. It is to be contrasted with purely *formal* reasoning on the basis of procedure and abstract legal rules without having any regard to deeper moral questions of value and principle that arise in particular cases.

Thus, a key question that arises, in the post-colonial and post-apartheid context, concerns how judges should adjudicate in light of the transformative aims of these constitutions. In order to address this question, this chapter and the next will engage with central debates in jurisprudence around how judges should adjudicate. This chapter will focus on theorists who are of the view that there can be a relatively objective approach to interpreting the law. The next chapter will address theories that provide a more thorough skepticism about the possibility of objectivity in the law and require strong reflection on the vantage point from which any judgment is made.

The following key questions will be dealt with in this chapter:
- Can a legal provision be interpreted simply on the basis of its language?
- Do 'hard' cases in law require a different interpretive approach than 'easy' cases?
- Is law made up only of rules, or also principles and values?
- To what extent must law be interpreted to be consistent with past legal decisions?

---

2   In South Africa, black people can be considered to include people of African, Indian and mixed race (or 'coloured') descent. All these groups were discriminated against, though the apartheid government also imposed different benefits and burdens upon them. People of African descent were at the receiving end of the worst measures of exclusion and discrimination.

3   Klare 1998 *South African Journal on Human Rights* at 155.

- To what extent must law be interpreted in light of moral and political philosophy? Does this make it subjective?
- What impact does the African context have on these theories? What values should be used in interpreting transformative constitutions?
- What does a transformative approach – as suggested by Justice Langa – which involves substantive reasoning, as opposed to formal reasoning, involve? How are we to understand the distinction between substantive and formal reasoning?

## 4.2   Rules, language and adjudication

In Chapter 3, we considered some of the arguments raised in the famous debate between Herbert Hart and Lon Fuller surrounding whether there is law within wicked political systems. As we saw, that debate focused on the merits of two main theories of law: positivism and natural law. The arguments for their theories also directly engage questions of adjudication. Text 1 is an excerpt from Hart's article and articulates his view on adjudication, which is influenced by a positivist theory of law.

**PRIMARY TEXTS**

### Text 1  Hart's core and penumbra theory

A legal rule forbids you to take a vehicle into the public park. Plainly this forbids an automobile, but what about bicycles, roller skates, toy automobiles? What about airplanes? Are these, as we say, to be called "vehicles" for the purpose of the rule or not? If we are to communicate with each other at all, and if, as in the most elementary form of law, we are to express our intentions that a certain type of behavior be regulated by rules, then the general words we use – like "vehicle" in the case I consider – must have some standard instance in which no doubts are felt about its application. There must be a core of settled meaning, but there will be, as well, a penumbra of debatable cases in which words are neither obviously applicable nor obviously ruled out. These cases will each have some features in common with the standard case; they will lack others or be accompanied by features not present in the standard case. Human invention and natural processes continually throw up such variants on the familiar, and if we are to say that these ranges of facts do or do not fall under existing rules, then the classifier must make a decision which is not dictated to him, for the facts and phenomena to which we fit our words and apply our rules are as it were dumb. The toy automobile cannot speak up and say, "I am a vehicle for the purpose of this legal rule," nor can the roller skates chorus, "We are not a vehicle." Fact situations do not await us neatly labeled, creased, and folded, nor is their legal classification written on them to be simply read off by the judge. Instead, in applying legal rules, someone must take the responsibility of deciding that words do or do not cover some case in hand with all the practical consequences involved in this decision.

We may call the problems which arise outside the hard core of standard instances or settled meaning "problems of the penumbra"; they are always with us whether in relation to such trivial things as the regulation of the use of the public park or in relation to the multidimensional generalities of a constitution. If a penumbra of uncertainty must surround all legal rules, then their application to specific cases in the penumbral area cannot be a matter of logical deduction, and so deductive reasoning, which for generations has been cherished as the very perfection of human reasoning, cannot serve as a model for what judges, or indeed anyone, should do in bringing particular cases under general rules. In this area men cannot live by deduction alone. And it follows that if legal arguments and legal decisions of penumbral questions are to be rational, their rationality must lie in something other than a logical relation to premises. So if it is rational or "sound" to argue and to decide that for the purposes of this rule an airplane is not a vehicle, this argument must be sound or rational without being logically conclusive. What is it then that makes such decisions correct or at least better than alternative decisions? Again, it seems true to say that the criterion which makes a decision sound in such cases is some concept of what the law ought to be; it is easy to slide from that into saying that it must be a moral judgment about what law ought to be. So here we touch upon a point of necessary "intersection between law and morals" which demonstrates the falsity or, at any rate, the misleading character of the Utilitarians' emphatic insistence on the separation of law as it is and ought to be.[4]

... It does not follow that, because the opposite of a decision reached blindly in the formalist or literalist manner is a decision intelligently reached by reference to some conception of what ought to be, we have a junction of law and morals. We must, I think, beware of thinking in a too simple-minded fashion about the word "ought." This is not because there is no distinction to be made between law as it is and ought to be. Far from it. It is because the distinction should be between what is and what from many different points of view ought to be. The word "ought" merely reflects the presence of some standard of criticism; one of these standards is a moral standard but not all standards are moral. We say to our neighbour, "You ought not to lie," and that may certainly be a moral judgment, but we should remember that the baffled poisoner may say, "I ought to have given her a second dose." The point here is that intelligent decisions which we oppose to mechanical or formal decisions are not necessarily identical with decisions defensible on moral grounds. We may say of many a decision: "Yes, that is right; that is as it ought to be," and we may mean only that some accepted purpose or policy has been thereby advanced; we may not mean to endorse the moral propriety of the policy or the decision. So the contrast between the mechanical decision and the intelligent one can be reproduced inside a system dedicated to the pursuit of the most evil aims. It does not exist as a contrast to be found only in legal systems which, like our own, widely recognize principles of justice and moral claims of individuals.

... We can now return to the main point. If it is true that the intelligent decision of penumbral questions is one made not mechanically but in the light of aims, purposes, and policies, though not necessarily in the light of anything we would call moral principles, is it wise to express this important fact by saying that the

---

4   Hart 1958 *Harvard Law Review* at 607–608.

firm utilitarian distinction between what the law is and what it ought to be should be dropped? Perhaps the claim that it is wise cannot be theoretically refuted for it is, in effect, an invitation to revise our conception of what a legal rule is. We are invited to include in the "rule" the various aims and policies in the light of which its penumbral cases are decided on the ground that these aims have, because of their importance, as much right to be called law as the core of legal rules whose meaning is settled. But though an invitation cannot be refuted, it may be refused and I would proffer two reasons for refusing this invitation. First, everything we have learned about the judicial process can be expressed in other less mysterious ways. We can say laws are incurably incomplete and we must decide the penumbral cases rationally by reference to social aims. I think Holmes, who had such a vivid appreciation of the fact that "general propositions do not decide concrete cases," would have put it that way. Second, to insist on the utilitarian distinction is to emphasize that the hard core of settled meaning is law in some centrally important sense and that even if there are borderlines, there must first be lines. If this were not so the notion of rules controlling courts' decisions would be senseless as some of the "Realists" – in their most extreme moods, and, I think, on bad grounds – claimed.

By contrast, to soften the distinction, to assert mysteriously that there is some fused identity between law as it is and as it ought to be, is to suggest that all legal questions are fundamentally like those of the penumbra. It is to assert that there is no central element of actual law to be seen in the core of central meaning which rules have, that there is nothing in the nature of a legal rule inconsistent with all questions being open to reconsideration in the light of social policy. Of course, it is good to be occupied with the penumbra. Its problems are rightly the daily diet of the law schools. But to be occupied with the penumbra is one thing, to be preoccupied with it another.[5]

### Questions

1. What method do judges use to interpret statutes according to Hart?
2. What is the difference between the approach adopted between the core and the penumbra? What argument does Hart provide for the distinction?
3. When adjudicating in the penumbra, why are the purposes that judges refer to not automatically morally good?
4. In what way does Hart preserve his positivist approach in his theory of adjudication?
5. According to Hart, why is it wrong to be preoccupied with the penumbra?
6. What is utilitarianism (see Chapter 6) and what role does it play in Hart's reasoning?

As we saw, a positivist theory of the nature of law is committed to the separation of law and morality: there is no necessary connection between the two. What does this mean for how to adjudicate a legal dispute?

Following from the positivist view, it must mean that judges do not need to have reference to morality when identifying the law to be applied in particular cases and deciding upon those cases. How can judges avoid referring to morality? Positivism requires that there be

---

5   Hart 1958 at 612–615.

sources of law that can be identified separately from morality. One such source would, for instance, be a statute passed by a parliament. If judges can identify clearly what parliament intended the law to achieve, for instance, they need not have reference to any moral ideas in determining what the law is.

To illustrate his point, Hart considers a simple statutory rule: 'no vehicles are allowed in the public park'. Consider an instance where Xolani parked his new Toyota Prius on the grass in the park whilst having a picnic. He was given a fine by a traffic officer. He, however, decides to contest the fine in court and argues that a Toyota Prius is not a vehicle as it has a hybrid engine (utilising both fuel and electricity to generate power). What should the judge do?

Hart argues that this is a simple case: the word 'vehicle' clearly includes all forms of motor car. Since a Toyota Prius is a motor car, Xolani should lose his case as a matter of law. Hart argues that there is what he terms a *core* of meaning that any competent individual who utilises English will understand: a vehicle includes a motor car. Most legal cases, argues Hart, are decided on the basis of the core of settled meaning. Many cases may not even reach court as people do not try to make arguments that fall within the core since they know they will lose. Another phrase for these would be, in Hart's view, 'easy cases'.

Hart provides one major argument for his claim:

> **Proposition 1:** If we are to communicate with one another (and be able to express our intentions in the form of general rules), general words must have a core of settled meaning that can be determined.
> **Proposition 2:** We can and do communicate with each other (and are able to express our intentions in the form of general rules).
> Therefore,
> **Conclusion:** General words must have a core of settled meaning that can be determined.

Hart, however, does not think that language is completely clear and transparent. He admits that sometimes we are unsure whether something falls within the meaning of a word. Would a bicycle or a toy motor car constitute a vehicle for purposes of the statute? Here, there is more uncertainty than in the case of the Toyota Prius. These examples share some features with the Prius, but are different in other ways. It is not entirely clear whether they fall within the scope of the word 'vehicle'. These more debatable cases of what falls within the meaning of a word are what Hart calls the *penumbra* of meaning. The word 'penumbra' is usually used in a scientific context and refers to the body of partial light that exists between the full light and the complete shadow (in an eclipse of the moon, for instance). It is an area that is on the fringes, not entirely easy to make out, and thus indeterminate. Hart believes words have a core of settled meaning but also outer edges which are not entirely clear and determinate. Real life experience provides examples that do not neatly fit into the core meaning of words. This problem affects law too, as we do not always automatically know whether a particular case falls under a prohibition in the statute. These are the 'hard' cases of law that are often reported in law reports. The fact that 'hard' cases are often studied in law school and fill the law reports provides a misleading impression that law consists principally of 'hard' cases. In fact, Hart argues, most cases are clear and can be settled by simply reading the words of the statute and understanding whether the concrete circumstances fit thereunder.

Cases in the core are relatively easily settled but, what happens in the penumbra? Here, there is no possibility of relying on words alone to resolve the question. In the penumbra,

Hart admits we require some understanding of the purpose at which the statute aims. Some of the time, the framers of legislation provide a clear understanding of what their intention was behind particular provisions; in many cases, however, there is a need for judges to construct the purpose behind a provision. The rule that there must be no vehicles in public parks could potentially have multiple reasons behind it. Such a rule preserves the quietness and recreational nature of the space; it also guards against dangers to adults and children that might be caused if vehicles were driving in the park. Bicycles, for instance, might well be a means for some people to enjoy themselves in the park; on the other hand, it might still be dangerous for people to be riding across all areas of the park, where adults and children are lying down and running around. Hart thinks that we must have regard to the social aims and purposes of the legislation when deciding cases in the penumbra. Hart often refers to utilitarianism in this passage: that would be the view that social policies and legislation should aim to achieve the greatest happiness possible in a political community. In Chapter 6, we will examine the utilitarian moral theory in more detail. For our purposes now, Hart seems to advocate judges deciding cases in the penumbra on the basis of which alternative would achieve the greatest happiness overall. Usually, judges will not have to do so and can rely on the core of settled meaning in the legislation; in hard cases, judges will need to exercise discretion through rationally reasoning about the purpose of the legislation in relation to the particular case (it is not possible, Hart thinks, simply to address these hard cases in a mechanical way).

Hart himself raises the objection as to whether he has departed from positivist reasoning by admitting that he needs to refer to social aims and purposes in constructing penumbral cases. In other words, when one looks at the purposes of a statute, does this not mean one is engaging in some form of moral reasoning? Hart denies this implication. He says it is possible to think about purposes in a way that is bad morally. He considers an example from Nazi Germany where the Nazi judges utilised law as a means to strike fear in the heart of the population and render them subservient. We could also add examples from apartheid legislation such as the Reservation of Separate Amenities Act,[6] which forced black and white people to use different toilets and even separate benches in parks. This legislation actively sought to distinguish between black and white people for purposes of entrenching white domination and black subordination. Positivists, such as Hart, argue that these forms of legislation were in fact law. Yet, they aimed at purposes that were morally bad. The fact that, in penumbral cases, we need to refer to purposes in adjudicating does not automatically mean that those purposes are good: they may be morally neutral or evil. As such, Hart claims he can admit that purposes are sometimes necessary to construct legislation without giving up on being a positivist.

In summary, Hart thus makes two main claims about adjudication: 1) in easy cases, there is a core of settled meaning which allows judges to decide simply by understanding the meaning of the words of a statute; 2) in hard cases, judges need to refer to social aims and purposes – such as achieving the greatest amount of happiness possible in the circumstances – to understand whether the concrete circumstances of the case fall within the words of the statute. Those aims and purposes, however, relate to the goals that can be ascertained in constructing the statute (and the intentions of the legislature if those are clear) and are not necessarily moral in nature.

---

6   49 of 1953.

## 4.3    Purpose in adjudication

Lon Fuller fundamentally disagrees with Hart about the manner in which adjudication takes place. We explore the main tenets of his critique below.

**PRIMARY TEXTS**

### Text 2  Fuller's critique of Hart

If I have properly interpreted Professor Hart's theory as it affects the "hard core," then I think it is quite untenable. The most obvious defect of his theory lies in its assumption that problems of interpretation typically turn on the meaning of individual words. Surely no judge applying a rule of the common law ever followed any such procedure as that described (and, I take it, prescribed) by Professor Hart; indeed, we do not normally even think of his problem as being one of "interpretation." Even in the case of statutes, we commonly have to assign meaning, not to a single word, but to a sentence, a paragraph, or a whole page or more of text. Surely a paragraph does not have a "standard instance" that remains constant whatever the context in which it appears.

If a statute seems to have a kind of "core meaning" that we can apply without a too precise inquiry into its exact purpose, this is because we can see that, however one might formulate the precise objective of the statute, this case would still come within it.

Even in situations where our interpretive difficulties seem to head up in a single word, Professor Hart's analysis seems to me to give no real account of what does or should happen. In his illustration of the "vehicle," although he tells us this word has a core of meaning that in all contexts defines unequivocally a range of objects embraced by it, he never tells us what these objects might be. If the rule excluding vehicles from parks seems easy to apply in some cases, I submit this is because we can see clearly enough what the rule "is aiming at in general" so that we know there is no need to worry about the difference between Fords and Cadillacs. If in some cases we seem to be able to apply the rule without asking what its purpose is, this is not because we can treat a directive arrangement as if it had no purpose. It is rather because, for example, whether the rule be intended to preserve quiet in the park, or to save carefree strollers from injury, we know, "without thinking," that a noisy automobile must be excluded.

What would Professor Hart say if some local patriots wanted to mount on a pedestal in the park a truck used in World War II, while other citizens, regarding the proposed memorial as an eyesore support their stand by the "no vehicle" rule? Does this truck, in perfect working order, fall within the core or the penumbra?[7]

Let us suppose that in leafing through the statutes, we come upon the following enactment: "It shall be a misdemeanor, punishable by a fine of five dollars, to sleep in any railway station." We have no trouble in perceiving the general nature of the target toward which this statute is aimed. Indeed, we are likely at once to

---

7    Fuller 1958 *Harvard Law Review* at 662–663.

call to mind the picture of a disheveled tramp,[8] spread out in an ungainly fashion on one of the benches of the station, keeping weary passengers on their feet and filling their ears with raucous and alcoholic snores. This vision may fairly be said to represent the "obvious instance" contemplated by the statute, though certainly it is far from being the "standard instance" of the physiological state called "sleep."

Now let us see how this example bears on the ideal of fidelity to law. Suppose I am a judge, and that two men are brought before me for violating this statute. The first is a passenger who was waiting at 3 A.M. for a delayed train. When he was arrested he was sitting upright in an orderly fashion, but was heard by the arresting officer to be gently snoring. The second is a man who had brought a blanket and pillow to the station and had obviously settled himself down for the night. He was arrested, however, before he had a chance to go to sleep. Which of these cases presents the "standard instance" of the word "sleep"? If I disregard that question, and decide to fine the second man and set free the first, have I violated a duty of fidelity to law? Have I violated that duty if I interpret the word "sleep" as used in this statute to mean something like "to spread oneself out on a bench or floor to spend the night, or as if to spend the night"?[9]

## Questions

1. What are Fuller's objections to Hart's view of adjudication?
2. What method do judges use to interpret statutes according to Lon Fuller?
3. What does Fuller think of the distinction between the core and penumbra of meaning?
4. For Fuller, why does reference to purposes in adjudication in all likelihood lead law towards being moral?
5. In what way does Fuller demonstrate that his view embodies a natural law conception of the nature of law?
6. According to Fuller, what role does the ideal of fidelity to law play in adjudication?

Fuller challenges Hart's idea that it is possible to determine a 'core' meaning of words. His first argument is that meaning is not determined by individual words on their own. Instead, meaning requires an understanding of a word in the context of a sentence, a paragraph and a full text. He considers, for instance, a statute which simply contains the words 'all improvements must be promptly reported to ...'. The meaning of the word 'improvement', he argues, will differ depending on whether the sentence ends with the word 'the head nurse' or 'the Johannesburg municipality'. In the former case, the word would refer to an upturn in the condition of a patient in the hospital; in the latter case, the word would refer to the upgrading of buildings. The meaning of the word alone changes as a result of the context and other words that are utilised. The construction of meaning in statutes involves considering not only individual words but the whole provision and text.

---

8   We draw attention to the fact that this language is troubling and demeaning to certain homeless persons. It may have been acceptable at the time Fuller was writing, but it is undesirable language we hope students will avoid.
9   Fuller at 664.

Hart, however, argues that there are cases that appear rather easily to fall within the domain of a particular statute like 'no vehicles in the park'. Fuller agrees that this is true but he provides a different reason, which he argues has greater explanatory power. Statutes, for Fuller, always require interpretation in light of the purposes thereof. 'No vehicles in the park' has a rather clear-cut purpose of ensuring the quietness of the space and ensuring individuals enjoying the park are safe from the dangers of motor vehicles. Certain cases, like the Toyota Prius mentioned above, clearly fall within that purpose. That is why we regard them as rather clear-cut cases. That does not mean, for Fuller, that we are simply interpreting words. It is rather that the concrete case quite clearly falls within the purpose of the statute. Fuller argues that his understanding has the benefit of actually giving some clarity to what is meant by a 'vehicle' for purposes of the statute. Hart relies on some kind of inherent intuitive understanding, which falls flat in a number of cases.

Fuller proceeds to illustrate his point by considering the placement of a truck in the park as a memorial to those who died in the Second World War. The truck is clearly a 'vehicle' in the 'core' sense utilised by Hart, but would it really be the target of an appropriately interpreted statute that prohibited 'vehicles in a park'? Parks are often utilised for memorials and the placement of such a vehicle in the park would neither affect the quietness or safety of those enjoying the outdoors for recreation. Fuller attempts to show that what is clearly a vehicle, in the ordinary sense of the term, is not included within the purpose of what should be prohibited by the statute.

As such, Fuller also attempts to show that there is a breakdown between Hart's notion of the 'core' and the 'penumbra'. Even a clear case of what constitutes a vehicle is not necessarily prohibited by the statute. He provides another example to illustrate this point: a statute prohibits individuals from 'sleeping in any railway station'. The purpose of such a statute would be to ensure, for instance, that seats on the platform of a train station are reserved for passengers rather than to provide a place to sleep for homeless persons. Fuller then considers two possible cases: Case 1 is of a passenger who is boarding a train in the middle of night, sits on a bench and happens to fall asleep. Case 2 is of a homeless person who brings a pillow into the train station, settles down but has not yet fallen asleep. On a strict construction of the statute on the basis of words alone, the prohibition is on 'sleeping' in a railway station. The law would thus require that the passenger in Case 1 be found guilty of the offence and the homeless person in Case 2 be acquitted (since he had not yet fallen asleep). Yet, if we have regard to the purpose of the statute (as it was constructed above), it would seem clear that the homeless person in Case 2 is much more the target of the prohibition than the passenger in Case 1. Once again, the purpose of the statute is essential in determining its meaning and application. At the same time, Fuller casts doubt on our capacity to determine when a case falls within the 'core' or 'penumbra'. Indeed, he contends that the concept of the core is not helpful as these examples illustrate how difficult it is to tell when the core ends and the penumbra begins.

What then is the connection between Fuller's approach to adjudication and his defence of natural law? Fuller, as we saw, is of the view that any sensible interpretation of legal texts involves reference to the purpose of the provision in question. To refer to the purpose is to refer to some conception of what ought to be the case. In other words, determining the purpose of a statute roots it in an attempt to achieve certain moral goals or ideals. If this is so, it is not possible to determine the meaning of a law, according to Fuller, without some moral conception of what ought to be the case. The very practice of making a legal decision thus requires reference to morality and the two are necessarily intertwined.

Hart, as we saw, accepts that there are times (in the 'penumbra', according to him) when purposes are necessary to interpret statutes. Yet, purposes he claims are not *necessarily* moral or good and there can be evil purposes behind laws – such as, for instance, in apartheid South Africa, where laws sought to entrench the inequality of black and white persons. Fuller does not deny the possibility of evil purposes. Yet, in his view, an approach that interprets law in light of purposes is not as morally neutral as Hart suggests. For Fuller, his approach requires judges to make explicit the purposes behind law. Doing so, says Fuller pulls 'those decisions towards goodness'.[10] In other words, by making clear the reasoning underpinning decisions and thus creating greater accountability for those decisions, judges are led to make morally better decisions. This view rests upon a view that open justification tends towards better moral decision-making. Unless one is dealing with a terribly wicked regime, the idea is that, in most cases, people will not wish to make explicit, reinforce or advance openly what is morally evil. The idea that justification tends towards goodness is an assumption underlying the classic contribution of Etienne Mureinik concerning the point of South Africa's new Constitution and the Bill of Rights.[11] Mureinik argued that one of the key goals of a new Bill of Rights was the creation of a 'culture of justification': in which every exercise of governmental power needed to be justified. The underlying idea must be that such a culture of justification will tend towards the direction of creating a morally better society. Mureinik, though, sees such justifications as being driven by clear substantive values enshrined in the rights of the Bill of Rights.

Fuller, indeed, sees the explicit identification of purposes as also likely to be embraced by vulnerable minorities. He contends that 'even in the most perverted regimes, there is a certain hesitancy about writing cruelties, intolerances and inhumanities into law'.[12] The reason for this lies in the fact that law is essentially an idea with an inherent moral content. Trying to place evil purposes into law thus undermines the very reasons people have to obey laws in society. Consequently, there is, once again, a pressure that when identifying purposes in the law, they will be those that are generally regarded as morally good.

This idea can be connected with the theory of law of William Idowu that was studied in Chapter 3. Law essentially for Idowu must be conceived of as seeking to achieve certain moral goals such as harmony, cohesion and reconciliation amongst human beings. Judges, when attempting to identify the purposes behind specific laws, would – if we utilise Idowu's theory – be required to consider the interpretation that would best achieve the goals of law (namely, harmony and social stability).

This raises a central feature of Fuller's thought that concerns the important idea of 'fidelity to law'. Fuller raises the question as to why we have a sense that we owe a duty to obey the law and honour it. The reason, he suggests, is that law is, ultimately, an idea that seeks to realise, at least, a minimum set of morally desirable goals. Without such a view, it is difficult to see why we see there as being any moral obligation to obey the law (other than coercion, which is not a moral, but is instead a justification rooted in self-interest and self-preservation). If this is so, for Fuller, it is vital that, once again, the law be interpreted in light of morally justifiable purposes. For, the notion that the law is just there and must be obeyed for its own sake fails to provide a basis for our allegiance to it. Interpreting in light of the purpose of a statute, renders the reasons for the law explicit which then can command

---

10  Fuller at 636.
11  Mureinik 1994 *South African Journal on Human Rights* at 31–33.
12  Fuller at 637.

our obedience. Law without a sense that it is rooted in any good reason is unlikely to provide grounds for obedience, for 'fidelity to law'.

In summary, Fuller makes the following claims about adjudication: a) it is a process that takes place through the construction of language within a wider textual setting; b) language alone is not sufficient but judges must determine the purpose of a provision in order to provide an adequate interpretation; c) purposes require some notion of moral reasoning to be infused within the law and, consequently, law and morality are necessarily connected; d) a purposive approach to adjudication is not morally neutral and likely to lead to morally desirable interpretations and encourage fidelity to law.

## 4.4 Consistency and morality in adjudication

Ronald Dworkin has proposed one of the most influential accounts of adjudication in law. He too is critical of the approach adopted by Hart, and this chapter begins with his early critique of Hart who fails, in his view, to recognise that law is not simply a system of rules, but also consists of principles. We then turn to consider Dworkin's 'chain novel' account of adjudication, which rests on an analogy between the interpretation of literary texts and the interpretation of law.

### 4.4.1 Dworkin's critique of Hart

In his early book, *Taking Rights Seriously* (1977), Dworkin outlines a detailed critique of Hart, arguing that his understanding of adjudication is fundamentally wrong. Dworkin disagrees with the idea that law is indeterminate even in hard cases. As we saw, Hart contends that judges must make decisions on the basis of purposes and policy reasons in hard (or penumbral) cases. Dworkin contends that judges do not understand their task differently in easy and hard cases and are always obliged to see themselves as making decisions in terms of the morally best understanding of the law.

When litigants come before judges, judges tend not to see themselves as creating new rights or law, but rather they see themselves as seeking to find the existing law. In other words, they seek to discover which litigant has a pre-existing right to win. Statements of law in these cases are not 'new' law, but improved reports about what the law actually is. Dworkin argues in this way, as he sees severe problems of fairness and justice arising from Hart's account:

- First, if judges make new law in hard cases, as Hart's view entails, the law would be applied retroactively to the case before the judge: this, in turn, would mean that the losing party would be liable though they had no legal duty at the time the events transpired which led to the litigation. Understanding the judicial task in that way would seem to go against basic standards of fairness that we cannot hold someone responsible for conduct he or she did not know was legally unacceptable.
- Second, laws are in fact meant to guide conduct. Retrospective laws would make it impossible to regulate our behaviour according to law, as we cannot guide our behaviour by something we do not know binds us.
- Third, judges are not elected, and it is unclear on Hart's account why they have the right to impose their policy choices on others through making new law each time they adjudicate.

In order to address these problems, Dworkin argues that there is more to law than rules found in authoritative sources. There are many cases where legal rules fail to provide clear guidance. In fact, Dworkin argues, law is not comprised of rules alone but also includes principles. What then is the difference between rules and principles?

Rules either apply or not. If it is clear a legal consequence falls under a rule, then it must automatically follow. Thus, if a statute states 'no vehicles in the park' and we know that a Toyota Prius is a vehicle, then it must automatically follow that the Prius is prohibited from entering the park. Of course, there might be exceptions. In an emergency to save someone's life, for instance, it might be justifiable for the Prius to enter the park. In this case, however, the rule that 'no vehicles are allowed in a park' is overridden by another rule of law, namely, that it is permissible to break legal provisions to avoid great harms to individual persons. This example illustrates that, when rules conflict, then one of them will have to be abandoned.

On the other hand, principles are different. Unlike rules, they are not either applicable or not. Principles are reasons in favour or against a particular legal outcome, but do not determine it. In each situation, a judge will need to weigh up how strong the principle is in the face of competing principles. If the principle does not prevail, it is not invalid.

Dworkin illustrates his views through referring to an old case of *Riggs v Palmer*[13] in the United States. We will utilise a similar case to illustrate his point that arose recently in South Africa, namely, *Makhanya v Minister of Finance*.[14] The case concerned regulations made in terms of the Government Service Pension Act.[15] The regulations provided for the payment to the widow of pension benefits that had accrued to the deceased, by virtue of his being employed by the South African Police Service. The language of the statute was quite clear that only the widow (as a dependant) was entitled to inherit. The problem was that the widow had been convicted of murdering the deceased: the question was whether she was still eligible to receive the pension benefits. What should the judge do in such a case?

Dworkin argues that the statute seems to allow for the inheritance by the murderer (the widow) in terms of its strict rule. Yet, there is a foundational *principle* that already exists in the law that one should not profit from one's own wrongdoing. In South Africa, this principle was derived from Roman-Dutch law which included the maxim '*der bloedige hand neemt geen erfenis*' (the bloody hand does not receive an inheritance). The principle had, in previous cases, only been applied to receiving a benefit in terms of the deceased's will but not in relation to a statutory benefit. Dworkin's view is that the judge must be allowed to read the statute in light of this foundational principle, and develop an exception that excludes a person from inheriting or receiving a statutory benefit if she murders her relatives. It is important to understand that there was no contrary rule, in this case, on the books to the effect that a widow, who is a murderer, cannot receive a pension benefit. The rule in the statute thus remained unchallenged. Dworkin, however, contends that there was a deep principle in law that meant that an exception needed to be determined to the statutory rule. The dependant relative (the widow above) would inherit unless she murdered the deceased. Dworkin argues, importantly, that if the statute is read in this way, one is not inventing new law: one is simply drawing on the deepest principles of law to express what the legal rule is.

Recognising that law involves principles, as well as rules, helps address some of the problems Dworkin finds in Hart's account. Principles can help supply answers when the rules of law run out. He demonstrates how judges can go beyond the settled rules of a case *according* to law. He argues that judges decide hard (or penumbral) cases by invoking the principles that provide the best moral and political justification for the established legal rules. This task requires judgement but is not simply a matter of determining which policies judges think personally will have the best consequences in the long term. It is still a matter

---

13   115 N.Y. 506, 22 N.E. 188 (1889).
14   2001 (2) SA 1251 (D).
15   57 of 1973.

of determining an outcome, based upon the principles already inherent in the law. We are not, therefore, holding people liable retrospectively. The widow should, for instance, have known that she could not expect the law to allow her to profit from murdering her husband.

Recognising principles in law adds a layer of complexity to adjudication. Judges are not simply tasked with deciding which legal rules apply. They also have to consider these other forms of reasons and standards when reaching a decision. Dworkin's recognition of principles thus requires answering the question: if principles are part of the law, how then are judges to decide cases? The theory he outlines in his later book, *Law's Empire* (1986), is designed to address this problem.

### 4.4.2 Dworkin's theory of constructive interpretation

**PRIMARY TEXTS**

**Text 3 Dworkin's chain novel**

We can find an even more fruitful comparison between literature and law, therefore, by constructing an artificial genre of literature that we might call the chain novel.

In this enterprise a group of novelists writes a novel *seriatim*, each novelist in the chain interprets the chapters he has been given in order to write a new chapter, which is then added to what the next novelist receives, and so on. Each has the job of writing his chapter so as to make the novel being constructed the best it can be, and the complexity of this task models the complexity of deciding a hard case under law as integrity. The imaginary literary enterprise is fantastic but not unrecognizable. Some novels have actually been written in this way, though mainly for a debunking purpose, and certain parlor games for rainy weekends in English country houses have something of the same structure. Television soap operas span decades with the same characters and some minimal continuity of personality and plot, though they are written by different teams of authors even in different weeks. In our example, however, the novelists are expected to take their responsibilities of continuity more seriously; they aim jointly to create, so far as they can, a single unified novel that is the best it can be.

Each novelist aims to make a single novel of the material he has been given, what he adds to it, and (so far as he can control this) what his successors will want or be able to add. He must try to make this the best novel it can be construed as the work of a single author rather than, as is the fact, the product of many different hands. That calls for an overall judgement on his part, or a series of overall judgements as he writes and rewrites. He must take up some view about the novel in progress, some working theory about its characters, plot, genre, theme, and point, in order to decide what counts as continuing it and not as beginning anew. If he is a good critic, his view of these matters will be complicated and multifaceted, because the value of a decent novel cannot be captured from a single perspective. He will aim to find layers and currents of meaning rather than a single, exhaustive theme. We can, however, in our now familiar way give some structure to any interpretation he adopts, by distinguishing two dimensions on which it must be tested. The first is what we have been calling the dimension of fit. He cannot adopt any interpretation, however complex, if he believes that no single author who set out to write a novel with the various readings of character, plot, theme, and point that interpretation describes could have written substantially the text he has been given. That does not mean his interpretation must fit every bit of the text. It is not disqualified simply because he claims that some lines or tropes are accidental, or even that that some events of plot are mistakes because they work against the literary ambitions the interpretation states. But the interpretation he takes up must nevertheless flow throughout the text, it must have general explanatory power, and it is flawed if it leaves unexplained some major structural aspects of the text, a subplot treated as having great dramatic importance or a dominant and repeated metaphor. If no interpretation can be found that is not flawed in that way, then the chain novelist will not be able fully to meet his assignment, he will have to settle for an interpretation that captures most of the text, conceding that it is not wholly successful. Perhaps even that partial success is unavailable, perhaps every interpretion he considers is inconsistent with the bulk of the material supplied to him. In that case he must abandon the enterprise, for the consequence of taking the interpretative attitude towards the text in question is then a piece of internal skepticism: that nothing can count as continuing the novel rather than beginning anew.

He may find, not that no single interpretation fits the bulk of the text, but that more than one does. The second dimension of interpretation then requires him to judge which of these eligible readings makes the work in progress best, all things considered. At this point his more substantive aesthetic judgments, about the importance or insight or realism or beauty of different ideas the novel might be taken to express, come into play. But the formal and structural considerations that dominate on the first dimension figure on the second as well, for even when neither of two interpretations is disqualified out of hand as explaining too little, one may show the text in a better light because it fits more of the text or provides a more interesting integration of style and content. So the distinction between the two dimensions is less crucial or profound than it might seem. It is a useful analytical device that helps us give structure to any interpreter's working theory or style. He will form a sense of when an interpretation fits so poorly that it is unnecessary to consider its substantive appeal, because he knows that this cannot outweigh its embarrassments of fit in deciding whether it makes the novel better, everything taken into account, than its rivals. This sense will define the first dimension for him. But he need not reduce his intuitive sense to any precise formula; he would rarely need to decide whether some interpretation barely survives or barely fails, because a bare survivor, no matter how ambitious or interesting it claimed the text to be, would almost certainly fail in the overall comparison with other interpretations whose fit was evident.

We can now appreciate the range of different kinds of judgments that are blended in this overall comparison. Judgments about textual coherence and integrity, reflecting different formal literary values, are interwoven with more substantive aesthetic judgments that themselves assume different literary aims. Yet these various kinds of judgments, of each general kind, remain distinct enough to check one another in an overall assessment, and it is that possibility of contest, particularly between textual and substantive judgments, that distinguishes a chain novelist's assignment from more independent creative writing. Nor can we draw any flat distinction between the stage at which a chain novelist interprets the text he has been given and the stage at which he adds his own chapter, guided by the interpretation he has settled on. When he begins to write he might discover in what he has written a different, perhaps radically different, interpretation. Or he might find it impossible to write in the tone or theme he first took up, and that will lead him to reconsider other interpretations he first rejected. In either case he returns to the text to reconsider the lines it makes eligible.[16]

### Text 4  Dworkin's chain model of adjudication

Judges who accept the interpretive ideal of integrity decide hard cases by trying to find, in some coherent set of principles about people's rights and duties, the best constructive interpretation of the political structure and legal doctrine of their community. They try to make that complex structure and record the best these can be. It is analytically useful to distinguish different dimensions or aspects of any working theory. It will include convictions about both fit and justification. Convictions about fit will provide a rough threshold requirement that an interpretation of some of the part of the law must meet if it is to be eligible at all. Any plausible working theory would disqualify an interpretation of our own law that denied legislative competence or supremacy outright or that claimed a general principle of private law requiring the rich to share their wealth with the poor. That threshold will eliminate interpretations that some judges would otherwise prefer, so the brute facts of legal history will in this way limit the role any judge's personal convictions of justice can play in his decisions. Different judges will set this threshold differently. But anyone who accepts law as integrity must accept that the actual political history of his community will sometimes check his other political convictions in his overall interpretive judgment. If he does not – if his threshold of fit is wholly derivative from and adjustable to his convictions of justice, so that the latter automatically provide an eligible interpretation – then he cannot claim in good faith to be interpreting his legal practice at all. Like the chain novelist whose judgments of fit automatically adjusted to his substantive literary opinions, he is acting from bad faith or self-deception.

Hard cases arise, for any judge, when his threshold test does not discriminate between two or more interpretations of some statute or line of cases. Then he must choose between eligible interpretations by asking which shows the community's structure of institutions and decisions – its public standards as a whole – in a better light from the standpoint of political morality. His own moral and political convictions are now directly engaged. But the political judgment he must make is itself complex and will sometimes set one department of his political morality against another: his decision will reflect not only his opinions about justice and fairness but his higher-order convictions about how these ideals should be compromised when they compete. Questions of fit arise at this stage

16   Dworkin 1986 *Law's Empire* at 228–232.

of interpretation as well, because even when an interpretation survives the threshold requirement, any infelicities of fit will count against it, in the ways we noticed, in the general balance of political virtues. Different judges will disagree about each of these issues and will accordingly take different views of what the law of their community, properly understood, really is.

Any judge will develop, in the course of his training and experience, a fairly individualized working conception of law on which he will rely, perhaps unthinkingly, in making these various judgments and decisions, and the judgments will then be, for him, a matter of feel or instinct rather than analysis. Even so, we as critics can impose structure on his working theory by teasing out its rules of thumb about fit – about the relative importance of consistency with past rhetoric and popular opinion, for example – and its more substantive opinions or leanings about justice and fairness. Most judges will be like other people in their community, and fairness and justice will therefore not often compete for them. But judges whose political opinions are more eccentric or radical will find that the two ideals conflict in particular cases, and they will have to decide which resolution of that conflict would show the community's record in the best light. Their working conceptions will accordingly include higher-order principles that have proved necessary to that further decision. A particular judge may think or assume, for example, that political decisions should mainly respect majority opinion, and yet believe that this requirement relaxes and even disappears when serious constitutional rights are in question.

We should now recall two general observations we made in constructing the chain-novel model, because they apply here as well. First, the different aspects or dimensions of a judge's working approach – the dimension of fit and substance, and of different aspects of substance – are in the last analysis all responsive to his political judgment. His convictions about fit, as these appear either in his working threshold requirement or analytically later in competition with substance, are political not mechanical. They express his commitment to integrity: he believes that an interpretation that falls below his threshold of fit shows the record of the community in an irredeemably bad light, because proposing that interpretation suggests that the community has characteristically dishonored its own principles. When an interpretation meets the threshold, remaining defects of fit may be compensated, in his overall judgment, if the principles of that interpretation are particularly attractive, because then he sets off the community's infrequent lapses in respecting these principles against its virtue in generally observing them. The constraint fit imposes on substance, in any working theory, is therefore the constraint of one type of political conviction on another in the overall judgment which interpretation makes a political record the best it can be overall, everything taken into account. Second, the mode of this constraint is the mode we identified in the chain novel. It is not the constraint of external hard fact or of interpersonal consensus. But rather the structural constraint of different kinds of principle, within a system of principle, and it is none the less genuine for that.[17]

---

17   Dworkin 1986 at 255–257.

**Questions**

1. What is a chain novel?
2. What constraints are placed on subsequent authors in a chain novel?
3. What is the relationship between a chain novel and how judges are to make decisions, according to Dworkin?
4. Which constraints are placed upon judges in adjudicating law, for Dworkin?
5. What is the relationship between the constraints?
6. Why does Dworkin refer to his theory as 'law as integrity'?
7. Does Dworkin's theory suggest he is a positivist or a natural lawyer? Why?

Dworkin attempts to understand the nature of legal adjudication through creating an analogy to a literary genre he calls a 'chain novel'. Whilst few novels have been written in this way, a modern equivalent of a chain novel would be the writing of a TV series like *Isidingo*, often written by numerous writers over many years. This idea involves a group of writers producing a novel or story one after the other. The first person writes the first chapter, the second the next chapter and the third the following chapter. Dworkin asks us to think, for instance, about how, if one were the third writer say in the series, one would proceed with this task. In order to create the sense that it is one novel (and not different novels), he argues that each writer would want to see himself as producing a unified work and the best possible novel it could be.

To achieve this goal, Dworkin suggests that there would be two important constraints upon this third novelist in the chain novel. These constraints are as follows:

1. *The dimension of 'fit'*: The novel must in some sense fit what has gone before; otherwise, it would be a new novel. The goal of subsequent writers is not to invent a new novel but to continue the existing one. In so doing, the story must be consistent with the characters and themes of what has gone before and be coherent overall.
2. *The dimension of 'value'*: It is possible there could be multiple directions the third author, for instance, could take in the chain. In deciding which path to take, the author should attempt to follow, what in his or her judgement would make the novel the best it can be. This judgement would be based on substantive aesthetic judgements, about what makes a novel good, beautiful and engrossing.

Dworkin claims that judges deciding cases (particularly common law ones) should see themselves as authors in the chain novel of the law. Law is an enterprise that involves language and interpretation. It is also a system that does not involve starting from scratch at this point in human history. The goal of judges, according to Dworkin, should be similar to that of a chain novelist: to make the law the best that it can be in a given jurisdiction.

In doing so, Dworkin argues there are two similar constraints to those imposed on the chain novelist:

1. *The dimension of fit*: A judge usually must make a decision that has a connection with other legal sources such as statutes, and other judgments. In other words, judges should usually make judgments that cohere with other parts of law that have already been developed. A judge interprets in light of the legal practices of a community. Were a judge to strike out in a wholly different direction, he or she would undermine the idea that he or she is acting in accordance with that practice.

2. *The dimension of value*: A judge may have different possibilities as to which rule fits with the legal practices of a community (Dworkin sees these as being what we term 'hard' cases). In deciding which approach to adopt, a judge will need to make judgements concerning which approach is best from the standpoint of political morality – this could involve, for instance, deciding which approach is more just or fair.

Judges will generally seek to ensure their judgments at least meet the dimension of fit before applying the dimension of value. Dworkin also recognises that there can be significant judgements as to whether something meets the dimension of 'fit' or not. As we know in a common law system, there are often attempts to distinguish precedents, and so it is not a mechanical decision as to whether a rule or principle fits the past record. It is also possible for something to fit the past record but clash with what is best from the perspective of political morality. In South Africa, for instance, against the backdrop of a past of inequality and racial exclusion, there are in fact undesirable features of the law that may be rejected. Dworkin recognises that judges will also have to make judgements, at times, about the weight to be given to each dimension. Sometimes, for instance, what is desirable from the perspective of political morality may well outweigh whether a legal rule coheres with past practice – particularly, in a context like South Africa where the past was suffused with injustice.

In utilising this method, Dworkin contends that judges must seek to achieve right answers to legal disputes. He does not deny that there will be differences amongst judges. The goal must be achieving the right answer as best as they each can. The 'chain novel' method Dworkin outlines means, he claims, that judges do not make law. They are not entitled to go outside the legal system and create new policy or legal duties. They also may not apply the law retrospectively. Instead, the method he outlined involves applying existing principles that are already in the law (perhaps merely implicitly) drawing out their implications and providing clarification of existing principles of law that renders the whole system the best it can be. Legal reasoning, though, remains complex and value-driven. It is not simply the formal application of rules.

Dworkin's approach is thus distinct both from that of Hart and Fuller. As we have seen, in contrast to Hart, Dworkin is of the view that law includes both rules and principles. He is also of the view that adjudication is not simply reading the words of a statute and applying them to a particular case, as Hart suggests occurs in the 'core' of a statute. Instead, it would involve a much more complex process of understanding the meanings accorded to similar provisions by courts in the past, the interaction of the statute with the underlying principles in the law, and considering the value dimension of which interpretation would render the law best from the standpoint of political morality. In contrast to Fuller, however, Dworkin is not of the view that the meaning of legal texts can be ascertained by reference simply to suitably constructed moral purposes that lie behind the law. It is necessary also to engage the dimension of 'fit': how a particular meaning connects with legal sources such as past precedent and understandings of a statute that must be factored into any adequate interpretation.

It is possible to object that Dworkin's method – and particularly the dimension of value – opens the door to judges utilising their personal preferences in deciding the law. Dworkin, however, does not think that the dimension of value is purely subjective. He believes there are objective answers to questions of political morality. A judge, therefore, could not simply decide against a litigant on the basis that he is a Christian who disapproves morally of something a litigant wants to claim. Moral judgements need to be justified by reference to reasons that can be shared by all in the political community. Judges also need to ensure their interpretations fit the legal record and must justify their decisions as being the best justification for a society's legal record. A Marxist judge, for instance, may think that the rich should share their wealth with the poor; the constraints of the legal record (the dimension of 'fit') may, however, prevent them from interpreting the law in exactly the way they wish. The brute facts of legal history thus place a limit also on the discretion of judges in adjudication.

It should thus become clearer why Dworkin refer to his theory as 'law as integrity'. Integrity in the personal life of individuals involves acting according to 'convictions that inform and shape their lives as a whole, rather than capriciously or whimsically'.[18] Integrity for political life requires the government to act in a coherent manner towards individuals in its domain, and to extend to everyone the same substantive standards of justice it uses. In adjudication, Dworkin argues that integrity requires seeing law as coherent and as if created by one author. Just like the chain novel, integrity means that there must be coherence and consistency in principle. Judges must conceive of the law as a holistic system in which the parts work together to advance social justice. Integrity also means that everyone must be treated equally and according to the same standards. The deep substantive political value underlying it is the moral ideal that everyone in the political community should be treated with equal concern and respect. Law needs to develop in light of that commitment.

The question then arises as to whether Dworkin is a positivist or natural lawyer. Interestingly, Dworkin's theory includes elements of both schools of thought. The dimension of fit involves reference to the sources and, thus, legal materials recognised in the community. Adjudication cannot take place, according to Dworkin, without an engagement with these sources. At the same time, the dimension of value recognises that a conception of substantive political morality is necessary to interpret the law. What Dworkin says about the value dimension, however, indicates that for him it is impossible to identify law without invoking moral reasoning. As such, there is no complete separation of law and morality and his perspective thus, ultimately, falls within the natural law school of thought. Whilst it is impossible to draw a sharp distinction between law as it is and law as it ought to be, Dworkin also shows the importance of including reference to source-based criteria in decision-making (which distinguishes his approach from that of Fuller).

In summary, Dworkin's view of adjudication is made up of the following dimensions: a) judges need to have references both to principles and rules in deciding what the law is in a political community; b) judges need to adopt a 'chain novel' approach to adjudication, seeing themselves part of a continuous process which has two main dimensions – there is the dimension of fit which includes a consideration of previous sources and an attempt to render the current law consistent in principle with the past, and the dimension of value whereby a judge must determine which interpretation of law is best from the standpoint of political morality and justice.

## 2.5 African transformative adjudication

We have thus far engaged with three highly influential theories on how judges should adjudicate that have been developed in the United States and the United Kingdom. What relevance do they have for the task facing African judges in the relatively new constitutional democracies on the continent?

---

18  Dworkin 1986 at 166.

Unfortunately, there are also many modern African societies where there is widespread political interference with the judiciary. Those conditions are not the focus of this section, as where there are conscientious and decent judges in those systems, they must always operate in a non-optimal manner, trying to do the best they can. In that sense, their task raises similar questions to those dealt with in the last chapter concerning the existence of law in wicked legal systems. In this chapter, we consider how judges should adjudicate within decent societies where they are able to exercise their independence.

African societies also have a recent experience of historical injustice and often the new constitutional orders represent sharp breaks with the past. How then is interpretation and adjudication to take place? We outline two extracts from the thought of leading South African legal thinkers and jurists, the former Chief Justice Langa and the former Deputy Chief Justice Moseneke. These texts are used as a basis to reflect on a range of questions surrounding adjudication in an African context. They also serve as a springboard for a critical discussion of the theories of Hart, Fuller and Dworkin in such a context with a focus on the particular challenges the African post-colonial context raises for these theories. Our focus here is on raising a number of questions that students and lecturers can develop further.

---

**PRIMARY TEXTS**

**Text 5 Langa CJ's transformative constititionalism**

At the heart of a transformative Constitution is a commitment to substantive reasoning, to examining the underlying principles that inform laws themselves and judicial reaction to those laws. Purely formalist reasoning tends to avoid that responsibility.

However, while it is vital that we embrace the idea of substantive adjudication, there is a distinct limit as to how far we can go. Judges do not have a free rein to determine what the law is. Laws, including the Constitution, do not mean "whatever we wish them to mean". This limit on judicial law-making is encapsulated in the idea of the separation of powers. The Constitution itself entrenches the notion of different roles for the different arms of Government: the legislature makes the law, the judiciary interprets the law and the executive enforces the law. Were the courts to completely discard any adherence to the text they would enter squarely into the domain of the legislature as creators rather than interpreters of the law. That is clearly not what the Constitution envisages.

This is not to suggest that the courts have no law-making responsibility. Upholding the transformative ideal of the Constitution requires judges to change the law to bring it in line with the rights and values for which the Constitution stands. The problem lies in finding the fine line between transformation and legislation. Overly activist judges can be as dangerous for the fulfilment of the constitutional dream as unduly passive judges. Both disturb the finely-balanced ordering of society and endanger the ideals of transformation.[19]

---

## Text 6  Moseneke DCJ's transformative adjudication

Few would contest that the imperative of the new legal order is the creation of a society different from our socially degrading and economically exploitative apartheid past. However, the meaning of transformation in juridicial terms is as highly contested as it is difficult to formulate. The legal content of the constitutionally entrenched rights is derived from the foundational values of the Constitution. The symbiotic relationship between these values and the legal content of the respective rights defies easy definition. This is to be expected because values are normative. Their worth and hierarchy is variable and contingent upon a given or predetermined value system.

However, in the case of our Constitution a specified set of values informs what is permissible in an open and democratic society based on freedom and equality. Perforce our constitutional interpretation is set against the backdrop of the values of the South African society. Constitutional adjudication must occur within that 'holistic, value-based framework'. The Constitution is a repository of 'the values which bind its people'.

The jurisprudence resulting from this value-drenched notion of constitutional adjudication will not be easy to develop. Justice Sachs reminds us that:

> Just as the transformation of our harsh reality is by its very nature difficult to accomplish, so it is hard to develop a corresponding and appropriate jurisprudence of transition.

Liberal legalism balks at the idea of transformative adjudication. The primary objection is that such jurisprudence invites judges to accomplish political objectives. The judicial mindset seeks a distinct differentiation between the legislative and the judicial function. On this approach, the judicial function primarily is directed at providing legal interpretation of texts of rules of law as distinct from imposing subjective intellectual, ethical or other preferred views. In liberal jurisprudence, a value driven adjudicative style which permits extra legal considerations is to be avoided.

Until 1994, the South African legal culture has been homogenous, conservative and predictable. It was informed by inflexible legal positivism predicated upon parliamentary sovereignty. Adjudication was rule based. Law drew its legitimacy from the very fact that it was state sanctioned. The material context or the social aftermath of the application of the rule was deemed irrelevant. In that scenario, judges were deemed to have no duty to dispense justice in any sense other than permitted by the law. Judicial activism had little or no place. That notion of the rule of the law is constrained to exclude intrusion of all extraneous considerations in adjudication.

Judicial interpretation under the Constitution has placed different imperatives upon the adjudicator. Austere legalism more suited to interpretation of statutes is not commendable to constitutional interpretation. The intention of the drafter is of little avail in constitutional interpretation as intimated earlier, the salutary approach to constitutional interpretation is one which provides the most adequate response to the countermajoritarian dilemma by giving effect to the underlying values of the Constitution. It seems to me that our constitutional design of conferring vast powers of judicial review to the courts becomes optimal only if the courts are true to the constitutional mandate. It is argued that, in their work, courts should search for substantive justice, which is to be inferred from the foundational values of the Constitution. After all, that is the injunction of the Constitution – transformation.[20]

**Questions**

1. How should adjudication be approached in an African constitutional democracy? For Langa? For Moseneke?
2. What is meant by 'transformative adjudication'?
3. What is the relationship between what Chief Justice Langa says and the theories of adjudication of Hart, Fuller and Dworkin?
4. What are the constraints on the exercise of judicial powers according to Justice Langa?
5. Moseneke refers to 'liberal legalism' as having a particular vision of the distinction between law and politics. What is that vision and how does a transformative vision differ?

Langa and Moseneke write against the backdrop of South Africa's transition from the rule by a white minority government, which imposed the system of apartheid on individuals (that sanctioned systemic discrimination against black people), to a constitutional democracy. Their articles are wide-ranging, but the selections of text focus on the question: what approach should judges adopt towards adjudication in the context of the new constitutional order?

## 4.5.1   Substance and values

Both Langa and Moseneke recognise that adjudication in a transformative context involves a commitment to engaging with the substance of legal disputes and reasoning openly and transparently. Such reasoning also involves reference to values and purposes with a clear goal in mind – changing South African society in the direction of greater social justice against a backdrop of historical inequality and discrimination. Indeed, section 39(1) of the South African Constitution specifically references the need to give expression to values in interpreting the Bill of Rights. It would seem, therefore, on the face of it that the approach of Langa and Moseneke is more closely allied to that of Fuller and Dworkin than Hart.

At the same time, Langa, particularly, recognises that law places certain constraints on the interpretations that can be developed by judges. He recognises that language is not infinitely elastic and judges cannot make legal texts mean whatever they wish them to mean. He provides a powerful argument for his position. In a democracy, it is the elected branches of government that are tasked with making laws. If judges were not to respect these laws, in general, they would in essence be acting undemocratically by imposing their own will over those of the people.

---

20   Moseneke 2002 *South African Journal on Human Rights* at 315–316.

Two different constructions can be given to Langa's views expressed in the text. On the one hand, he could be agreeing with Hart that there is a 'core' of ordinary meaning in statutes which must be respected by the judiciary and that places constraints on any interpretation that can develop. Moreover, he could well be taken to be arguing that text places some restrictions on what interpretations may develop. A 'no-vehicles-in-the-park rule' may have a purpose of preventing noisy and dangerous activities in the park. Yet, such a rule could never be used as the basis for preventing fireworks in a private home even though the same purpose may apply. Such a legal rule could only be applied to those things that constitute 'vehicles' or, are in 'parks'.[21] On the other hand, he might be saying that judges are constrained to develop interpretations that are consistent with the purposes that have been given expression to by the legislature, a view more consistent with Fuller's approach. Either way, Langa does not see judges as being unconstrained to develop whichever interpretations they wish. Their duty overall is to bring law in line with the rights and values in the Constitution but, in doing so, they also need to respect the democratic pedigree of the legislature.

These disputes are not just theoretical and arise in concrete case law. The Constitutional Court of South Africa, right at the outset of its work, was faced with the challenge of how to approach adjudication. In the case of *S v Mhlungu*,[22] the Court had to interpret a provision of the Interim Constitution which, whilst not entirely clear, seemed to provide that, for cases that were already in progress prior to the coming into force of the new Constitution, the law would be applied as if the Constitution had not been passed. In practical terms, the issue that arose concerned the law of confessions in criminal matters. Prior to the Constitution being passed, in order to be inadmissible an accused had to show that a confession he or she had made was not given voluntarily; after the Constitution was passed, it was the onus of the state to show that the confession was freely and voluntarily made. This change in the law could make the difference between an accused person being found innocent and guilty.

The judgment in the case was split between a majority and a minority. The majority claimed that there was an alternative interpretation that was possible for the interim provision that would not prevent the new law concerning confessions from being applied in pending criminal trials. Its reasons were strongly substantive in nature. The court saw it as arbitrary that an accused could be convicted in the same court in a trial that commenced prior to the coming into force of the interim constitution but be acquitted afterwards. Mahomed J stated that:

> What must be avoided, if this is a constitutionally permissible course, is a result which permits human rights guaranteed by the Constitution to be enjoyed by some people and denied arbitrarily to others.[23]

Interestingly, the majority too felt constrained by language. It simply used the purposes lying behind the Constitution to arrive at a more strained interpretation of the provision. Its reasoning can more strongly be related to Fuller's approach to interpretation with the purpose affecting the manner in which statutes are read. The minority, on the other hand, was of the view that there was no alternative viable interpretation of the interim provision other than that it preserved the old law in the new constitutional order for trials that were not completed. Even though perhaps the result sought by the majority was desirable,

---

21   See Fagan 2010 *South African Law Journal* at 615 for this example.
22   1995 (3) SA 867 (CC).
23   Ibid at para 8.

there was a 'core' meaning of the provision that meant that judges could not deviate from it. Kentridge AJ stated that:

> There are some provisions, even in a constitution, where the language used, read in its context, is too clear to be capable of sensible qualification. It is the duty of all courts, in terms of section 35, to promote the values which underlie a democratic society based on freedom and equality. In the long run, I respectfully suggest, those values are not promoted by doing violence to the language of the Constitution in order to remedy what may seem to be hard cases.[24]

The minority view is, of course, much more connected to the theory of adjudication outlined by Hart.[25]

Moseneke is also concerned about how to capture the task of adjudication in a society undergoing transformation. He, too, sees such a task as requiring an approach rooted in the foundational values of the Constitution and being focused on achieving a transformative change in society. Moseneke contrasts a view he terms 'liberal legalism' with a 'transformative' approach to adjudication. Liberal legalism, he claims, wishes strictly to separate law and politics. Moseneke uses the word 'liberal' to reference this form of adjudication, though his usage of this term is rather puzzling as it bears a very limited relationship to what is meant by 'liberalism' in political philosophy (some liberal theories are dealt with in the second half of this book). Judges, under this view, he argues are confined to a task of interpreting legal rules and no considerations outside the law should enter into their considerations, irrespective of the consequences. As such, this view could be termed 'formalist' in Langa's usage of the term as it rejects reference to the substantive values at stake in a case and to ensuring that just consequences flow from a decision. A 'transformative' approach to adjudication, on the other hand, requires judges to aim at achieving substantive justice in their interpretive work rather than simply attempting to apply the law in a narrow manner.

These thoughts by Deputy Chief Justice Moseneke require further elaboration though, as it is not clear what such a substantive approach involves. He suggests that the intention of the legislature is not very important. If this is so, what should judges utilise when constructing the law? Moseneke's approach appears to be quite close to Dworkin's theory but it appears only to utilise or reference the 'dimension of value' rather than the 'dimension of fit'. Judges, for Moseneke, must attempt to achieve the legal result that best achieves the political morality underlying the South African legal community. To unpack his view in this regard, it is important to consider both of the dimensions of Dworkin's theory in a transitional context like that of South Africa.

### 4.5.2   The dimension of fit and historical injustice

Dworkin attempts to place constraints on judges by requiring any interpretation to 'fit' or cohere with deep principles of law that have been developed in the past, as well as the legal sources relevant to the dispute. An interesting question arises in contexts like South Africa concerning the importance of this dimension where there is a legal rupture between the past and the present. If we take the analogy of the chain novel, is there in fact a story we wish to continue or do we wish to begin again? If we want to start again, then are the judges shortly after the institution of a new system in a situation where they are like the first authors of the chain novel?

---

24   Ibid at para 84.
25   An academic debate was generated by the case, see Fagan, A 1995 *South African Journal on Human Rights*; Fagan, E 1996 *South African Journal on Human Rights;* Davis 1996 *South African Journal on Human Rights;* Fagan, E 1997 *South African Journal on Human Rights*; Davis 1997 *South African Journal on Human Rights*.

If one is in the position of a first author in a chain novel, then the dimension of fit does not seem properly to apply. It is possible to begin the story in any direction that one wishes. As Stanley Fish has pointed out, however, this freedom is not quite as absolute as it appears.[26] A first author would still be functioning within the constraints of the practice of developing a novel – drawing a picture and nothing more, for instance, would not count as writing a novel. The same is true of judges. It would be hard to imagine a judge ruling on the constitutionality of the death penalty, simply by saying, 'I am Christian and believe in the death penalty; therefore, it is constitutional'. Such an approach would dispense with the duty of giving adequate reasons, which is central to our understanding of the law. Moreover, in a secular constitutional democracy, it would fundamentally contradict a requirement to provide reasons all people can in principle accept. Such a judge would likely be dismissed from his or her position or not be recognised as acting legally. As such, there are constraints inherent in the enterprise of law that even the first bench of judges after a revolution must take into account.

Even if we accept this argument, it is not quite clear that judges in post-apartheid South Africa, for instance, were clearly in the position of first authors. The law during apartheid South Africa contained many dimensions that have rightly been rejected by the new order. Judges, clearly, cannot be expected to 'fit' any new interpretation with those features of the law that existed but are repugnant to the current constitutional order. However, South Africa also did not simply replace its legal system completely during the transition to a constitutional democracy. There has, in fact, in many areas of the law – such as delict and contract – been a legal continuity from the past. Indeed, case precedents prior to the 1994 transition are often still referred to. This is true of many other countries in Africa, too, which continued to utilise many parts of the legal systems of those who colonised them.

The question that arises and has challenged the academic community in South Africa is the right approach to be adopted towards the existing common law. The common law often drew from Roman-Dutch law sources with some aspects of English law too. It was, of course, also developed during the time of the systems of colonialism and apartheid. Is the common law simply to be discarded as a whole or can it be rendered fit for purposes of the new order?

Section 8(3) of the South African Bill of Rights clearly envisages the need to develop the common law to give effect to rights in the Bill of Rights. Section 39(2) also expressly places a duty on courts to develop the common law in light of the 'spirit, purport and objects of the bill of rights'. What is clear is that South Africa did not choose to begin its legal journey from scratch and the common law was not discarded entirely. Nevertheless, it was recognised that it had to be made consistent with the new order and developed.

Serious academic debates have arisen as to how these requirements are to be understood. Anton Fagan argues – on the basis of several constitutional provisions – that the development of the common law must, as primary matter, take place with reference to the rights in the Bill of Rights, justice considerations as well as the rules of the common law itself. Reference to the 'objects of the bill of rights' is vague and less clearly rooted in the intentions of the constitution drafters than reference to specific rights provisions, which compel the development thereof. Courts, in Fagan's view, should only resort to the 'objects of the bill of rights' where there is no clear answer from other sources and they need to choose between possible alternative routes for the development of the common law that arise.[27]

Dennis Davis, on the other hand, contends that it is of importance for judges to have an overarching understanding of the purposes and objects of the constitutional order as a

---

26   Fish 1982 *Texas Law Review* at 553.
27   Fagan 2010 *South African Law Journal* at 611–627.

whole. To ensure coherence of the new constitutional project as well as its commitment to constitutional values, it is of importance to develop the common law with reference to this broad, holistic vision (something section 39(2), in his view, contemplates).[28] Both accept the need to develop the common law and recognise a role for judicial discretion. They place emphasis on different ways of doing so. The debate between them highlights the difficulty for the development of common law when there is very limited value alone in consistency with past principles. What is needed is some method of determining how the law should develop in future which, unavoidably it appears, must reference moral questions. As the law becomes more settled and conforms better to the values underlying the constitutional order, the dimension of fit may become of more importance. In the early days of a new constitutional order, however, it appears that the dimension of value will be primary and it is to an understanding of this dimension that we now turn.

### 4.5.3   The dimension of value and the African context

Both Langa and Moseneke recognise the importance of having reference to the values underlying the new constitutional order in South Africa. Yet, reference to these values, itself, raises a number of complexities. The South African Constitution refers in its foundational values to dignity, equality and freedom. If judges are seeking to develop a jurisprudence rooted in the African context and that connects legitimately with our society, how are they to proceed?

One view would contend that there are certain universal values which apply in all societies and which all people should strive for. Dignity is about asserting the value of every person; equality about the fact that no-one is more valuable than any other; and freedom about respecting the ability of people to make decisions about their own lives. Any decent society, one might suggest, would respect this triad of values. Whilst they may have different implications and relate to different contexts, the judicial task is to advance them in the best way they see possible. Doing so would not differ between judges in Europe, North America, Asia or Africa.

The critique of this view is that it can be out of touch with the discourse and discussion within particular societies. It abstracts from the values that many people in society recognise as their own and places concepts and ideas in language that feels foreign. That, in turn, fails to enhance the legitimacy of human rights discourse in that society.

An alternative view – not necessarily in conflict with the first – sees the importance of embedding values in a particular context. It also sees the importance of drawing on local values to support universal ones. This view is perhaps exemplified by the concurring opinion of Justice Mokgoro in the case concerning the constitutionality of the death penalty in South Africa.[29] Mokgoro contends that one of the central tasks of judges is to balance rights and freedoms: that, she argues, can only be done by reference to values extraneous to the constitutional text itself. The South African Constitution requires taking account of international law and comparative foreign approaches when judges interpret the rights in the Bill of Rights. However, she states that:

> I am of the view that our own (ideal) indigenous value systems are a premise from which we need to proceed and are not wholly unrelated to our goal of a society based on freedom and equality.[30]

---

28   Davis 2012 *South African Law Journal* at 59–72.
29   *S v Makwanyane* 1995 (3) SA 391 (CC).
30   Ibid at para 304.

She quotes from the European Court of Human Rights to the effect that the law cannot afford to be out of touch with the moral consensus of the political community in which it takes place – otherwise, it is brought into disrepute. She argues that the common values in South Africa can form the basis of a new human rights jurisprudence. One such value, she contends, shared by all South Africans is the value of '*ubuntu*':

> *ubuntu* translates as *humaneness*. In its most fundamental sense, it translates as *personhood* and *morality*. Metaphorically, it expresses itself in *umuntu ngumuntu ngabantu*, describing the significance of group solidarity on survival issues so central to the survival of communities. While it envelops the key values of group solidarity, compassion, respect, human dignity, conformity to basic norms and collective unity, in its fundamental sense it denotes humanity and morality. Its spirit emphasises respect for human dignity, marking a shift from confrontation to conciliation.[31]

Mokgoro recognises that there are major similarities between the notion of *ubuntu* and the notion of dignity. Yet, her view is that it is of importance to connect the values courts use in their jurisprudence with those people in society generally hold. Court decisions will be more readily comprehensible and persuasive if they connect with these particularly African values. Developing a jurisprudence rooted in Africa thus requires connecting with these values – even though the constitutions of post-colonial Africa often fail to provide them with pride of place.

Indeed, this discussion has implications for how we understand the 'value dimension' in Dworkin. One question that may be asked concerns which values should be used in determining what is morally best for the political community when judges are making decisions. One plausible answer to this question would require making references to values that are most prominent in a particular jurisdiction and give expression to the requirements of political morality therein. The South African Constitution clearly indicates the need to consider dignity, equality and freedom, but a value such as *ubuntu* (and the philosophy surrounding it) also has a strong claim to guiding judicial decision-making.

One potential difficulty for Mokgoro's view concerns the extent to which notions such as *ubuntu* are shared across a diverse country like South Africa. It is a value which emerges from traditional African communities. The majority of South Africans, of course, emerge from these communities. There are, however, many South Africans from other communities for whom the notion of *ubuntu* may not be well understood. It could be argued, on the one hand, that building a unified society requires reference to a more 'neutral' value like dignity which all can recognise or that stands apart from any particular tradition and represents common ground between the African and Western traditions of thought. On the other hand, the under-valuing of African thinking and philosophy in the past may well be a particularly good reason for developing particularly African values, which have a universal dimension – such as *ubuntu* – and giving them pride of place in the new jurisprudence of the country.

A more radical view may also contend that the discourse of fundamental rights and constitutionalism is itself 'Western' in nature and should be discarded. Instead, African societies should develop their own governance systems and the values that are utilised in judgments should be specifically those emanating from such societies. Post-colonial Africa needs to reject the shackles of thinking of the colonial past and start anew.

---

31    Ibid at para 308. The philosophy of *ubuntu* is dealt with elsewhere in this book in Chapters 6, 7 and 8.

This view though is not supported by the fact that most post-colonial African societies have in fact chosen to commit themselves in their founding documents to principles of fundamental rights and constitutionalism, which are framed in a manner that connects with international discourse. These ideas are not seen as Western but part of what decent African societies aspire to. African societies also are not isolated and their views and attitudes have developed through their engagement with a range of different perspectives from different places: it is not clear what is in fact an 'essential' African perspective. African societies are also diverse and there are a range of disagreements and different value commitments therein. Moreover, the fact that values have a particular source (rooted in Africa) does not automatically entail they are desirable or undesirable. There is still a need to provide arguments for why people should assent to them (as we saw Bodunrin argues in the first chapter). Unfortunately, often claims around the need for specific African values to be dominant have not been used progressively to achieve the advancement of African societies, but rather to legitimise authoritarian rulers, and against the fundamental rights of groups such as women and LGBTQ persons.

### 4.5.4   Objectivity, transparency and adjudication

We have seen how the task facing the judge in a transformative African constitutional democracy is one that often requires pride of place to be given to the dimension of value in adjudication. Ronald Dworkin is of the view that judges must seek to do what is best from the point of view of political morality of their community. Whilst this injunction involves a judgement, ultimately, political morality, in his view, is objective. A major line of critique challenges this assumption and suggests the unavoidable subjectivity of judicial judgments around adjudication, even if the task is understood along the lines of Ronald Dworkin. This issue is simply mentioned here but will be developed in more detail in the next chapter.

## 4.6   Conclusion

In this chapter, we began with the question as to how judges should adjudicate within the context of the constitutions of post-colonial Africa, with a particular focus on South Africa. The question led us to examine three theories of adjudication:

1. *Hart's theory.* It is possible, in general, to determine a 'core' meaning of the law from the language employed therein. In the penumbra, judges must utilise their discretion and base their decisions on moral and political values and determine what will have the best consequences for society. That approach, generally, allows law to be determined separately from morality.
2. *Fuller's theory.* The law can be determined only with reference to the purposes behind the law. This approach conceives of such a purposive approach as generally leading to morally desirable understandings of the law. That approach tends to lead law to coincide with the demands of morality.
3. *Dworkin's theory.* The law is made up of both principles and rules. In adjudication, judges are required to adopt the best interpretation which must have regard to two dimensions: the dimension of 'fit' (it must cohere with past legal decisions/materials), and the dimension of value (the interpretation must be found that is best from the perspective of political morality, perhaps the one of the community).

We then considered the thought of two leading justices in South Africa that set the scene to engage with a number of particular issues and critiques that arise in the African context in relation to these theories. The issues covered involve the following:

- The constraints language imposes on judges in a transformative jurisdiction
- The impact of historical injustice on legal method
- The manner in which the values underlying a constitution are to be constructed and the degree to which they should be particular to the African constitutional context
- Whether the reasoning of judges should be understood to be objective or subjective in adjudication, which will be dealt with in more detail in the next chapter.

Both justices considered that judges are faced with a task in the post-apartheid (and, by extension, post-colonial) context of adjudicating in a manner that engages with substantive reasoning and values, and seeks to achieve justice in the circumstances of the case and more widely. Purely technical and formal legal reasoning was rejected by both jurists. The advent of constitutional democracy is recent in Africa and the methods of adjudication are still developing. Students are encouraged to debate these questions and work out which theories are best for the African context (if any). The next chapter investigates a number of other theories around adjudication which contend, in their various ways, that adjudication is much more subjective than the theories in this chapter suggest and, inherently, require reference to the animating ideologies and profiles of judges.

## POINTS TO CONSIDER

1. Can judges adjudicate simply by using the plain meaning of a statute?
2. Does reference to purposes automatically mean the law will be moral?
3. Is the analogy between a chain novel and the process of adjudicating law apposite?
4. Are there points in the adjudication process where particularly African conceptions of value can come in?
5. What is the problem with the requirement of 'fit' in Dworkin where a new constitutional order is formed against a backdrop of historical injustice?
6. If purposes and values are to be utilised, which purposes should be used? According to whom?
7. In what sense should adjudication be conceived of in an objective manner or does reference to values inherently lead to a high level of subjectivity in the process?

# Chapter 5

# Is legal interpretation subjective?

## 5.1 Introduction

Whereas Chapters 2 and 3 sought to answer the question of what law is, Chapter 4 and the present one address the question of how to interpret it. One major distinction in Chapter 4 was between non-moral and moral interpretations of law. Recall that for HLA Hart it is sometimes possible and desirable for a judge to make a ruling based on the plain meaning of a statute, which might not include any moral considerations, whereas for Ronald Dworkin a judge should always have moral considerations in mind (though not only those), which could in principle mean going against the plain meaning of a statute.

Chapter 5 addresses a different major distinction between accounts of legal interpretation, the subjective and the objective. For something to be objective in general is for it to be independent of the mind and yet to be known by at least some minds. The fact that the earth is round is objective. It was round even when people thought it was flat, and these days many of us know that it is indeed round. People coming to the realisation that it is round did not make it round; it would have continued to be round even if they had not thought that it was round. And those who believe the earth is flat are making a mistake. When something is objective then there is a fact of the matter about which our beliefs can be more or less correct, with at least some people being correct.

In contrast, for something to be subjective can mean one of two different things. On the one hand, and most strongly, it could mean that something is dependent on the mind for its truth. Do carrots taste good? It depends entirely on the subject, that is, on whether the particular person eating them likes them or not. There is no fact of the matter about whether carrots taste good. If a person did not like the taste of carrots, he or she would not be making any sort of mistake; similarly, if a person did like the taste of carrots, he or she would not be making any sort of mistake.[1]

A second, weaker form of subjectivity would consist of there being certain facts that exist independently of a person's judgement but those facts failing to influence his or her judgement substantially. To illustrate this condition, consider whether there is just one universe, or whether this universe is just one of many universes in a 'multiverse'. There is a fact of the matter about this; believing one way or the other cannot make it the case. However, there is currently so little evidence one way or the other that no one knows. If a person were firmly to believe that there is a multiverse, his or her judgement would be subjective in the sense that the real fact of the matter has not determined his or her thinking. The person has judged in this way not because he or she is in touch with the truth, but because of something else like a random guess, or what feels good to believe, or what he or she expects to gain him or her some attention.

Now, the core question of this chapter is roughly this: is legal decision-making more like apprehending the shape of the earth, appraising the taste of carrots, or contending that there is a multiverse? Concretely, think about when judges make rulings, say, about whether the use of force by police or in self-defence was 'reasonable', or about whether a level of noise constitutes a 'nuisance' or is instead 'acceptable'. Are judges doing something that is capable of error, or does the validity of their rulings depend entirely on their various viewpoints? And if judges are doing something that is capable of error, do they routinely avoid error and rule in the light of the evidence that points towards the truth? Or are judges so influenced by other things that they rarely track the truth about how they ought to rule?

A second major question considered in this chapter supposes that objectivity is possible, and then considers what, if anything, could be done to make legal interpretations more objective. Which institutional mechanisms and judicial practices could be adopted, particularly in the South African context, to make it more likely that judges will track the truth in their decisions?

This chapter first considers the subjective/objective distinction in more detail, suggesting a variety of ways in which legal interpretation might fail to be objective (section 5.2). Then the chapter addresses extreme forms of subjectivism according to which in principle there can be nothing beyond a legal decision by which to consider it correct or incorrect. After briefly discussing classic legal realism, the view that law is nothing other than what judges enforce, the chapter considers the more recent influence of postmodernism, one strand of which is the view that there are no moral or other normative facts that could or should constrain an interpretation of the law (section 5.3). Next, the chapter addresses more moderate forms of subjectivism, including Critical Legal Studies, Critical Race Theory and Feminist Legal Theory. According to these views, legal interpretations in principle could be correct in virtue of tracking moral and other facts, but too often they are not, and are instead influenced by factors such as politics and discriminatory beliefs and practices (section 5.4). Discussion of this cluster of perspectives will include consideration of whether a state might be able to select judges and change the way they make their rulings so as to advance objectivity in legal interpretation. The chapter concludes by noting that it forms the end of Part 1 of this book and by indicating how the topics of Part 2 will be different (section 5.5).

---

1   For another example of subjectivity, see the discussion of rudeness in Chapter 3.

## 5.2   The subjective/objective distinction

The previous section gave two examples of subjectivity: there was liking the taste of carrots, where there is no fact of whether carrots taste good or not, and there was believing in something, such as the nature of the universe, where there is a fact of the matter but the evidence about it does not yet exist (or has not determined one's beliefs). These examples were drawn from outside the law to serve as analogies. This section, in contrast, uses legal examples to make more concrete sense of what subjectivity – and, conversely, objectivity – might involve when it comes to judicial decision-making.

There are five major respects in which philosophers of law have deemed legal interpretation to be subjective. This section merely expounds them as possibilities, leaving for later sections consideration of the extent to which they obtain in the South African legal context.

First, an interpretation of the law is sensibly deemed to be subjective insofar as it neglects to consider some patently relevant materials. Suppose that a judge simply misinterpreted what a witness said, or forgot to apply a certain body of law that clearly speaks to the matter. Then his or her ruling would lack some objectivity.

A second kind of subjectivity plausibly involves certain emotions or moods influencing a judge's decisions. Suppose, as appears to be the case, that tired and hungry judges mete out harsher sentences than those who are not experiencing these physiological states.[2] The more that judicial decision-making was influenced by such factors, rather than by the evidence in the case, the more subjective it would be.[3]

Pressure from other people seems to count as a third form of subjectivity. Imagine that politicians threatened to withdraw funding for a judicial body if a judge did not rule a certain way. Or consider judicial peers commenting on the case and trying to persuade a judge to decide a particular way. Or, most crassly, suppose that a criminal defendant threatened a judge with harm to him or her or their family, lest the defendant not be acquitted.

A fourth instance of subjectivity is discrimination, such as racist or sexist beliefs. If a judge thinks that members of a racial group or gender inherently manifest undesirable traits, or if he or she values their lives less than those of other groups, one would reasonably say that his or her decision-making was not objective insofar as such a mind-set influenced it.

A fifth suggestion about what subjectivity might involve concerns moral, political and related values. Judges normally must interpret the law, as opposed to apply it in a merely mechanical fashion. Whenever someone interprets, though, especially terms such as 'reasonable' or 'acceptable', he or she cannot avoid bringing in their own value judgements. Even if he or she invokes the values stated in a legal document, he or she will view them through a specific belief system, one that not everyone shares. Some philosophers contend that interpretation is therefore inherently subjective, although this account of law's purported subjectivity is more controversial than the previous four.

Consider some different implications of these conceptions of subjectivity. If all interpretation is unavoidably subjective, then it appears that law is shot-through with subjectivity and cannot become more objective. In contrast, insofar as subjectivity consists of factual mistakes, emotional influences and outside pressures, it appears that in principle law could become more objective. Perhaps the most interesting case is discrimination: what (if anything) could be done to substantially reduce racism and sexism in South Africa's judiciary?

---

2   Corbyn 2011 *Nature*.
3   A much more controversial claim would be that any decision made consequent to a feeling, emotion or attitude is necessarily subjective. Is objectivity sacrificed whenever a judge feels sympathy or, conversely, resentment?

## 5.3 Extreme subjectivism: Legal realism and postmodernism

Some philosophers of law maintain a strong form of subjectivism according to which law is unavoidably subjective to a large degree. According to extreme subjectivists, legal interpretations cannot be objective in the sense that there simply are no facts 'out there' on which judges could and should try to base their decisions about what is reasonable, acceptable or the like. According to more moderate subjectivists, addressed in the fourth section, there are moral and other facts 'out there', but judges are too influenced by other factors for these facts to influence decisions very much.

### 5.3.1 Legal realism

Legal realism, or specifically American legal realism, was the first notable form of extreme subjectivism to emerge in Western philosophy of law. Realism gets its name from the idea that an understanding of law should focus on how it is actually practised as a behavioural phenomenon. Instead of supposing that law is essentially constituted by abstract moral principles, or that law consists of what a general rule adopted by the legislature entails for a particular case before a judge, realists propose looking at how members of judiciary in fact make decisions and relate to others in society. Such an approach downplays the respects in which legal decisions are viewed as rational or formal, and instead highlights their unpredictable, emotional and haphazard nature, roughly in terms of how judges affect society.

According to one philosophically interesting version of realism, law is nothing other than what judges decide or, somewhat more broadly, law is whatever gets enforced by the courts and the police. Notice the strength of this claim about the essence of law.[4] It is not that most often parliamentarians make law and that sometimes judges and police do, too, for instance when judges add in reasoning that now serves as precedent. Instead, the conceptual claim ascribed to realism is that parliamentarians *never* make law, and that *only* judges and other court and corrections officials do.

Such a view is suggested by elements of the works of Oliver Wendell Holmes Jr, John Chipman Gray, Jerome Frank and Karl Llewellyn,[5] who were writing at the end of the nineteenth century and the first half of the twentieth century in the United States. For example, Holmes Jr wrote, 'The prophecies of what the courts will do in fact, and nothing more pretentious, are what I mean by the law',[6] and similarly Llewellyn stated that what judges and law enforcement officials 'do about disputes is, to my mind, the law itself'.[7] This view remains somewhat influential, with one philosophically sophisticated contemporary American judge having expressed sympathy for it when he said:

> [L]aw is the activity of licensed persons, the judges, rather than a body of concepts (rules, principles, whatever) ... The law is not a thing they discover; it is the name of their activity.[8]

---

4  Note that realism, as construed here, is a rival to the naturalist and positivist theories of law's nature from Chapters 2 and 3.
5  Representative texts include Holmes Jr 1897 *Harvard Law Review*; Gray 1921 *The Nature and Sources of the Law*; Frank 1930 *Law and the Modern Mind*; Llewellyn 1930 *The Bramble Bush: On Our Law and Its Study*.
6  Holmes Jr 1897 at 461.
7  Llewellyn 1930 at 3.
8  Posner 1990 *The Problems of Jurisprudence* at 21, 225.

Realists invariably acknowledge that theirs is not the dominant view of law, which is instead that courts pronounce what the law is, that courts apply the general rules that a legislature has created. However, realists contend that this view is a myth or some other kind of false consciousness. Instead, realists suggest that a legislature provides a 'source' or 'occasion' for law, where law itself is in fact created by courts upon rendering particular decisions or prescribing certain allocations of benefits and burdens.

Why believe this claim? One rationale is that, since law is nothing other than a physical phenomenon, it should be an event amenable to scientific analysis which, in turn, means looking at the effects of an activity on the rest of society. Gray seems to be making this sort of argument in the following:

> Practically in its application to actual affairs, for most of the laity, the law, except for a few notions of the equity involved in some of its general principles, is all *ex post facto*. When a man marries, or enters into a partnership, or buys a piece of land, or engages in any other transactions, he has the vaguest possible idea of the law governing the situation, and with our complicated system of Jurisprudence, it is impossible it should be otherwise. If he delayed to make a contract or do an act until he understood exactly all the legal consequences it involved, the contract would never be made or the act done. Now the law of which man has no knowledge is the same to him as if it did not exist.[9]

Gray suggests that insofar as something does not influence people's lives, it does not exist, and insofar as law does influence people's lives, it does so in the form of courts making decisions about how to distribute resources. Now, if law is reducible to the activities of courts, then there is nothing objective, nothing independent of the minds of judges, on which to base their decisions. It follows that legal interpretation, not merely about terms such as 'reasonable' but also in general, is utterly subjective if philosophical realism is true.

One might reply to Gray by pointing out that legislatures routinely influence people's lives without the mediation of the courts. For example, new statutes tend to educate people about what the political community deems legitimate and to discourage certain acts, and they do so prior to their enforcement. However, rather than question this rationale for philosophical realism, consider some *prima facie* problems with realism itself.

One way to question realism is to appeal to the rationales for positivism or naturalism from Chapters 2 and 3. For example, the naturalist Lon Fuller would object to realism on the ground that it cannot account for the respects in which a legal system essentially includes rules that are intuitively moral for tending not to apply *ex post facto* (that is, in retrospect), not to contradict each other, and so on. Whatever evidence there is for positivism, too, will naturally provide some reason to reject realism.

Another common strategy for casting doubt on realism is to note that it seems unable to make any sense of the idea that it is possible for a judge to make a mistake. Although in some jurisdictions there might not be any mechanism by which to overturn a court's decision, which is final, it still seems conceivable that a judge could have read the law incorrectly and sensibly be criticised for that. However, if law were nothing beyond what judges decide, then there would be no legal basis on which to evaluate their decisions, as there appears to be.

A third way to question realism is to consider whether it can make sense of what a court is without appealing to an independent notion of law. For philosophical realism, law is

---

9   Gray 1921 at 100.

defined in terms of whatever the courts decide. For this analysis of law to be thorough and to avoid circularity, we need to know what a court is, and that of course must not be defined in terms of the law at all. However, the natural way to differentiate a court from other institutions, such as universities or police forces, is to say that it is what interprets the law so as to determine whether it was broken. Instead of defining law in terms of what the courts do, as per realism, it is more natural (and perhaps unavoidable?) to define courts in terms of their orientation towards the law.

### 5.3.2   Postmodernism

These days, realism is not the most popular way to defend extreme subjectivism. Instead, the more common way to contend that there is no way for courts to be objective is to appeal to a postmodern account of interpretation. Roughly, according to this viewpoint, whenever one interprets something, whether it is a text or a work of art, one is unavoidably bringing in one's own values, which render it irremediably subjective. Another way to put the point: there are no objective values, but value judgements are inherent to the activity of making a judicial decision. Postmodernism is often identified with French philosophers such as Jacques Derrida, Michel Foucault and Jean-François Lyotard (even if some of these intellectuals do not use the term themselves).[10]

Notice the main difference between postmodernism and realism. A postmodern approach to legal interpretation can grant that, *contra* realism, legislatures routinely make law. What the postmodernist would say is that, even if there is an independent law that parliamentarians have created, when judges have to make a decision about whether a particular law applies, how to understand its key terms, how much weight to give it compared to other laws, and so on, there is nothing objective to which to appeal. No one judicial interpretation is truly better than any other; it is simply up to the judge to decide what counts as a *reasonable* amount of force or an *acceptable* level of noise.

To begin to make sense of this position, consider what the word 'postmodern' means. To understand it, one must of course first know what 'modern' is supposed to mean. Talk of the 'modern' and 'modernity' have many senses, and are usually associated with the Enlightenment period of Europe (roughly, the eighteenth century). Enlightenment thinkers tended to think that European society had progressed in various ways compared to not merely the previous, medieval period there, but all other societies as well. They have tended, for example, to think that science has been an epistemological improvement over faith, and that a secular and democratic state committed to human rights has been a political improvement over, say, a state ruled by self-appointed religious authorities punishing people for things such as blasphemy and heresy.

In the present context concerning values, what stands out are two major ideas regarding Enlightenment thought or modernity. One is that it is possible for human reason to apprehend values, particularly concerning justice, that are objective in some way. It is characteristically modernist to believe that by deliberating carefully, we can discover moral norms that are binding on everyone and that are not merely a function of personal belief or taste, social custom or other subjective factors. A typical modernist would maintain that we can know that it is wrong for anyone to torture babies for fun, just as we can know that $2 + 2 = 4$ or that the earth is round.

---

10   Representative texts include Foucault 1977 *Discipline and Punish*; Lyotard 1984 *The Postmodern Condition*; Derrida 2002 *Acts of Religion*.

A second salient feature of modern thought about values is that they can be captured in the form of a principle or a theory. There are many particular duties that seem to exist, for example not to steal, not to break agreements, not to exploit and not to torture. Modernists are inclined to think that these can all be reduced to a single property or to one basic duty. For example, utilitarians, exemplars of Enlightenment thought *par excellence*, maintain that what ultimately makes an action wrong is its failure to promote the general welfare as much as some other action could have.[11] Similarly, Kantians, also quintessential Enlightenment adherents, maintain that all wrong actions are in essence a matter of failure to treat people's autonomy with respect.[12] Likewise, consider John Rawls' claim that distributive justice for any society is identical to whichever principles would be agreed to in a certain social contract.[13]

A postmodernist in general is basically someone who is not as optimistic as modernists have been about the power of reason to provide insight or to help humanity. A postmodernist will tend to find scientific practices, supposedly the most epistemically rational, to be riddled with coercion, cheating and bias. He or she will also tend to find secular, democratic and liberal states, supposedly the most reasonable and free, to be oppressive in their own ways.

When it comes to moral values, a typical postmodernist denies the modern claims that there are any objective ones for our reason to grasp or that our reason can reduce them to a basic principle. First, many postmodernists instead hold value *scepticism*, according to which claims about right and wrong, just and unjust, and the like either lack truth altogether or at most are 'true for' only some people or societies. Instead of there being universally binding values, there are at best ones that are true relative to a given society's beliefs or ways of life. If someone claims that certain values are objectively or universally true, there is always room for doubt and for instead viewing the person as imposing his or her preferred values on others, preventing them from articulating and living by their own values.

Second, if a postmodernist were inclined to grant that there are any objective values, he or she would then probably deny that they can be captured in a systematic, that is, theoretical, way. Instead, the postmodernist would hold *particularism*, contending that the most we can know about values is contextual. We might be able to know what should be done in a specific situation, but we are rarely, if ever, in a position to make justified claims about what to do that would be valid for all societies or all times.

Why do postmodernists hold value scepticism and particularism? Two arguments have been particularly influential. In the reading below Patrick Lenta alludes to one of them, specifically the idea that postmodernists are impressed by the idea that we are not certain about values, that there is no 'rational foundation' on which to base our value judgements. In the second reading Dworkin notes another source of sympathy for postmodernism, and particularly value scepticism, namely, the thought that it is hard to obtain consensus about values. There seems to be a lot of disagreement about which value claims are true, which might suggest that none is objectively true or that we do not know which ones are.

---

11   Considered in Chapters 6, 7 and 10.
12   Addressed in Chapters 7, 8 and 10.
13   Explored in Chapter 6.

### Text 1  Patrick Lenta on postmodern jurisprudence[14]

Patrick Lenta is one of South Africa's most prolific jurisprudential scholars, having written on a wide variety of topics in the philosophy of law, particularly as it pertains to the South African context. He is Associate Professor of Philosophy at the University of KwaZulu-Natal.

[P]ostmodern jurisprudence [is] the attempt to create the conditions of possibility for reason(s), ethics and law once all the strategic moves of modern philosophy and jurisprudence to ground them on some single principle, form or meaning have been discredited ... [T]he modern view that a single form of reason could guide humanity towards social progress has been largely discredited. A disavowal of one (European, androcentric, etc) type of rationality has resulted from the various forms of rebellion to the multi-faceted subjugation of Western modernisation and a polyphony of oppressed voices – an 'indefinable wail' – has successfully eroded a sustained belief in the purity of Western rationality.

The Enlightenment universalism of liberalism, the political dispensation of post-apartheid South Africa, purportedly unaffected by political context and insistent on the foundationalism of rationality, cannot legitimate the discourses of political and epistemological transition. Moreover, the modern conception of law and justice is both misconceived and inadequate to the task of providing a just transformation. The following formulation of justice is typical of the modern outlook, both in its over-confident tone and its abstraction from cultural particularity:

The truth is – it is a truth which will bear a great deal of reiteration – that it is of the essence of both notions of justice in particular and morality in general that to appeal to such considerations is to appeal to principles logically independent of all particular and group interests or tastes.

I want to argue against this modern formulation, with its echoes of John Rawls's postulated Original Position, for the postmodern formulation of justice as contingent and particular ... This is to say that justice will always be contingent and contextual, emerging from uniquely South African 'forms of life' ... Postmodernism rejects the idea that justice can be universal or divorced from the context in which subjects conduct themselves. Postmodernism insists that to talk about justice in universalist terms is inauthentic; justice must be conceived as relating to situated subjects.

The European Enlightenment emphasised the capacity of science and rationality combined with faith in unilinear progress and liberal democracy, to lead towards the ideals of civilisation and the emancipation of humanity. On this account, law is accorded a privileged position as the guardian of the boundary between state and citizens and between citizens *inter se*, boundaries constructed through the creation of legal rights.

Postmodernism argues contrary to these rhetorical assertions that rationality is social and instrumental; that it operates as a vehicle of power and is only totalising by virtue of its exclusions. The 1996 Constitution does not reflect the shared aspirations of the nation but rather those of the elite who negotiated it. The law's civilising pretensions are undermined by the bogus evolutionary assumptions on which such a conception rests. The law's creation of legal subjectivity may be deconstructed to reveal subjects who have rights but lack equality and material well-being. In fact, far from ensuring freedom, the rules, structures and mechanisms of legal modernism, such as rights litigation and the rule of law, are revealed by postmodernism often to be conduits of power and mechanisms of subjection and domination.

Foucault argues that all-encompassing concepts like 'reasonableness' and categories like 'the reasonable man' or 'reasonable expectations' almost invariably exclude ... With the application of the legal concept of 'reasonableness' concrete individuals are turned into legal subjects, unique and unchangeable characteristics are subsumed under types, singular and contingent events transformed into model 'facts' and scenes in impoverished narratives with the limited imagination of evidence and procedure.

The legal system is founded not upon reason or justice but upon an interpretative act of violence. It may be asked of any particular law: What is its authorisation? It may be answered: 'The Constitution', which leads to the rejoinder, 'What is the authority for the Constitution?' and so commences a ... regress as the chain of authority is followed backwards in time. It must finally be admitted that law is based on nothing other than custom. The founding law (for instance the 1996 Constitution) is merely a construct installed by an act of violence.

The Constitution, as legitimator of all laws, cannot itself be legally legitimated: it is neither legal nor illegal, rather it is extra-legal, which is to say that in the South African case there was no legal authority for the constitutional negotiations which took place between 1989 and 1994, within the historically specific domain formed by the prevalent relations of power. Rather, the interim and 1996 Constitutions came about as a resolution to the longstanding and violent struggle for political power between opposing political forces. Derrida has pointed out elsewhere that there is a tendency for the creative establishing act to be forgotten, so that a higher moral justification (God, reason, natural law) is thought to ground the state and the law within it. This may constitute a failure to realise that law is groundless.

## Questions

1. Can you think of any claims, either descriptive or prescriptive, that seem to be rationally justified, despite us not being absolutely certain they are true?
2. Against the idea that there is a single human reason that Westerners have tended to tap into more than others, Lenta suggests that there is a 'polyphony', a wide range of voices from different cultural backgrounds that have some claim to truth. How do you think one should proceed when these views appear to contradict each other?
3. Lenta points out that any given legal system is usually the product of conquest or some other kind of force. Does that mean that no one legal system is better than any other? Why or why not?

### Text 2  Ronald Dworkin on value scepticism[15]

Ronald Dworkin is, perhaps after Lon Fuller, the most influential natural law theorist of the twentieth century. He is well known for arguing that the best way to interpret the law in a society includes appealing to the most objectively justified principles of justice that fit with that society's legal history.

Can beliefs about value – that it is wrong to steal, for instance – actually be true?... If some value judgments are true and others false, how can we human beings discover which are which? Even friends disagree about what is right and wrong; and of course we disagree even more strikingly with people of other cultures and ages. How can we think, without appalling arrogance, that we are right and others are just wrong? From what neutral perspective could the truth finally be tested and settled?

Someone who sticks pins into babies for the fun of hearing them scream is morally depraved. Don't you agree? You probably hold other, more controversial opinions about right and wrong as well ... You think that your opinions on these matters report the truth and that those who disagree with you are making a mistake ... You also think, I imagine, that sticking pins into babies or torturing terrorists would be wrong even if no one actually objected to it or was repulsed by the idea. Even you. You probably think, that is, that the truth of your moral convictions does not depend on what anyone thinks or feels. You might say, to make plain that that is what you think, that torturing babies for fun is 'really' or 'objectively' wicked.

[Some] learned scholars and great philosophers reject different aspects of [this] ordinary view. I shall call those who do that 'skeptics,' but I use that word in a special sense to include anyone who denies that moral judgments can be objectively true ... An unsophisticated form of skepticism, which is often called 'postmodernism,' has been much in vogue in ... faculties of art history, comparative literature, and anthropology, for example, and for a time in law schools as well. Devotees declare that even our most confident convictions about what is right or wicked are just emblems of ideology, just badges of power, just the rules of the local language games we happen to play ... [Some skeptics] say that the historical and geographical diversity of moral opinions shows that no such opinion can be objectively true ... It seems arrogant, in the face of great cultural diversity, to claim that everyone who disagrees with us is in error.

But any form of error skepticism seems out of the question. We can't really believe that there is nothing morally objectionable about suicide bombers or genocide or racial discrimination or forced clitoridectomy ... Of course it should give us pause that others disagree with what we find so plain. How can I be sure that I am right when others, who seem just as intelligent and sensitive, deny that I am? But we cannot take the fact of disagreement itself to count as an argument that our moral convictions are mistaken. We would not count the popularity of any of our other convictions as evidence for their truth.

---

15   Extracted from Dworkin 2011 *Justice for Hedgehogs*.

Morality is an independent domain of thought ... [A]ny argument that either supports or undermines a moral claim must include or presuppose further moral claims or assumptions ... If we think that our reasons for accepting any such moral claim are good ones, then we must also think that we are 'in touch with' the truth of the matter, and that its truth is no accident.

Many people and some philosophers ... hope to find a litmus stick: a test for good moral argument that does not beg the question it tries to answer by already presupposing some controversial moral theory ... [However] that is not a reasonable hope ... there is no way I can test the accuracy of my moral convictions except by deploying further moral convictions.

[I]f I am faced with someone who holds moral opinions radically different from my own, I cannot count on finding anything in my set of reasons and arguments that he would be irrational not to accept. I cannot demonstrate to him that my opinions are true and his false.

But I can hope to convince him – and myself – of something else that is often more important: that I have acted responsibly in reaching my opinions and acting on them ... I may be right about affirmative action when I flip a coin and wrong when I reflect carefully, but I am irresponsible in the first case and responsible in the second.

**Questions**

1. Dworkin provides an example of sticking pins into babies just to hear them scream as something we cannot help but think is objectively wrong, that is, wrong not merely because some society happens to think so, but wrong for everyone regardless of what they currently believe. Can you suggest an additional example of a moral judgement that appears similarly unreasonable to reject?

2. Dworkin says that 'we cannot take the fact of disagreement itself to count as an argument that our moral convictions are mistaken'. Is this point true in the case of scientific claims? For instance, does the fact that someone believes the earth is flat count as a reason to doubt your belief that it is round? If not, is there some relevant difference between a scientific judgement and a moral one?

3. At the end of the reading, Dworkin suggests that what ultimately matters when thinking about morality is not being correct or showing that another person would be unreasonable to disagree, but 'being responsible' when thinking about it, attempting to deliberate with integrity. How might the postmodernist respond to this suggestion?

There appear to be two distinct arguments for value scepticism in the above readings. On the one hand, Lenta questions the 'foundationalism of rationality'. In doing so, he is contending that a given legal system cannot be rationally supported or justified with good reasons. Why not? Roughly because when we exercise our reason we do not discover any claims that are certain or have any kind of unquestionable support behind them, such as God. Although you might believe in certain moral claims or the existence of God on faith, faith is not evidence, let alone indubitable evidence. You cannot be sure your moral beliefs are true, and you cannot be sure that God exists (or that you know His mind if He does exist).

Instead, legal interpretation involving an appeal to justice is 'groundless', that is, always open to reasonable questioning, revision and even rejection.[16]

On the other hand, Dworkin notes a distinct rationale for value scepticism, the idea that there are widespread differences of opinion about right and wrong. When there is objective knowledge, then there tends to be agreement amongst enquirers. If I ask people whether there are any trees still alive, everyone who understands me and is answering sincerely will say, 'Yes'. We will all agree that there are trees, and the best explanation of our unanimity is the fact that there *really are* trees. There is a mind-independent fact of the matter that trees exist, which our minds have all been able to apprehend.

Things are different if I ask whether it is proper to drive on the right or the left. Here, answers will differ, depending on the society doing the answering. South Africans will say that it is appropriate to drive on the left, whereas Americans will say that one should stay to the right. Substantial differences between people here are well explained by the absence of any objective fact of the matter; it is instead merely a social convention which side is appropriate to keep to when driving.

The argument for value scepticism that Dworkin considers is more or less the idea that our epistemic situation when it comes to morality is more like the driving case than the tree case. We do not encounter a lot of agreement about what is just and unjust, and the best explanation of the lack of agreement is that there is no objective fact of the matter, or at least that we do not have knowledge of such.[17]

Both arguments, from the absence of certainty and the presence of disagreement, purportedly entail that there are no objective moral facts that judges can and ought to grasp, ones that are analogous to the real shape of the earth that scientists have apprehended. Instead, there are at most truths about right and wrong that vary from society to society.

Part of the way that Dworkin objects to the lack of agreement argument is by suggesting that there is more agreement than one might have thought. If asking people about what is right and what is wrong, surely nearly everyone who understands the question would agree that it is wrong to stick pins into babies just to hear them scream. Dworkin suggests that these kinds of cases can be multiplied. He need not maintain that there is no disagreement. It would be enough for him to show that there is not substantial disagreement, or that there is not substantial disagreement that is reasonable.

Some objectivists might appeal to similar kinds of cases to respond to Lenta. Perhaps some of us are certain that it is wrong for anyone anywhere to torture babies for fun.

A second way that Dworkin objects is by contending that, even to the extent that there are differences of moral opinion, the mere fact that people disagree does not provide reason for doubt. What matters, according to Dworkin, is not the bare existence of different views, but rather whether those views are defensible or not. This point seems powerful in the context

---

16  Another facet of Lenta's reasoning supports particularism, when he suggests there are often exceptions to generalisations. If so, then we do not truly know that any purportedly basic and comprehensive moral principle is true, and to assert that one is true merely involves foisting one's views onto others or objectionably excluding other perspectives in some way. This approach is considered below in the sub-section on Feminist Legal Theory.

17  One might think that these two arguments amount to the same point; perhaps if a claim is certain then everyone will assent to it, and if everyone assents to a claim then it is certain. However, there are occasions in which everyone agrees to the same claim, but the claim is not certain. In a jury trial, a large group of people might all come to the same agreement that a defendant is guilty, not because it is indubitable that he or she is, but merely because they are confident beyond a *reasonable* doubt. Conversely, sometimes one can be certain of a claim that not everyone accepts. Logicians are sure that the *modus tollens* inference is valid, for example, but about half of varsity students surveyed since the 1970s have failed to grasp it. Consider this reasoning: if she has coffee, then she is happy; she is not happy; therefore, she does not have coffee. I am certain that she does not have coffee, given the other conditions, but many readers of this passage will not be sure, thinking that she may or may not have it.

of mathematics and science. If those who are not experts in these fields judge differently, that does not give the mathematician or scientist any reason to change his or her mind. Instead, the latter should retain their views because they, unlike the former, are familiar with the evidence. Similar remarks apply to morality, one might suggest on behalf of Dworkin.

At this point the question becomes whether there is evidence in moral deliberation of a sort that is comparable to evidence in mathematics and science. Dworkin seems to suggest that we cannot help thinking that there is. He remarks:

> If we think that our reasons for accepting any such moral claim are good ones, then we must also think that we are 'in touch with' the truth of the matter.

For all we can tell, there are plenty of good reasons for thinking that it is wrong to torture babies for fun. It is wrong to inflict unnecessary suffering on any being; it is wrong to treat an innocent party in an unloving way; it is wrong to cause grave harm for a trivial reason to non-rational beings that rational agents love; it is wrong to treat as unimportant beings that, in the normal course of affairs, will develop into persons. Even if some of these rationales are more compelling than others, the point is that it is extremely difficult to come up with *any* reasons for thinking that it is *permissible* to stick pins in babies just to hear them scream.

This sort of objection can be extended to apply to Lenta's rationale. Although we might not be absolutely certain that it is wrong to torture babies for fun, that claim arguably merits belief nonetheless in the light of the evidence we are currently able to marshal. We might not be 100% sure whether the evidence is correct, but there are cases in which the evidence is strong, strong enough to warrant belief. Analogous remarks appear to apply to at least many scientific claims; they seem to be aptly believed on the basis of probabilities, not certainties.

Turning away from objections to the two arguments for postmodernism, consider now some *prima facie* problems with postmodernism itself. One is that many postmodernists implicitly do not think that 'anything goes' when it comes to morality. Many of them, including Lenta, are critical of coercion, oppression and marginalisation, appealing to them to reject modernism. But where do these value judgements come from? What grounds them? On what basis can the postmodernist advance them as preferable if there are no objective moral facts that we can and do know? It might be that postmodernists are appealing to deep modernist principles to criticise modernist practice (even if they do so in a more particularist manner).

Another problem with postmodernism is that it appears to be self-refuting. On the one hand, postmodernists claim that there are no objective and universal moral facts, ones that apply to everyone regardless of their cultural backgrounds and belief systems. On the other hand, postmodernists maintain that no reader would be correct to believe in modernism. Postmodernists implicitly hold that that are good reasons that readers might not currently appreciate for changing their minds to hold postmodernism, and that all readers should believe in the truth of postmodernism if they currently do not. But if there are objective and universal truths about what one should believe, why deny that there are similar truths about what one should do?

Another way to see the apparently self-refuting nature of postmodernism is to note that postmodernists suggest that you are justified in believing in postmodernism even though it is not certain. No one is sure that postmodernism is true, and yet postmodernists think it should be believed anyway. But if postmodernism should be believed despite the absence of a rational 'foundation' or 'ground', then why not also believe certain moral claims in the absence of such?

This section has critically explored two major arguments for thinking that legal interpretation is inherently subjective. Some realists contend that law is nothing other than what judges decide, meaning there are no facts 'out there' about the correct interpretation of law beyond the minds of judges. Some postmodernists grant that law exists independently of what judges decide, but contend that there are no objective values to invoke when interpreting the law, where interpretation is unavoidable. In contrast to these extreme views, the next section addresses more moderate ones, according to which objective interpretations of law are possible in principle, but elusive in practice.

## 5.4 Moderate subjectivism: Critical Legal Studies, Critical Race Theory and Feminist Legal Theory

This section considers three major theories about the nature of legal interpretation that have been influential in twentieth-century Anglo-American jurisprudence and that South African legal thinkers have applied in various ways to the post-apartheid context. One thing all three approaches have in common is the idea that the backgrounds of judges substantially influence their interpretations. A judge's psychology, upbringing, culture, race/gender/sexuality, and political allegiances are routine factors that affect the way he or she thinks about justice and more generally about how to adjudicate disputes. In addition, these three theories contend that judicial rulings influence class, race and gender dynamics in society in ways that are often unrecognised but are pernicious.

Implicit in these approaches is usually the idea that a legal interpretation could admit of some objectivity but that the backgrounds of, or constraints on, judges tend to get in the way of that. Specifically, it has been common to maintain that it is objectively wrong for judges to be biased in favour of white males, or objectively unjust for law to distribute benefits and burdens in a way that disfavours black people and women. Judges and legal systems are to be evaluated on the basis of egalitarian or progressive moral views, and are often found wanting in the light of them. The question then becomes how racial and gender discrimination might be mitigated when interpreting the law.

### 5.4.1 Critical Legal Studies

This theoretical approach to law was salient in the United States from the late 1970s to the 1990s, with influential exponents including Duncan Kennedy, Karl Klare, Mark Tushnet and Roberto Unger.[18] Critical Legal Studies, or CLS as it is often abbreviated, grew out of the realist movement that had been prominent before World War II. Recall that realists often suggested that law is nothing but the activities of judges, where their decisions are unpredictable, based on emotions, and fail to cohere with each other, as opposed to being rational or formal articulations of a system of rules. Adherents to CLS tended to let go of the claim that law is identical to whatever judges do, but retained and developed the realist idea that what judges do is far from comprehensible in terms of some inner logic of law or mechanical application of general rules.

Instead, according to one dominant theme of CLS, judicial decisions are rarely fixed by what a legal text says, providing great interpretive leeway. Often this is called law's 'indeterminacy'. Instead of a legal statute or other rule being determinate in the sense of clearly entailing a single outcome, it is open to judges to interpret it in any number of ways, which they often do. This point seems particularly true for terms such as 'reasonable' or 'acceptable'.

---

18  Representative texts include Kennedy 1982 *Journal of Legal Education*; Tushnet 1984 *Stanford Law Review*; Unger 1986 *The Critical Legal Studies Movement*; and Klare 1998 *South African Journal on Human Rights*.

Another salient idea of CLS is that judicial interpretations are commonly constrained and influenced by extra-legal factors. A decision that might be truly just will not be made because it would conflict with present ownership patterns governing an economy. The way a judge was trained in a law school, perhaps to think that the law is apolitical and that there is a plain meaning of the law that should be prioritised, affects the way he or she interprets legal texts. A judge's status as a comparatively wealthy member of society's elite leads the judge to avoid social conflict and to favour the status quo in his or her readings of the law.

Notice, here, the *political* influences on a judge. Many CLS scholars and activists would accept the existence of non-political influences, such as the proverbial matter of what the judge had for breakfast, but what is characteristic of CLS is critiquing judicial practice in the light of Marxian or more generally leftist values. That is, issues of class have been central to CLS, with many of its adherents maintaining that law ideally ought to be used to help redistribute wealth away from those who own and control major sectors of the economy and towards those at the bottom.

However, CLS advocates are generally sceptical about the extent to which judges and lawyers can do that on their own. Instead, they highlight respects in which a given legal system serves ideological functions, that is, serves to legitimate injustice or oppression, particularly as it concerns those with power and money in relation to those without.

For one example, many CLS advocates believe that the category of individual rights is inappropriate when thinking about how to respond to social conflicts. Inspired by the views of Karl Marx,[19] they contend that resolving disputes in terms of rights is wrong, say, because claiming a right selfishly advances one's own interests against those of others, or because deciding on the basis of rights tends to neglect the interests of the large majority. Imagine that someone has become incredibly wealthy by virtue of having inherited money or won the lottery. The person did not harm anyone in the process of acquiring the money, let us suppose, and so intuitively may be said to have a right to keep it. However, when he or she claims a right to retain a vast amount of wealth, he or she is being selfish, and if his or her rights-claim were upheld by a court, it would neglect the disproportionately great influence he or she could have on politicians and the amount of suffering that could have been avoided had his or her wealth been redistributed.

For another example of how law tends to facilitate class oppression according to mainstream CLS, appeals to ideas about the rule of law or equality before the law are said to mask relationships of inequality. People in broadly liberal societies are inclined to believe that they are on an equal footing with others insofar as the law is meant to apply to everyone, including those who make it, and insofar as all are entitled to equal treatment in a court. However, these egalitarian ideals are rarely fulfilled. Furthermore, even when they are, they tend to make people forget about grossly unequal relationships when it comes to the distribution of wealth and the consequent influence of the rich on politics and society.

Broadly speaking, CLS advocates seek to undermine the supposed neutrality and objectivity of legal practice. Many judges and lawyers think of themselves as politically neutral and seeking legally sound outcomes, but, according to CLS, much of what they in fact do is not fixed by an independent law, is influenced by political factors, inclines people not to question economic injustice, and serves to reinforce class inequality.

In the South African context, ideas from CLS have been central to debate about how judges ought to adjudicate in the light of a new constitutional order that is 'transformative',

---

19   For example, 1843 *On the Jewish Question.*

that is, is roughly meant to overcome the injustices of apartheid.[20] South Africa's Constitution explicitly allows for land reform, obligates the state to meet socio-economic rights, and grounds a democratic political framework. A number of legal theorists who have engaged with South Africa,[21] including Akinola Akintayo in the following text, have argued that because there is a strong degree of choice involved in legal interpretation and a judge's values inevitably influence his or her interpretation, a judge should be explicit about what his or her values are if transformative goals are going to be met.

**PRIMARY TEXTS**

**Text 3  Akinola Akintayo on the pliability of legal texts[22]**

Dr Akinola Akintayo is a lecturer in Public Law at the University of Lagos, Nigeria. He has published on socio-economic rights, criminal justice and legal interpretation. He wrote the article from which the following is extracted when studying for his doctorate in law at the University of Pretoria in South Africa.

A long-standing thorny controversy is whether legal texts constrain judges or whether extra-legal factors influence judges in spite of the provisions of law. There is evidence to suggest that most legal practitioners trained under the conservative common law culture do believe in the objective reality of the law and the constraining power of legal texts. There are others, however, like the scholars of the Critical Legal Studies movement (CLS scholars), who believe that legal texts do not constrain judges.

The main argument of the CLS scholars is that, when confronted with a legal dispute, the judge invariably has to interpret the applicable law. According to them, this interpretive function of the court is influenced by many factors outside of the provisions of the law. These factors may include the judge's view of how the case should come out, the judge's legal culture, the judge's knowledge, the material available to the judge, the time available to the judge to research the law applicable to the issue in dispute, and the political climate, among other things. These extra-legal influences ... reduce or negate the assumption of the constraining power of legal texts.

In a situation where courts continue to validate the plasticity and pliability of legal texts, the question and immediate worry of legal theorists ... should be: What becomes of the transformative objectives and goals of a transformative constitution like that in South Africa, which requires that its provisions be interpreted in a certain way?

Do we appoint judges based on their perceived ideological or political leanings with the hope that the appointees will carry into effect the objectives and goals of a transformative constitution? Or do we expressly recognise extra-legal influences like ideology and politics in adjudication and constitutionally require judges to avail us of the ideological and political underpinnings of their decisions for more robust accountability and democratic participation?

---

20  On which see Chapter 3.
21  See Klare 1998 *South African Journal on Human Rights*; Madlingozi 2008 *Constitutional Court Review*.
22  Extracted from Akintayo 2012 *Southern African Public Law*.

I am of the opinion that acknowledgement of the 'esoteric morality' behind the decisions of courts is a constitutional imperative under a transformative constitutional regime. This is so not only because it will ensure judicial openness, responsibility and accountability, which is a constitutional imperative under a transformative constitutional regime, but also because it will enable the engagement and participation of citizens, which is another constitutional imperative under South Africa's democratic regime. Judicial openness and accountability, and participation and engagement by citizens are, I think, two sides of the same democratic coin. This is because while judicial openness and accountability enables participation and engagement by citizens in judicial decision-making, participation and engagement by the populace also promotes the openness, responsibility and accountability of the judiciary.

Judicial decisions are species of expert systems and knowledge and a variant of public decisions in which citizens are entitled to participate through comments, critiques and dialogues. In order for citizens to participate effectively, however, court decisions will have to be devoid of legal sophistry. Judges will have to be more honest and open about the political, ideological and the moral premises of their decisions and avail the citizens of the same, and not merely reel off constitutional or statutory provisions as the bases for their decisions. This is the only way that the twin ideals of citizen engagement and judicial accountability in a democratic regime will be realized. It is also the only way to expose the latent transformative issues in adjudication.

### Questions

1. Akintayo contends that greater transparency from judges about their moral and political values would improve citizen participation in governance. How might it do so?
2. Akintayo argues that greater transparency from judges about their values would enhance transformative Constitutionalism when it comes to judicial accountability and citizen participation. Is there any reason to think that it would also help with economic transformation? Why or why not?
3. Do you think it is possible to have too much democracy? Why or why not?

Notice how Akintayo's discussion of legal interpretation does not presume that seeking out objectivity is a hopeless endeavour. He can be read as presuming that a better, that is, more just, interpretation of the Constitution and law in general is one that advances a transformative agenda. For Akintayo, the issue is that judges will not necessarily interpret in ways that do so, and he proposes a solution to help remedy that problem.

Democratic norms are central to a transformative Constitutionalism, for Akintayo. He mentions two of their dimensions in this extract, namely, judicial accountability and citizen participation. A polity is more democratic, in one major respect, the more that people can and do hold their government officials accountable, perhaps by criticising their decisions and making requests for different ones in the future. Akintayo suggests that holding officials accountable is in itself a form of citizen participation or engagement. However, an additional form of citizen participation is plausibly the opportunity to vote for those who hold public office.

Akintayo contends that in order to enhance judicial accountability and citizen participation, judges need to be more transparent about their decisions. Specifically, he maintains that judges should be explicit about the contingent moral and political values that are behind their decisions, instead of pretending that a legal text is demanding a particular reading.

A friendly amendment to Akintayo's suggestion is that judicial rulings should also be widely publicised, not cloistered away in law reports. A further idea is that they should be written in a way that is not too complex and does not use a lot of jargon:

> [J]udgments that require the reader to enter into a highly sophisticated and technical reconstruction of a judgment – some would say a *sangoma*-like exercise – do not advance the cause of ensuring that ordinary people are part of the 'principled' – or at least transparent – constitutional dialogue to which the Court is ostensibly committed.[23]

Were South Africa's Constitutional Court Justices, and judges more generally, to reveal their moral and political values, to print or post online their decisions in forums that the public can easily access, and to write in ways that the public could readily understand, then it does appear that judges could be held more publicly accountable than they currently are. Citizens not only could critically engage with judicial decisions to a larger extent, but also could vote for parties or representatives responsible for judicial appointments in a more informed and hence meaningful way.

How might one question Akintayo's argument for greater transparency about which judicial decisions are being made and why? One concern is whether it is realistic. Judges have not been trained in moral and political philosophy, and so are not able to articulate their values in a coherent way. In addition, judges are extremely busy, and might not have the time to write longer and simpler opinions; it is quicker to speak to other experts familiar with the law.

Deeper criticisms contend that, even if judges could in practice make their decisions more transparent to the public, perhaps they in principle should not. One consideration is whether there are certain kinds of aims behind judicial decisions that would be frustrated if those aims were publicised. For example, perhaps it is appropriate for a judge to rule in a specific way at least in part because the public needs to retain confidence in the judiciary. However, telling the public that he or she is doing so would seem likely to undermine such confidence.

Another factor is whether greater public involvement in judicial decision-making would on the whole advance a transformative agenda. One can grant that transformation would be promoted in one respect by greater accountability and participation, but note that it might be retarded in other, perhaps more serious ways.

In particular, a Constitution with a Bill of Rights that protects minority liberties and interests, such as the one in South Africa, might be less likely to be protected, the greater the influence of the majority on the judiciary. If, for example, a majority of the public favours the death penalty, believes abortion should be illegal, and thinks the state should prevent newspapers from printing cartoons that are disrespectful of senior politicians, then, upon adopting Akintayo's recommendation, judges would face greater pressure to conform to these views, contrary to the currently dominant interpretation of the Bill of Rights in South Africa.

Are the views of the public any less subjective than those of judges? In fact, might they on average be more subjective, in the sense of being less understanding of the values of equality and dignity that underlie South Africa's Constitution?

---

23  Madlingozi 2008 at 69. A *sangoma* is someone who has been initiated into a traditional African healing practice and is thought to have knowledge, e.g. of what ancestors want, that others cannot access.

This sub-section has expounded some core elements of CLS, including the idea that legal interpretation is often subjective in the sense of being substantially influenced by judges' varying moral and political values. It has also explored a proposal about how this sort of subjectivity might be mitigated: if judges had to publicise their value judgments, they would thereby advance democratic transformation and would also have to consider which of their judgments could survive critical scrutiny from the public. The next sub-section addresses two other kinds of subjectivity, namely, the presence of racial bias and the ignorance of constitutional norms.

## 5.4.2   Critical Race Theory

Just as Critical Legal Studies grew out of realism, so Critical Race Theory (often abbreviated CRT) grew out of Critical Legal Studies. According to CRT, it is not merely the case, as per CLS, that legal texts are indeterminate and that judges are influenced by extra-legal, and specifically political, factors when reading them, but it is also true that some of these factors are racialised and racist. Broadly speaking, whereas CLS has focused largely on class, CRT has of course done so on race, particularly blackness, contending that failure to engage with race would make any critical account of law inadequate.

In the 1970s a number of scholars in the United States began to reflect systematically on ways in which race there influences the law and is influenced by it. CRT's inauguration is often attributed to Derrick Bell, the first tenured African-American professor at the Harvard Law School, Alan Freeman, a white civil rights and academic lawyer, and Patricia Williams, an African-American professor who currently holds an endowed chair at the Columbia Law School.[24] Despite CRT having become an established and large field by the early 1990s,[25] one scholar has more recently noted that it has yet to receive the attention in South African legal discourse that postmodernism, CLS and Feminist Legal Theory have.[26]

Although Critical Race Theorists are diverse in their approaches, recurrent themes and sympathies can be identified, as was done above with other broad collections of views (namely, postmodernism and CLS). Four are mentioned here.

One is the idea that anti-black racism is something pervasive. Racism is not reducible to the malevolent intentions of individual white people that are occasionally manifested in insults, discrimination or violence. Instead, it has unintended social and institutional dimensions that routinely harm and degrade black people in serious ways.

As an example in the South African context, although jobs are formally open to anyone who is qualified, so that there is a kind of equality of opportunity, black people are often in a weak position to obtain qualifications because of historical injustice and hence not truly able to compete on an equal footing for jobs. For a second example, although white academics or employers might sincerely espouse non-racial values, they often harbour implicit (unconscious) biases that lead them to react differently to white and black applicants who have comparable abilities. For a third example, being a white person tends to carry with it certain cultural privileges, such as being treated fairly when it comes to seeking to rent a dwelling, being sympathised with and cared for in medical settings, seeing other white people held up as exemplars of success, and feeling at home in meetings where 'white' norms, such

---

24   Representative texts include Freeman 1978 *Minnesota Law Review*; Bell 1992 *Faces at the Bottom of the Well*, 1995 *University of Illinois Law Review*; and Williams 1992 *The Alchemy of Race and Rights*. For additional classic works, see Crenshaw et al 1995 *Critical Race Theory*.

25   About 25 years ago two scholars noted several books and more than 200 articles, on which see Delgado & Stefancic 1993 *Virginia Law Review*.

26   Modiri 2012 *Southern African Public Law* at 232.

as a certain kind of spoken English, are accepted by default. Fourth, and finally for now, white people do not have to bear what are often called 'microaggressions', such as a person of mixed race being asked 'What are you?' or a black person being told that he or she 'speaks well' like a white person.

A second salient feature of CRT is an impatience with incremental change. Because anti-black racism is viewed as pervasive, limited and small-scale reforms are viewed as inadequate. This kind of attitude was prevalent amongst South African students during the 2015–2016 upheavals on university campuses. Although the government, controlled by the African National Congress, had adopted a loan scheme for impoverished students and succeeded in getting substantial numbers of black students admitted to tertiary studies, students were dissatisfied because of the oppression they continued to encounter day to day. They wanted fee-free education, accommodation that is more affordable, a curriculum that includes more African sources and perspectives, a professoriate that is more demographically representative, a medium of linguistic instruction that is accessible and does not feel alien, the removal of symbols of colonial heritage, the creation of mechanisms by which managers would listen to students, and still more. And they wanted it all immediately.

A third salient facet of CRT is a greater sympathy towards the normative category of rights than one usually encounters in CLS. Recall that CLS adherents have tended to believe that appealing to individual rights objectionably means supporting a selfish, atomistic society and a capitalist economy. In contrast, many of those sympathetic to CRT, while not dismissing these points, believe that sometimes rights are useful theoretical and practical categories to use when thinking about race.[27] It is plausible, for example, to think that many of the injustices done under apartheid (on which see Chapter 3) consisted of violations of people's rights to political participation, access to resources, equal opportunities and civil liberties. Similarly, many would say that black people's right to reparations for the wrongs of apartheid continue to be violated.

A fourth common theme is that a 'colour blind' or race neutral approach in law is often counterproductive, having the effect of entrenching racial injustice. Although one might be tempted to think that, after apartheid, the best anti-discriminatory approach to legal thought would be not to infuse it with racial categories, it is in fact failing to think and act in the light of race that means that the effects of historical injustice directed towards black people go unaddressed. Instead, for most CRT adherents, one must be 'race conscious' when interpreting the law in a post-apartheid context. This is one major point of the following reading.

| PRIMARY TEXTS | **Text 4  Joel Modiri on race in legal adjudication**[28] |
|---|---|
| | Dr Joel Modiri is the leading academic to have applied Critical Race Theory to South African jurisprudence. He lectures in the University of Pretoria Faculty of Law, and is an editor of the *South African Journal on Human Rights*. |
| | This case [of BoE Trust Limited] dealt with an appeal against the judgment of Mitchell AJ ... in which he dismissed an application to have the word 'White' – which was used to identify the group entitled to benefit – severed from a trust provision in a will. The provision empowered the trustees to apply the part of the trust's income ... for the provision of small bursaries to assist White South African |

---

27  Williams 1992 *The Alchemy of Race and Rights* is the *locus classicus*.
28  Extracted from Modiri 2013 *Potchefstroom Electronic Law Journal*.

students who have completed an MSc degree in Organic Chemistry at a South African University and are planning to complete their studies with a doctorate degree at a University in Europe or in Britain ... The trustees applied to the High Court for a *rule nisi* inviting interested parties to show why the word 'white' should not be deleted from the will.

Mitchell AJ dismissed the application, basing his decision mostly on the common law principle of freedom of testation and its relation to the constitutional right to property, which includes the right to dispose of one's property as one wishes. The main legal issue in the SCA [Supreme Court of Appeal – ed.] was whether or not to uphold the appeal against Mitchell AJ's judgment and to allow a deletion of the word 'white' from Ms de Villiers' last will and testament.

Erasmus AJA specifically points out that the two rights that are pertinent in this case are the rights to property and the right to dignity. In his view, the right to property, as enshrined in section 25(1) of the Constitution, which provides that no one may be arbitrarily deprived of property, also protects a person's right to dispose of their assets as they wish upon their death. Dignity further comes into play because ... 'the right to dignity allows the living, and the dying, the peace of mind of knowing that their last wishes would be respected after they have passed away'.

It is of course trite that South African law places a high premium on the common law principle of freedom of testation. But it is equally trite that the freedom of testation has a number of common law limitations. A testamentary provision will not be given effect to if it is (1) unlawful; or (2) contrary to public policy (*contra bonos mores*) ... [P]ublic policy is now rooted in the Constitution. Section 9(4) of the Constitution provides that no person may unfairly discriminate directly or indirectly against anyone on the grounds inter alia of race ... Further ... I contend that the unfairness of the racially exclusive trust provision is considerably aggravated by the fact that it was designed with the aim of protecting and advancing persons who were and still are vastly advantaged by past and present forms of unfair discrimination, racial exclusion and white privilege.

Erasmus AJA justifies his decision for the most part by simply remaining within the bounds of the common law ... [H]e never confronts the question of how the Constitution alters the fundamental legal concepts of the law of succession, especially freedom of testation. Drucilla Cornell and Nick Friedman have made a powerful argument that 'the Constitution mandates that the common law be deeply infused with constitutional values' ... On Cornell and Friedman's argument, the judge was under 'a non-conditional obligation' to interpret the common law of succession in a way that would have given expression to the equality clause (and specifically the injunction against unfair discrimination based on race) and to the ideal of 'non-racialism' embedded in the Constitution ... Because the trust established in this case would have involved acceptance by public institutions (universities) and thus could not, by definition, be purely private, the judge had an affirmative constitutional obligation and a political responsibility, due to the well-established and frequently proclaimed public policy against racial discrimination, to invalidate and alter the provisions of the trust ...

In this case, depoliticisation is achieved by eschewing the question of white racial power and the history of apartheid, dispossession and racial inequality in the representation of the legal dispute at hand. In the judge's elision of power and history, private and personal vocabularies come to stand in for and replace public and political ones; the language of individual choice, private ownership and respect for the last wishes of the dead and their peace of mind in knowing that those wishes will be respected after they pass away replaces an enquiry into the public implications of universities carrying out racist testamentary clauses [and] the law's explicit endorsement of the continuation and transfer of white privileges ... On my reading, the judgment can be seen as a defence of private racism and a refusal to see or even challenge white privilege.

**Questions**
1. Suppose that Ms de Villiers had instead created a will in which funds were reserved for black students. Would that have counted as unfair discrimination for Modiri? For you?
2. Modiri does not suggest that it is always unfair discrimination for race to enter into people's choices, only those that have a public dimension. Can you give an example of a choice that does not have a public dimension (or only a minimal one)?
3. Suppose that Ms de Villiers had instead created a will in which funds were reserved for white students not at a public university but at a privately funded one. Do you think that the logic of Modiri's reasoning would still apply? That is, is funding the only respect in which a university has a public dimension?

In this case, the Supreme Court of Appeal (SCA) in South Africa had to decide whether to allow a trust to retain a racially exclusive provision, one that would have allowed only white students at certain public universities to apply for a bursary to study. None of the universities was willing to accept a bursary with such a restriction, but all were willing to do so if the restriction were removed. Those in charge of administering the trust therefore approached the courts to see whether they were permitted to change the terms of the will. The SCA ruled unanimously that they were not.

The opinion, composed by Judge Erasmus but signed onto by all four of his peers, did not lead to the bursary being adopted.[29] Since the will included a clause indicating that if the bursary scheme were 'impossible' to adopt the funds should go to certain charities, and since the Court noted that it was indeed 'impossible' to adopt the bursary scheme given the universities' unwillingness to accept it, the Court ruled that the funds should be distributed to the charities.

Although Modiri favours this outcome, he finds the reasoning that led to it problematic in the light of themes from Critical Race Theory. The Court ruled, largely on the basis of common law, that the trustees could not rightly remove the racial restriction because of the need to respect the property rights and dignity of the testatrix. Modiri contends that such considerations were outweighed by less individualist factors that were not addressed in the ruling.

---

29   Supreme Court of Appeal of South Africa, *BoE Trust Limited NO & Another* (846/11) [2012] ZASCA 147 (28 September 2012).

Specifically, Modiri argues that the common law must be infused with constitutional values, which include the avoidance of unfair discrimination in the public sphere. The adoption of the bursary scheme would have consisted of unfair discrimination, in part because it would have singled out a race to benefit from it, but also, and probably mainly for Modiri, because of the particular race favoured. White students have substantially benefited from past injustice and do not need bursaries nearly as much as black students. Plus, one might add that the adoption of such a bursary scheme would have expressed support for apartheid-era, that is, racist, norms. Modiri complains that the Court did not consider South African history and politics in its decision, and relied on 'colour blind' or 'race neutral' considerations of an individual's right to property and dignity that were to the harm and denigration of black people.

Suppose that Modiri is correct about his analysis of the case, that it is poorly reasoned because there is no engagement with the Constitution's implications for the racial dimensions of a bursary scheme meant for public universities and restricted to white students. What is to be done in order to avoid these kinds of narrow decisions?

One thing is to publish critical discussions of cases in the way that Modiri has done, and to work to get judges to read them. Relatedly, one might suggest that the judiciary in South Africa should systematically train judges at all levels to interpret constitutional provisions and the values underlying them. The common law is often called 'judge-made' law; it consists of precedent and principles that make good sense of it. Now, which judges made this body of law?

The answer is: largely white males during apartheid. It was only in 1991 that the first black person was appointed to the South African bench, and in 1994 'of the 165 judges, 160 were white men; three were black men, and two were white women. At that stage, there was no black woman judge in South Africa'.[30] Given that a certain body of law was developed in a racially skewed society (and, it must be added, a gendered one), it is imperative to interpret this law in the light of constitutional norms. And since many judges have been unfamiliar with South Africa's new constitutional order, and so rendering subjective decisions in the sense of ones uninformed by relevant (indeed, overriding) law, they should be thoroughly educated about it.

Educating white men about how to interpret common (as well as statutory, customary and other) law in the light of egalitarian principles, human rights and the like is probably not enough to advance the kinds of decisions that Modiri believes would be more just. In addition, the people making the decisions also need to change.

As one advocate has pointed out of the apartheid bench:

> **The judiciary was deprived of the services of persons who had life experiences similar to those of many of the litigants who appeared before them, persons who understood the language, culture and ways of doing and saying things of such litigants.**[31]

The suggestion here is that, with more black, and particularly African, people being appointed to the bench, black interests and perspectives are more likely to be given their due. In other words, the subjectivity of white judges, in this case meaning their limited understanding of the black (especially African) experience, would be best corrected by the significant appointment of black (African) judges.

---

30   Mokgoro 2010 *Advocate* at 44.
31   Moerane 2003 *South African Law Journal* at 710.

This point, about the epistemology of judges, is one major rationale for section 174(2) of South Africa's Constitution, which says the:

> **need for the judiciary to reflect broadly the racial and gender composition of South Africa must be considered when judicial officers are appointed.**

Two additional rationales for changing the demographics of the bench include making it more likely that a largely black public would perceive judicial decisions as impartial and acknowledging 'symbolic value', roughly expressing a message to the public that black people are capable and merit inclusion.[32]

The controversy at this point concerns how much weight to ascribe to race (and gender) when appointing judges. Virtually no one thinks that race is a sufficient criterion for appointment. Surely, a candidate must have other qualifications such as experience, integrity, technical capacity and ability to understand constitutional norms.

Conversely, few believe that race should be ignored when making appointments in the hope that enough black people would be appointed when looking solely at these other kinds of qualifications. Apartheid's effects on educational institutions where black people have tended to reside mean that their non-racial qualifications on average might not be as strong, but that they nonetheless have potential to improve their knowledge and skills while on the job.

There is one obvious approach that remains and that has been widely accepted in South Africa. It is to seek out some kind of balance when making appointments, weighing race against other kinds of qualifications to come to an overall judgement in a particular situation. There has been debate, however, about whether the South African Judicial Service Commission (often abbreviated JSC), which is responsible for interviewing candidates for the bench and making recommendations, has consistently struck the right balance. Some critics have contended that it has given too much weight to race and not enough to other qualifications (and to gender).

In particular, consider a case in which a black candidate is sufficiently, albeit minimally, qualified when it comes to experience, technical capacity and so on, while a white candidate is much better qualified in these latter terms. Which should the JSC chose, supposing that only one can be picked?

A complaint of 'unfairness' to the white candidate might not resonate with many readers. After all, if he or she is indeed extremely well qualified, then he or she was probably lucky enough to benefit from an unjust distribution of educational resources in the past, and is in any event very likely to find some other good job in the future.

However, equal opportunity to compete for a job is not the only *prima facie* moral consideration. If judicial appointments routinely failed to give much weight to non-racial qualifications, then not only might the public lose faith in the judiciary, but chances are that the public would also be served worse by it.

There is no suggestion here that white candidates are routinely strong when it comes to non-racial qualifications and black ones are weak. Such an empirically unjustified proposition is not what is at stake, which is instead a normative point: how in principle should the likely benefits of 'equity' or 'affirmative action' when appointing judges be weighed against its potential drawbacks? Giving race some independent consideration in judicial appointments is one important way to reduce subjective judicial interpretations, in the sense of those

---

32  For mention of symbolism, see Moerane 2003 at 714; and Judicial Service Commission 2010 *Politicsweb*.

insufficiently informed by the perspectives of black people appearing before courts. How much weight should the need to avoid this form of subjectivity be given in relation to other considerations that might compete with it?

### 5.4.3   Feminist Legal Theory

Feminist jurisprudence followed in the wake of both CLS and CRT. Class and race are not enough on their own to understand what affects legal interpretation and how it, in turn, affects society; in addition, gender is an important variable.

Feminist Legal Theory took off in earnest in the 1980s in the United States, with pioneers including Drucilla Cornell, Catharine MacKinnon, Deborah Rhode, Robin West and Joan Williams.[33] Other critical or anti-discriminatory approaches arose hot on the heels of these and related feminist thinkers publishing their views. For example, sexual orientation was soon deemed another variable for evaluating law, with what is widely known as 'Queer (Legal) Theory', which questions heteronormative assumptions and biases in law, arising in the 1990s.[34] Disability also came to ground a way to critique law, with Critical Disability Theory having likewise recently grown out of CLS and these other movements in the early 2000s.[35] Most recently, in the past ten years, there has emerged the field of what is called 'Elder Law Jurisprudence' or 'Jurisprudential Gerontology', which theoretically explores respects in which discrimination against the elderly is present in law.[36]

The rest of this chapter focuses strictly on Feminist Legal Theory, which has become enormous, with a wide variety of topics, styles, positions and philosophical foundations. Many of the topics have concerned what the content of law should be. For example, nearly all feminists believe that abortion should be legal (even if some have moral qualms about it) and that marital rape should be illegal. There is debate amongst feminists about whether the law should permit various forms of surrogacy, and whether prostitution should be decriminalised. Feminists invariably want sexual harassment in the workplace to be against the law[37] as well as for the law to require equal pay for equal work. Many feminists also want the economy changed by law so that mothers do not have to choose between pursuing a career and knowing their children are well cared for, and so that domestic work, such as cleaning and childcare, becomes routinely compensated.

One particularly large area of enquiry about which laws and policies should be adopted has concerned how to understand equality. Supposing that people should be treated as equals or have a right to equality, what does this mean for how to distribute goods? Feminism is often credited with demonstrating that merely 'formal' equality can be unjust, and that some kind of 'substantive' equality is essential. Formal equality is roughly a matter of giving the same thing to everyone, regardless of their gender and the differences associated with that. Substantive equality instead consists of giving different things to people, so that their differences are responded to in such a way that they achieve some kind of equal condition.

Initially Western feminists focused on the formal kind of equality, seeking the same rights to vote, to hold public office, to get an education, to hold jobs and to participate in sports as

---

33   Representative texts include MacKinnon 1987 *Feminism Unmodified*; West 1988 *University of Chicago Law Review*; Rhode 1989 *Justice and Gender*; Williams 1989 *Michigan Law Review*; and Cornell 1991 *Beyond Accommodation*.

34   For example, Valdes 1995 *California Law Review*; and Leckey & Brooks 2010 *Queer Theory*.

35   For example, Pothier & Devlin 2006 *Critical Disability Theory*; and Hosking 2008 *Critical Disability Theory*.

36   For example, Doron 2008 *Theories on Law and Ageing*; and Doron & Meenan 2012 *Gerontology*.

37   In the United States it was only in 1964 that discrimination based on sex (gender) was made against federal law, and it took time for the courts to treat sexual harassment as a form of such discrimination.

men had enjoyed (this approach, of seeking the same rights as men, is sometimes called 'liberal feminism'). In addition, feminists at first wanted to be treated as individuals with the same kinds of valued capacities as men, for example rationality and strength.

However, in time feminists argued that formal equality is not enough and that it can lead to injustice in many circumstances. For example, women can reproduce the species with their bodies while men cannot. Being treated in the same way would mean that an employer, for example, might not give women time off to deal with pregnancy, birth and the initial stages of looking after a newborn infant.

Another area where mere formal equality appears insufficient concerns the opportunity to compete for a job. Formal equality would mean removing any legal barriers to employment and enforcing laws against a hostile workplace and the like. However, this sort of equal treatment is arguably not enough. Suppose that women are socialised to look after vulnerable parties such as the young, the elderly and the sick, and suppose further that there are few or no female role models in a certain profession. Then, treating men and women the same way would plausibly count as failing to do justice to women when it comes to having a real chance for them to get a job in that profession. In order to make up for the disadvantages women face when it comes to being able to picture themselves in a certain job, members of that profession might be obligated, say, to give them extra encouragement and training, and academics might be obligated to give weight to gender when hiring lecturers.

The central topic of this chapter is the interpretation of law, and specifically respects in which it is subjective, and, on this score, Feminist Legal Theory has made at least three major contributions. One is about the kinds of basic values that should determine the way that burdens and benefits get distributed in a society and hence invoked with adjudicating disputes. A major strain of feminist philosophy identifies individual rights- or desert-claims as a characteristically male way of thinking about morality and caring relationships as, in contrast, characteristically female.[38] Relatedly, some feminist philosophers have maintained that an impartial approach to morality, typified by utilitarianism or social contract theory (see especially Chapter 6), is male, whereas a partial approach, in which bonds of family and friendship are central, is female. Yet another point about values has come from African womanists, who often contrast their perspectives with those of Western feminists. The former are, for example, inclined towards communal-relational values that would prescribe co-operation with, and not distance from, men, purportedly unlike the latter.[39]

Debate continues about whether women and men do tend to think differently about morality, why they might do so (that is, whether nature or nurture is responsible), and what gendered value judgements should mean for how to make moral decisions in a public context such as judicial interpretation. Would an objective interpretation of the law be one that is, say, grounded on characteristically female values since they are true or justified whereas the male ones are not? Or would it mean invoking female values when dealing with women and male values when dealing with men? Or would it mean balancing them in some way?

A second large contribution from feminism to thought about law's interpretation concerns how to understand terms such as 'reasonable'. For example, consider whether a use of force was reasonable for purposes of self-defence or not. For a long while, legal systems spoke of what a 'reasonable man' would have judged in the situation, although that in time

38   Classic sources include Gilligan 1982 *In a Different Voice*; Noddings 1984 *Caring*; West 1988.
39   See, for example, contributions to Nnaemeka 1998 *Sisterhood, Feminisms, and Power*; and to Osha 2006 *Quest: An African Journal of Philosophy*.

became an appeal to a 'reasonable person'. Some feminists, however, claim that even talk of a 'reasonable person' has tended to smuggle in a characteristically male perspective.

This sort of claim has been salient in debate about how judges should respond to women who kill their abusers, but not when the abusers are immediately threatening them in any way.[40] Although from a typically male or allegedly 'neutral' perspective, it might not be reasonable to kill a husband who has been abusive when he is sleeping, from the perspective of a woman who has been repeatedly battered and denigrated and who lacks economic opportunities, it might appear to be her only option. Should a reasonable judgement be one constituted by a reasonable person in general, or a reasonable person of a particular gender who, because of that gender, is in a particular situation?

A third significant influence of feminism on legal interpretation has concerned what is often summed up as 'difference'. Drawing on postmodern scepticism about general categories, some versions of feminism, especially those influential in South Africa, have criticised legal decisions for being insufficiently sensitive to particularity, that is, respects in which individual women have interests or are in situations that are different from those of men or from what is considered 'normal'.

Sometimes the suggestion is that just as 'colour blindness' can lead to racial injustice, so a failure to apprehend differences between men and women and their respective situations can mean oppression or other injustice for women. This sort of recognition of difference was discussed above in the context of substantive justice.

Other times the dichotomy or 'binary' of male/female, and related ones such as rational/ emotional and free/unfree, are questioned for occluding awareness of ways of living that are neither just one nor the other. Speaking and thinking in terms of male/female tends to make one forget that people instantiate these traits to varying degrees, and doing so often involves prioritising one opposite, the male, over the other. 'Deconstruction' is a process of interpretation that, amongst other things, reminds the reader of the fluidity of such distinctions and encourages one to question their hierarchical order.

Still other times feminists point out that attempts to recognise gender differences between groups can 'backfire' in that they tend to homogenise women. Here, the concerns are that using a general category such as 'women' can objectionably lead to treating all members of this group as the same when they are not. Not all members of the group might in fact share the traits associated with it, and, even if all members of the group did share those traits, some members would have or lack additional ones, making them and their situations distinct. These kinds of interpretive concerns are salient in the following reading.

| PRIMARY TEXTS | **Text 5 Karin van Marle on feminism and difference in legal interpretation[41]** |
| --- | --- |
| | Karin van Marle is Professor of Law and Head of the Department of Jurisprudence at the University of Pretoria. Often collaborating with Drucilla Cornell, she is a leading voice of feminist jurisprudence in the South African context. |
| | Feminist theory has travelled a long way since the liberal feminist demand for the right to equality based on the yardstick of neutrality and sameness. One of the most significant shifts from modern and liberal feminist theories to postmodern |

---

40   For example, Cahn 1992 *Cornell Law Review*; Walker 2012 *Notre Dame Journal of Law, Ethics & Public Policy*.
41   Extracted from van Marle 2003 *Feminist Legal Studies*.

and critical theories was the switch in focus from a search for abstract universal conceptions of equality and justice to context and the particular. Western feminists, most notably, have come to accept the claim that many feminist theories repeat the harms of patriarchal society by accepting only one view of reality and thereby excluding many women.

I ... consider the protection of equality under the South African Constitution and come to argue that the inherent structure of law inevitably leads to a denial of difference and a support for generalisation and universalism based on sameness, even where there is an attempt to recognise difference ... Most, if not all, law and legal reform are reflections of universal thought processes based on notions of sameness and symmetrical reciprocity rather than on an open-ended acceptance of difference and asymmetrical reciprocity. One reason for this is that the law and legal reform are directed at a general level – in the case of the protection of women, women are regarded as representing a certain group or community of individuals. I wish to argue that law and legal reform, even though it has (and must have) formalist and institutional restrictions can nevertheless benefit from feminist deliberations on heterogeneity and difference. Law and legal reform should approach women by recognising difference and by acknowledging that it is impossible to know all and therefore fully to cater for difference and diversity.

We see attempts in the South African protection of equality to expand formal universal models of law and legal reform ... Section 9 of the Constitution of South Africa protects the right to equality. It is generally accepted that this section should be understood as not only protecting formal equality but also substantive equality. In other words, a court will accept that in some instances individuals must be treated differently in order to protect their right to equality. An approach based on substantive equality takes the concrete circumstances of an individual into account in contrast to a formal abstract approach based on sameness.

In *President of the Republic of South Africa and Another v. Hugo* the facts were as follows: Hugo was imprisoned at a time when the former president, Nelson Mandela (in the Presidential Act 17 of 1994) pardoned certain categories of prisoners. One of these categories was all women in prison on the tenth of May 1994 who were single mothers to children under the age of twelve years. Hugo, a widower and the father of a son under the age of twelve, applied for an order declaring the Presidential Act unconstitutional on the grounds that it discriminated unfairly against him on the basis of gender. The majority in the Constitutional Court held that there was discrimination against Hugo, but that it was not unfair. Justice Goldstone argued that the court followed a substantive approach to equality by focussing on the differences between the genders.

Justice O'Regan, concurring in Hugo, argued that the presidential pardon did not discriminate unfairly against Hugo, primarily because he, as a man, was not a member of a group that had previously suffered from discrimination. She pointed out that, even though it would be better in the long run for equality if the responsibilities of child-rearing were shared fairly between fathers and mothers, the reality at present and in the near future is that mothers bear primary child-rearing responsibility. In this light the pardon benefited a particular group of women in a material way, despite its reliance on what might be a harmful stereotype.

A question to consider is whether this decision truly protected and enhanced equality. To my mind the court affirmed unfair discrimination against Hugo and other single fathers with children under the age of 12 as well as against children under 12 who were in the precarious position of having only a father as single parent. Further the court's decision negatively affected the dignity and respect of women by affirming the harmful stereotype and generalisation that only women are to be considered the primary care givers of children. To reiterate: The court's approach of substantive equality, which aims to represent a way of regarding difference, by taking a 'universal'/general or stereotyped view of reality as its starting point, harmed the dignity of and respect for women and men.

I am concerned that in our attempts to address substantive, material conditions, we harm and violate by not truly regarding difference and otherness, by assuming symmetrical reciprocity, by being presumptuous about our own abilities to understand context, by placing individuals in groups, and, ultimately, by ending up doing the very same thing we wanted to break with, namely universalising the experiences and contexts of each other.

### Questions

1. Explain how, in the Hugo decision, the Court was trying to avoid reliance on merely formal equality and instead seeking to advance substantive equality.
2. As indicated prior to the reading, normally feminists believe in substantive equality. Why is van Marle therefore unsatisfied on feminist grounds with the Court's decision?
3. Would pardoning women with children also discriminate unfairly against women without children? Why or why not, in your view?

In the case that van Marle discusses, the South African Constitutional Court had to decide whether to allow a presidential pardon to retain a gendered provision, one that allowed only single women with children, and not also single men with them, to be pardoned. The Court ruled that the gendered nature of the pardon did not constitute unfair discrimination.

If equal treatment were merely formal, then men were treated unequally, that is, unfairly discriminated against, by virtue of being excluded from the group that was pardoned. Men and women were not treated the same way. However, the Court contended that equal treatment is in this case a substantive matter, requiring judges to consider the different situations that women and men typically face. Since women in South African society are normally those accorded the responsibility of child-rearing, pardoning them is not unfair to men.

Although van Marle welcomes the Court's inclination to think in terms of substantive equality, she finds its reasoning flawed in the light of other themes from Feminist Legal Theory, particularly as they pertain to difference. She objects to the way the Court categorises women as responsible for child-rearing and men as not, identifying three distinct ways in which doing so fails to recognise difference.

First, the Court's reasoning affirms the stereotype that women are and should be primary caregivers of children, not doing enough to acknowledge that some women are not and reasonably do not want to be. Second, it wrongs the children of men who are single parents, not giving them the care that they need because of an arbitrary factor, namely, the gender of the caregiver. Third, it unfairly discriminates against men who are single parents, for, although not many of them are in that situation, some are, and their unusual circumstances should not have been ignored. According to van Marle, the Court would have treated everyone affected with more respect, presumably an objectively correct moral norm, had it instead removed the gendered provision and extended the pardon to anyone who was a single parent.

A large challenge posed to the feminist philosophy of difference has come from another strand of feminism, and particularly the work of academic lawyer Catharine MacKinnon. The objections are, first, that it is not clear which differences merit respect and which do not, and, second, that many differences that might seem to merit respect in fact do not when they have themselves been created by a patriarchal society:

> **Women value care because men have valued us according to the care we give them, and we could probably use some. Women think in relational terms because our existence is defined in relation to men.**[42]

> **When difference means dominance as it does with gender, for women to affirm differences is to affirm the qualities and characteristics of powerlessness ... [W]hat women have been and thought is what they have been permitted to be and think.**[43]

For MacKinnon, dominance should be the central feminist concept, not difference. What should matter, according to her, is women's ability to choose how to live their lives, not the respect of ways in which women are different, at least when they are different because of lives they have not chosen.

Is MacKinnon correct to think that women tend to value relationships such as child-rearing merely or mainly because they have been forced into caring roles? If she were correct, would it follow that these values should not be respected? Or might the fact that women identify with these values provide some reason to acknowledge them? Does it matter whether women can shed themselves of certain differences or whether they are stuck with them? Is it relevant whether the differences are objectively important or are merely subjective preferences? These and related questions have been the subject of much debate in Feminist Legal Theory over the past 30 years.

## 5.5 Conclusion and transition to Part 2

The large question this chapter has sought to address is the extent to which legal interpretation is subjective and whether it can and should be made more objective. On the one hand, there are legal realists and some postmodernists who, very roughly, maintain that when judges make rulings they are doing something akin to appraising the taste of carrots. For these thinkers, there are no mind-independent standards to guide a legal adjudication and to deem it to be either correct or incorrect.

On the other hand, there are adherents to CLS, CRT and Feminist Legal Theory, who usually do not deny that there are objective standards such as equality and respect for

---

42  MacKinnon 1987 at 39.
43  MacKinnon 1989 *Toward a Feminist Theory of the State* at 51.

human dignity, but who maintain that they often fail to influence legal decisions adequately. In particular, the economic, racial and gender backgrounds of judges affect their interpretations of legal documents, often in discriminatory ways. Furthermore, even when these features are not influencing interpretations, judges routinely do a poor job of thinking about how their decisions might have unjust social implications when it comes to the poor, black people and women.

Some suggestions about how legal interpretation could become less discriminatory, and presumably more objectively just, have included requiring judges to be more transparent about the values behind their decisions, training judges in constitutional values, diversifying the bench so that it is not overpopulated by one group such as white males, and encouraging judges to appreciate differences between and within genders when making rulings. Perhaps by employing these kinds of strategies, legal interpretations would more often home in on good moral reasons and thereby become more like apprehending the shape of the earth, where there is a real fact of the matter about its shape and many humans have come to learn that it is round.

This chapter concludes Part 1 of this book, the two core issues of which have been what the nature of law is (Chapters 2 and 3) and how judges should interpret it (Chapters 4 and 5). Part 2 of the book focuses on issues that fall under the broad heading of 'justice', namely, what justice requires when it comes to the distribution of benefits and burdens (Chapters, 6, 7 and 8), and how courts should respond when injustice has been done (Chapters 9 and 10).

## POINTS TO CONSIDER

1. What do you think is the strongest argument for what has been labelled 'extreme subjectivism' in this chapter? Is it sound?
2. It is hard to deny that South Africa needs more black and female judges. What do you think would be the best ways of attracting them?
3. Imagine you are a judge having to decide whether a certain use of force in the context of self-defence was reasonable or not. How would you go about it? Do you think your decision could be objective or not? If not, why not? If so, what would make it so?

# PART TWO

# Theories of justice

# Chapter 6

# What is a just distribution of resources?

DAVID BILCHITZ

## 6.1    Modern questions of justice in African states

Gugu is a mother of two children living in rural South Africa. She is married to Thabo who went to Johannesburg to find work and never returned. It is rumoured that he found another woman and formed a new family with her. Gugu has no means of earning a living, and the small, subsistence crops she planted this year have failed due to the drought. Her children are starting to develop malnutrition illnesses. Thabo's family is no longer happy for her to stay with them and has threatened to evict her from the family homestead, as they feel she must contribute to the costs of the household. All the land around the homestead is owned either privately or by the state. Gugu's plight is so desperate that she has removed her children from school so that they can beg on the side of the street for a little money for food.

Gugu's story is not unique in South Africa and across the African continent, but rather is representative – to various degrees – of the plight of many people who often lack sufficient food for themselves and their children and, even, a place which they can legitimately claim as their own. Indeed, the Food and Agriculture Organization of the United Nations estimates that 233 million people in sub-Saharan Africa are hungry or undernourished, translating into one in every four people in this region.[1] Almost half the population of sub-Saharan Africa lives in extreme poverty (defined as having less than R15 per day to live on).[2] In South Africa, millions of people who migrate to the urban areas live in informal settlements where they build small shacks, which remain exposed to the rain and cold, on land which they cannot call their own.

This state of affairs is clearly one where many individuals are suffering. This leads many people to claim that this situation is unjust and human beings are obligated to take all the necessary measures to improve the conditions of these people. It is important, however, to distinguish between two types of claims about why the situation of Gugu and her family is unjust. The first type of argument is that Gugu's plight arises due to a history of wrongful actions, which include particularly the effects of colonialism and apartheid. As a result of a tax imposed by colonial authorities on all men over the age of 18, many African men were forced from their rural homes into the cities to find work (often in the mines). This situation had a major social effect in breaking up families. Historic wrongs such as these caused Gugu's plight and thus call for actions to compensate her (and her family) for her losses. Arguments such as these which are rooted in historical wrongs, which call for compensation, are referred to as 'reparative justice' arguments. They are of great importance in dealing with the plight of individuals in the African continent and will be dealt with in Chapters 9 and 10 of this book.

A second type of argument around justice, however, is not focused on the historical causes of the plight of individuals such as Gugu. It is rather concerned, irrespective of how an individual's situation arose, as to whether the existing distribution of resources in society is fair or just. Let us imagine that an Afrikaans woman – Erika – and her two children landed up on the streets without shelter when her husband died of a sudden heart attack. Erika and her children were not the subject of historical wrongs (they, in fact, have benefited from them) but they are destitute. Is it unjust for anybody – no matter how the situation arose – to be without shelter, food or adequate healthcare? This question is about what we term 'distributive justice' – what a fair distribution of resources would look like, abstracted from any historical circumstances.

To understand this question, let us imagine a simple example where we have eight members of a family and each stands around the table waiting for a piece of birthday cake for Khomotso. Which distribution would be just? Most people initially think that a fair distribution is an equal one. This would involve cutting the cake into eight equal slices. Things, however, quickly become more complicated. Does Khomotso, whose birthday it is, deserve more? Do we need a special cake to cater for Lerato, who cannot digest sugar? Is it fair to give Lebogang – a small child who has a small appetite and goes to many birthday parties – the same amount of cake as Thabo – an adult of 25 who is ravenous and has not had cake for a year due to his poor financial circumstances? As we can see, there are complexities even in relation to a simple example such as this. Things become even more difficult when we seek to consider how resources across a particular society (or the world as a whole) should be distributed. This is the question of distributive justice and it is the focus of the next three chapters.

---

1   See Africa Hunger and Poverty Facts, available at http://www.worldhunger.org/africa-hunger-and-poverty-facts/
2   This is the equivalent of 1,25 US dollars per day. Statistic is drawn from Poverty in Africa. Facts available at http://borgenproject.org/10-quick-facts-about-poverty-in-africa/

It is also important to recognise that Gugu's situation described above is an example of what the current status quo is like; but, most of us would agree, it is not what a decent, just world *ought* to look like. This raises an important distinction between the descriptive (what the world is like) and the prescriptive or normative (how the world *should* be or *ought* to be). It is a descriptive fact that some human beings are violent towards other human beings; but, from a normative point of view, that is wrong. It is a descriptive fact that some people suffer from conditions associated with poverty; but, from a normative point of view, society should ensure that everyone has enough to live a decent life.

We have already engaged in previous chapters with the debate about the relationship between law and morality. Natural lawyers, as we saw, believe there is a necessary connection between the two, whilst positivists think that law and morality are conceptually distinct domains. Even so, positivists recognise that morality is of practical importance in guiding how law (as it is descriptively) *ought* to be (normatively). Morality is thus relevant to the question of which laws to adopt on both views of the nature of law.

The next section of this book examines important questions around what law ought to be and how law ought to be constructed. Since law often concerns very fundamental matters in relation to individual lives, the morality connected with law is often framed in terms of the idea of justice. This part of the book will thus deal specifically with what we term 'theories of justice'. A number of important questions arise in this regard:
- What is justice and how is it conceived in different theories?
- Are there different kinds of justice?
- What do the different theories of justice require in relation to the distribution of resources?
- What is the relationship between justice and the idea of fundamental rights?
- Are there distinctively African theories of justice and what are their characteristics?
- What would a just distribution of resources look like for African societies?

The structure of the discussion in this book will be as follows: Chapters 6–8 deal with distributive justice, namely, the manner in which resources in society must be distributed. Chapter 6 will discuss a number of key theories of justice and examine the question as to how a state should be organised to ensure a just distribution in the society. Chapter 7 will discuss the question as to who has duties flowing from the demands of justice. In particular, it will focus on the duties of individuals (and corporations) and how extensive these duties are. In the case of Gugu, it will ask whether the duties are only those of the state or do individuals around her and her family also have obligations? What about the duties of companies? Chapter 8 will examine the question concerning who is included within the domain of justice: to whom do we owe duties? It will raise questions of those outside our political communities (foreigners/refugees) as well as those beyond the human species (non-human animals).

Chapters 9–10 concern different kinds of justice, the civil and the criminal as opposed to the distributive. In other words, they will ask what must be done to repair wrongs that have been done in the past, and how, if at all, should wrongdoers be punished? Chapter 9 will examine the question of major historical wrongs, such as the confiscation of the land from the majority of black people in South Africa. What does reparative justice require to right these wrongs? Chapter 10 will deal with wrongs on a more individual level, such as where someone perpetrates a crime. Which penalty would be just to mete out for a given crime?

In approaching theories of justice, it is important to be aware that each distinct theory engages the following key components:

- *A theory of value.* This concerns what the theory regards as being of value in society and in individual lives.
- *General principles as to how society ought to be structured.* These are principles which tell us, for instance, the pattern of distribution of those things that are of value.

It will be useful to bear in mind this distinction between what to allocate and how to allocate it when engaging with the different theories in question.

## 6.2   Utilitarianism

The first theory of justice we will study is known as utilitarianism. It forms part of one of the central schools of ethics, which evaluates what is just in relation to the consequences that flow from an action or policy. This theory can be seen to be a feature of human thinking across societies and, in its written form, has received expressions going back to Ancient Greece. In the nineteenth century, it was developed philosophically by two famous British philosophers, Jeremy Bentham (1748–1832) and John Stuart Mill (1806–1873). Both were involved in social reform movements and advocated, amongst other things, for causes such as the abolition of the death penalty, equality of men and women, decriminalisation of homosexuality and the decent treatment of animals. The text below comes from John Stuart Mill's excellent and clear outline of the theory of utilitarianism.

| PRIMARY TEXTS | **Text 1  Mill: Utilitarianism and justice** |
| --- | --- |

The creed which accepts as the foundation of morals, Utility, or the Greatest Happiness Principle, holds that actions are right in proportion as they tend to promote happiness, wrong as they tend to produce the reverse of happiness. By happiness is intended pleasure, and the absence of pain; by unhappiness, pain, and the privation of pleasure. To give a clear view of the moral standard set up by the theory, much more requires to be said; in particular, what things it includes in the ideas of pain and pleasure; and to what extent this is left an open question. But these supplementary explanations do not affect the theory of life on which this theory of morality is grounded – namely, that pleasure, and freedom from pain, are the only things desirable as ends; and that all desirable things (which are as numerous in the utilitarian as in any other scheme) are desirable either for the pleasure inherent in themselves, or as means to the promotion of pleasure and the prevention of pain … .

… According to the Greatest Happiness Principle, as above explained, the ultimate end, with reference to and for the sake of which all other things are desirable (whether we are considering our own good or that of other people), is an existence exempt as far as possible from pain, and as rich as possible in enjoyments, both in point of quantity and quality; the test of quality, and the rule for measuring it against quantity, being the preference felt by those who in their opportunities of experience, to which must be added their habits of self-consciousness and self-observation, are best furnished with the means of comparison. This, being, according to the utilitarian opinion, the end of human action, is necessarily also the standard of morality; which may accordingly be defined, the rules and precepts for human conduct, by the observance of which an existence such as has been described might be, to the greatest extent possible, secured to all mankind; and not to them only, but, so far as the nature of things admits, to the whole sentient creation ...[3]

... To have a right, then, is, I conceive, to have something which society ought to defend me in the possession of. If the objector goes on to ask, why it ought? I can give him no other reason than general utility. If that expression does not seem to convey a sufficient feeling of the strength of the obligation, nor to account for the peculiar energy of the feeling, it is because there goes to the composition of the sentiment, not a rational only, but also an animal element, the thirst for retaliation; and this thirst derives its intensity, as well as its moral justification, from the extraordinarily important and impressive kind of utility which is concerned. The interest involved is that of security, to every one's feelings the most vital of all interests. All other earthly benefits are needed by one person, not needed by another; and many of them can, if necessary, be cheerfully foregone, or replaced by something else; but security no human being can possibly do without on it we depend for all our immunity from evil, and for the whole value of all and every good, beyond the passing moment; since nothing but the gratification of the instant could be of any worth to us, if we could be deprived of anything the next instant by whoever was momentarily stronger than ourselves. Now this most indispensable of all necessaries, after physical nutriment, cannot be had, unless the machinery for providing it is kept unintermittedly in active play. Our notion, therefore, of the claim we have on our fellow-creatures to join in making safe for us the very groundwork of our existence, gathers feelings around it so much more intense than those concerned in any of the more common cases of utility, that the difference in degree (as is often the case in psychology) becomes a real difference in kind. The claim assumes that character of absoluteness, that apparent infinity, and incommensurability with all other considerations, which constitute the distinction between the feeling of right and wrong and that of ordinary expediency and inexpediency. The feelings concerned are so powerful, and we count so positively on finding a responsive feeling in others (all being alike interested), that ought and should grow into must, and recognised indispensability becomes a moral necessity, analogous to physical, and often not inferior to it in binding force exhorted.[4]

## Questions

1. According to utilitarianism, what makes an action right or wrong?
2. What is of value in life and the world, according to the utilitarian?
3. Is the metric of value only quantitative or qualitative too? How is quality measured?
4. What is a right according to the utilitarian? How is it connected to utility?
5. What is the reason for the special feeling and attention given to fundamental rights?
6. What is the relationship between justice (the domain of rights) and utility?
7. What does utilitarianism imply about the distribution of resources in society?

---

3   The first two extracts are from Mill 1863 *Utilitarianism* Chapter two, available at https://www.utilitarianism.com/mill5.htm

4   The final extract is from Mill 1863 Chapter five, available at https://www.utilitarianism.com/mill5.htm

The central principle of utilitarian ethics is the following: *acts are right insofar as they promote the greatest amount of happiness (utility)*. In understanding what this principle means there is a need to clarify a number of points.

## 6.2.1 The utilitarian theory of value

First, it is important to understand what is of value in life for the utilitarian. What is meant by happiness or utility? According to John Stuart Mill, happiness is understood in terms of pleasure, and unhappiness in terms of pain. This is what we term a 'mental state' or 'hedonist' account of utility. Our happiness or unhappiness is constituted solely by whether we subjectively have good experiences (pleasure) or bad experiences (pain). In Bentham's formulation of utilitarianism, what mattered was merely the *quantity* of pleasure or pain that was experienced. If I have to decide whether to go drinking tonight or to a concert of my favourite artist, the decision should be determined by what will bring the most amount of pleasure. Bentham points out that this is more complicated than is ordinarily thought. Some experiences like drinking alcohol may initially be pleasurable but later cause pain (a hangover). Drinking in excess may also inhibit the experience of other pleasures (like going to a concert, which is compatible with drinking in moderation). These examples are rooted in individual lives. When we attempt to calculate the overarching quantity of pleasure and pain caused by a legislative measure, for instance, the calculation becomes very complicated indeed.

For Mill, however, it is not simply the quantity of pleasure that matters but the quality of pleasure too. For him, maximising happiness will involve taking account of the type of pleasures experienced. For human beings, Mill states that there are intuitively higher pleasures – like intellectual stimulation and aesthetic experiences of art and music – and lower pleasures – such as eating and sex. What is a higher or lower pleasure for a human being is revealed by individuals who have experienced both and self-consciously recognised which is qualitatively better. After all, who could reasonably judge between two pleasures who has not felt both of them?

Utilitarianism does not, of course, require that one abstain from lower pleasures but would emphasise (on Mill's account) the higher quality pleasures. Importantly, utilitarianism must take account of the pleasures of all those that can experience pleasure or pain – including non-human animals (an issue we will discuss in Chapter 8). Some critics of Mill's theory question whether he can really succeed in distinguishing between higher and lower quality pleasures where pleasure is the only metric of value.

## 6.2.2 The utilitarian principle and its operation

When we look at the general principle as to what ought to be done, utilitarianism tells us that we must act so as to maximise happiness overall, taking everyone's interests into account. The principle thus requires us to achieve the most amount (it is a *maximising* principle) of what is valued (happiness), giving weight to all individual beings (who experience pleasure or pain). This must be distinguished from achieving the principle of the egoist who acts to promote the greatest happiness of herself. For the utilitarian, we must act to promote the greatest amount of happiness no matter whose happiness it is, that is, regardless of her race, gender, nationality or even species. Utilitarianism thus includes in it an idea of equality or impartiality. Every individual's pleasure or pain is equal and is calculated and included in deciding what to do. It is as, we have said before, *consequentialist*. The morality or otherwise of an action is determined by its consequences, not the intentions of the party in question or the actions in themselves.

Utilitarianism can be applied to individual acts, as well as decisions of a society or state on how to legislate or act. Let us consider the case of Gugu mentioned at the start of this chapter and how utilitarianism would apply to it. As we saw, Gugu and her children are suffering from malnutrition and the threat of eviction, and she has removed her children from school. What would utilitarianism require of the government? It seems that Gugu and her children are experiencing a large degree of pain. If all other things were equal, the government should adopt measures to ensure that Gugu has a place for her children to go, has adequate food for herself and her children, and can send her children to learn and study at school.

However, the problem comes with the clause 'if all other things were equal'. We know that in South Africa, millions of people are suffering from similar conditions to Gugu. This means that the government could not justify addressing her condition alone but would have to provide similar treatment for others. That would involve a significant amount of expenditure by the government and, for instance, require increased taxation of the middle and wealthy classes in the society. Such taxation could reduce the earnings of these people and thus cause them some degree of pain. The government may have to shift resources from say fixing roads in middle class areas and looking after parks to providing welfare and housing benefits for people like Gugu and those similarly situated. Utilitarianism would require us to try and maximise overall happiness. It might, initially, seem obvious that the small amount of pain caused to a wealthy minority is worth a large increase in the happiness of the needy majority. At the same time, such a calculation often involves some degree of complexity. If the measures introduced by the government to help those in need lead the rich minority to leave the country, foreign investors to take their capital elsewhere, and inflation to run wild, everyone will be worse off.

Ultimately, what must be done for the utilitarian must maximise happiness, which will involve a weighing of interests and consequences: who will benefit the most and who will lose the least? This example highlights the fact that utilitarianism in principle can seem to allow a rather easy conclusion, where everyone benefits from a particular measure. The problem is that often some benefit and others lose, which causes a conflict between them. Utilitarianism requires us to focus on the maximisation of utility; but, in doing so, some people's interests may be disregarded. For utilitarianism, the correct distribution of goods in society is whichever one achieves maximum happiness or utility. That, however, is consistent with some people being very miserable. It does not matter how the maximum happiness is distributed amongst people, or even if some people are happy *because* others are sad (a racist, for instance, may in fact derive pleasure from pain or harm caused to individuals who belong to the race they are biased against). This leads to the difficulty that the greater gains of some can compensate for lesser losses of others.[5] Another example will highlight how this problem arises and creates a difficulty for utilitarianism and its compatibility with fundamental rights.

### 6.2.3   Utilitarianism and fundamental rights

Joe is a South African homeless person, who lives on the streets of Johannesburg. He has become severely depressed and drinks a lot. He does not have any family who can assist him in his plight. Recently, there has been a gruesome murder of a black South African. The community is convinced that the perpetrator is a Nigerian. This has led to an upsurge of xenophobic sentiments, with many people in the community calling for reprisal attacks on all foreigners. The police are under pressure to arrest someone and to try to avoid further

---

5   Rawls 1999 *A Theory of Justice* at 23.

murders and violent assaults. They decide to frame Joe for the murder and reason as follows on utilitarian grounds: if we arrest Joe for the murder, Joe will experience significant disutility and be deprived of his freedom. The society, however, will feel safer. He is also South African and so this will help to reduce the negative xenophobic attitudes that have arisen. Joe's arrest could also help reduce any further xenophobic violence, which could harm more people than simply Joe. They therefore arrest Joe and announce that the murderer has been found. The people, for the time being, are placated.[6]

Whilst arresting Joe has had positive effects on the society, most people would object: it is unfair to arrest wrongfully and frame an innocent man. It also violates the intuitive fundamental rights of Joe. The South African Constitution in section 12 provides for the right to freedom and security of the person, which includes the right not to be deprived of freedom arbitrarily and without just cause. The objection is that utilitarianism encourages the sacrifice of Joe's liberty and happiness due to the positive consequences of doing so for the vast majority of the community. The greatest happiness or general welfare overrides the deep unfairness of the police's actions to the individual. In fact, the utilitarian would have to deny there is any unfairness at all, as happiness is maximised overall and Joe's individual interests are simply outweighed by the many others who benefit from his arrest. Utilitarianism, the claim goes, thus has a problem recognising the fundamental rights of individuals.

There are a number of responses that can be made to this claim by those wishing to defend utilitarianism. The first would be to say that the police, in fact, did not do their calculations properly and utilitarianism would not encourage arresting Joe. If what the police did were to be uncovered, then the community as a whole would feel even less safe. They would recognise that the police were not doing their job properly and also could potentially arrest any innocent person. Such a scenario would lead to deep feelings of insecurity across the society and thus high levels of unhappiness. Of course, the guilty murderer would also still be on the loose and thus possibly strike again, which would create more pain and suffering. A proper evaluation of the consequences of the police's actions would thus not lead to utilitarianism sanctioning the arrest of an innocent person.

The critic could, however, respond that perhaps the police were pretty sure that the public would not find out, given that only one or two of them were involved in the framing. They also regarded it as pretty unlikely they could find the murderer. The essential point of the critic is that it is not certain on a utilitarian theory whether arresting an innocent person is wrong. This, it would be claimed, is problematic for a theory of morality. Ultimately, the question will always involve whether happiness is maximised by one outcome or the other, which renders the fundamental rights of individuals always potentially in peril.

A further series of responses is provided by John Stuart Mill in the passage quoted above. He first notes how severe the experience is for someone to have an interference with his or her fundamental rights. As such, when we look at the utilitarian calculations, we need to place a strong weight on the side of individuals who have their rights infringed that, in general, would outweigh any weaker benefits to others. Thus, in the example relating to Joe, the harms to him are so severe, it is claimed, that they would outweigh the benefits to the community the police see as flowing from their actions.

This response is not, however, entirely convincing. We might, for instance, point out that some in the community might have their lives and bodies assaulted if Joe is not arrested and so interests of a similar weight are at stake. Utilitarianism could then still allow similar harms to a greater number of people to mandate arresting and framing an innocent person.

---

6   Nozick 1974 *Anarchy, State, and Utopia* at 41, amongst others, raises these kind of problems with utilitarianism.

Mill provides another response, which is a fascinating development of the utilitarian theory. For him, utilitarianism is entirely compatible with fundamental rights and not at odds with it. Rights, for him, are those things that would maximally benefit society were individuals in the possession of them. Fundamental rights for Mill are deeply connected to the notion of security and ensuring that people are protected from having the very basis of their existence taken away by others. Their fundamental importance to individuals leads to their being seen to have a very special and priority space within moral thinking. If we want to achieve the greatest happiness for society, it is then imperative that we, in fact, protect the fundamental rights of individuals. For Mill, therefore, a society where everyone is worried about arbitrary arrest would be a society that has a low utility in comparison to one where that possibility is taken off the table. Utilitarianism for Mill, therefore, requires and justifies the recognition of certain fundamental rights that cannot easily be overridden by considerations of the welfare of a greater number.

Thus, this line of thinking suggests that the question should not be in every situation – is this particular action (like arresting Joe) justified by advancing the greatest amount of happiness overall? The theory that promotes evaluating whether particular acts are compatible with the utilitarian principle is known as *act utilitarianism*. Apart from the problems raised above, namely that act utilitarianism could not adequately recognise fundamental rights, philosophers point to several other problems with this view. To evaluate each act against the principle of utility in each situation is likely to lead people to make mistakes in their calculations of what will achieve the greatest utility. When faced with particular circumstances, people often lack adequate information and enough time, and also are subject to particular biases and pressures flowing from the situation itself (the pressure on the police, for instance, to calm the community down and arrest someone).

An alternative version of utilitarianism is suggested. It involves looking at matters in a wider way and attempting to develop certain *rules* or *principles* that are justified by the principle of utility and cover most individual cases. This approach – which requires a longer-term evaluation of utility and its impact on the rules and principles of morality – is referred to as *rule utilitarianism*. Rule utilitarianism involves developing principles and rules which guide day-to-day decision-making that we decide on serious reflection and after long-standing evidence generally maximise utility or happiness. Knowing that societies where people are constantly afraid of wrongful arrest have a low level of utility, we thus develop a general principle that individuals have a right to be free from arbitrary arrest. That right is likely to maximise utility in a society and so will forbid the arrest of a person like Joe. Similarly, we know that societies in which people are fearful that they are not going to be able to have enough food at the end of the month involve low levels of utility. Thus, we create a general right to adequate food, which the state must provide if an individual cannot.

In general, in rule utilitarianism, we decide in advance which rules or principles we should follow which guide us in day-to-day decision-making. Thus, the police when confronted with the scenario of whether to arrest Joe would not be entitled to do so as they are bound to respect his right to be free from arbitrary arrest. In rule utilitarianism, the only time we need to refer directly to the principle of utility and calculate overall happiness is when there are conflicts of rights or principles in a particular case. For instance, to resolve a clash between the right to freedom of expression and the right to dignity of an individual, we need to have reference to what would achieve the greatest happiness in the long run if one right were prioritised over the other.

Rule utilitarianism is a more plausible version of the theory. Nevertheless, there are some critics who do not think it fully solves the problem utilitarianism has with fundamental rights. Consider, for instance, the law in many countries that sexual intercourse between members of the same sex is illegal. Recently, Uganda proposed a law that increased penalties for such behaviour to include life imprisonment and the death penalty. Gay and lesbian people – whose human expression of love and affection is given effect through romantic and sexual connections with members of the same sex – are permanent minorities in virtually all societies in the world including Uganda. The criminalisation of same-sex sexual intercourse has been condemned in most of the respected courts around the world as violating basic fundamental rights to equality, dignity, privacy, and freedom and security of the person.

Let us accept that the vast majority of Ugandans are firmly opposed to individuals being allowed to express their sexual orientation through engaging in sexual intercourse with members of the same sex. The question for the rule utilitarian would be whether a law that criminalises same-sex sexual intercourse (and indeed increases the penalties for such behaviour) advances the overall happiness? In a society where there is a high degree of homophobia and a small minority of gay and lesbian people, it is conceivable that the answer to this question would be that such a law does maximise the general happiness. If that is so, then the rule utilitarian would still have a major problem with fundamental rights, as it is quite clear that any such law violates the rights to equality, dignity, privacy, and freedom and security of the person.

Given these difficulties with utilitarianism, we will now consider a leading modern theory of justice developed by the philosopher John Rawls, which has been proposed as a leading alternative to utilitarianism.

## 6.3 Justice as fairness

John Rawls is regarded as one of the most important and influential political philosophers of the twentieth century. He spent most of his life at Harvard and sought to articulate a theory of justice that many have found compelling. Rawls' first important book that deals with justice in the sphere of a particular society is called *A Theory of Justice* (1971). He later developed his thinking in *Political Liberalism* (1993). He also developed a theory of international justice in the *Law of Peoples* (1999). For Rawls, the principles of justice are those that flow from a particular procedure, which he calls the 'original position'.

| PRIMARY TEXTS | Text 2 John Rawls: The original position |
| --- | --- |

Let us begin with how we might be led to the original position and the reasons for using it. The following line of thought might lead us to it: we start with the organizing idea of society as a fair system of cooperation between free and equal persons. Immediately the question arises as to how the fair terms of cooperation are specified. For example: Are they specified by an authority distinct from the persons cooperating, say, by God's law? Or are these terms recognized by everyone as fair by reference to a moral order of values, say, by rational intuition, or by reference to what some have viewed as "natural law"? Or are they settled by an agreement reached by free and equal citizens engaged in cooperation, and made in view of what they regard as their reciprocal advantage, or good?

Justice as fairness adopts a form of the last answer: the fair terms of social cooperation are to be given by an agreement entered into by those engaged in it. One reason it does this is that, given the assumption of reasonable pluralism, citizens cannot agree on any moral authority, say a sacred text or a religious institution or tradition. Nor can they agree about a moral order of values or the dictates of what some view as natural law. So what better alternative is there than an agreement between citizens themselves reached under conditions that are fair for all?

6.2 Now this agreement, like any other, must be entered into under certain conditions if it is to be a valid agreement from the point of view of political justice. In particular, these conditions must situate free and equal persons fairly and must permit some to have an unfair bargaining advantage over others. Further, threats of force and coercion, deception and fraud, and so on must be ruled out. So far, so good. These considerations are familiar from everyday life. But agreements in everyday life are made in determinate situations within the background institutions of the basic structure, and the particular features of these situations affect the terms of the agreement reached. Clearly, unless those situations satisfy the conditions for valid and fair agreements, the terms agreed to will not be regarded as fair. Justice as fairness hopes to extend the idea of a fair agreement to the basic structure itself. Here we face a serious difficulty for any political conception of justice that uses the idea of contract, whether or not the contract is social. The difficulty is this: we must specify a point of view from which a fair agreement between free and equal persons can be reached, but this point of view must be removed from and not distorted by the particular features and circumstances of the existing basic structure. The original position, with the feature I have called the "veil of ignorance" (Theory, §24), specifies this point of view. In the original position, the parties are not allowed to know the social positions or the particular comprehensive doctrines of the persons they represent. They also do not know persons' race and ethnic group, sex, or various native endowments such as strength and intelligence, all within the normal range. We express these limits on information figuratively by saying the parties are behind a veil of ignorance. One reason why the original position must abstract from the contingencies—the particular features and circumstances of persons—within the basic structure is that the conditions for a fair agreement between free and equal persons on the first principles of justice for that structure must eliminate the bargaining advantages that inevitably arise over time within any society as a result of cumulative and social historical tendencies. "To persons according to their threat advantage" (or their *de facto* political power, or wealth, or native endowments) is not the basis of political justice. Contingent historical advantages and accidental influences from the past should not affect an agreement on principles that are to regulate the basic structure from the present into the future.

6.3 The idea of the original position is proposed, then, as the answer to the question of how to extend the idea of a fair agreement to an agreement on principles of political justice for the basic structure. That position is set up as a situation that is fair to the parties as free and equal, and as properly informed and rational. Thus any agreement made by the parties as citizens' representatives is fair. Since the content of the agreement concerns the principles of justice for the basic structure, the agreement in the original position specifies the fair terms of social cooperation between citizens regarded as such persons. Hence the name: Justice as fairness.[7]

### Text 3  John Rawls: Two principles of justice

13.1 To try to answer our question, let us turn to a revised statement of the two principles of justice discussed in Theory, §§11-14. They should now read:

(a) Each person has the same indefeasible claim to a fully adequate scheme of basic liberties, which scheme is compatible with the same scheme of liberties for all, and

(b) Social and economic inequalities are to satisfy two conditions: first, they are to be attached to offices and positions open to all under conditions of fair equality of opportunity, and second, they are to be to the greatest benefit of the least-advantaged members of society (the difference principle).

As I explained below, the first principle is prior to the second; also, in the second principle fair equality of opportunity is prior to the difference principle. This priority means that in applying a principle (or checking it against test cases) we assume that the prior principles are fully satisfied. We seek a principle of distribution (in the narrower sense) that holds within the setting of background institutions that secure the basic equal liberties (including the fair value of the political liberties) as well as fair equality of opportunity. How far that principle holds outside that setting is a separate question we shall not consider.[8]

... To conclude: given the conception of the person in justice as fairness, we say that the parties assume that, as persons with the two moral powers and a determinate complete conception of the good, citizens have, among other interests, certain religious, philosophical, and moral interests, and that the fulfillment of these interests must, if possible, be guaranteed. There are some things we cannot give up; they are not negotiable. If the advocate of average utility rejects this, then for the moment we have reached an impasse.

It is essential that the two principles are an available and satisfactory alternative which does not impose excessive strains of commitment. They not only protect the basic rights and liberties but provide an adequate complement of the primary goods required for exercising and enjoying those freedoms. There are indeed situations in which there is no way to avoid putting our basic freedoms in jeopardy, but with the two principles available, the original position is not one of them. To agree to the principle of average utility would be to aim for still greater well-being while jeopardizing those rights and liberties without sufficient reason.[9]

---

7   Rawls 2001 *Justice as Fairness: A Restatement* at 14–16.
8   Rawls 2001 at 42–43.
9   Rawls 2001 at 104.

**Questions**
1. Why do the principles of justice not flow from religious law?
2. Where do the principles of justice come from?
3. What are the characteristics of the original position and the ideas connected with it?
4. What does Rawls mean by the term the 'veil of ignorance'?
5. What is the value of the original position in determining principles of justice?
6. What are the principles of justice according to Rawls that should guide the way society is structured?
7. Why would decision-makers in the original position not support utilitarianism as the correct theory of justice?
8. Why would decision-makers support the two principles of justice?

## 6.3.1   Foundational ideas in constructing Rawls' theory of justice

John Rawls asks the fundamental question: where do principles of justice come from? He considers three main possibilities. The first is a response many people give and say that justice flows from the laws given by a religious authority such as God. This answer has problems on its own terms, which cannot be discussed here. Nevertheless, the fundamental difficulty is that societies like South Africa include a diverse range of people who have different religious views. Some people are atheists, but others identify as engaging African spiritual traditions as well as Christian, Jewish, Hindu and Muslim traditions. People disagree about whether there is a God and also about what God's laws are. Even if we recognise there is a majority of South Africans who are Christian, for instance, there are differences within Christianity. It is thus not possible in a diverse society to use religion as the basis for determining with some broad agreement what constitutes justice or not.

The second answer Rawls considers is that justice flows from a notion of 'natural law' that is out there which determines how laws ought to be constructed. The problem he raises is that just like with religion, there is often a problem with identifying these natural laws and there is fundamental disagreement about many important moral questions.

The third alternative that he favours is that justice flows from an agreement that would be reached between people under fair conditions. Determining principles of justice is itself a special kind of project. It is one that relates to the determination of the basic rules of society, which he terms *the basic structure of society*. In legal terms, we can imagine this project as being similar to attempting to develop a constitution, which is the most fundamental law in a society.

To determine these principles, Rawls thus believes it is necessary to set up a procedure that would enable all the people in society to reach a fair agreement about them. The goal of setting up this procedure and principles is to establish what he terms a *well-ordered society*. Such a society is one that is established on the basis of fair terms of co-operation between people and guided by publicly recognised rules. The idea of co-operation is very closely connected to the idea of fairness. Such a society is one in which individuals can participate on a basis that everyone can reasonably accept.

It is also of importance to Rawls to understand the individuals (or persons) who will live in such a society and accept the principles of justice. Such individuals must be ones who can agree to fair terms of co-operation. As such, they have two important capacities. The first is a *capacity for a sense of justice* – this means that they understand and can act upon the principles of justice they determine; the second is that they have a *capacity for having a conception of the good* – this means they have some idea of what is valuable for them in life (for instance, living with a same-sex partner, following Islam, becoming a judge). The ability to have a conception of the good, to think about it and reason about it renders individuals *free*. The fact that they all have this ability to the requisite degree renders them *equal*.

If we conceive of a society in this way, and a person in this way, how are we to develop principles of justice? Rawls suggests we imagine a situation in which the fair terms of co-operation are agreed to between free and equal citizens, who are born into the society in which they lead their lives. This situation is called the original position. We can imagine this as a kind of constitutional convention. It is important to understand it is a conceptual, imaginary situation, not an actual one. The question posed to each person sitting in the convention is: what would you agree to if you were trying to do the best for yourself but still wanted to co-operate on fair terms with others?

Now, if we start today and create such a convention, Rawls worries that the situation will not be fair. There are two main problems he identifies in this regard. First, there is the *problem of differential power positions*. People who are in positions of privilege will wish to preserve those privileges. The wealthy, for instance, will seek to preserve their wealth. Similarly, we know that race, gender and many other factors have conferred advantages on individuals. If you are in a better and stronger position than others when we begin the discussion on principles of justice, you will not agree to rules that place you in a lower position. The problem is that we are already playing the game and the question is how can we avoid entrenching existing privileges in setting up the basic principles and rules?

This point also leads to a major question concerning the fairness of entrenching privileges that were not deserved. A lot of privileges and benefits flow from natural or social factors, which one has no role in bringing about. In relation to natural factors, consider the fact that people with particular talents often are able to receive greater financial benefits than those without those talents. For example, Sibongile Khumalo is widely regarded as an outstanding South African opera singer. Yet, she was just fortunate to be born with a beautiful voice. Whilst she might have worked hard to develop her voice, ultimately, it is not clearly fair that she should have more opportunities to earn wealth in society than other people who simply lack such a voice. It is thus not clear why people deserve to benefit from their talents simply because they were born with them. Some contend that the benefits flow from the fact that there is a lot of hard work involved in developing one's talents. Yet, some people put in the hard work but simply lack the talents – is it fair that they are disadvantaged simply because of the natural luck that some people have? A similar point can be made in relation to social advantages. Is there any reason it is fair for an individual to benefit from being born into a wealthy and loving family? Or for having a certain race, gender or religion?

To address these problems, which he sometimes labels 'arbitrariness', Rawls suggests that the agreement entered into in the original position must be concluded under certain conditions. These require excluding certain information about participants in order to situate them fairly. Excluding information prevents some from having bargaining advantages and helps remove threats of deception or coercion. Rawls calls this feature the '*veil of ignorance*': parties in the original position are behind a veil, knowing nothing about their particular positions in society (whether they are wealthy or poor; talented or untalented). They also do not know whether they adhere to particular doctrines (Judaism, Christianity, Islam or Buddhism) nor any information concerning their race, ethnic group, sex and gender. They also do not know whether they have various talents such as strength and intelligence. People also do not know how various alternatives will affect their own particular case and, in fact, they could land up being anyone in a given society. Since we are symmetrically situated to others and equal in the original position, the fact that we occupy a particular social position is not a reason to expect others to accept a conception of justice that favours that position. The fact that we affirm a particular religious, philosophical or moral doctrine is not a reason for us to propose or expect others to accept principles of justice that favour those who adhere to that doctrine.

If we deprive people of all knowledge about their situations, the question then arises: how are people in the original position to make decisions about principles of justice? They cannot base their judgement on specific conceptions of the good of individuals and they cannot choose principles of justice without understanding what people value. It is thus necessary to have some idea of what people value. In order to address this problem, Rawls creates what he terms a 'thin' conception of the good. It does not require reference to specific values of individuals but covers what we all must generally value. To understand this point, let us recognise that every individual has a conception of the good (of what it is to live well). In order to realise this conception of the good, every individual needs certain goods. Consider health: because humans are biological beings, they cannot achieve anything in life without such a good. Rawls refers to these things as '*primary goods*' – the things we need in order to realise our individual particular goals and purposes. Rawls thinks we need certain *natural* primary goods such as health and basic intelligence. We also need certain *social* primary goods in order to function as citizens within any given society. These social primary goods include the following:

a)  basic rights and liberties
b)  freedom of movement and choice of occupation against a range of diverse opportunities
c)  ability to hold office and responsibility in the political and economic institutions of a society
d)  income and wealth
e)  self-respect.

Thus, we cannot achieve our goals and purposes if the government tells us what we must do and where we must go. We also need resources, such as income and wealth, to achieve most purposes. Interestingly, Rawls also recognises that we need a certain psychological attitude of self-respect to be able to achieve our goals. He means by this that we need a belief that our aims are worthwhile, as well as a sense of confidence that it is possible to achieve them. In later work he also claims that leisure time and freedom from pain are social primary goods, things we need in order to pursue any number of conceptions of the good. Rawls believes that justice is about the distribution of the social primary goods. The natural ones – such as health – are not something that the state can or should distribute as this would involve, for instance, the forcible allocation of organs, a serious violation of the bodily integrity of individuals.

## 6.3.2   Why utilitarianism would be rejected and Rawls' alternative principles of justice

So, we have in the original position, no information concerning our particular positions in society. We do have information about needing social primary goods. With these ideas in place, the question asked of all those in the original position is which principles of justice would you – as free and equal persons – agree to? You could, importantly, land up anywhere in the society once the veil of ignorance is removed.

Rawls first considers the possibility that individuals in the original position would choose the utilitarian principle to maximise the greatest happiness. This principle importantly enshrines a basic equality that every individual must be counted in the ultimate equation of interest satisfaction. The problem, however, is that some individuals could possibly lose out really badly in the maximising process. As we saw, individuals like Joe could be subject to arbitrary arrest and prevented from realising their conceptions of the good. If you are the weakest person, would you accept a situation where you could be killed or tortured for the interests of the majority? Rawls thinks that such a situation is not one that any sane person acting in their self-interest (understood in terms of securing primary goods) would accept. Indeed, he does not believe anyone could realistically live up to an agreement that would risk such an outcome. This is what he means by the 'strains of commitment'. It would push people beyond the bounds of an agreement that they could commit to honour.

Rawls goes further to say that utilitarianism is problematic because it allows for an argument of the following sort: slavery is unjust in that the advantages to the slaveholder do not counterbalance disadvantages to the slave and society at large. We could imagine a similar argument to say that apartheid is unjust because the advantages to white people do not outweigh the disadvantages to black people. Rawls argues though that some benefits should not be weighed at all. His theory would reject reasoning that would place any values on the gains to a slaveholder or white people under apartheid. The reason for this is that individual persons in the original position could land up anywhere. They could land up as the slaveholder or the slave, the white person or the black person under apartheid. As such, they simply would refuse to accept that the benefits to the slaveholder or white person have any weight in determining the principles of justice as they would be rejected out of hand. Such benefits could never be justified to the slave or black person under apartheid, as they could never accept them as having any legitimacy. For Rawls, some benefits should not be weighed as they cannot be mutually affirmed. One would thus be unreasonable to agree in the original position to any principle that permitted slavery or apartheid, since doing so would not ensure for oneself an adequate amount of social primary goods, including liberties, opportunities, wealth and self-respect.

If utilitarianism is rejected, what is the alternative? Rawls puts forward a series of principles of justice that he thinks would be accepted in the original position. They are:

> **Principle 1:** Each person has an equal claim to a fully adequate scheme of basic rights and liberties, compatible with a like scheme for all (**equal basic liberties principle**)
> **Principle 2:** Social and economic inequalities are to satisfy two conditions:
> a) they are to be attached to positions and offices open to all under fair equality of opportunity (**fair equality of opportunity principle**)
> b) they are to be to the greatest benefit of the least advantaged (**difference principle**).

Rawls suggests these principles would be accepted by people in the original position. Why? Well, no matter which conception of the good one has, one will need protection for liberty to achieve it. The first principle essentially ensures equal protection for rights and liberties of persons. That principle also recognises that liberties are meaningless without certain basic protections for socio-economic goods that enable people to take advantage of their liberties. If one lacks any income or wealth and is starving, it becomes difficult, for instance, to muster the energy to gather together and protest one's situation, even if one has freedom of association guaranteed in the constitution. It would also therefore support protecting certain basic socio-economic rights.

Rawls, however, considers how social and economic goods in society should be distributed overall. He imagines that the first thought individuals would have is that everyone should have an equal bundle of social and economic resources. If we could land up anywhere when the veil of ignorance is removed, we would want at least the same as others. It is possible though that such an equal sharing of resources might involve a very minimal level of well-being with no-one going above a very small amount.

Rawls wonders, however, if it is possible that introducing a certain level of inequality could lead everyone to do better than a situation of equality. Could it be possible that with some inequality in the distribution of resources everyone could have more social primary goods than pure equality? This is the foundation of what he terms the 'difference principle'. If I were in the original position, and I could do better for myself by allowing some inequality of wealth (for instance), it would be rational for me to do so. Why would such a circumstance be a likely scenario? Rawls imagines a society in which everyone is purely equal and there are no incentives to do better. In such societies, productivity often goes down (as was shown in some of the communist countries that experimented with this model). Everyone is on the same level and has no incentive to improve. Let us say then that a society introduces some incentives for hard work or entrepreneurship. This would, of course, involve some level of material inequality between people. Yet, Rawls argues, if everyone is materially better off, that is, if the worst off group where there is some inequality would be better off than where there is a strict equality, no one has a reason to complain in the original position.

Let us take the example of mobile phones. They have revolutionised people's lives in society and innovations continue to expand access to knowledge (the internet) and communications. Across Africa, almost 82% of the population has a mobile phone.[10] Prior to their invention, communications for poor individuals were very difficult and they often lacked fixed lines due to a lack of infrastructure or the inability to pay. With the invention of mobile phones, most poor people were enabled to communicate much more easily and, more recently, gain access to knowledge sources that were previously impossible for them. Much of the innovation that has taken place in the mobile phone sector has occurred through private initiatives, which people took to be able to earn money from their inventions. That money they earned, of course, was more than those who had not innovated in the same way and so created material inequality. The argument though is that this is a form of inequality that helps improve the lives of everyone. Even though the wealthy phone innovators have much greater wealth and income than others due to their inventions, a system which enabled such inventions helped increase the primary goods of everyone, including the poor. The difference principle would thus be met in this case as allowing financial benefits to private individuals in the telephony industry does still provide the greatest benefit even to those who are least advantaged.

This example highlights how people would think in the original position. Since an individual could land up anywhere, the individual would want to assess what would happen if they landed up as the weakest individuals in the society. They would therefore want to create either a situation of equality or, better according to Rawls, allow for inequalities that would render them better off than the state of equality.

Understanding this point also allows us to recognise that there will be limits placed on inequalities by the difference principle. Consider the example of pharmaceutical companies that develop new drugs. They often claim that they place huge amounts of money into research and development of new drugs. Their hope is to be able to reap financial rewards

10   See http://www.itwebafrica.com/mobile/339-africa/237068-85-mobile-subscription-penetration-in-sub-saharan-africa

from any new discoveries of cures to diseases. The legal system has allowed them to exploit any discoveries by enabling them to place patents on those discoveries. Patents mean that they are allowed to be the sole provider of a drug for a set period of time (20 years). This means that they can create a monopoly over the production of these drugs; since they are the only supplier, they can charge the price that they wish. Pharmaceutical companies have often charged huge amounts of money for HIV/AIDS drugs and, recently, for new cancer treatments. For instance, pharmaceutical companies were charging over R180 000/year to provide the promising new drug for breast cancer treatment called Herceptin.[11]

These huge amounts of money of course provide incentives to make new discoveries and cures. Yet, the majority of people in a place like South Africa cannot gain access to medicines at such high prices. This means that individuals suffering from life-threatening conditions such as breast cancer can literally die before being granted access to such a cure. These people are the least advantaged. It is unlikely individuals in the original position who could land up in the situation of these persons would accept a situation where pharmaceutical companies can make massive profits at the expense of people's healthcare (and thus lives). The current legal regime of allowing uncapped profits from patents would be condemned by the difference principle. Inequalities that fail to advance the position of those worst off (and there can be no advance if one is simply left to die) would not be allowed. Rawls thus provides us with principles that can critique a number of our current institutions and render them more just.

Rawls recognises another principle that applies to socio-economic inequalities. That is, that they must be attached to positions and offices that are open to all and offer equal opportunities to all to occupy them. This principle can be thought of in relation to political offices, for instance. It is necessary to have leaders in a society who make policy. Many democracies also have representatives who give expression to the thoughts and ideologies of particular parts of the population. These political positions often come with economic benefits as well as having a particular status. Whilst these positions are necessary for the functioning of a society, and people in the original position would recognise that, Rawls contends that individuals would want equally to have a chance to occupy these positions. No one can claim to occupy a political office, for instance, without allowing others the opportunity to do likewise. Ultimately, the principle enshrines again a certain idea of equality.

It is important to recognise that Rawls thinks people would agree to a principle of 'fair' as opposed to merely 'formal' equality of opportunity. 'Formal' equality of opportunity would mean prohibiting, for instance, individuals from being excluded from running for political office on the basis of their race or gender. Yet, even if no formal discrimination exists, people might be prevented from running for such a political office due to receiving a poor education or lacking the money to run for political office. 'Fair' equality of opportunity requires ensuring that every individual really has the ability to run for political office. This would require ensuring individuals are provided with sufficient education to enable them to run for political office. It would also involve requiring the public to provide at least a minimum degree of funding that would make it possible to run for political office. To achieve this fair equality of opportunity, it would be permissible, according to Rawls, to tax those who have more to ensure equality of opportunity is fairly distributed in society.

Rawls, therefore outlines principles of justice which give expression to what might be termed an egalitarian form of liberalism. There is the equal protection of rights and liberties, and material inequalities are only allowed when they are to the benefit of those least

---

11     ALL4WOMEN 'Herceptin: Hopeful New Breast Cancer Treatment' (March 25, 2014), available at http://www.all4women. co.za/176637/health/herceptin-hopeful-new-breast-cancer-treatment

advantaged. These principles are the outcome of a procedure of decision-making – called the original position – which is set up in a certain way (the veil of ignorance and primary goods) so as to reflect the situations in which fair agreement can be reached between persons.

### 6.3.3   What are the implications of Rawls' theory for the distribution of resources?

What would Rawls' principles of justice imply for Gugu's situation? It is useful to try and think through the implications in this concrete context to understand what the principles would imply. The first principle, as we saw, protects certain basic rights and liberties. Whilst traditionally conceived to involve freedoms, Rawls recognises that a level of resources is required in order for one's freedoms to mean anything. If one is literally starving and too weak to function, one cannot really participate in the political community or exercise freedoms such as those of association and religion. Rawls' theory would therefore support the recognition of certain basic socio-economic rights that protect the access of individuals to some resources. Gugu and her family seem to be below this minimum and could therefore claim access to adequate food and a space in which to stay securely.

The fact that Gugu has had to take her children from school will, of course, also affect their fair equality of opportunity in later years. It is thus necessary that Gugu be placed in a position where she has enough income to enable her children to go to school and receive a decent education.

Finally, the existing state of South Africa is one in which there is a high degree of inequality between rich and poor, with some being very wealthy and some very poor. In a situation where Gugu is not able to provide adequate food for her children and herself, it is clear that these inequalities are not to the greatest benefit of the least advantaged. The government, therefore, would be required by the difference principle to take urgent measures to ensure that inequalities are lessened and that the process of doing so ensures that the plight of the least advantaged is speedily improved. The urgency of Gugu's situation means that the government will have a strong obligation to do so as a matter of priority.

At the same time, one of the difficulties with the difference principle is understanding how much inequality in the distribution of socio-economic resources is in fact to the greatest benefit of the least advantaged. It is perhaps a difficulty with the principle that it admits of different readings that lie on a spectrum and could lead to vastly different visions of society. Which kind of society would be the one in which the worst-off group is the best off?

A *strong capitalist* reading would essentially place great emphasis on the incentives argument discussed above and contend that a society in which people are willing to take risks for their own economic benefit will ultimately lead to the advancement of all, including the least advantaged. Roughly, the poor under capitalism would be much better off than the poor under socialism, an argument that the African National Congress, for instance, in South Africa accepted after the demise of apartheid. Such an interpretation might also make the argument – often made by defenders of capitalism – that the capitalist system has thus far been the only one that has shown the capacity over the long term to lift large numbers of people out of poverty. Such a reading would thus be consistent with high levels of inequality.

A *strong socialist* reading would contend, however, that social and economic inequalities are generally harmful to the least advantaged in terms of education, access to general opportunities and also their sense of their own position in society. High levels of inequality also lead to less stable societies, which can undermine the primary goods of everyone. Such a reading would tend towards very little inequality in the distribution of resources in society. It is possible to make arguments that fall between these two extremes on the spectrum.

As such, the concrete implications of Rawls' view for the distribution of resources in society are relatively unclear. Rawls' own writing appears to support a middle position. That would entail allowing for a capitalist system and the inequalities that flow from it with a heavily redistributive taxation system that limits the degree of inequality and provides resources for economic support to the least advantaged, and protects democratic processes from being manipulated by the super-rich.

### 6.3.4 A social contract?

As we saw, the original position attempts to model the idea of reaching an agreement between people in society who do not know their current positions or where they would land up. The agreement, however, is different from some other versions of the social contract. These versions imagine an actual contract between people in society. Sometimes, this contract could be an express one. In South Africa, for instance, people voted in 1994 for a parliament that was expressly designed to pass a final constitution. When their representatives passed the Constitution in 1997, it could be said that they – on behalf of all the people – reached a clear social contract as to the basis on which South Africans would live together. Of course, the problem with such an express contract is that the consent to it would be valid at the time, but what happens across time? Twenty years later, a large number of people have been born and have reached voting age who never had a say in the original election. Does this mean that the Constitution is now no longer legitimate? There are few moments in history where countries have express social contracts and, arguably, it would be destabilising to have continual votes on the basic document that regulates social interactions.

In light thereof, other theorists speak about a tacit social contract. Even though people in 2017 have not expressly agreed to the social contract, by continuing to live in South Africa, for instance, and abide by its laws, they implicitly agree to the legitimacy of the constitutional order. This argument, however, has many problems. Once a constitutional order has been set up, people may feel coerced to follow the laws on pain of criminal sanctions or imprisonment. It is hard to infer consent from people in these circumstances, where they may feel coerced. Tacit theories of consent also struggle to determine what people are consenting to. Do they simply accept that the rule of law must be followed or do they accept all the provisions of the constitutional order?

Rawls attempts to avoid these problems with both express and tacit versions of the social contract by focusing on an imaginary or hypothetical situation – the original position – in which people would be reasonable to reach agreement. He argues that if we imagine ourselves into this position and we construct it in a particular, intuitively fair way, people will choose the two principles of justice. Ronald Dworkin, however, questioned the force of this argument. We understand, he tells us, that there is force in holding people to an agreement they voluntarily reached. Yet, the agreement in the original position is not an actual agreement – it is a hypothetical one. There is no actual constitutional convention or vote. It is what we imagine people would agree to under the conditions of the original position. A hypothetical agreement, Dworkin tells us, is, however, 'not simply a pale form of an actual contract, it is no contract at all'.[12]

Rawls responds to say that the original position is not of significance because it is a hypothetical *agreement* between parties. Instead, it is a way of modelling two important things: a) it provides an understanding of what fair conditions would be for reaching agreement between people about the fair terms of co-operation in society. We thus imagine

---

12  Dworkin 1977 at 151.

that people are all equal in the original position with no-one being able to force anyone else to adopt their point of view. Each has to make arguments that others can reasonably accept; and b) it models restrictions on the reasons that people may put forward for acceptance of their proposals. Thus, it recognises that the fact that someone is wealthy or poor, black or white, is no reason on its own to accept a social arrangement favouring any particular group. In order to capture this point, people are understood to be behind a veil of ignorance, meaning that they could land up in any social position and thus must reason in ways that could be accepted by anyone. The original position thus provides a model for thinking through whether principles of justice are fair or not. Think about it: is it perhaps a useful device, for instance, to consider the laws and actions of the government in South Africa today by determining whether everyone in society could reasonably accept those actions?

### 6.3.5   The distribution of natural talents

One of the controversial aspects of Rawls' theory is his view, as we saw, on the natural talents of individuals. Rawls is of a view that these flow from a 'natural lottery' and that no-one deserves the talents they have. As such, they ideally should not benefit economically from having those talents. Whilst we may play a role in developing our talents, of course, we would not have been able to do so without having the talents in the first place. Rawls also thinks that the desire to develop also arises from features of the self – motivation – and perhaps the environment in which one grew up – ambitious or, conversely, ineffectual parents – which one did not choose. As such, the original position is meant to offer a way in which to ensure that the benefits from the talents of individuals are distributed across society and not only in relation to a particular individual.

Robert Nozick was a famous critic of John Rawls from the 'libertarian school' and he developed a very interesting alternative theory of justice in his book *Anarchy, State and Utopia* (1974). Nozick's work will be engaged further in Chapter 7. One of his strong critiques of Rawls is in relation to his treatment of natural talents. He denies the fact that holding a natural talent is arbitrary and automatically leads to injustice of distributions that result from talents. To illustrate his point, he gives the example of grades for examinations. He suggests we imagine that a group of students are asked to decide how to distribute grades for examinations. There would be a temptation, for instance, for students to agree that everyone would equally receive the same high grade.[13] Yet, Nozick argues that such a distribution of grades would make a nonsense of the notion of grading itself. Grades, he contents, are not the kind of thing that can simply be distributed equally. They are linked to an evaluation of the performance of students in an examination and the knowledge and skills they demonstrate. The very point of grading becomes lost if we move towards an equal distribution of grades. Even though some people may naturally be fortunate to have a higher level of intelligence than others, we cannot change the process of grading to ignore a quality such as intelligence.

Nozick argues that the distribution of wealth in society is similar to grading. Rawls treats wealth, he says, as if it falls from heaven and is unconnected to what one has a right to in virtue of past transactions. Nozick, however, contends that the distribution of wealth and resources in society is fundamentally connected to the past manner in which it has been acquired. He gives an example that we can modify by considering the famous South African opera singer Sibongile Khumalo mentioned earlier.[14] Nozick imagines everyone starts off

---

13   See Nozick 1974 *Anarchy, State, and Utopia* at 199–204 for his detailed discussion of this example.
14   Nozick utilises a famous basketball player called Wilt Chamberlain to illustrate this argument in Nozick 1974 at 161–164.

with an equal amount of money, say R1 000. One thousand people, however, want to see Sibongile Khumalo sing and each are willing to pay R10 to do so. Each of these 1 000 people now has R990 and Sibongile Khumalo – who receives their ticket fees – will have R11 000. Whilst Khumalo may not have deserved her singing talent, people voluntarily have transferred money to her. As such, the new distribution of wealth – though unequal – is fair and just as it flow freely from people's choices, regardless of whether it helps the worst-off group in the long run. This argument has attracted much debate in the philosophical literature and students who are interested can read some of the literature mentioned in the bibliography. Try to think through what responses Rawls could provide to this argument.

Having explored utilitarianism and the theory of John Rawls about the distribution of resources in society, we now turn to consider certain theories of justice from Africa and their implications for the distribution of resources in society.

## 6.4 Theories of justice in Africa

In exploring African theories of justice, we will have reference to a number of African thinkers. We start off with Text 4 from one of the most famous judgments of the Constitutional Court in South Africa, dealing with the constitutionality of the death penalty. In it, Justice Yvonne Mokgoro outlines an understanding of the key African value of *ubuntu*. Text 5 is by Oritsegbubemi Anthony Oyowe, a lecturer in the Department of Philosophy at the University of the Western Cape. He is also the Secretary of the Philosophical Society of Southern Africa. Oyowe provides an exploration of the important relationship between individuals and communities in African philosophy. Text 6 is by the famous Ghanaian political philosopher, Kwame Gyekye, who is Professor of Philosophy at the University of Ghana. It grapples with the implications of African philosophical thinking for the distribution of resources in society. The thought of further philosophers, which develop some of these ideas, will be engaged in the discussions on each of these texts.

| PRIMARY TEXTS | **Text 4 Yvonne Mokgoro on the idea of *ubuntu*** |
| --- | --- |
| | Although South Africans have a history of deep divisions characterised by strife and conflict, one shared value and ideal that runs like a golden thread across cultural lines, is the value of *ubuntu* – a notion now coming to be generally articulated in this country ... |
| | ... Generally, *ubuntu* translates as 'humaneness'. In its most fundamental sense, it translates as personhood and 'morality'. Metaphorically, it expresses itself in *umuntu ngumuntu ngabantu*, describing the significance of group solidarity on survival issues so central to the survival of communities. While it envelops the key values of group solidarity, compassion, respect, human dignity, conformity to basic norms and collective unity, in its fundamental sense it denotes humanity and morality. Its spirit emphasises respect for human dignity, marking a shift from confrontation to conciliation. In South Africa *ubuntu* has become a notion with particular resonance in the building of a democracy. It is part of our 'rainbow' heritage, though it might have operated and still operates differently in diverse community settings.[15] |

---

15  *S v Makwanyane* 1995 (3) SA 391 (CC) at paras 307–308.

**Text 5  Oritsegbubemi Anthony Oyowe on the priority of the collective in some African philosophy and a critique thereof**

Perhaps, the most common and widely cited conception of human nature discussed in the African literature on self is the idea that the human being depends both descriptively and normatively on the community. Consider John Mbiti who debunked the idea of the lone individual in African thought suggesting that the existence of the individual human subject could not be rendered intelligible without first presupposing the collective. 'The individual', he says, 'does not and cannot exist alone except corporately.' And the reason is that 'he owes his existence to other people ... He is simply a part of the whole' so that the '... community must therefore make, create, or produce the individual'[16] (1969, p. 108 ...).

Additionally, it is typical of proponents of the view that the community takes priority over the individual to insist that there is a normative element to the idea of a human being. Menkiti (1984), for instance, argues that 'the various societies found in traditional Africa routinely accepted this fact that personhood is the sort of thing, which has to be attained, and is attained in direct proportion as one participates in communal life through the discharge of the various obligations defined by one's stations' (p. 176). Elsewhere, Wiredu (2009) adds that the African conception of a human being is one of 'a morally sound adult who has demonstrated in practice a sense of responsibility to household, lineage and society at large' (p. 16). That is to say, human nature is also a function of approximating certain cultural cum moral ideals.

... All of the foregoing seems attractive. But there are very good reasons as to why we might want to reject this conception of human nature and the human rights conception it supposedly engenders ... the idea of the collective as 'producing' the individual implicates a questionable idea of community i.e., the idea of community as a natural formation. It is the idea of the community as some fixed, unchangeable entity existing independently of the individual ... It is questionable because in order for the community to create or produce the individual its existence must be independent of and prior to the existence of individual human beings.

I should note that my criticism here raises two critical questions:

(a)  Is the community prior to the individual?

(b)  Is the community a fixed entity?

These questions are fundamentally related. In response to the first question, I have noted that an answer in the affirmative necessarily involves an idea of community as some fixed and unchangeable entity that exists independently of individuals. With regards to the second question, it is worth pointing out that if the community is a fixed and unchanging entity then it is quite difficult to account for the ways in which individual actions continually shape the community. It seems

16   Mbiti 1969 *African Religions and Philosophy.*

rather odd to conceive of community as an empty set as it were, existing independently of individual members. This is because the very existence of a community and its realisation is dependent on individuals who constitute that community. Adherents of this idea of community as fixed, unchanging entity fail to consider that individual human beings have multiple interests and do not neatly fit into rigid wholes. Instead, they are part of more fluid communities that are always changing, which changes and the overall nature of community is dependent ultimately on the creative inputs of individual members ...

... [This conception of community] prioritises collective or people's rights over individual rights ... by construing collective rights and interests as existing over and above individual ones, this conception of human nature yields the undesirable consequence that individual rights must always make way for collective rights. It seems to me that the litmus test for any serious conception of human rights is its performance over a range of conflict situations; so-called African conceptions of human rights readily imply that human rights always give way to traditional values (e.g. communal harmony, kinship relations, etc.) whenever these values conflict. Moreover, prioritising collective rights over individual ones may summarily exclude non-conforming individuals and minorities.

These upshots of the preference for collective rights are not particularly desirable if a conception of human rights is to be regarded as plausible ... This is because they show human rights to be of less value and incapable of protecting the dignity of human beings (that is, if they are readily overridden by other non-rights considerations). A conception that yields these results cannot be a plausible conception of human rights.[17]

### Text 6  Kwame Gyekye on African socialism

The caring ethos of traditional African society is stressed in statements by Nyerere: "In our traditional African society we were individuals within a community. We took care of the community, and the community took care of us."[18] His perception of the traditional society as a caring society appears also in his seeing society "as an extension of the basic family,"[19] the implication being that the care and compassion demonstrated among the members of the basic family find similar expression in the sensitive attitudes members of the wider society have (or, will or should have) toward the needs of other members. Nyerere also makes the following noteworthy observation about the ethical nature of the traditional society:

> Both the "rich" and the "poor" individual were completely secure in African society ... Nobody starved, either of food or of human dignity, because he lacked personal wealth; he could depend on the wealth possessed by the community of which he was a member. That was socialism. This is socialism.[20]

17   Oyowe 2014 *Human Rights Review* at 332–334.
18   Nyerere 1968 *Ujamaa: Essays on Socialism* at 6–7.
19   Nyerere 1968 at 12.
20   Nyerere 1968 at 3–4; emphasis in original.

Thus, for Nyerere socialism is ministering to the needs—especially the material needs—of the individual members of the society. And when he adds almost immediately after the foregoing quoted statement that "socialism is essentially **distributive**,"[21] he is certainly alluding to the ethical, rather than the productive (economic) nature of an ideological system. This is because, as I said, distribution of the wealth of a society is the function essentially of the socioethical norms and ideals cherished by a society. Even though it may be true, as Nyerere avers, that the individual in the traditional society can depend on the wealth of the community, there is no implication whatsoever that the wealth possessed by the community is "socialistically" produced, that is, produced by the whole community into a kind of public or communal barn into which any individual can, as it were, dip her hands when she is in some material need. The individual's dependence on the wealth of the community derives from—and is an aspect of—the practice of social and humanist morality, from the fulfillment of the moral obligations of people to their fellow human beings. In his articulation of "African socialism" Nyerere employs such expressions as "caring," "familyhood," "wellbeing" "reciprocity," "togetherness," "human equality," "a sense of security," and "universal hospitality."[22] These expressions are patently and essentially socioethical, rather than economic.[23]

... The foregoing analysis of the articulations of African socialism suggests the deep conviction that the African advocates of the ideology of socialism understood it in terms of the original sense of the Latin word *socialis*, which means "belonging to companionship, or fellowship," "fellow feeling." This root meaning of socialism suggests the idea of people living together, helping one another, caring for one another, and being just to one another. This meaning is unambiguously social or ethical but has hardly anything to do directly with an economic arrangement, such as a centrally planned economy. I am not suggesting, to be sure, that a choice of a socialist economy cannot or should not be made by an African nation. But I doubt that the premises of the arguments for such a choice should essentially be derived from the African socioethical communitarian doctrine. The socioethical sense of the word socialis, however, is on all fours with the communitarian and humanist interpretations provided by the advocates of African socialism in the postcolonial era. It is, as I have said elsewhere, the humanist ethic of the traditional African society that spawned the communitarian social structure; for, insuring the welfare and interests of each member of society can best be accomplished within the communitarian social and ethical framework.[24] I conclude that the use of the term "socialism" in reference to understanding the nature of the society envisaged by the African political leaders and thinkers under the inspiration of the African tradition is a misnomer. That term was undoubtedly used as a surrogate for "humanism."[25]

---

21  Nyerere 1968 at 4.
22  Nyerere 1968 at 1–12.
23  Gyekye 1997 *Tradition and Modernity: Philosophical Reflections on the African Experience* at 160.
24  Gyekye 1997 at 162.
25  Gyekye 1997 at 162.

**Questions**

1.  How do African traditions of thought approach questions of justice?
2.  What does the notion of *ubuntu* mean, according to Justice Mokgoro?
3.  Is *ubuntu* an ethic that focuses on individuals or the community?
4.  According to Oyowe, what is the way in which – in many African systems of thought – the individual is conceived of in relation to the community?
5.  Why, according to Oyowe, is this conception of the relationship between the individual and the community unattractive?
6.  What, according to Oyowe, are the moral implications of this idea of the individual in relation to the community for human rights? Why would such an African conception struggle to give a plausible account of human rights?
7.  What alternative view of community is articulated by Gyekye and how would it support the idea of fundamental rights?
8.  According to Nyerere, what approach to the economic organisation of society characterises African societies in relation to the distribution of resources?
9.  According to Gyekye, what does Nyerere mean by socialism?
10. According to Gyekye, do African approaches to distributive justice necessarily involve socialism? What two meanings of socialism does he distinguish?

## 6.4.1   *Ubuntu*, personhood and ethics in African philosophy

There are of course a diversity of ethical ideas and concepts in Africa. A central key idea, however, which has run through many diverse groups is often captured by the term '*ubuntu*'. Indeed, the South African philosopher, Mogobe Ramose, claims that '*ubuntu* is the basis of African philosophy'.[26] In explaining the notion of *ubuntu*, the Constitutional Court Judge Yvonne Mokgoro refers to an Nguni saying *umuntu ngumuntu ngabantu*, which is often translated as 'a person is a person through other people'. There is a similar saying in Sotho '*Motho ke motho ka batho babang*'. As stated, the principle can have both a metaphysical and an ethical interpretation, which are elaborated upon in the Oyowe excerpt above. The metaphysical understanding – which deals with the place of human beings in the world – recognises that individual human beings can only become persons through their relationships with other people. Mbiti expresses this idea by recognising the role of the community in shaping the individual. On a basic level, children could not survive without their connections to their parents and a community, and who they are as individuals is constituted by the group of which they are a part. This saying, therefore, indicates the fundamentally social nature of human beings.

The ethical understanding of this idea is connected to this but different. It suggests that we only truly realise our potential to be what we ought to be – a real person – through the manner in which we relate to other people. There are two different interpretations that we can give of this idea. The one is that all human beings simply by virtue of existing within society are persons through relating to others. Menkiti and Wiredu (quoted by Oyowe above) suggest another view – that being a person in African thought is not a fixed state but rather it is something that one develops into. Personhood is not something, for these thinkers, that we are born with. It is something to be attained through realising our responsibilities towards

---

26   Ramose 1999 *African Philosophy through Ubuntu* at 35.

others. Only through acting in a morally praiseworthy manner do we fully realise our natures and become full persons. As we will see further below, this understanding of the person is controversial, particularly as it relates to human rights.

On either view of the person discussed above, ethics begins not just with the individual but the relationship between individuals. The ethical command would be for individuals to create harmonious forms of relationships between themselves that exhibit the respect to be accorded to other persons. Since our identities and relationships are formed in connection with one another, we must not undermine the personhood or well-being of anyone else and instead should seek to contribute towards their fulfilment. This vision of ethics sees individuals as intimately tied together in relations of interdependence. A diminishment of one person involves a diminishment of the personhood or moral virtue of others.

In attempting to understand these ideas more fully, Metz has suggested that we think of the ethical obligations imposed by *ubuntu* as involving two relational dimensions: identity and solidarity. To *identify* with others involves conceiving of ourselves as connected, as part of the same group, as a 'we'. It also involves engaging together in joint projects and co-ordinating our behaviour to realise shared ends. People who fail to meet these standards conceive of themselves as strictly separate from others, and often aim to undermine other people's ends. To adopt an attitude of *solidarity* involves a psychological state where people are sympathetic towards others and seek to help them for their own sake. Solidarity also involves an action-component of engaging in mutual aid so as to seek to benefit others. A failure of solidarity happens when people are indifferent towards the well-being of others or, worse, they take active actions that demonstrate ill-will through being hostile and cruel to others.[27] As Mokgoro has said elsewhere, '(H)armony is achieved through close and sympathetic social relations within the group – thus the notion *umuntu ngumuntu ngabantu*'.[28]

### 6.4.2   The relationship between the community and the individual in African philosophy

The value of *ubuntu* is often connected with particular practices in African societies. Thus, traditionally, many small-scale African communities have practised wide-ranging forms of home hospitality to visitors from another village, which are seen as expressions of the ethos underpinning *ubuntu*. The YouTube video in the footnote provides a clip of former president of South Africa, Nelson Mandela, explaining that *ubuntu* involved communities providing food for a traveller passing through a village, without him even having to ask for it.[29]

In more recent times, the value has been appealed to on a wider political scale to offer a philosophical vision as to how a very large and heterogeneous community should act. Mokgoro J, in the above passage, appeals to *ubuntu* in the context of deciding on whether the death penalty is constitutional or not, with her suggesting that it requires treating others with dignity, which the death penalty would fail to do. It is also utilised in the context of interpreting the rights in the Constitution. Inherent in this understanding is the idea that the notion of fundamental rights and *ubuntu* can be reconciled.

The relationship between protections for the individual and the community is one of the fundamental tensions that has been explored by a number of African philosophers. Some contend that *ubuntu* and African philosophy essentially is based upon an ethic which

---

27   Metz 2011 *African Human Rights Law Journal* at 538.
28   Mokgoro 1998 *Potchefstroom Electronic Law Journal* at 3.
29   See http://www.youtube.com/watch?v=HED4h00xPPA

recognises that the community is primary, and the individual is completely constituted by their relationship with others. We see this view expressed in Text 5 above by Oyowe who recognises the many African thinkers who have taken this approach. In this view, the community takes precedence over the individual and the individual is conceived of as simply existing to promote the ends of the community.[30] The primary moral notion, in this regard, is the idea of the duties owed by individuals to their community. Such a view would seem to run counter to the idea that individuals have fundamental rights that they can claim must be respected even if at some cost to the community.

This view, on first glance, would seem to have strong similarities with the utilitarian approach discussed above which could see the sacrifice of individual interests for the sake of the community. However, two different ideas of community are at play between utilitarianism and African thought. The problems utilitarianism has with fundamental rights arises from its *aggregation* of individual interests. The philosopher, Ifeanyi Menkiti, refers to this understanding of a collective as more like an association of separate individuals rather than a true community. In African thought, on the other hand, Menkiti argues, communities are collectivities in the truest sense which he suggests involves an 'organic dimension' to the relationship between the component individuals.[31] This seems to involve a tighter connection between individuals and an identification of themselves as one with the community. In addition to thinking of oneself as a part of the whole, it might also involve others in society relating to one in a harmonious manner and doing what they can to ensure that one is living well.

However, as Oyowe points out there are a number of deep problems with this view. He raises two important challenges in the above passage. First, the idea of community that is drawn on is problematic. It suggests that a community somehow exists naturally, is fixed, unchangeable and somehow exists independently of individuals. Only such a notion of community could be responsible for 'creating' individuals. Yet, communities seem to be dependent upon the individuals that make them up in all sorts of ways. Would a community exist without individuals? It does not seem that it would; the two are intimately intertwined. Oyowe provides a further argument on the basis of the fact that if the community is to be prior to the individual, it must be fixed and unchangeable. Yet, this is simply not true. Communities, in fact, change and these changes are brought about by the creativity and actions of individuals who shape the communities of which they are a part.

The second challenge concerns the prioritisation of the interests of the collective over those of the individual. Since the community is prior and the focus of value on this view, individual interests must yield when they clash with those of the community. If a community, for instance, holds the view that the expression of same-sex sexuality is wrong, a gay or lesbian individual will have to deny their natural sexual orientation and engage in relationships with members of the opposite sex, as the community norms take precedence over the rights of individuals to express themselves freely. This would apply to all minorities and those with a different view from prevailing community norms. Such a view would not adequately give expression to the value of individuals and thus be unable – according to Oyowe – adequately to respect individual rights. Of course, there is also a major question of what is in the interests of the community, which this approach needs to answer: is it what the majority wants? Or what prevailing social norms dictate? A majoritarian approach would,

---

30   Menkiti 1984 *African Philosophy: An Introduction* at 171, 180.
31   Menkiti 1984 at 179–180.

of course, always prejudice those who are minorities; focusing on prevailing social norms would lead African societies to become fundamentally conservative and continually to prioritise existing approaches and attitudes.

In light of these weaknesses in an approach that prioritises the community over the individual, an alternative view has been developed known as moderate communitarianism (a term coined by Kwame Gyekye). It recognises that community remains important in African ethics but that cannot be understood without having reference to the interests and well-being of individuals. The common good, for Gyekye, for instance, refers to 'a political or moral notion – not an exotic or weird notion – embracive of fundamental or essential goods, to which all individuals desire to have access'.[32] The common good is thus to be understood in relation to those features of a social system that enhance the well-being of all individuals, or at least without degrading or harming some in the process. Individuals are also to be understood as both communal in nature, but also having their own free will and vision of the life they wish to live. A community based on an ethic of *ubuntu* must be committed on this view to a recognition of the intrinsic value or dignity of the self that makes up the community. A commitment to the intrinsic value of the self will, in turn, require respect for the individuals and projects that they have: in other words, a commitment to respecting the fundamental rights of individuals.

Justice Mokgoro clearly subscribes to this understanding of *ubuntu* as she sees it as entirely compatible and linked to a notion of human dignity, which is focused on respect for the value of each individual. This view, however, differs from other notions of dignity, which tend to focus all moral thinking upon the nature of the individual and their claims. African theories can be compatible with a recognition of fundamental rights but they also foundationally recognise the value that exists in the *relationship* between individuals. As such, their focus is on building harmonious, amicable connections between individuals, which develop a particular type of community. That vision of community flows from and connects with a respect for the importance of individuals – it is not an instance of harmony to try to force someone to adopt a different vision of his or her life than he or she has created. It is also a vision of community that can embrace and deal with the difference amongst human beings. Thus, this vision of African philosophy, could well require African societies to respect minorities such as gays and lesbians. Requiring people to act against their deep natures or beliefs would not be an instance, on this view, of a decent community. The African ethos also makes demands on individuals to consider what is good for others and not to act in a manner that destroys the relationship between individuals. In this way, a balance is arguably achieved between the individual and the community.

The vision articulated by Gyekye and Mokgoro, which seeks to reconcile a respect for fundamental rights with a communitarian ethic, seems to assume that deep conflicts between individual and collective interests can always be avoided. However, that assumption is questionable as human societies often involve difficult clashes between individuals themselves and between individuals and the community.

Consider, for instance, the painting *The Spear* of the president of South Africa, Jacob Zuma. The painting depicts the President in a position reminiscent of the Soviet leader Lenin with his genitals exposed. The artist saw this as part of his freedom of expression to critique the form of masculinity and power that Jacob Zuma represents. There were many objections to the work, one of which suggested that it was highly inappropriate as in African tradition,

---

32   Gyekye 1997 *Tradition and Modernity: Philosophical Reflections on the African Experience* at 46.

a central value is to demonstrate some respect for elders. This did not mean that a leader like Jacob Zuma was immune from criticism, but simply that such criticism should be expressed with due respect for his dignity. The depiction of Jacob Zuma with his genitals exposed failed to offer such respect for his dignity and thus the community was entitled to prevent the picture from being shown. Such an argument would see the interests of the individual in free expression clash with the interests of the community in promoting an attitude of respect for elders.

It is interesting to contrast the approach of Rawls to such an example to that of the African theories discussed. Rawls would, as we saw, require protection for the liberties of individuals in his first principle. Consequently, the liberty of the artist would, arguably, trump that of the community. On the other hand, the African philosophical approach that prioritises the collective over the individual would clearly require the painting to be censored in the interests of the community. The implications of the moderate communitarian approach of Gyekye are less clear. They would recognise both the interests of the individual and the community and try to harmonise them. However, it is not easy to see how the interests of individuals in these circumstances could simply be reconciled with those of the community. As Oyowe points out in a critique of this position (not reproduced above), it appears that the moderate communitarian approach often simply restates the tension between the individual and the community rather than offering us a way to resolve it.[33] It thus fails to offer us a clear resolution to the tension that arises in cases such as the *The Spear* articulated above.

### 6.4.3 Are African views of distributive justice identical with socialism?

With this broad understanding of African theories of justice, we can now attempt to understand their implications for the distribution of resources in society. If individuals are fundamentally connected to one another, they must be concerned about the well-being and dignity of each other. The value of *ubuntu* thus gives rise to a fundamentally caring ethic between one individual and another. Since how we relate to each other partially constitutes one another's personhood, we cannot simply disconnect from each other.

Julius Nyerere, who led Tanzania to independence and became the first prime minister of Tanzania, thus recognises the idea that traditional African societies strongly took care of their members. He conceives of the manner in which individuals should treat one another as the way in which family members ideally treat one another. He thus demonstrates the manner in which a small-scale ethic might be extended to a wider political community. Families do not generally allow their members to starve and so, in traditional African communities, individuals could rely on the communal store of resources to claim a reasonable share for themselves. Great disparities between rich and poor were thus not common and there was a guarantee that basic resources would be provided to all.

Nyerere sees this approach of care for individuals' socio-economic position as being equivalent to socialism. In fact, he was a key proponent of the notion of African socialism, which in the case of Tanzania involved forcibly transferring people to collective farms which produced food. In this, he gave expression to the African view that strongly prioritised the collective (as he defined it) over the individual. This elicited resistance amongst the people and led to brutal crackdowns with villages being burnt and Tanzania becoming dependent on food aid. The disastrous nature of these policies (accepted even by Nyerere himself in the end) and the resistance of local people raised questions about whether in fact Nyerere had

---

33 Oyowe 2014 *Human Rights Review* at 339.

accurately created an equivalence between an African ethic of *ubuntu* and care with a socialist form of production. His failure to take account of the interests and views of individuals also demonstrated how such an approach elicits strong resistance and can fail to promote social harmony.

Kwame Gyekye, in Text 6 above, challenges the identification of these two things. He agrees with Nyerere about African societies caring about every individual in the society. Yet, he suggests that this ethic of care is completely distinct to the mode of production of resources in society. Socialism is often understood to involve a centrally planned economy with collective productive systems and collective ownership of land. Gyekye seeks to show how in fact traditional African agriculture and modes of production had key similarities to capitalist forms of organisation. There was a notion, he contends, of individual or family private ownership of land, a high value placed on the notion of wealth, and a focus on improving the accumulation of such wealth by particular individuals or at least families. Individuals and families were also entitled to trade with other individuals and families from within or without their communities freely. This, of course, did not mean that individuals had no ethical obligations to others in their community, but that the modes of production in society were not necessarily inherently communal or planned in nature.

Gyekye thus challenges the idea that African views of justice require a socialist economic method of organising society. The African approach, however, would also clearly not be compatible with unrestricted capitalism. It is not possible for individuals on the relational ethical view simply to dissociate from one another and claim that they have no responsibility for the welfare of other people. If a capitalist mode of production is utilised, an African ethic would counsel, on Gyekye's view, at least that all individuals be properly cared for. It seems that, in such a society, individuals could indeed make strong claims to the resources necessary for each to live an adequate life. As such, it seems, that an African ethic would strongly support the socio-economic rights, for instance, that are included in the South African Constitution.

Indeed, Henry Odera Oruka, Kenya's most influential philosopher in the 1980s and 1990s, who was a founder of the Department of Philosophy at the University of Nairobi and sought to record the philosophical thinking in traditional communities in Kenya, develops a theory of justice (applicable both in the domestic and international sphere) which expressly recognises what he terms the 'right to a human minimum'.[34] This right involves the 'justified demand by anybody that the world (not just his society) has the duty to ensure that he is not denied a chance to live a basically healthy life'.[35] To deny someone such a right would be to place them in a continued state of desperation in which we cannot expect people to act in rational ways. Thus, to fail to respect this right to a basic minimum would mean that we cannot require individuals to respect others and it could lead thus to the collapse of a community. Oruka engages with Rawls' theory but suggests that it places too much emphasis on liberty, which can compromise socio-economic equality. We could think, for instance, of the example of Sibongile Khumalo above and how unrestricted liberty can lead to a vast difference in the amount of resources people have. He suggests that the difference principle in Rawls' theory be given priority over the other two principles, which would allow limitations on liberty in the interests of the worst off.[36]

---

34   Oruka 1997 *Practical Philosophy* at 88.
35   Oruka 1997 at 88.
36   Oruka 1997 at 123–124.

Indeed, Oruka's view suggests another interesting contrast between African approaches and Rawls' theory. Too much inequality in society would, on African views, harm the relationships between individuals. People, on such approaches, should be willing to forego perhaps added financial benefits in order to ensure more equal and harmonious relationships in society. Rawls conceives of the greatest benefit to the least advantaged in terms of primary goods and, perhaps particularly, in relation to how much income/wealth is consistent with improving the lives of the worst off economically. African theories of justice would, however, point out that the quality of relationships between people are not adequately taken account of in the primary goods and need more emphasis in a theory of justice. Students can perhaps think how Rawls would respond to such a charge and whether certain of the primary goods Rawls identifies could account for developing decent quality relationships between persons.

If we return to the example of Gugu provided at the beginning of this chapter, what would the implications of the African perspectives we have studied be for her? The focus of such a view is on the relationships between individuals and, as such, each person must care for and respect every other person. Since relationships are also central to African views on justice, the connection that exists between individuals could also affect how resources should be distributed. A parent or spouse, for instance, may have greater obligations to some persons (their child or partner) than others. This stands in strong contrast with the other views we have studied, which are strictly impartial in nature. In terms of those views, the duties we owe to one another do not differ depending on the relationship in which we stand to them. This is a matter that will be covered in more detail in the next chapter.

Thabo's behaviour then in abandoning his wife would be condemned by such an African ethic that is modelled on an ideal familial relationship of identity and solidarity. Similarly, the threat by Thabo's family to evict her from the family homestead would go against the value of *ubuntu*, so long as she has been making an effort and not taking advantage of them. If we move from an ethical value to a theory of justice as to how society should be organised, *ubuntu* would clearly require that society not abandon individuals in the position of Gugu. Gugu must be enabled to earn a living and provided with opportunities to work for income for herself and her family. If she is unable to do so, she should be provided with the resources necessary to have adequate food for herself and her children. She would also need to be guaranteed a place where she and her family can live which is adequate and can meet their needs. The society would also need to guarantee her children a decent education and to ensure that they need not be kept home for fear of lacking adequate food.

Certain socio-economic rights would definitely be guaranteed to Gugu. The question is whether such an ethic would require a much more extensive distribution than just guarantees for a basic minimum. An African ethic would attend, it seems, very carefully to the relationship of dependency that Gugu and her family are in. Indeed, it would seek to create the conditions to remove her from such a situation and try and ensure that her relationships with others are characterised by an interdependence and a fundamental equality and respect. This may well require a highly extensive attempt to reduce strongly the inequality of the distribution of resources in society. How extensive this would be is not entirely clear but is worthwhile as a matter of debate for thinking through carefully, and it is likely that some of the philosophers discussed in this section will differ in that regard.

## 6.5   Conclusion

This chapter began the discussion of what constitutes justice in society. Three theories were considered:

1. *Utilitarianism.* This focuses on achieving the consequences that provide the greatest happiness in the long run, taking everyone's interests into account.
2. *Justice as fairness.* The background to this theory was explained as well as its key ideas. It focuses on ensuring equality in the basic rights and liberties of individuals; fair equality of opportunity; and that any socio-economic inequalities are to be to the greatest benefit of the least advantaged.
3. *African theories of justice.* The focus of this section was on the idea of *ubuntu* which was seen to require an ethic founded in the importance of creating relationships between individuals that are respectful, harmonious and akin to those of an extended family.

In each of these theories, we saw a range of different perspectives from which the justice or otherwise of a social arrangement must be judged. Utilitarianism we saw focuses on the aggregation of the happiness for individuals; justice as fairness focuses on the perspective of the least advantaged; African theories focus on the primacy of relationships between individuals.

The focus of this chapter went beyond merely outlining theories of justice to consider how resources should be distributed in society. By focusing on a concrete example of Gugu's plight, it sought to make clear the implications of the theories of justice considered in the chapter for at least the distribution of wealth and opportunities:

- We saw that it was not entirely clear how act utilitarianism would respond to Gugu's plight. A more sophisticated rule utilitarianism was likely to require the recognition of at least certain socio-economic rights that were due to her.
- Justice as fairness too had a degree of unclarity as to its exact implications for the distribution of resources in society (particularly of the difference principle for Gugu). It was likely to ensure that she also be guaranteed certain basic socio-economic rights, perhaps by giving incentives to people to be productive and then taxing them and redistributing resources to the poor.
- The idea of *ubuntu*, we saw, strongly embodies an ethics of care and would certainly require protection for Gugu's socio-economic rights. In fact, the idea might go beyond this level and how extensive the provision would be was unclear. We also saw a division between philosophers who think that African ethics requires a particular form of economic system (socialism) and those who think it is compatible with a wider variety of approaches including moderate forms of capitalism.

These theories each provide useful methods of thinking through the complex question of which distribution of resources in society is just and how to organise our social structures accordingly. The focus of this chapter has been on the implications of these theories for how the state should respond to the plight of Gugu. The next chapter elaborates further on theories of justice and, to do so, focuses on the duties of individuals and non-state actors to respond to the plight of individuals such as Gugu.

## POINTS TO CONSIDER

1. Can utilitarianism adequately protect fundamental rights? Does rule utilitarianism perform better than act utilitarianism in this regard?
2. What examples of current and past practices can you think of that would be restricted by the two principles of justice of John Rawls?
3. What is the force of the original position? Does it flow from being a hypothetical social contract?
4. What distribution of resources does the theory of justice of John Rawls promote? How would it differ from that promoted by utilitarianism?
5. Have any of the African theories you studied adequately resolved the tension between the rights of individuals and the overall good of the community? If not, can you think of a better way to approach the matter?
6. Can African theories of justice provide an alternative and compelling vision of how resources should be distributed in society?

# Chapter 7

# Who has duties flowing from justice?

ORITSEGBUBEMI OYOWE

## 7.1 Introduction

The notion of duty is integral to the idea of justice. Any conception of justice would be incomplete if it stopped short of specifying who has the duties that flow from justice, as well as the nature and scope of these duties. For example, suppose that justice requires that all university students should receive free quality education. It is reasonable to ask whose job it is to provide university students with free quality education.

That question invites us to identify the actor, or otherwise duty-bearer, that is, who is responsible to do what justice requires. This, in part, involves explaining why some person or entity, and not others, has this duty. Perhaps, they are related to university students in some way, or they simply have the capacity to fulfil that duty. It also provokes us to think deeply about what exactly the duty-bearer is being asked to do. Is the duty-bearer merely required not to prevent students from accessing free quality education or is he or she required to take active steps to ensure that they do? And finally, we have to consider the extent of the duty. How far should the duty-bearer go? Should he or she be wary of costs to himself or herself or rather set aside his or her own interests?

In the previous chapter, we engaged some of these issues, focusing primarily on the state. Indeed, it is typical to attribute the duties that flow from justice to state actors. But perhaps states are not the only responsible subjects of justice. Modern constitutional democracies like ours often provide that duties of justice flow to non-state actors as well. For instance, the South African Constitution clearly states that the provisions of the Bill of Rights:

> binds a natural or a juristic person if, and to the extent that, it is applicable, taking into account the nature of the right and the nature of any duty imposed by the right.[1]

Similar declarations can be found in other constitutions, including the Kenyan one, which explicitly states that the Bill of Rights binds persons, and not only the state. Further, state actors may turn out to be instruments of injustice either because they are corrupt, are simply too weak, or otherwise they simply lack the relevant capacity and resources to realise the aims of justice. These cases seem to suggest that we need 'a diversity of agents and agencies … that can contribute to justice'.[2]

In this chapter, we will examine whether and to what extent obligations of justice apply to non-state or private actors. In particular, we will examine not only the appropriate criteria for identifying duty-bearers, but also what these duties really amount to and the extent to which non-state actors are bound. To do this, we will consider various approaches to justice and their implications for three sets of concerns: the nature and extent of duties of justice and the identification of duty-bearers. First, we will consider an individualist perspective of justice by Robert Nozick, with a view to drawing its implications for the three concerns (section 7.2). We will then contrast this view with a Welfarist one, which, according to its proponent, Peter Singer, yields a different set of judgements regarding the three concerns (section 7.3). Our discussion of Singer will be followed by an evaluation of Kwame Gyekye's ostensibly moderate African communitarian perspective on justice, which purports to capture what it deems to be essentially lacking in the individualist and Welfarist approach (section 7.4). Initially, and up to this point, our focus will be on individual agents, in part because the idea of justice 'ultimately operates in the realm of freely chosen and accountable human action'.[3] Towards the end (section 7.4), however, we will extend the discussion to a different kind of non-state actor namely, the corporation. Specifically, we shall engage with the issue of whether and to what extent corporations as juristic persons have duties of justice. As will become clear, corporations are interesting in part because of the significant economic and financial power they wield, making them potential bearers of the duties flowing from justice.

More clearly, this chapter will engage with the following questions:

1. Do non-state actors have obligations of justice at all and to what extent?
2. What is the nature of the obligations flowing to private, non-state actors? Can we reasonably distinguish between duties of justice and duties of charity?
3. Are duties of justice necessarily correlated with rights?

---

1  Section 8(2).
2  O'Neill 2001 *Metaphilosophy* at 194.
3  Wettstein 2009 *Multinational Corporations and Global Justice* at 117.

4.  What criteria are appropriate for identifying duty-bearers and how do they impact our thinking on the nature and extent of duties of justice?
5.  Do corporations have legally binding obligations of justice and to what extent?

## 7.2   Justice, entitlements and negative duties

**PRIMARY TEXTS**

### Text 1   Robert Nozick's entitlement notion of justice[4]

Robert Nozick (1938–2002) was an American philosopher and until his death, Professor at Harvard University. He is widely known for his defense of libertarianism in *Anarchy, State and Utopia* (1974). The following extract is from that book.

> The central core of the notion of a property right in X, relative to which other parts of the notion are to be explained, is the right to determine what shall be done with X; the right to choose which of the constrained set of options concerning X shall be realized or attempted. ... My property rights in my knife allow me to leave it where I will, but not in your chest. I may choose which of the acceptable options involving the knife is to be realized. This notion of property helps us to understand why earlier theorists spoke of people as having property in themselves and their labor. They viewed each person as having a right to decide what would become of himself and what he would do, and as having a right to reap the benefits of what he did.
>
> When end-result principles of distributive justice are built into the legal structure of a society, they (as do most patterned principles) give each citizen an enforcible claim to some portion of the total social product; that is, to some portion of the sum total of the individually and jointly made products. ... It is on this batch of individual activities that patterned distributional principles give each individual an enforcible claim. Each person has a claim to the activities and the products of other persons, independently of whether the other persons enter into particular relationships that give rise to these claims, and independently of whether they voluntarily take these claims upon themselves, in charity or in exchange for something.
>
> Whether it is done through taxation on wages or on wages over a certain amount, or through seizure of profits, or through there being a big *social pot* so that it's not clear what's coming from where and what's going where, patterned principles of distributive justice involve appropriating the actions of other persons. ... If people force you to do certain work, or un-rewarded work, for a certain period of time, they decide what you are to do and what purposes your work is to serve apart from your decisions. This process whereby they take this decision from you makes them a part-owner of you; it gives them a property right in you. Just as having such partial control and power of decision, by right, over an animal or inanimate object would be to have a property right in it.

**Questions**

1.  What are the key principles of Nozick's entitlement theory of justice?
2.  How does Nozick characterise end-state and patterned theories of justice, and in what respects are they different?

---

4   Nozick 1974 *Anarchy, State and Utopia* at 171–172.

> 3. According to Nozick, a person's right to use the things he or she owns has certain limits. What determines the limit of that right?
> 4. In Nozick's view, under what condition is someone a part-owner of another?

## 7.2.1    Entitlements and the scope of justice

Robert Nozick adopts what may broadly be described as a rights-based approach to justice. In general, such approaches specify the range of entitlements that individual agents may reasonably claim against not only the state but also non-state actors. The discussion in the text is set in the context of distributive justice. The central issue concerns whether or not in seeking to distribute resources justly it is justified to interfere in the personal freedoms of others. In doing this, Nozick distinguishes between theories of justice that are end-state and patterned, on the one hand, and those that are historical and unpatterned, on the other. A theory of justice is end-state and patterned if it seeks to attain some just state of affairs correlated to some pre-determined metric. For example, a view of justice according to which justice entails that resources are distributed according to people's needs, or on the basis of merit would be both end-state and patterned. A historical and unpatterned theory of justice does not correlate just distribution with anything else; instead some distribution of resources is just in so far as people have come to possess what they have in the right way. This can occur in two separate ways. One can acquire things that have not been previously owned. For example, Sanele might come to own a well by digging one. If so, then Sanele owns it justly and is entitled to it. Alternatively, one might come to own something that was transferred to one. So, for example, Nozipho inherits a mine from her dad. If so, she is entitled to it and owns it justly (at least supposing that her dad also had done so). These two ways of coming to own something correspond respectively to Nozick's two principles: justice in acquisition and justice in transfer.

Nozick does not specify the principles of justice in acquisition and justice in transfer in detail. But he is clear that people are entitled to things that have been transferred to them and to things that they have produced or appropriated from nature, as long as enough is left in nature for others or the appropriation does not leave them worse off than they would be without it. This latter point is often referred to as the 'Lockean proviso' in Nozick's entitlement theory of justice. The condition is violated, according to Nozick, if any one person acquires all of something necessary to life such that there is no more left for others to possess.[5] For example, it would be wrong if some people acquire all of the water in South Africa as private property, leaving others without any or then charging exorbitant rates for it.

For Nozick, the subject of justice and the duties it imposes can be explained by reference to these fundamental entitlements people have and the constraints they place on what others may do relative to them. Since end-state or patterned principles of justice, which seek to redistribute resources in terms of some pattern, for example need and utility, would typically involve taking what belongs to some people and giving it to others in order to address the need or achieve greater utility in society, they undermine the fundamental entitlements of people. For example, if we took some of Patrice Motsepe's fortune and distributed it to poor South Africans in order to meet their needs, we would be depriving Patrice Motsepe of his fundamental entitlement – that is, his right to use his wealth, which he presumably acquired without harming others or being unfair, as he pleases. If such a principle were legally

---

5   Nozick 1974 at 179.

enforced, it would threaten the entitlements of people. And if we undermined the fundamental entitlements of others in order to realise some end, we would be using them as a mere means to that end. Nozick goes as far as claiming that this would imply that people do not really own themselves. That is, to the extent that someone can compel you to aid others, and you are not free do as you please with what you own, you may be said to be partly owned by someone else.

## 7.2.2   Duty, negative and positive

As we have seen, for Nozick justice requires that we honour the entitlements that people have. In making this point, he is mostly concerned with the limitations of the state towards individual entitlements. Even so, he does not deny that there are similar constraints on non-state actors. It is important to think about what these constraints are and what they reveal about Nozick's position on the nature of the duties of justice. His example does shed some light. 'My property rights in my knife', he writes, 'allow me to leave it where I will, but not in your chest'.[6] In other words, my right to do as I wish with my knife ends at the point where your rights are at stake. So, I may not interfere with your own rights. This is because each person has what Nozick regards as a right to self-ownership, which is an absolute right. The absolute right of each person thus places some limitation on what others can justifiably do to them.

Because it specifies what one should *not* do in relation to another, Nozick's account entails that duties of justice are essentially negative in character. A duty is negative if it obliges the duty-bearer to forebear from performing certain actions. For example, the duty not to kill is a negative one insofar as it requires non-interference towards another. Such duties are distinguished from positive ones. A positive duty requires the duty-bearer to perform, rather than refrain from performing, some action towards another. For example, the duty to aid Syrian refugees is positive in that it requires people to *do* something as opposed to not doing something. It is worth noting, however, that the claim that Nozick's account entails that the duties of justice are negative does not mean that it precludes positive duties, like giving to charity organisations, like Oxfam, or volunteering their time to the care of the needy and so on, for individuals. On the contrary, Nozick allows that individuals have positive duties in accordance with the demands of morality, but not justice. He simply denies that the state may rightly *force* people to live up to their positive duties.

## 7.2.3   Duty, justice and charity

As we have seen, Nozick's account suggests that positive duties fall outside the scope of justice. This observation relates to another pair of distinctions, namely, between duties of justice and duties of charity. The traditional way of distinguishing them requires us to separate those duties that are correlated with rights, and those that are not – duties of justice are associated with rights, whereas duties of charity are not.[7] In making sense of the distinction, the nineteenth-century British philosopher, John Stuart Mill, observes that:

> Justice implies something which it is not only right to do, and wrong not to do, but which some individual person can claim from us as his moral right. No one has a moral right to our generosity or beneficence because we are not morally bound to practice those virtues toward any given individual.[8]

---

6   Nozick 1974 at 171.
7   O'Neill 1996 *Towards Justice and Virtue: A Constructive Account of Practical Reasoning* at 139.
8   Mill 2001 *Utilitarianism* at 50.

The key idea is that whereas some duties are correlated with rights, others need not be so. For example, Sipho's negative duty not to kill Thabang is associated with Thabang's right to life, whereas Sipho's duty to aid a beggar on the street need not be based on the beggar's right to Sipho's money. This latter duty to the beggar is a matter of Sipho exhibiting generosity towards the beggar. Now consider that those obligations correlated with rights can be claimed by the bearer of the relevant rights, because they are morally owed these duties. That is, because Sipho's duty is based on something Thabang is entitled to, namely, Thabang's life, he is not merely being kind to Thabang when honouring this duty; instead, it is something he *owes* Thabang. In other words, duties correlated with rights are duties owed to particular individuals, or can be legitimately claimed by the right holder, who, in our example, is Thabang. Alternatively, the point is that morally owed duties are not merely optional, discretionary or expedient. Instead, the duty-bearer is obliged unconditionally to perform duties of this sort, in a way one may not be obliged to give alms to this particular beggar, leaving one free to help some other impoverished person.

Duties of justice are morally owed duties, of the sort Sipho has towards Thabang, precisely because they are associated with entitlements people have and can legitimately claim against others. In addition, they are unconditionally binding in that duty-bearers cannot justifiably exempt themselves from such duties and failure to perform them is always accompanied by moral blame. To see this, consider a slight modification of the above example. Sipho cannot claim from Thabang the same degree of generosity, for example requiring Thabang to pay for his drinks, as we would expect him to show to himself. This is not something that Sipho has a right to or that Thabang owes Sipho. Nor should anyone consider Thabang blameworthy for not buying Sipho drinks. This is not a duty of justice. And so, Thabang is not unconditionally bound to do it. As friends, though, this may be expected of Thabang. In that case, Thabang has a duty of charity towards Sipho. Just as in the earlier example, Sipho has a duty of charity towards the beggar – a duty not based on the beggar's rights, but on the generosity of Sipho. Duties of charity are not morally owed to others because they are not associated with rights or entitlements people have. Although expected, and performing them is morally praiseworthy, duties of charity are not unconditionally binding; Thabang may reasonably relieve himself from this obligation for whatever reason, precisely because Sipho is not entitled to his generosity. As such, they merely bind individual agents in conscience.

It is worth noting that this way of making sense of the distinction coincides with Immanuel Kant's distinction between perfect and imperfect duties. He specifically defines imperfect duties as lacking corresponding rights, that is, they are duties of charity, and perfect duties are instances of duties that are owed to others, that is, they are duties of justice. On this view, then, 'insofar as duties of charity are imperfect, you need not discharge them on all occasions; you only have a *pro tanto* reason to discharge them on some occasions', whereas 'insofar as duties of justice are perfect, you have a *pro tanto* reason to discharge them on all occasions on which they arise'.[9]

For our present purposes, however, the implication is that for Nozick, the scope of justice encompasses negative and perfect duties, but not positive and imperfect duties. This is because negative and perfect duties clearly correspond to the entitlements of individual agents, which define the scope of justice. Since duties of charity or imperfect duties are not associated with entitlements, Nozick's account implies that they fall outside the domain of justice; they are beyond what the state may rightly enforce.

9   Goodin 2016 *Political Studies* at 268.

## 7.2.4    Identifying duty-bearers I: The causality principle

Thus far, we have seen that from the perspective of Nozick's entitlement theory of justice, the duties that flow from justice are essentially negative in character. We have, however, not yet considered, on Nozick's account, the criteria for identifying who, beyond the state, has the duties flowing from justice. Nozick's entitlement theory of justice provides some clues. One such clue relates to the circumstances under which issues of justice typically arise in Nozick's framework. Since, for Nozick, individual entitlements determine the scope of justice, the violation or possible violation of these entitlements determine circumstances in which people can legitimately demand justice. To return to our previous examples: because some entitlement of Thabang's is at stake where Sipho threatens to wield Sipho's knife, the situation is one of justice – Thabang's right to life is being threatened – whereas because there are no rights at stake in the duty to give alms to the beggar, this is not a circumstance of justice.

This consideration allows us to neatly work out some criterion for deciding who has duties flowing from justice by simply tracking which non-state actor stands, by virtue of his or her action, in some causal relation to the violation or anticipated violation of the relevant fundamental entitlements. In other words, duties of justice flow to private actors to the extent that they have contributed or will contribute by virtue of their actions to bringing about injustice, where this, as we have seen, amounts to the violation of the fundamental entitlements of individuals. Alternatively, the negative duty, on the part of Sipho, not to kill Thabang, flows to Sipho by virtue of the fact that Sipho's action will causally bring about the violation of Thabang's fundamental entitlement to life.

This is the causality principle for identifying who has duties of justice. Since it identifies duty-bearers by way of tracking their causal contribution to injustice, the principle allows that duties of justice can apply not just to human agents, but also to non-human agents. So, for example, on the causality principle, because the activities of big multinational oil companies, like Shell and Chevron, in the Niger Delta region of Nigeria is causally related to the widespread environmental degradation that has negatively impacted on the livelihood of the local population, they have duties of justice to *refrain* from degrading natural resources, which ultimately undermines the rights of individuals in this region to freely pursue their own ends. Moreover, these duties apply uniformly to all causally linked private actors.

We shall return later to examine whether big corporations have positive, and not just negative, obligations with respect to fundamental rights. In the meantime, it is worth noting that something like the causality principle has been given expression by the South African Constitutional Court. In *Governing Body of the Juma-Masjid Primary School v Essay N.O.*,[10] in which a private trust sought to evict from its premises a government school as a result of its failure to pay rentals, the Court found that although the private trust in the case had no obligation to take active steps to fulfil the right to education as enshrined in the Constitution, that is, no positive duties (for example, build schools), it nevertheless had negative obligations, for example, not to harm the rights of learners to education through its actions. In other words, the Court took into account the likely contribution of the private trust by virtue of its actions to frustrate that right, in allocating constitutional duties to the private trust. David Bilchitz has described the Court's approach as the 'nature of the duty' criterion and it broadly coincides with what we have described as the causality principle.[11]

---

10    [2011] ZACC 13.
11    Bilchitz 2017 *Business and Human Rights: Context and Contours.*

## 7.2.5 Duties and correlative rights

The idea that the scope of justice is defined by individual entitlements and that therefore the duties of justice are limited only to those duties that are correlated with entitlements is not without problems. The first is that it tends to rely on a rather simplistic analysis of the relation between rights and duties.[12] It implies that the duties of justice are present only where some right is at stake. In doing so, however, it ignores a whole range of circumstances where one might have significantly strong duties to one's family, community and nation that are not at all correlated with rights. These duties may give rise to questions of justice even if there are no claimable rights. For example, a South African citizen may have duties towards other citizens simply on the basis of national belonging and identification. At least, individual citizens often view themselves as bearers of substantial duties to a wide range of people for reasons other than entitlement.[13]

It is open to a friend of Nozick to argue that these other duties of citizens are simply duties of charity, or some other kind of duty rather than of justice. But why should we accept the distinction between justice and charity? Alternatively, why should we draw the line at the point where duties are correlated with rights? This question takes on added significance since, as we shall see, the assumed distinction between justice and charity is potentially revisable.

Moreover, if duties of justice flow to private actors because of their causal role in hindering some fundamental right, then Nozick's account does not quite provide guidance on how to deal with cases in which these causal roles are unclear. For example, it is extremely difficult to track who is causally responsible for global poverty. Should we simply accept in the face of global poverty that private actors have no duties of justice at all, even if they have the capabilities to alleviate global poverty?

Finally Nozick's approach appears to rest on the implicit assumption that duties of justice only arise in the context of interactions between rough equals.[14] In particular, he presumes that the problem of justice arises for individual agents who have more or less the same range of entitlements that they can claim against each other. The context is one of rough equality with 'none able to dominate the others and none asymmetrically dependent upon the others'.[15] But not only does this fail to capture the complex nature of human relationships, including especially asymmetrical relationships, that intuitively occasion problems of justice, but it also seems to entail that more powerful non-state actors, like abled individuals and big businesses, do not have duties of justice to people with varying degrees of need and dependency. For example, we intuitively think that there are duties of justice towards people with severe mental impairments, simply on the basis of their needs and dependency rather than entitlements they can claim against others. If cases of asymmetrical relationships give rise to questions of justice, then Nozick's entitlement approach seems to exclude them.

In the next section, we examine an alternative approach that takes these issues a bit more seriously.

12  Ulriksen & Plagerson 2014 *World Development* at 758–759.
13  Ulriksen & Plagerson 2014 at 757.
14  Ulriksen & Plagerson 2014 at 758.
15  Nussbaum 2003 *Feminist Economics* at 51.

## 7.3   Justice, welfare and duties of charity

PRIMARY
TEXTS

### Text 2   Peter Singer on famine, affluence and morality[16]

Peter Singer (born 1945) is an Australian philosopher at Princeton University. He is also a Laureate Professor at the Centre for Applied Philosophy and Public Ethics, University of Melbourne and a renowned utilitarian.

I begin with the assumption that suffering and death from lack of food, shelter, and medical care are bad. I think most people will agree about this, although one may reach the same view by different routes. I shall not argue for this view. People can hold all sorts of eccentric positions, and perhaps from some of them it would not follow that death by starvation is in itself bad. It is difficult, perhaps impossible to refute such positions, and so for brevity I will henceforth take this assumption as accepted. Those who disagree need read no further.

My next point is this: if it is in our power to prevent something bad from happening, without thereby sacrificing anything of comparable moral importance, we ought, morally, to do it. By "without sacrificing anything of comparable moral importance" I mean without causing anything else comparably bad to happen, or doing something that is wrong in itself, or failing to promote some moral good, comparable in significance to the bad thing that we can prevent. This principle seems almost as uncontroversial as the last one. It requires us only to prevent what is bad, and not to promote what is good, and it requires this of us only when we can do it without sacrificing anything that is, from the moral point of view, comparably important. I could even, as far as the application of my argument to the Bengal emergency is concerned, qualify the point so as to make it: if it is in our power to prevent something very bad from happening, without thereby sacrificing anything morally significant, we ought, morally, to do it. An application of this principle would be as follows: if I am walking past a shallow pond and see a child drowning in it, I ought to wade in and pull the child out. This will mean getting my clothes muddy, but this is insignificant, while the death of the child would presumably be a very bad thing.

... neither our distance from a preventable evil nor the number of other people who, in respect to that evil, are in the same situation as we are, lessens our obligation to mitigate or prevent that evil. I shall therefore take as established the principle I asserted earlier. ... The outcome of this argument is that our traditional moral categories are upset. The traditional distinction between duty and charity cannot be drawn, or at least, not in the place we normally draw it. ... I am not maintaining that there are no acts which are charitable, or that there are no acts which it would be good to do but not wrong not to do. It may be possible to redraw the distinction between duty and charity in some other place. All I am arguing here is that the present way of drawing the distinction, which makes it an act of charity for a man living at the level of affluence which most people in the "developed nations" enjoy to give money to save someone else from starvation, cannot be supported.

**Questions**
1. Can you identify the central principle underlying Singer's approach to justice?
2. For Singer, do duties of justice necessarily correlate with rights?
3. What precisely is Singer's analogy of the drowning baby meant to illustrate? Does it hold any significance for his argument?
4. Singer clearly intends to 'redraw' the line between justice and charity 'in some other place'. How might that distinction be re-drawn?
5. Why does Singer insist that one's distance from 'a preventable evil' does not lessen one's duty to prevent evil?

### 7.3.1   Social welfare and the scope of justice

Whereas Nozick's account focuses on the particular entitlements that individual agents have and the manner in which these entitlements condition obligations towards others, for Singer the duties of justice, whatever these turn out to be, are not grounded on entitlements. Instead considerations about who has obligations of justice flow directly from the need to alleviate morally bad situations. Singer is particularly concerned with the challenge of global poverty. In South Africa, as with many other parts of Africa and the world, the gap between the rich and the poor has significantly widened. Who beyond the state has the duty to lessen the scourge of poverty?

Singer's argument in the text develops in stages. First, he begins by stating what he deems uncontroversial namely, that global poverty is morally bad. Specifically, the lack of food, shelter and healthcare is morally bad. He then adds what seems to resonate with our common sense intuition, that if people are in a position to prevent something bad from occurring, without in the process sacrificing something of comparable moral importance, they ought, morally, to do it. Singer's own example is illuminating. One would be, on this account, obligated to save a drowning child, as long as this does not, for instance, involve one's own death and/or the child's, or any other comparable harm. The analogy illustrates the intuitive force of Singer's argument. If you have a duty to save the drowning child, why can you not give say R50 to relieve global hunger?

The next step in Singer's argument is that we, and especially the wealthy members of the global community, can alleviate global poverty without sacrificing anything of comparable worth. For example, many wealthy people are capable of giving of what they have to alleviate global hunger without thereby having to starve. Thomas Pogge puts the point more succinctly, noting that:

> for the first time in human history it is quite feasible, economically, to wipe out hunger and preventable diseases worldwide without real inconvenience to anyone.[17]

If this is the case, then the wealthy members of the global community ought as a matter of justice to lessen global poverty, that is, to give towards alleviating the lack of food, clothes, shelter, and so on. Therefore, wealthy members of the global community ought to be maximally generous or at least give much more than they do presently.

Notice that there is a utilitarian element in the argument. It comes in at the point where Singer suggests that in the event that the negative consequences of carrying out the duty

---

17   Pogge 2001 *Metaphilosophy* at 14.

outweigh the positive ones, one is not obliged to perform that duty. The primary consideration is alleviating the bad condition and improving overall welfare.

## 7.3.2   Identifying duty-bearers II: The capability principle

Earlier, we noted that the causality principle seems unreliable in cases in which the injustice is systemic and pervasive but opaque, so that 'it is often impossible to connect [the problem] causally to specific, clearly identifiable harmful actions or to particular agents'.[18] We also noted that the causality principle omits from consideration potential duty-bearers who might have the capability to prevent injustice. Singer's approach suggests an alternative way of allocating duties in the 'increasingly common cases in which our information about the causal chains between actions and outcomes is incomplete'.[19] We can infer from Singer that the key element in determining who has duties of justice is consideration about capabilities to positively alter bad situations for the better. His point that we ought morally to do so if it is in our power to prevent something bad without comparable harm to ourselves speaks to considerations of the capabilities of potential duty-bearers. It indicates that justice is 'as much about the capabilities to prevent and alleviate misery as it is about not causing it'.[20]

To see this, consider a slightly modified example of the drowning baby. Suppose that Sipho and Siya witness Thandi drowning in a pool much deeper than the one in Singer's original example. Suppose also that unlike Siya, Sipho is an exceptional swimmer. Moreover, neither Sipho nor Siya are causally responsible for Thandi's drowning. Recall that Nozick's view entails, on this modification, that Sipho and Siya have only duties of charity towards Thandi; the state may not punish either of them if they choose not to save her. On the capability principle, in contrast, the decisive consideration is that Sipho has the ability to prevent Thandi's drowning – something that Siya crucially lacks. So, whereas Siya's diving into the pool and attempting to save Thandi would be heroic and beyond the call of duty, since it would involve incurring huge costs to herself, the same is not true of Sipho, who, on this analysis, ought as a matter of justice to save Thandi. Failing to do so, would merit censure.

So, Singer's central idea seem to be that a duty of justice exists for a private actor insofar as the private actor possesses the capability to reverse or prevent some bad situation from occurring. A 'capability derives from the combination of personal capacities (for example, talents) and adequate external circumstances and arrangements to put them to use favourably'.[21] The capability principle entails that 'if we want bad situations put right, we should give the responsibility to those who are best placed to do the remedying'.[22] Conversely, where the relevant capability is absent the potential actor does not have similar duties.

In the case of *Khumalo v Holomisa*,[23] which involved a politician suing a media house for defamation, the Constitutional Court of South Africa determined the duty of a private party with respect to the right to freedom of expression, in a way that sheds light on the capability principle. It found that a media agency has not just constitutional rights but also obligations deriving from its role to impart information in a way that honours the dignity of a person and that person's sense of self-worth. According to Bilchitz, in this case the Court relied on 'agent-relative' considerations in allocating appropriate obligations.

---

18   Wettstein 2009 at 135.
19   Wettstein 2009 at 136.
20   Wettstein 2009 at 139.
21   Wettstein 2009 at 138.
22   Miller 2005 *Global Responsibilities: Who Must Deliver on Human Rights?* at 102
23   2002 (5) SA 401 (CC).

Some consideration is agent-relative just in case it is dependent on facts about the party involved, in this case, the media house. Bilchitz's point is that the view of the Court was that 'there might be particular factors which provide grounds for certain agents [in this case, the media house] to have obligations which others do not ...'[24] For Singer, it would seem that one such agent-relative consideration is the capability of the private actor, which creates special obligations for it that others may not have.

### 7.3.3 Justice and charity revisited

The idea that duties of justice flow to private actors with relevant capabilities seems to suggest that some duties of justice are positive, and not all negative. That is, since the capability principle entails that duty-bearers ought to *do* something, rather than simply refrain from doing something, it envisages positive duties of justice. Moreover, the focus on capability suggests that one has duties of justice that are not necessarily based on another's rights. If *Person A* has a duty to give maximally to *Person B* simply because *Person A* has the capability, then the duty is not necessarily correlated with some entitlement that *Person B* has. This means that the focus on capability allows us to include imperfect duties, that is, duties that are not correlated with rights, in the scope of justice. But if positive and imperfect duties fall within the scope of justice, then not only is Singer's position in conflict with Nozick's but, more importantly, the supposed distinction between justice and charity has been called into question. This is because positive and imperfect duties that were excluded by that distinction from the scope of justice have, on Singer's alternative approach, been brought into it.

Even so, Singer is not necessarily opposed to the idea that we can reasonably distinguish between charity and justice, but only that we should rethink the basis of the distinction. Whereas Nozick draws the line between justice and charity at the point where duties correlate with rights, Singer would rather have it elsewhere. For him, duties of justice exist where there is capability to improve overall utility. As such, his account is able to go beyond Nozick's and redraw the distinction between charity and justice 'in some other place', that is, at the point where capability exists to positively impact utility, rather than merely where fundamental rights are at stake.

To reiterate, Sipho's duty to save Thandi from drowning is not merely a charitable act. To the extent that it is distinguishable from Siya's, on the basis of capability, it is, on Singer's view, a matter of justice. Moreover, Sipho's duty requires him to do something to save Thandi, as opposed to merely refraining from doing something. So, not only is Sipho's duty in this regard not a negative one, it is also not based on consideration of whether Thandi has some right that Thandi may claim against Sipho. Instead, the duty is based entirely on consideration of Sipho's capability to avert some morally bad outcome.

### 7.3.4 Assessing Singer's welfarist approach

One challenge for Singer relates to the idea that people who can, should do a great deal to alleviate global poverty. The cut-off is the point at which giving is likely to bring suffering to oneself. However:

> from this genuinely utilitarian perspective, one ought to keep giving until one reaches the level of marginal utility at which the suffering caused to oneself is greater than relief provided to others.[25]

---

24  Bilchitz 2017.
25  Wettstein 2009 at 139.

Yet, this seems to be too demanding on individuals. Because it requires individuals in comparatively affluent nations to always act in the interest of others, it seems to significantly constrain their freedom as individuals to act or do things that advance their own personal goals. For example, Singer's approach appears to require Karabo who lives in Johannesburg to suspend her planned trip to the Canary Islands, presumably of less moral importance, in order to contribute to some poverty relief programme in Sudan. This does not seem fair on Karabo. Perhaps, individuals should be free to make their choices.

Further, although Singer's approach, unlike Nozick's, takes seriously the unequal standing of individuals in wealthy and poorer nations. It also recognises that social and economic empowerment play a crucial role in determining why some agents have remedial obligations of justice, where others may not. However, he seems to leave us with a framework in which it is unclear whether the poor, or individuals in poorer nations, have any duties at all and, if they do, what these obligations are. Not only is this an inaccurate depiction of poor citizens, who often see themselves as duty-bearers in some way, it also crucially denies them agency – a view of 'the poor as passive claimants unwilling to make an effort'.[26] Perhaps the poor have duties as well. As former president of South Africa, Thabo Mbeki, says, the poor should not think that:

> it is sufficient merely to hold out their hands and receive a hand-out, but to understand that all of us, as South Africans, have a shared responsibility to attend to the development of the country.[27]

Singer's account does not seem to capture this fact.

Moreover, Singer's approach excludes rights, including socio-economic rights, altogether. But if there are such rights at stake, it would be possible to enforce them, while at the same time not placing an unrestricted obligation on individuals. Perhaps there is some benefit to correlating duties of justice to rights, which may indicate not only that they are salient but also that they can be enforced. Singer, however, does not seem to entertain socio-economic rights at all. Lastly, Singer is explicit that distance has no impact at all on whether one has duty to aid others. So, it makes no difference morally whether one is far away or unrelated to the impoverished people; one has duty to do as much as one is able to do regardless. But perhaps people have stronger obligations to people to whom they are related. For example, one has stronger duties to one's fellow citizens, relatives and friends, and so on, than to non-citizens, non-relatives and strangers respectively. If so, Singer's view is unable to explain the intuition that relationships may impact on the nature of duties.

In the next section, we consider an approach that ostensibly fares better in the areas in which Singer's approach seems unable to cope.

---

26   Ulriksen & Plagerson 2014 at 756.
27   Cited in Ulriksen & Plagerson 2014 at 756 and Marais 2011 *South Africa Pushed to the Limit: The Political Economy of Change* at 253.

## 7.4 Communitarianism, relationality and justice

PRIMARY TEXTS

**Text 3 Kwame Gyekye's communitarianism and supererogation[28]**

Kwame Gyekye is a Ghanaian philosopher. He is currently Professor of Philosophy at the University of Ghana and visiting Professor of Philosophy and African-American studies at Temple University. The following selection is from his widely cited book, *Tradition and Modernity* (1997).

The communitarian ethic acknowledges the importance of individual rights but it does not do so to the detriment of responsibilities that individual members have or ought to have toward the community or other members of the community. ... Responsibilities to the community as a whole or to some members of the community would not derive from a social contract between individuals ... In a communitarian framework ... responsibilities will derive from the communitarian ethos and its imperatives. ... The relational character of the individual by virtue of her natural sociality immediately makes her naturally oriented to other persons with whom she must live. Living in relation to others directly involves an individual in social and moral roles, obligations, commitments, and responsibilities, which the individual must fulfill. ... It is true that if I have a right to education, then it is the responsibility of someone– a parent or a local authority ... to provide what is necessary for my education; similarly, if I have the right to work, it is the responsibility of the state to make jobs available to me. In such cases, where rights are asserted ... against some persons in specific social or political or public roles or positions, the correspondence or correlation between rights and responsibilities will clearly be on track.

But it is possible for a person to carry out a responsibility to some one else without our having to say that the responsibility was carried out because of the right of this other person, that is, the person for whose sake some responsibility was fulfilled. If I carry out a responsibility to help someone in distress, I would not be doing so because I think that that someone has a right against me, a right I should help defend or realize. If I give my seat on a bus to an older person, I do not do so because this older person has a right against me. In such situations, the fulfillment of responsibility would not be based on the acknowledgment of someone's right. I would be carrying out that responsibility because I consider that person worthy of some moral consideration by me, someone to whose plight I ought to be morally sensitive ... Responsibilities to such fellow human beings, then, are not grounded on their rights. ... Social life, which follows upon our natural sociality, implicates the individual in a web of moral obligations, commitments, and responsibilities to be fulfilled in pursuit of the common good or the general welfare.

The scope of the responsibilities and obligations will expectably be extensive and not clearly circumscribed. Thus the communitarian concept of moral responsibility will encompass what are known in other moral theories as acts of super-erogation. ... Implicit in supererogationism is a clear assumption that there are

---

28 Gyekye 1997 *Tradition and Modernity: Philosophical Reflections on the African Experience* at 66–68, 71–73.

limits to what we, as human beings, can reasonably consider as our legitimate moral responsibilities and obligations, those responsibilities that we naturally feel we are morally obliged to fulfill. ... The problem that immediately arises is: how do we set the limits, that is, what criteria are we to establish in order to set those limits, to demarcate responsibilities from those responsibilities that are sort of quasi-responsibilities and, thus, beyond the call of duty?

One major set of criteria will relate to the practicability of certain acts, that is, whether or not those acts are such as we, as human beings, have the ability or are in a position to perform. ... I think, however, that it would be necessary to distinguish acts that we should regard as moral responsibilities but which for some practical or other reasons we cannot carry out from those moral responsibilities the fulfillment of which is relatively easier. Yet our inability to fulfill the former set of responsibilities does not- should not- make them supererogatory. There are indeed some responsibilities that we recognize as within our moral limits, that is, not "beyond the call of duty," but which, nevertheless, we are not able to carry out ... A harmonious cooperative social life requires that individuals demonstrate sensitivity to the needs and interests of others, if that society is to be a moral society. The reason is that the plight or distress of some individuals in the society is likely to affect others in some substantial ways. If social arrangement is to maximize the good for all, then that arrangement will have to include rules the pursuit of which will conduce to the attainment of communal welfare.

**Questions**

1. What does Gyekye mean by the 'communitarian ethic'? Can you identify its principal features?
2. Are duties necessarily correlated with rights in Gyekye's moderate communitarian approach? If not, why not?
3. What is supererogation? What are the reasons Gyekye provides for recoiling from distinguishing between duty and supererogation?
4. How does the focus on 'relationships' in Gyekye's account impact the question of who has the duties flowing from justice?

## 7.4.1   Moderate communitarianism

Gyekye's focus in the text is on the nature and extent of the moral duties individuals have to each other. To fully understand these points, it is important to notice that Gyekye is committed to the view he describes as moderate communitarianism. It is his response to what he takes to be extreme individualism, on the one hand, and extreme communitarianism, on the other. While extreme individualism prioritises the rights and entitlements of individuals to the detriment of the duties they have towards each other, extreme communitarianism focuses exclusively on the duties individuals have to the detriment of rights. Although they may not describe their positions in this way, the views of Nozick and Singer that we have so far examined seem to fall under these broad generalisations. As we saw, Nozick focuses on the rights of individuals and ended up limiting the obligations of individuals to negative duties only. Singer, on his part, begins with claims regarding the duties individual agents have to others, with no mention of rights at all. For Gyekye, it is possible to balance the competing claims of individual rights and responsibilities to the community, rather than prioritise one over the other. The possibility for doing so, in the moderate communitarian view, rests on understanding the proper nature of individual persons. On this view, persons are composites of two basic features, individual and communal features; therefore a proper approach should equally regard these aspects.[29] This is essentially the basic claim of moderate communitarianism.

For Gyekye, the key to this mutual balancing is in the recognition that rights and duties emerge out of the complex social relationships in which individuals are necessarily embedded. Because relationships are dynamic and multi-layered, and not simply static and one-dimensional, there are various ways of making sense of duties and rights that emerge from them. Some relationships are between rough equals, for example the relationship between experts in some field, say medicine; other kinds of relationships are asymmetric and marked by dependency, for example the relationships between parent and child, a mentally impaired person and his or her caregiver, and so on. Gyekye thinks that given the complex nature of relationships in a community, it is possible for some members to have duties to others on the basis of rights that others have, as well as duties to others that do not correlate with any rights. Of the duties that are not correlated with rights, some of these emerge from the recognition that others need help or are dependent, while others are based on considerations of realising the common good. Slight modifications of his examples are helpful. Nandipha has a right to education that correlates with the duty of someone, say her parent (and the state), to provide education, for example pay her fees (build schools), and so on. But she too has a duty to rescue another in distress (recall Singer's case of rescuing a drowning baby), without any correlative right, or to contribute quite generally towards the good of her community by providing educational programmes for children.

In essence, Gyekye's moderate communitarianism seeks to account for all these different sorts of duties emerging from social relationships, including those duties that are correlative with rights (also known as perfect duties) and those that are not (also known as imperfect duties). He maintains that there are no reasonable grounds for distinguishing between these two sets of duties, or between duties of justice and duties of charity. If we approach the question of duties and rights from the perspective of relationships, we find that the sort of relationships we have towards each other are very many indeed, embracing so-called duties of justice and duties of charity, which are all essential to our moral life. The reason for not distinguishing between justice and charity is that in order for shared social and moral life to be successful, each member will have to exhibit a 'high degree of moral responsiveness and sensitivity to the needs and well-being of other members', which requires fulfilling all of one's obligations rather than some of them (for example, only perfect duties).[30] This is why Gyekye says in the text that:

> the scope of the responsibilities and obligations will expectably be extensive and ... encompass what are known in other theories as acts of supererogation.[31]

### 7.4.2 Justice and supererogation

Like Singer, Gyekye maintains that justice should aim at improving welfare, although he does not mean simply maximising utility for the majority. Rather than merely aiming to benefit the majority, Gyekye's notion of the common good envisages harmonious coexistence for all.

29  Oyowe 2013 *Philosophia Africana* at 119.
30  Gyekye 1997 at 67.
31  Gyekye 1997 at 71.

A major difference concerns the nature of duties of justice. For Singer, duties of justice do not correlate with rights and one is obligated up to the point where discharging the duty would cause comparable suffering to oneself. For example, fire-woman Buhle getting herself badly burnt in a fire in a bid to rescue Amy; although Buhle is capable of rescuing Amy, the suffering and likely death for Buhle makes the act non-obligatory or optional. Such an act would be supererogatory. An act is supererogatory if it goes beyond what is morally required of any individual. At issue in the idea of supererogation is the extent one ought to go in carrying out one's duties; a supererogatory act goes beyond the call of duty. And like duties of charity, although they are usually morally good and performing them is deserving of praise, failing to perform them is not considered morally objectionable.

Gyekye's moderate communitarianism implies that we should:

> not make a distinction between moral responsibility and a supererogatory act, the former being obligatory and the latter being non-obligatory and optional, but instead ... collapse the two.[32]

In other words, for Gyekye, there is strictly speaking no category of supererogation – that is, we need not limit the extent to which an individual may go in order to improve the situations of others. By recoiling altogether from drawing a line between the duty imposed by justice and acts of supererogation, his view seems to suggest that duties of justice, on the one hand, overlap with duties of charity, on the other. In arriving at this position, Gyekye first wonders whether there are in fact reasonable grounds upon which the distinction may be established. He considers and then rejects two possible grounds for limiting the extent of duties.

The first is what Gyekye calls 'practicability'. In this way of limiting the extent of obligations of justice, we say that one has no duty because it is impractical for one to perform the duty. Such acts would be supererogatory and fall outside the scope of justice. Gyekye disagrees. For him not being able to do something does not mean that the act is supererogatory. To return to an earlier example, if Siya, who cannot swim, decides not to dive into the deep end of a pool in order to save Thandi, this does not make the act optional. It is instead an acknowledgment of Siya's limitation, rather than a judgement on the nature of the duty to save Thandi. The second criterion relates to whether the rights of an individual to pursue his or her own ends should limit the extent of his or her obligation to improve the welfare of others. That is, Siya is not obligated to save Thandi because doing so would impact on Siya's right to do as she wants. However, Gyekye thinks that this view rests on the problematic assumption that 'some form of self-sacrifice cannot be expected of individuals'.[33] It is problematic because, for Gyekye, it is unclear which forms of self-sacrifice are just too much to require since what counts as self-sacrifice is typically subjective and context-dependent. For example, it may involve huge sacrifice for some to aid the poor, but not so much for others who live in a society where the giving of aid is normal. Gyekye thinks that morality always demands self-sacrifice – that is, 'the loss of one's time, money, strength, and so on'. As such, he concludes that there is no need to place limits on 'the extent of our moral responsibilities'.[34]

It should be clear then that in relation to supererogatory acts, Gyekye's view diverges significantly from Singer's. Whereas for Singer we should distinguish between duty and supererogation in that one is not duty-bound if the suffering to oneself is greater than the

---

32   Gyekye 1997 at 71.
33   Gyekye 1997 at 73.
34   Gyekye 1997 at 73.

welfare to others, Gyekye does not distinguish them, insisting instead that one is obligated even up to the point of sacrificing oneself. But this seems counterintuitive. Am I really obligated, for example, to kill myself and distribute my organs so that those who would die without them will live? Is this not a case of going beyond the call of duty (that is, supererogation)? In other words, because it permits self-sacrifice, Gyekye's view seems to be even more demanding than Singer's. As such, one might reasonably question whether his view is as moderate as he claims.

In response, however, a friend of Gyekye might argue that the view is still moderate, and is not extreme communitarianism. This is because it is able to provide a delicate balance between rights and duties in relation to the common good. That is, I still have rights against others not to be used for the greater good, even if I have a duty to use myself, including indulging in self-sacrificial acts, for the greater good.

### 7.4.3 Identifying duty-bearers III: Capability and relationality

One other point of comparison between Singer and Gyekye relates to the criterion for identifying duty-bearers. Recall that for Singer, the wealthy Karabo in Johannesburg has a duty to contribute to alleviating the hunger of people in Sudan, even if she has never and perhaps will never meet them. Her duty is not affected by distance or by the fact that she is in no way related to them. Gyekye's account yields a different judgement. Specifically, it is that the relationship between the duty-bearer and the recipient of relief makes a basic moral difference. This follows from the earlier point that moderate communitarianism sees obligations as essentially grounded in and flowing out of a complex web of relationships between people. And to the extent that one's relationships are typically stronger towards one's relatives and friends, and relatively weaker towards strangers, the implication is that for Gyekye duties of justice may vary accordingly.

One reason why relationality might be regarded as a useful criterion for identifying duty-bearers is that it enables us to explain why poor citizens might have duties of justice. As we saw, in relation to Singer, focusing solely on (especially economic) capability might imply that duties of justice do not flow to poorer citizens. However, for Gyekye, to the extent that they are related to others in important ways, and obligations emerge from a complex web of communal relationships, poorer members of community also have duties of justice.

Notice that Gyekye need not deny that capability plays a role in determining who has duties of justice. Instead, he sees both capability and relationality as equally crucial. So, more clearly, the interaction between capability and relationality seems to imply that although duties of justice may flow to one in virtue of one's capability to improve the welfare of others, the strength of that obligation may vary depending on the nature of the relationship. To return to our most recent example, the wealthy Karabo may have duties to alleviate global poverty on the basis of her capability to prevent a bad situation from occuring. However, her duty to alleviate poverty in the townships bordering the city of Johannesburg or to members of her family may be much stronger than her duty to alleviate poverty in the Sudan, say. Likewise, although poorer members of the community also have an obligation to alleviate poverty however they can, and on the basis of their relationship to others in greater need, it is still the case that wealthier members have stronger obligations because they have greater capabilities.

We have now considered three different approaches to justice, each entailing different judgements regarding the nature and extent of the duties of justice and how we might identify who beyond the state has duties flowing from justice. In what follows, we draw on these insights in examining whether and to what extent corporations as juristic persons have duties of justice.

## 7.5   The nature and obligations of a corporation

**PRIMARY TEXTS**

**Text 4   David Bilchitz's 'Do corporations have fundamental rights obligations?'** [35]

David Bilchitz (1975) is a South African academic, who specialises in the intersection between political philosophy and constitutional law with a specific focus on fundamental rights. He is currently Law Professor at the University of Johannesburg and Director of the South African Institute for Advanced Constitutional, Public, Human Rights and International Law (SAIFAC). The selection below is from his paper.

... The very economic focus of corporate entities embeds them in the process of acquiring resources and property rights. Indeed, since their inception, as entities they have been the sites of accumulation of large amounts of wealth. Property rights have certain harms attendant upon them which in turn forms the basis of duties to avert those harms on the part of those who wish to claim such rights. The qualifications on property rights also give expression to certain conditions that must be met in order for them legitimately to be held. An entity that has, amongst its key purposes, the possession and accumulation of wealth must thus have duties to ameliorate the harms caused by the very system of property rights that enables it to achieve this purpose. In societies where many individuals are deprived of even very limited property holdings, it is necessary to protect their rights to those resources which are preconditions for them to survive and exercise their autonomy. The very economic purpose of corporations and their success in accumulating wealth thus highlights their crucial role in the property system and provides the basis for recognising an obligation upon them to make a contribution to alleviating at least the worst effects of such a system: the exclusion of individuals from having the resources necessary to realise their fundamental rights. We may term this the 'argument from the limits of property rights'.

... The second argument seeks to draw out the implications of the social perspective that lawmakers must adopt. Of great importance here is a deeper elaboration upon this societal perspective and the notion of social benefit. Where lawmakers are tasked with creating laws for an entire society in a democratic system, they are not expected to make such laws with the view of privileging particular individuals. The rules governing a society are by their very nature not concerned with the actions of a particular individual but are designed to regulate the distribution of benefits and burdens to a group of individuals ... Law-makers thus must go about their task through adopting an impersonal perspective that requires every individual to be treated with equal importance. ... A society committed to the principle of treating each individual with equal importance must provide rights to individuals that their most basic interests in such 'freedom' and 'resources' will be met. Without the resources to be free from starvation or malnourishment, for instance, no being can live a valuable life ...

How does this all relate to the obligations of corporations? As has been argued, the corporation is an artificial institution created by law-makers who must adopt a societal perspective towards what they do. That societal perspective requires them to advance the equal importance of individuals in the institutions and legal

35   Bilchitz 2010 *Theoria* at 15–16, 19, 21, 23.

rules they create. ... Thus, a key criterion from the societal perspective against which to assess the social advantages brought by a particular structure such as the corporation is the impact that it can have upon fundamental rights. ... Understanding the implications of the societal perspective that law-makers must adopt in designing the corporation thus leads to the recognition that such a structure should have positive obligations to contribute to the realisation of rights. We can term this the 'argument from social benefit'.

**Questions**

1. According to Bilchitz, what is the nature of a corporation? Does the nature of a corporation modify its obligations?
2. How far do corporate obligations extend, according to Bilchitz? Specifically, do they encompass positive duties or are they limited only to negative ones?
3. How does Bilchitz motivate the view that corporations have fundamental rights obligations?
4. According to Bilchitz, what is the significance of adopting the 'societal perspective' towards corporations?

## 7.5.1    The nature of a corporation

Bilchitz's principal aim is to demonstrate that corporations, conceived of as legal persons, have not just negative duties, but also positive duties. In order to do this, he articulates a view of the corporation, which he sets as a foil against a well-known libertarian one, aligned to the free-market system.

On the latter, a corporation is essentially an artificial entity set up primarily to fulfil some economic aim, specifically to provide goods and services in view of maximising profits for its owners and investors. This picture of a corporation ultimately reduces it to the private economic interests of the individuals that own and manage it. That is, it is simply an expression of their basic rights to property and to pursue their economic interests. It is because 'these individuals have property rights in the corporation', that they are 'entitled to use their property to achieve greater wealth'.[36] So, the MTN Group, for example, is the private property of its owners who invest in it primarily for the purpose of providing high-grade telecommunication services to its clients with the ultimate aim of maximising profits for its investors.

Milton Friedman has given one of the clearest expressions to these ideas. He famously remarked that:

> there is one and only one social responsibility of business – to use its resources and engage in activities designed to increase its profits so long as it stays within the rules of the game, which is to say, engages in free and open competition, without deception or fraud.[37]

He adds that 'only people can have responsibilities. A corporation is an artificial person and in this sense may have artificial responsibilities'.[38] In other words, a corporation is constrained by its economic nature in that it is a means to increase profits. It is not set up to

---

36   Bilchitz 2010 at 6.
37   Friedman 1970 *Ethical Theory and Business* at 55.
38   Friedman 1970 at 51.

advance the aims of justice. So, the MTN Group has no obligation to provide access to clean water, healthcare and so on, although it may do so entirely on a voluntary basis.

For Bilchitz, that view is mistaken. A purely economic analysis of a corporation does not adequately capture its various facets. He proposes instead a notion of the corporation as comprising a distinctive legal understanding and a broader social perspective. On the latter, a corporation is a juristic person, having a 'separate legal personality' in the eyes of the law and which makes it 'bearer of rights and liabilities in its own right'.[39] Its 'separate legal personality' undercuts any attempt to see it as merely an extension of the property and economic rights of its owners. It has its own rights and bears liabilities independently of the individuals constituting it.

There are three ways to account for this. First, a corporation enjoys the 'benefit of perpetual succession', whereas the individuals constituting it do not. So, for example, MTN Group may carry on even if its current investors and owners are gone. Second, the liability of investors and owners is limited to their investment in the corporation and does not extend to their personal wealth, thus separating them from the corporation. So, a director of a company may not suffer personal financial losses were the company to become insolvent. Third, corporations are typically more powerful than individual investors and managers. A multinational company may possess the capabilities to lobby and influence the policies of powerful governments, whereas individuals in the corporation lack these capabilities.[40]

For Bilchitz, comprehending the legal status of a corporation involves recognising it as an independent agent with rights and responsibilities. But, in addition to its legal status, Bilchitz adds a broader social conception of its purpose. That is, a corporation is not set up simply as a means to generate profit. Instead, lawmakers adopt an impersonal and impartial perspective in enacting the relevant statutes that enable its creation. As such, they would consider the interests of all individuals in society, rather than merely the economic interests of the individual investors and owners, as they would when passing laws. Bilchitz refers to this impartial and impersonal attitude as the societal perspective. In his words, lawmakers would establish:

> whether that very structure [i.e. the corporation] will be of benefit to all members of society and determine in what respect it can either hinder or advance the purpose of treating each individual with equal importance.[41]

## 7.5.2   The nature of corporate obligations

If a corporation is, in the eyes of the law, an agent in its own right and, more importantly, if its objectives are broadly social, and not just economic, then the scope of corporate obligations is likely to encompass not just negative but also positive duties. Bilchitz offers two reasons in support of the view that corporations have positive obligations.

The first argument rests on the idea that there are reasonable constraints that may be placed on the right to property. According to Bilchitz, the current system of property rights is potentially harmful to the extent that it excludes others, especially the poor, from ownership. For example, copyright laws, which safeguard the rights of some individuals to educational resources, equally precludes access to others. If something is potentially harmful, we should place certain reasonable limits on it in order to forestall or to alleviate the harm. Therefore, the current system of property rights should be reasonably limited.

---

39   Bilchitz 2010 at 7.
40   Bilchitz 2010 at 7–8.
41   Bilchitz 2010 at 10.

Moreover, Bilchitz thinks that one of the foremost beneficiaries of the current system of property rights is the big corporation. So, appropriate constraints should be imposed on corporations. One way to impose this burden is to require of them to take active steps to ensure that poor individuals have the basic resources they have been deprived of as a result of the illegitimate property rights system. Therefore, big corporations have positive duties with respect to the fundamental rights of the poor to basic resources.

The second argument from social benefit draws on the other aspect of the nature of a corporation – the idea that the statutes that bring a corporation into existence envision it in part to contribute towards creating social benefits for everyone, rather than merely profits for its owners and investors. Moreover, these benefits ought to be made equally available to all. In other words, Bilchitz thinks that the societal perspective entails that in thinking about the social benefits of a corporation, lawmakers have to treat each person's interest equally and treat each individual with equal importance. That is, 'no one individual must be privileged over others'.[42] For Bilchitz, to treat each person with equal importance entails that basic freedoms are protected and basic resources, including food, shelter, healthcare, and so on, are guaranteed up to a level that ensures a dignified life. This is because individual importance could not be made sense of without the availability of these goods.

Bilchitz's arguments strongly advocate positive duties for corporations to realise fundamental rights. This relates to two key considerations in the previous sections. The first relates to the importance of expanding the scope of the duties of justice to encompass both negative and positive duties. So, for Bilchitz, where a pharmaceutical company develops a new medicine, which it has patented, the property rights and social benefit arguments both imply that it ought to make the medication accessible to all since not doing so and just profiting from it instead essentially involves (1) passing on the harms of the property ownership system to the poor, who are excluded because of the right of some to own, and (2) failing to treat each one's interest equally and to create social benefit for all. These reasons suggest that corporations have positive duties to ensure that the fundamental rights of citizens are realised. In this way, Bilchitz's case for corporate obligations to incorporate positive duties as well comes as close as anything to Singer's and Gyekye's. In other words, whereas Nozick's account implies that the duties of justice are essentially negative, Bilchitz's view of corporate obligations, like Singer's and Gyekye's, envisages positive duties of justice.

The second relates to the importance of correlating duties with rights. As we saw, this was a crucial element in Nozick's and Gyekye's account, but not in Singer's. In line with Nozick and Gyekye, Bilchitz acknowledges the importance of legally enforceable obligations for corporations. His reason is that since a corporation is also partly set up to make profits, it is likely that this objective may from time to time conflict with its duty to create social benefit, especially the realisation of fundamental rights, for all. For example, the interest of a pharmaceutical company in maximising profit might instead lead it to monopolise some medical innovation and make it inaccessible to all. Again, this would mean depriving some the rights to proper healthcare. Legislation would thus be required to ensure that corporations balance these two potentially conflicting aims, namely, profit-making and realising the fundamental rights of those affected by its activities. For him, correlating corporate obligations with rights that people can claim makes it likely that these obligations can be enforced.

It is worth highlighting that Bilchitz's insistence that a corporation's positive duties should be balanced with its economic objectives suggests that there are reasonable limits on the extent of those duties. That is, unlike Gyekye and like Singer, Bilchitz places some

---

42   Bilchitz 2010 at 19.

limit on the positive duties of justice. More clearly, the idea of balancing entails that a corporation is not obligated to the point that it is no longer economically sustainable.

### 7.5.3   Causality, capability and relationality

We are yet to consider how the three criteria for identifying duty-bearers might shed further light on Bilchitz's view that corporations are appropriate bearers of the duties of justice.

Take the causality principle. As we saw, it identifies duty-bearers purely in terms of their causal contribution to some violation or potential violation of fundamental rights. Since justice requires that responsible subjects desist from bringing such violations, the causality principle envisions duties of justice as essentially negative. If, however, as Bilchitz argues, some corporate obligations are positive, then the causality principle would not be entirely sufficient. Moreover, focusing on causal contribution only might prove difficult in the case of corporations, since they are made up of several individuals and often various layers of responsibility. This makes it especially hard to determine when and track who in particular might be causally implicated in corporate violation of fundamental rights.

We would do well then to turn to the capability principle, on which the primary consideration is the capacity of a private actor to positively alter an otherwise bad situation. In this regard, Bilchitz explicitly claims that corporations 'wield significant economic power', and have obligations towards realising fundamental rights, which is consistent with the capability principle. Moreover, because the principle requires duty-bearers to act in particular ways, rather than to forbear, it anticipates positive duties. Unsurprisingly, Bilchitz argues, in a language similar to Singer's regarding improving the welfare of deprived persons, that:

> **for purely consequentialist reasons relating to the improvement of the well-being of individuals across the world, the recognition of some positive obligations upon such actors makes sense and is of importance.**[43]

Finally, although Bilchitz does not explicitly discuss it, consideration of relationality is as well crucial and can be seen in his reference to the likelihood that corporations 'should have stronger not weaker obligations than individuals'.[44] This remark, as well as Gyekye's reference to relationality as crucial for understanding duties of justice, corresponds with what we may regard as a robust intuition that obligations may sometimes come in degrees and may be stronger towards those closer or related to us. Moreover, it allows us to explain why a corporation in some locality (and not others outside that locality) might have an obligation, and for that matter stronger obligations, to the people in that locality rather than to those far away. So, for example, Shell and Chevron might have stronger obligations to people in the Niger Delta where they operate than to people elsewhere, where they do not operate, and this difference is not based on capability but on something like Gyekye's relationality principle.

## 7.6   Conclusion

In summary, this chapter has explored three different accounts of the duties of justice. It specifically covered the nature of these duties, the extent to which they bound duty-bearers and finally the criteria for deciding who counts as an appropriate bearer of the duties of justice.

---

43   Bilchitz 2010 at 19.
44   Bilchitz 2017.

We began with Nozick's account of justice as entitlements. As we saw, it sought to limit the interference of private actors on the legitimate entitlements or rights of others. As such, it specifies what an agent should not do rather than what they should do. We noted that this implies that it takes the duties of justice to be essentially negative in character. Moreover, it entails that those who are causally related in virtue of their action to the violation of some entitlement have the relevant negative duties of justice. Amongst other things, our evaluation of Nozick's account foreshadowed the possibility of positive duties and of duties that are not correlated with entitlements or rights at all within the scope of justice. So, we turned to Singer's Welfarist account, according to which one is duty-bound to aid those who are deprived as much as one can by positively altering the bad situation. Not only did we highlight its potential to account for positive duties, we also noted that it evinced a different criterion for deciding who should bear the duties of justice. Specifically, we noted that having the capability to prevent or otherwise reverse a bad situation, rather than causing or being able to cause it, is enough to make one a bearer of the duties of justice. Even so, we noted that Singer's account has no place for rights, which might make those duties salient and perhaps enforceable, and that it does not quite distinguish between cases in which proximity and relationality to a bad situation might impact the extent of a bearer's duties.

Gyekye's moderate communitarian account of justice sought to fill these gaps. Not only does it promise to combine considerations of rights and welfare, it also sheds light on why considerations of proximity and relationality might impact the strength of duties of justice flowing to appropriate bearers. Specifically, it locates duties in the context of a complex web of communal relationships, which encompasses a large swathe of duties, including those correlated to rights and those that are not, but instead are grounded in the need to improve overall welfare. This way it is able to account for positive duties. Moreover, the idea that duties arise in the context of a complex set of relationships suggests that considerations of relationality, in addition to capability, play a key role in deciding who has duties of justice. One difficulty with Gyekye's account, we noted, is that although it purports to be moderate, it recoils, unlike Nozick and Singer, from placing any limit on the extent of the duties that flow to duty-bearers, even permitting self-sacrifice in the process of discharging duties of justice. The idea that duties of justice have no limit at all had no place in our discussion of Bilchitz's conception of the corporation as a juristic person, endowed with a societal perspective. We noted specifically that on this view, the positive obligations of a corporation are to be balanced with its economic objective. In addition, corporations not only have negative duties in terms of the causality principle, but also positive (enforceable) duties to realise fundamental rights and are appropriate bearers of those duties, in terms of the capability and relationality principle.

## POINTS TO CONSIDER

1. What do you make of the distinction between justice and charity? Do you think that the duty, if it is a duty, to alleviate global poverty is a matter of justice – in the sense that victims of global poverty have a right to it?
2. Is Gyekye right that there should be no limits at all to how far one should go in discharging duties of justice? Perhaps, a lover still has a duty to his or her partner even if it requires self-sacrifice? Do you think self-sacrifice may be permitted under certain conditions?
3. One of the main contentions in this chapter is whether or not private actors have positive duties of justice. Do you think that Bilchitz is right that corporations should seek to provide basic resources to deprived people beyond the tax they already pay?

# Chapter 8

# Whom do rights protect?

*David Bilchitz*

## 8.1 The 'who' question and exploring the reach of justice

Between 1525 and 1866, over 12,5 million people were taken forcibly from their homes in Africa and shipped to form part of the slave trade in North and South America.[1] Of these people, around 10,7 million survived the sea voyage across the Atlantic, with many dying in the terrible conditions on the ships taking them across the ocean.[2] Many more died at various other stages of the trade. These people were not treated as individuals deserving of respect. They were traded as commodities on a market, when they arrived in the Americas, and regarded legally as the property of the slave-holder who bought them. Slaves were human beings who lacked any claims they could make in their own right. In short, slavery involved treating human beings as simply 'things' who lacked fundamental rights and to whom the concept of justice did not apply.

Today, the slave trade is regarded as being a classic example of a clear-cut terrible injustice. Individual human beings with valuable lives of their own – who were deserving of respectful and decent treatment – were treated as lacking any value in their own right and deprived of their freedom and hope of living fulfilling lives. Those who had value were treated as if they had none. This is a moral mistake that has been made countless times throughout human history. Beings that are valuable are excluded from the domain of rights and justice without any good reason.

A more recent example is the Holocaust that took place in the Second World War from 1939–1945. Jewish people suddenly found themselves being forcibly removed from their homes and being sent to concentration camps, where they were either forced to work for no pay or killed in gas chambers. Similar treatment was meted out to the Roma people as well as gays and lesbians. The extermination of these people involved the denial of all rights to them and, effectively, placed them outside the domain of justice.

South Africa, of course, experienced slavery as well until its abolition in 1834. Yet, the abolition of slavery did not suddenly lead to a recognition of the fundamental rights of all in South Africa. Segregationist policies continued in relation to white and black people and, with the advent of the Union of South Africa, one of the most notorious pieces of legislation, the Natives Land Act[3] denied black people the ability to hire or buy land across 93% of South Africa (later decreased in 1936 to 87%). When the National Party came to power in 1948, it implemented an apartheid policy which fundamentally sought to maintain black people in an inferior position to white people. Apartheid was premised on according higher value to white people in comparison to black people. From that basic idea flowed differential treatment between the two groups. The fundamental injustice and moral mistake which is recognised today involved treating one group – black people – in an inferior way to another group – white people – simply on the basis of the colour of their skin, an irrelevant moral characteristic.

These historical examples demonstrate the importance highlighted by the African context for providing a compelling answer to two central questions:

1. Who is entitled to be considered as being of value and therefore being included in the domain of justice and having rights accorded to them?

---

1  Gates, HL Jnr 'How Many Slaves Landed in the US?' (1 June 2014), available at http://www.theroot.com/how-many-slaves-landed-in-the-us-1790873989 (accessed 26 February 2017). The most comprehensive study of the numbers of slaves boarding ships and disembarking in the trans-Atlantic slave trade is available on a website titled Voyages: The Trans-Atlantic Slave Trade Database and accessible at this website: http://www.slavevoyages.org/assessment/estimates
2  Ibid.
3  27 of 1913.

2.  If an individual is of value, is he or she entitled to equal treatment? What does that equal treatment involve?

These questions remain of importance in relation to a number of groups in society. In light of the historical injustices discussed above, they challenge us not to exclude from the domain of justice and rights, those who are of value and entitled to make claims on our society. Our focus in this chapter will largely be on the first question as to who falls within the domain of justice, though some of the discussion will be relevant to whether individuals are entitled to equal treatment or not. To focus our minds on the contemporary issues that these questions raise, we will keep in mind two important groups.

A lot of our focus will be on the foundational question of what property or feature of the world entitles an individual to moral consideration. That question can be productively engaged by considering whether animals (who are not human) should be considered as having rights and within the domain of justice. In response to the Holocaust, the global community recognised that every human being had value and was entitled to certain fundamental rights (protected in the *Universal Declaration on Human Rights*). Yet, human beings share the earth with many other creatures. Do they have any entitlements and, if so, what are these? Africa has an incredibly rich array and diversity of creatures. How we answer these questions will thus affect the lives of many individuals and our treatment in relation to them.

Some of the discussion in this chapter will also be relevant to considering the approach to be adopted towards the rights of foreigners in a political community: individuals who come to visit or live in a particular society but are not originally from that society. If a foreign individual has a heart attack in South Africa, should he or she be treated in a public hospital? Can foreign individuals rightly claim access to social grants in the same ways that South Africans can? These questions require understanding principles which help us determine the rights and entitlements of those who are not clearly part of our political community.

In considering the theories in this chapter, it will be useful to think through a number of questions:

• What is the basis for being recognised as an individual who has worth and therefore rights?
• Who is excluded from the particular theory?
• Are there good reasons for any exclusion?

## 8.2   Kant and rationality

The first approach we will consider flows from the philosophy of Immanuel Kant (1724–1804). Kant is regarded as one of the greatest modern philosophers. His writings span across most spheres of philosophy including the theory of knowledge, metaphysics, ethics and aesthetics. In the sphere of ethics and political philosophy, he wrote a famous short book called the *Groundwork of the Metaphysics of Morals* (1785) from which our extract is derived. Kant articulates an approach to morality that is often regarded as the leading alternative to a utilitarian approach. Indeed, his form of ethics is often referred to as *deontological*. It is focused on the duties we have and are required to perform, irrespective of the consequences of our actions. Thus, for Kant, we are forbidden to lie even if others would never find out and would be happier believing falsehoods. Kant's philosophy is widely regarded as influencing some of the core ideas behind the recognition of human rights internationally: we must observe the rights of people whether that will bring about the best consequences overall or not. It has also been referred to, at times, by judges in the South African Constitutional Court.

---

**PRIMARY TEXTS**

**Text 1 Kant: Dignity and rationality**

... All objects of the inclinations have only a conditional worth; for, if there were not inclinations and the needs based on them, their object would be without worth. But the inclinations themselves, as sources of needs, are so far from having an absolute worth, so as to make one wish to have them, that it must instead be the universal wish of every rational being to be altogether free from them. Thus the worth of any object **to be acquired** by our action is always conditional. Beings the existence of which rests not on our will but on nature, if they are beings without reason, still have only a relative worth, as means, and are therefore called **things**, whereas rational beings are called **persons** because their nature already marks them out as an end in itself, that is, as something that may not be used merely as a means, and hence so far limits all choice (and is an object of respect)...

If, then, there is to be a supreme practical principle and, with respect to the human will, a categorical imperative, it must be one such that, from the representation of what is necessarily an end for everyone because it is an **end in itself** it constitutes an **objective** principle of the will and thus can serve as a universal practical law. The ground of this principle is: **rational nature exists as an end in itself**. The human being necessarily represents his own existence in this way; so far it is thus a **subjective** principle of human actions. But every other rational being also represents his existence in this way consequent on just the same rational ground that also holds for me; thus it is at the same time an **objective** principle from which, as a supreme practical ground, it must be possible to derive all laws of the will. The practical imperative will therefore be the following: **So act that you use humanity, whether in your own person or in the person of any other, always at the same time as an end, never merely as a means ....** [4]

... In the kingdom of ends everything has either a **price** or a **dignity**. What has a price can be replaced by something else as its **equivalent**; what on the other hand is raised above all price and therefore admits of no equivalent has a dignity. [5]

**Questions**

1. What is the capacity that individuals must possess, to be regarded as having worth for Kant?
2. Why is this capacity so important for Kant?
3. If an individual has this capacity, how must he or she be treated?
4. What does Kant mean by dignity and who has dignity?

## 8.2.1 Kant's theory of value

Immanuel Kant considers different possible features of ourselves as the grounds of assigning value. He mentions what he terms 'inclinations' or, in more modern times, we might call them desires. Kant sees our desires for things like food or sex as simply existing naturally but being parts of ourselves over which we have no real control. They move us to act in various

---

4  Kant 1785 *Groundwork of the Metaphysics of Morals* at 79–80.
5  Kant 1785 at 84.

ways in an almost robotic manner. It is for this reason he states that rational beings would rather be free from these desires. Similarly, Kant thinks that creatures that are not rational lack the ability to control their actions and behaviour. As such, they are simply under the forces of instinct or nature and so blindly seek to realise whatever goals have been essentially programmed into their DNA.

The ability to reason, however, fundamentally changes the nature of individuals for Kant. Reason for Kant, in this context, is conceived of as allowing individuals to weigh up and evaluate the considerations in favour or against acting in a particular manner. It also involves being able to act upon the reasons one decides are persuasive. Of course, the capacity to exercise rational agency in this way also comes with the ability to think abstractly about matters and to utilise language in a complex manner.

These capacities mean, for Kant, that human beings are not simply at the mercy of their desires. Instead, they are able to control their own actions and act out of their own free will. They are not simply subject to the laws of nature but, in a sense, are self-legislating. They can give laws to themselves as to how they should behave or not. The capacity for rational agency is a basic condition for morality according to Kant. We cannot claim someone has a moral duty without their ability to recognise such a duty and act accordingly. This capacity is also necessary to attribute moral blame or praise. Someone can only be guilty of a moral wrong if they have the ability to choose between right and wrong.

Given the importance of these capacities for morality, Kant believes they are the basis upon which we recognise that an individual has essential moral worth or not. Recognising moral worth, of course, has consequences for the manner in which we can treat individuals that possess it. Kant adopts a famous principle or categorical imperative which reflects the manner in which we must act in relation to those with rational agency:

> **So act that you use humanity, whether in your own person or in the person of any other, always at the same time as an end, never merely as a means.**[6]

What does this principle mean?

## 8.2.2   Kant's key principle of morality and the notion of dignity

The essential characteristic of humanity that Kant focuses upon is the capacity for rational agency. Thus, this principle can be taken to mean that whenever we engage with another rational agent, we must do so in a manner respectful of their rational agency. Thus, I cannot use force to require another individual to do something. That would treat them merely as a 'means' and someone who is under the control of external forces. Instead, I must provide them with the reasons to comply with what I want them to do and they must freely choose to follow this course of action. As such, I treat them with respect as people who are able to make their own decisions. A similar point can be made about why Kant regarded lying as so problematic. To lie to someone is to provide someone with false information or arguments, usually in order to make them perform some action one regards as desirable. Yet, that is to circumvent their rational abilities to decide which course of action they wish to perform.

Importantly, the principle does not state that we can never use another individual as a means: rather, it says, *merely* as a means. In modern society, we use individuals to achieve our ends all the time. Think about going to the grocery store and the till-operator enabling you to acquire your goods. You are using such an individual to achieve your ends but you are not treating him or her merely as a means. The individual must be given the ability to

---

6   Kant 1785 at 80.

decide whether to work in such a job or not. Kant will also require that the attitude with which you engage with the individual behind the till is respectful and recognises the worth of the person in question.

The importance of rational agency for Kant leads him to make another distinction which has been very influential. On the one hand, there are things he states that can be replaced by something else and that are regarded as having a 'price'. On the other hand, there are individuals that have no equivalent and cannot be replaced. These features of the world have what Kant calls 'dignity'. Those parts of the world that have dignity are the very basis upon which we confer value on any other thing. They, therefore, have a type of absolute or incomparable worth. The central characteristic that confers value for Kant is the ability to make decisions for oneself on the balance of reasons. It is thus only rational agents that have dignity. Since the only type of fully rational agents we know are human beings, it follows that it is only human beings that have dignity. These ideas have had a strong influence and led to the inclusion in the *Universal Declaration on Human Rights* of the idea that 'all human beings are born free and equal in dignity and rights'.[7]

The absolute or incomparable worth of an individual that has dignity can also be seen to provide the justification for the non-utilitarian (or deontological) features of Kant's thinking. Since we cannot replace one individual with another and each has absolute worth, it is not therefore correct to think that we could justify harming one individual for the benefit of another. Whatever the consequences, individuals cannot be traded off against one another and must be respected in each individual situation.

### 8.2.3   Implications of Kant's theory

In terms of the groups we started considering in the introduction, Kant's theory would give strong grounds to oppose slavery of human beings. Individuals with rational agency must not be reduced to the mere property of others – that would be a central case of not treating individuals as ends in themselves. It would clearly be against the treatment of Jews, Roma and gays and lesbians in the Holocaust as well as black people in South Africa under apartheid, for example.

In relation to foreigners, the theory would require that they be treated as having dignity and thus as ends in themselves. Foreigners would be treated as every other human being and not be subject to differential treatment. The theory seems to require impartial concern for all human beings. It would struggle, it seems, to allow for distinctions on the basis of nationality. Whilst this may be regarded as a good thing by many, there is a question as to whether, for instance, those who are in the country for a short amount of time should be entitled to the same social grants as those who have lived in the society for a long period. Kant's theory does not seem well-equipped to address that issue. It could be argued, however, that Kantian fairness requires distributing goods in proportion to the contribution people make to a society (from those able to do so); otherwise, those who do not contribute could be said to be free-riding or exploiting those who do (assuming they are able to do so).

In relation to animals, Kant's theory seems, on first glance, to exclude them from the domain of justice and morality. Kant sees animals as lacking rational agency and as such not subject to moral concern in their own right. They are beings with only conditional value and, as such, can be treated as means to our ends. Kant, however, has a clever argument why we should nevertheless not treat animals cruelly and still seek to meet their needs. He argues that treating animals in cruel way will lead human beings to treat each other in a cruel way.

---

7   The *Universal Declaration on Human Rights* is available here: http://www.un.org/en/universal-declaration-human-rights/

Why should this happen? Kant recognises that animals can suffer and, as such, if we turn our back on their suffering, we will develop characteristics which make us hard-hearted and cruel more generally. If that happens, then our cruel and heartless actions will not be confined to animals but affect other human beings too. Kant thus says we should not treat animals cruelly in order that we treat human beings – who have real value and worth – properly. As such, he is regarded as articulating an 'indirect' duty view in relation to animals. Our duties to them are indirect as we only have duties to them through our direct duties towards human beings.[8]

### 8.2.4    Is rationality the only ground of value?

As we saw, Kant places central importance on the capacity for rational agency as a ground for individuals to have value. Kant seems to be correct that we require rational agency in order to have duties, in other words, in order to be *moral agents*. However, he seems to make a jump from this claim to the idea that only moral agents count in our moral considerations and place duties upon us.

Consider, for instance, the case of infants: as human beings we all go through a stage in our lives where we are entirely dependent upon our parents. We also lack the ability to exercise rational agency. If we are thirsty or hungry, we cry but have no control over our inclinations. Kant's theory would seem to suggest that young infants fall outside the domain of moral concerns and that we lack moral duties towards them. They also are not to be considered as having dignity or incomparable worth.

Similar reasoning would apply to those with severe psychosocial disabilities. Consider an individual who is in the midst of a psychotic episode. The individual is not able to exercise rational agency and decisions must be made for them. Some individuals throughout their lives never develop the ability to exercise rational agency. Kant's theory would seem to imply that we do not owe them duties directly and that they can claim no rights.

In the cases of both the infant and the individual with severe psychosocial disabilities, Kant's view runs counter to our moral intuitions that these vulnerable individuals are deserving of respectful treatment in their own right. It also goes against the idea that all human beings are deserving of respectful treatment and fall within the domain of our moral concern. The South African Constitution, for instance, would recognise the fundamental rights of both infants and those with severe psychosocial disabilities. The capacity for rational agency cannot then be essential if we are to recognise these individuals as falling within the domain of our moral concern and being entitled to rights. There, therefore, seem to be a class of individuals who lack the capacity to exercise rational agency (and therefore have moral duties) but who place duties on those of us who do have rational agency. Philosophers refer to these individuals as *moral patients*.[9]

This conclusion does seem to accord with common sense reasoning. Rational agency indeed seems of vital importance when we consider the importance of the right to vote, for instance. It is necessary to have the capacity to consider and evaluate different positions regarding the nature of a political community in order to be able to participate effectively in elections. That explains why young infants are not given the right to vote. Yet, when it comes to a right to be free from violent attacks or harm (often protected by a right to freedom and security of the person or the right to bodily integrity), young infants have such rights just as

---

8    Kant 1963 *Lectures on Ethics* at 239–240.
9    See Regan 1983 *The Case for Animal Rights* at 151–152.

much as adults do. Rational agency does not fully explain our interests in these rights. There appears to be something else at stake.

Before we move on, it is important to consider briefly Kant's argument in relation to animals (which could be extended to these human beings who lack rational agency) that cruel treatment to these moral patients will lead to cruel treatment to moral agents. Whilst some empirical studies suggest there is some truth to this argument in terms of its effects,[10] the problem lies in explaining the connection. We do not think hitting a table hard will lead us to harm other moral agents. If this is so, why therefore will kicking a dog or child do so? The reason must be that there is a sufficient similarity between the dog or the infant and the adult human beings – the kicking leads to pain and suffering. If this sufficient similarity is the reason to fear a spill-over from cruel behaviour to dogs or infants, then it seems what matters in these circumstances are the interests of both animals and humans in avoiding suffering. If the interest is sufficient to ground a prohibition against cruel behaviour in the case of human beings who are rational agents, why is it not sufficient to ground such a prohibition in the case of sentient animals and young children? If there is no good reason to distinguish these two cases, then it seems that the indirect duty argument collapses into an argument that we have direct duties to those who share the relevant similarity with moral agents.[11] Once again, this raises the question as to what this similarity is and the next texts provide some ideas of what that might be.

## 8.3 Singer and sentience

We encountered Peter Singer's thought in the previous chapter on the positive duties of individuals to assist others living in conditions of poverty. Singer has also been an extremely influential philosopher on the question of the manner in which we are required to treat non-human animals. His book *Animal Liberation* (1975)[12] made powerful arguments that catalysed the development of a whole field considering the treatment of non-human animals. Singer's thinking is of importance not only to non-human animals but also provides a significant discussion of the question that is the subject matter of this chapter and has relevance, for instance, to the question as to what point, if any, a human fetus must be considered morally in its own right.

---

**PRIMARY TEXTS**

**Text 2  Singer: Sentience and the argument against categorical thinking**

... Most people draw a sharp moral line between humans and other animals. Humans, they say, are infinitely more valuable than any "lower creatures." If our interests conflicts with those of animals, it is always their interests which should be sacrificed. But why should this be so? To say that everyone believes this is not enough to justify it. Until very recently it was the common view that a woman should obey her father, until she is married, and then her husband (and in some countries, this is still the prevailing view). Or, not quite so recently, but still not all that long ago, it was widely held that people of African descent could properly be enslaved. As these examples show, the fact that a view is widespread does not

---

10   Lockwood 1999 *Animal Law* at 85; Lacroix, CA 1998 *Animal Law* at 7; Dryden 2001 *Idaho Law Review* at 185.
11   Bilchitz 2009 *South African Journal on Human Rights* at 48.
12   Singer 1975 *Animal Liberation*.

make it right. It may be an indefensible prejudice that survives primarily because it suits the interests of the dominant group.

How should we decide whether a widely held view is justifiable, or a prejudice based on the interests of the dominant group? The obvious answer is that we should consider what reasons are offered for the view. Putting aside religious grounds that would force us to examine the foundations of the particular religions of which they are a consequence, the reason given usually refers to some kind of human superiority over animals. After all, are not human beings more rational, more self-aware, more capable of a sense of justice, and so on, than any nonhuman animals? But while this claim may be true if limited to normal mature human beings, it does not help us to defend the place where we now draw the moral line, which is between all members of our species and all nonhuman animals. For there are many humans who are not rational, or self-aware, and who have no sense of justice – all humans under one month of age, for a start. And even if infants are excluded on the grounds that they have the potential to become rational, self-aware, and have a sense of justice, not all humans have this potential. Sadly, some are born with brain damage so severe that they will never be rational or self-aware, or capable of a sense of justice. In fact, some of these humans will never possess any intellectual or emotional capacities that are not also possessed by any normal, non-infant chimpanzee, dog, cat, pig, cow, or even laboratory rat.

Hence it seems that no adequate reason can be given for taking species membership, in itself, as the ground for putting some beings inside the boundary of moral protection and others either totally or very largely outside it. That doesn't mean that all animals have the same rights as humans. It would be absurd to give animals the right to vote, but then it would be no less absurd to give that right to infants or to severely retarded human beings. Yet we still give equal consideration to the interests of those humans incapable of voting. We don't raise them for food, nor test cosmetics in their eyes. Nor should we. But we do these things to nonhuman animals who show greater rationality, self-awareness, and a sense of justice than they do.

Once we understand that in respect of any valuable characteristic we can think of, there is no gap between humans and animals, but rather an overlap in the possession of that characteristic by individuals of different species, it is easy to see the belief that all humans are somehow infinitely more valuable than any animal is a prejudice. It is in some respects akin to the prejudice that racists have in favor of their own race, and sexists have in favor of their own gender (although there are also differences, as with any complex social phenomena). Speciesism is logically parallel to racism and sexism, in the sense that speciesists, racists, and sexists all say: Never mind what you are like, if you are a member of my group, you are superior to all those who are not members of my group. The speciesist favor a larger group than the racist, and so has a larger circle of concern, but all of those prejudices use an arbitrary and morally irrelevant fact – membership in race, gender, or species – as if it were morally crucial.

The only acceptable limit of our moral concern is the point at which there is no awareness of pain or pleasure and no conscious preferences of any kind. That is why pigs are objects of moral concern, but lettuces are not. Pigs can feel pain and pleasure; they can enjoy their lives, or want to escape from distressing conditions. To the best of our knowledge, lettuces can't. We should give the same weight to the pain and distress of pigs as we would give to a similar amount of pain and distress suffered by a human being. Of course, pigs and humans may have different interests, and there are some human interests that a pig is probably incapable of having – like, for example, our interest in living to see our grandchildren. There may, therefore, sometimes be grounds for giving preference to the human over the pig – but if so, it can only be because in the particular circumstances the human has greater interests at stake, and not simply because the human is a member of our own species.[13]

**Questions**
1. Why is it unjustifiable simply to think categorically in terms of who is included within the domain of justice: to say, simply that humans are included and non-humans are excluded?
2. What is the relationship in Singer's view between speciesism, racism and sexism?
3. What, in Singer's view, is the problem with the Kantian approach?
4. Why does the recognition of humans who lack rational agency as having rights provide reasons for the recognition of animals as having rights?
5. What is the only justifiable basis upon which to include individuals within the domain of moral concern, according to Singer? Why?
6. Why can we still distinguish between the rights we afford to moral agents and moral patients?

### 8.3.1 The problem with categorical thinking

Singer starts by asking: what is the basis upon which we can decide who lies within the domain of our moral concern? He considers the fact that many people answer the question by saying all humans count and animals do not. Indeed, many legal systems (including that of South Africa) have often regarded only humans as persons – and thus capable of having rights – whilst animals are considered as things – without any rights in their own right.[14] Drawing the line in this way of who counts morally is based on a type of categorical thinking: if you belong to one category (the human species), then you count; if not, you do not.

Singer points out the way in which this type of thinking has played out in various contexts. African people were regarded as being outside the domain of moral concern and therefore could be enslaved. If you were European you counted morally; if you were African you did not.

Singer attempts to show that this form of reasoning is in fact fundamentally flawed and simply the result of prejudice. It is hard to see why the colour of one's skin, for instance, or origin in Europe has any bearing on how one should be treated. The colour of one's skin or one's national origin are simply facts about one which appear to have no moral relevance as to whether one counts morally or not.

---

13  Singer 2004 *Animal Rights: Current Debates and New Directions* at 78–80.
14  See my discussion of this question in Bilchitz, 2009. The position may have changed with the ground-breaking judgment of *National Society for the Prevention of Cruelty to Animals v Minister of Justice and Constitutional Development* (2017) 1 SACR 284 (CC).

A similar point can also be made about whether one should be treated in an equal manner with others or not. Racism and xenophobia are wrong as they focus on an irrelevant characteristic as the ground for treating people differently. There is simply no good reason why black people should be treated differently simply because of the colour of their skin. The same is true of the sex and gender of an individual. The fact that one belongs to a particular category cannot in itself provide the basis for differential treatment. One needs to show why such a category is morally relevant to treating an individual differently.

Singer argues that the same reasoning applies to the differentiation between humans and animals. The fact that one belongs to a particular species – a particular biological category – provides no reason in and of itself why humans deserve to be counted morally or treated preferentially to other creatures. Singer coins the term 'speciesism' for such thinking which he claims is similar to the thinking underpinning racism and sexism. There is no rational explanation why simply belonging to a particular category is the basis for attributing value to a being or not.

### 8.3.2   The argument from marginal cases

However, some people think that humans count morally and animals do not (or that humans count more than animals) and attempt to provide a justification for the distinction. The most common argument is that it is justifiable to distinguish between the two on the basis of the fact that humans generally have more sophisticated mental capacities than animals. We have already seen the manner in which Immanuel Kant outlines this view in relation to rational agency.

Singer contends that when we break down the problems with Kant's view, we are led to recognise a strong argument as to why species is not an adequate basis upon which to differentiate between individuals morally. He recognises that there are many humans – young infants and those with severe psychosocial disabilities – who do not have sophisticated mental abilities. Some human individuals may never develop such abilities. Yet, we recognise that these human individuals fall within the domain of our moral concern and are entitled to equal consideration of their interests.

If we admit humans that lack rational agency within the domain of our moral concern, then we must – on pain of arbitrariness – also admit non-humans who lack rational agency within the domain of our moral concern. In a similar manner, they will also be entitled to equal consideration for their interests. Equal consideration for Singer does not mean identical rights or treatment. He recognises that young infants and animals will not be entitled to a right to vote. Nevertheless, they will be entitled to equal consideration of their interests which matter to them such as those relating to their lives, bodily integrity and well-being.

This powerful argument suggests that we must find a non-arbitrary basis upon which to decide who falls within the domain of our moral concern and that the species boundary does not provide an adequate answer. What then is Singer's view in this regard?

### 8.3.3   Sentience

Singer was influenced in his view by the famous philosopher, Jeremy Bentham, whom we encountered in Chapter 6 (and will encounter again in Chapter 10). Bentham wrote 'The question is not, Can they *reason*? nor Can they *talk*? But, Can they *suffer*?'[15]

---

15   Singer 1995 at 7.

Singer is of the view that the only basis upon which we can distinguish between those who count morally and those who do not relates to whether they are sentient creatures or not. Sentience involves the idea that there is something it is like from the inside, to be an individual of a particular type. In other words, an individual has a consciousness and is capable in his or her own right of experiencing pleasure or pain. An individual that lacks sentience has no interests of their own; as such, they can simply be acted upon. An individual that has sentience has a point of view from which we can judge good or bad. Irrespective of what anyone else thinks, from the point of view of that creature, there is something that goes better or worse for them.

Thus, Singer states that pigs are the object of our moral concern whilst lettuces are not. Lettuces lack the ability to feel pain or pleasure, whereas pigs can feel these sensations but also can enjoy their lives or be subject to severe suffering. We can judge these matters from the point of view of the pig: it has interests of its own. The same of course is true of infants, those with severe psychosocial disabilities and adult human beings without those disabilities. Sentience for Singer is a non-arbitrary basis upon which to draw the line between those who count and those who do not.

There is also no non-arbitrary reason to treat the interests of some sentient individuals as being more important than the interests of other sentient individuals and, so, according to Singer, they should be treated equally. Of course, he recognises that the interests of pigs and humans will sometimes be different and it will be legitimate to take into account these different interests when making decisions as to what we should do. This means we sometimes can give a preference to a human over a pig but the reasons for doing so are not simply related to the species of the individuals – which is arbitrary – but in relation to the balance of interests under consideration. Singer is a utilitarian and therefore concerned with achieving the best overall happiness for all concerned. It is, though, also possible to create a non-utilitarian theory which accepts sentience as the ground of value too.[16]

How would Singer's theory apply to foreigners? Once again, his approach is one which requires equal consideration to be afforded to all those who are sentient. Since foreigners are clearly sentient, their interests would be taken into account in any moral evaluations. As we saw in Chapter 7, Singer's views are strictly impartial. He does not think there is a difference between how we should treat a child who we see falling into a pond or a foreign individual starving in a country far away. We also saw that, on his approach, individual duties are extensive in relation to those who are distant too. Proximity does not make a difference. As such, foreigners would be entitled to equal consideration with citizens and, ultimately, the question would be which policies would lead to the greatest overall happiness. It might be that there are some reasons to give preference to citizens in relation to social benefits. Those would arise from thinking more generally about how to design a global system that ensures everyone has access to a decent social minimum of benefits. If such a system were designed in a way that requires nation states to provide social benefits for their own citizens, it could legitimately be argued that foreigners should claim such benefits from the states in which they were originally from. Unfortunately, as is evident from our world today, many states across the world and on the African continent particularly are not able to provide these required social benefits for their citizens. The question then becomes whether there is then greater obligations on wealthier states to assist those people unable to gain access to such benefits in their home states – including foreigners from outside their borders. Since Singer's theory is impartial and includes all sentient individuals, it is likely he would strongly

---

16   See, for instance, Regan 1983.

advocate for such enhanced responsibilities towards foreigners for countries which are better off. This of course poses a major moral challenge to many such societies which often, rather selfishly, are seeking to exclude refugees from Syria and North Africa whose home states are in terrible conditions.

## 8.3.4   Is sentience inclusive enough?

Singer's views on sentience of course extend the domain of our moral concern more widely. Some, however, particularly from the environmental movement, regard this criterion as still being too restrictive. We live in a world in which there is the biological kingdom and the question arises about the manner in which human beings should treat plants and trees. On top of that, there are major questions relating to such beautiful features of the world such as rivers and mountains. Environmental ethicists often want to extend the domain of our moral concern beyond only sentient creatures to the many other features of the world around us.

A *biocentric* view seeks to extend the domain of our moral concern to all living things. Paul Taylor, for instance, argues that:

> [w]e can think of the good of an individual nonhuman organism as consisting in the full development of its biological powers. Its good is realized to the extent that it is strong and healthy.[17]

The idea of having a good applies irrespective of whether that biological being is aware of its interests or not. Taylor thinks we can harm trees and plants (through depriving them of water or cutting their roots) even though they lack desires or feelings.

The question of course is from what perspective we judge harm in these cases. If the plant or tree is not aware of being harmed, then it seems there is a good case to argue that it is human beings that are imposing the notion of harm on the natural world. Indeed, the view seems so extensive that it would include inanimate objects such as tables or machines within its domain of moral concern. We seem to be able to 'harm' a table by chopping it up. Yet, this seems to take matters much too far: do we really have moral obligations to inanimate objects? One crucial question for a biocentric view will be whether it can adequately distinguish between life forms – which lack sentience – and other inanimate objects. If we reject the biocentric view, however, that does not mean we have no duties to the environment. The manner in which we treat plants, rivers and mountains affects humans and other animals and so we will need to care for the environment if we are concerned for these individuals.

An *ecocentric* view, on the other hand, challenges the individualist assumption of the ethical theories considered thus far. The theories we have studied, generally, focus on a particular capacity that rests in individual animals and human beings. Instead, the ecocentric view regards value as resting in the 'biotic community' as a whole or perhaps, in more modern terms, in the ecosystem as a whole. This view was famously developed by Aldo Leopold who held that:

> a thing is right when it tends to preserve the integrity, stability and beauty of the biotic community. It is wrong when it tends otherwise.[18]

Thus, to illustrate this view, it is worth considering the major discussion in South Africa about whether there were too many elephants in the Kruger National Park. Elephants, in the

---

17   Taylor 1981 *Environmental Ethics: Readings in Theory and Application* at 140.
18   Leopold 1977 *A Sand County Almanac: And Sketches Here and There* at 224–225; Callicott 1987 *Environmental Ethics: Readings in Theory and Application*.

natural course of finding food, eat a lot and destroy many trees. It is sometimes argued that having too many elephants in an area destroys the plant life and also affects other species of animals. An ecocentric ethic would regard it as permissible to kill some individual elephants in order to preserve the good of the whole 'biotic community'. What matters fundamentally is not the individual but the whole ecosystem.

There are two main challenges and problems raised with such a view. First, there is the question as to what value lies in the 'biotic community' as a whole. It is not puzzling to understand why individual human beings or animals have value; but, why should we attribute value to a whole system which is made up of these many individuals that have lives that can be better and worse? These accounts find significant difficulty in answering this question.

Second, in a related manner, the problem also is raised as to how to justify overriding the interests of individuals for the ecosystem as a whole. Of course, the reasoning contained therein may apply equally to humans as well as other creatures. If there are too many humans, is it permissible to kill some to restore the balance of the whole? Indeed, these accounts seem to have parallel problems to utilitarianism in accounting for the value and rights accorded to individuals and have been charged with 'environmental fascism' – akin to ordinary fascism, they allow for the good of the whole (which as we saw is difficult to specify) to override individual interests.[19]

## 8.4   Sen, Nussbaum and capabilities

We now turn to an alternative view which finds value not in rationality or sentience but in what is referred to as 'capabilities'. The approach was developed by the Nobel prize-winning economist and philosopher, Amartya Sen, as well as the philosopher Martha Nussbaum.

**PRIMARY TEXTS**

**Text 3  Sen: Functionings and capabilities**

The well-being of a person can be seen in terms of the quality (the 'well-ness', as it were) of the person's being. Living may be seen as consisting of a set of interrelated 'functionings', consisting of beings and doings. A person's achievement in this respect can be seen as the vector of his or her functionings. The relevant functionings can vary from such elementary things as being adequately nourished, being in good health, avoiding escapable morbidity and premature mortality, etc, to more complex achievements such as being happy, having self-respect, taking part in the life of the community, and so on. The claim is that functionings are constitutive of a person's being, and an evaluation of well-being has to take the form of an assessment of these constituent elements.

Closely related to the notion of functionings is that of the capability to function. It represents the various combinations of functionings (beings and doings) that the person can achieve. Capability is, thus, a set of vectors of functionings, reflecting the person's freedom to lead one type of life or another. Just as the so-called 'budget set' in the commodity space represents a person's freedom to buy commodity bundles, the 'capability set' in the functioning space reflects the person's freedom to choose from possible livings.[20]

---

19   Regan 1983 at 362.
20   Sen 1992 *Inequality Re-Examined* at 39–40.

### Text 4  Nussbaum: Dignity beyond rationality

A second fundamental departure from contractarianism pertains to the notion of dignity, and thus to Rawls's Kantian conception of the person, which makes a notion of dignity basic. Kant contrasts the humanity of human beings with their animality. Although Rawls does not do so explicitly, he does make personhood reside in (moral and prudential) rationality, not in the needs that human beings share with other animals. The capabilities approach, by contrast, sees rationality and animality as thoroughly unified. Taking its cue from Aristotle's notion of the human being as a political animal, and from Marx's idea that the human being is a creature "in need of a plurality of life-activities," it sees the rational as simply one aspect of the animal, and, at that, not the only one that is pertinent to a notion of truly human functioning. More generally, the capabilities approach sees the world as containing many different types of animal dignity, all of which deserve respect and even awe. The specifically human kind is indeed characterized, usually, by a kind of rationality, but rationality is not idealized and set in opposition to animality, it is just garden-variety practical reasoning, which is one way animals have of functioning. Sociability, moreover, is equally fundamental and equally pervasive. And bodily need, including the need for care, is a feature of our rationality and our sociability; it is one aspect of our dignity, then, rather than something to be contrasted with it.

Thus, in the design of the political conception of the person out of which basic political principles grow, we build in an acknowledgment that we are needy temporal animal beings who begin as babies and end, often, in other forms of dependency. We draw attention to these areas of vulnerability, insisting that rationality and sociability are themselves temporal, having growth, maturity, and (if time permits) decline. We acknowledge, as well, that the kind of sociability that is fully human includes symmetrical relations, such as those that are central for Rawls, but also relations of more or less extreme asymmetry; we insist that the nonsymmetrical relations can still contain reciprocity and truly human functioning.[21]

... The purpose of social cooperation, by analogy and extension, ought to be to live decently together in a world in which many species try to flourish. (Cooperation itself will now assume multiple and complex forms.) The general aim of the capabilities approach in charting political principles to shape the human-animal relationship, if we follow the intuitive ideas of theory, would be that no sentient animal should be cut off from the chance for a flourishing life, a life with the type of dignity relevant to that species, and that all sentient animals should enjoy certain positive opportunities to flourish. With due respect for a world that contains many forms of life, we attend with ethical concern to each characteristic type of flourishing, and strive that it not be cut off or fruitless.

Unlike contractarianism, this approach involves direct obligations of justice to animals; it does not make these derivative from or posterior to the duties we have to fellow humans. It treats animals as subjects and agents, not just as objects of

---

21   Nussbaum 2006 *Frontiers of Justice* at 159–160.

compassion. Unlike Utilitarianism, it respects each individual creature, refusing to aggregate the good of different lives and types of lives. No creature is being used as a means to the ends of others, or of society as a whole. The capabilities approach also refuses to aggregate across the diverse constituents of each life and type of life. Thus, unlike Utilitarianism, it can keep in focus the fact that each species has a different form of life and different ends; moreover, within a given species, each life has multiple and heterogeneous ends.[22]

... Given the fact that pleasure and pain are not the only things of intrinsic value for the capabilities approach, the approach, strictly speaking, should not say that the capacity to feel pleasure and pain is a necessary condition of moral status. Instead, we should adopt a disjunctive approach: if a creature has either the capacity for pleasure and pain or the capacity for movement from place to place or the capacity for emotion and affiliation or the capacity for reasoning, and so forth (we might add play, tool use, and others), then that creature has moral standing. Science fiction reminds us that there are intelligent creatures who lack the ability to feel pleasure and pain. So does religion: God, in many traditional views, is a rational being who lacks sentience. But nature as we know it is not like science fiction or theology. All the creatures that have one of the other salient capabilities mentioned above also have the capacity to feel pleasure and pain. Aristotle reminds us that this is no accident: for sentience is central to movement, affiliation, emotion, and thought. We may, however, admit the science fiction possibility for theoretical purposes.[23]

**Questions**

1. For Amartya Sen, what is the basis upon which we assess value in life?
2. What is the difference between functionings and capabilities?
3. What are some of the benefits of the capabilities approach in contrast with other approaches?
4. What approach does the capabilities approach, as Nussbaum describes it, adopt towards dignity in contrast with the Kantian approach?
5. Which capabilities are important for Nussbaum?
6. What is the relationship between human capabilities and the capabilities of animals who are not human?

## 8.4.1 The capabilities approach of Sen and its motivation

The capabilities approach has its origins in attempting to understand how to measure the quality of life for individuals. This is important if, for instance, we want to know how to improve the conditions of life and what to focus on. Achieving an understanding of such a metric will assist in developing social policies and laws which advance that quality of life.

The capabilities approach situates itself in contrast to two existing approaches. The first approach assesses the quality of life in terms of whether individuals express satisfaction with what they have. The idea behind this view is the understanding that the best way to find out if people are experiencing a decent quality of life is to ask them directly about it.

---

22  Nussbaum 2006 at 351–352.
23  Nussbaum 2006 at 362.

One major problem with this account is that people's desires often adjust to the circumstances in which they live. Karl Marx gives an example of a 'contented slave': someone who has never known any reality other than slavery may express satisfaction with their situation. Yet, we know that slavery is wrong and freedom is valuable. If we accept that people come to adjust to their circumstances which may be undesirable, a purely subjective account will be unable to challenge the circumstances that shaped the satisfactions which people express. This is called the 'adaptive preference problem'. Nussbaum gives another example of women in India who have become accustomed to being malnourished and only having a quantity of food which is well below the United Nations requirements for adequate nutrition. The women have never known another reality and so express satisfaction with their lot. If we want to recognise that the state of their lives is not optimal, we need to go beyond a purely subjective account focused on whether they express satisfaction with their lives. A purely subjective account also leads to problems for policy. It is a difficult goal to ensure everyone is equally satisfied. Equal satisfaction will also mean giving vastly different amounts of resources to some people over others. Think, for example, about some people who, in order to move around, are happy to use public transport versus those who want a Mercedes Benz.

These problems with a subjective account lead philosophers to posit more objective accounts of well-being and value. One such account focuses on understanding quality of life in terms of the resources individuals can command. Resources are a more quantifiable metric than satisfaction and would allow us broadly to ensure individuals have an equal amount thereof. The problem, however, as Amartya Sen points out, is that we do not value resources in and of themselves; rather we value what we can do with them. Consider an example of a person who requires a wheelchair to move around and receives an equal pension to a person who is able to move around unaided. The person who is unable to walk by themselves needs more resources than the able-bodied individual. If we give each an equal amount of resources, it seems to be unfair to the disabled person who may not be able to afford the wheelchair to enable her to move around.

These considerations lead Amartya Sen to propose an objective account that lies somewhere in between the two views discussed. What matters, according to Sen, for individuals is what they can do or be with any resources they have. He terms this idea the *functionings* of an individual. Crucial functionings for individuals are being adequately nourished and being healthy. Being in these states leads individuals to be able to act in ways that they wish, as well as to achieve such objectively desirable functionings as participating in the life of one's community.

*Capabilities* represent alternative sets of functionings individuals can attain. This notion includes the idea that there are different ways in which individuals can be fulfilled and that it is important for individuals to be able to choose between them. Thus, the idea of capabilities seeks to distinguish between the poor person and a monk – who chooses to fast for several days of the week – who are both malnourished. The monk has adequate food at his disposal and actively chooses not to eat. He thus has the capability to be adequately nourished but the freedom to choose otherwise. The poor person lacks the capability to be adequately nourished and has no freedom to choose to remain in that state or not. Capabilities thus importantly take account of the freedom or lack thereof of individuals to choose alternative paths in life.

The capabilities view also recognises that there are limitations on the things individuals can do which come from a range of sources. Individual abilities, for example, vary and thus one person can be a brilliant soccer player whilst another cannot; one has the capability to be a Benni McCarthy whereas another does not. Our social, environmental and physical constraints also affect the capabilities we can attain. If I live in a rural area, I may be able to attain a greater connection with the natural world but I may also lack opportunities to go to the movies or the theatre.

The capabilities approach thus assesses value in terms of whether an individual is capable of doing something or not. As we saw, there are multiple factors in determining whether someone has a capability. One criticism with the approach, as it was developed by Amartya Sen, is that there are many functionings and capabilities in individual lives. The mere existence of a functioning or capability does not seem to attest to its being valuable. Consider the fact that an individual may be obsessive. Is that a valuable functioning? Usually, we think such a state hinders an individual's ability to achieve his or her goals. Similarly, we also have the opportunities to choose between many things. Do we think it is critical, for instance, to have the capacity to choose between multiple brands of cereal?[24] That seems like a rather trivial capability. A central problem for the capabilities approach is thus to provide us with a criterion to determine which capabilities are valuable or not.

### 8.4.2 Nussbaum's development of the approach and the importance of flourishing

Martha Nussbaum develops the approach in order to answer these questions. She builds on insights drawn from the famous Greek philosopher Aristotle who suggests that when we evaluate what is of value, we need to understand the goals or ends which a particular individual being wishes to achieve. On a simple level, we can think of a utensil such as knife. What makes a good knife? We understand that the purpose of a knife is to be able to cut. A good knife is a knife that realises its purpose and cuts well. In the natural world, we might think of the purpose of a bee as being able to pollinate plants. It would harm the good for bees if there are conditions which prevent them from realising their end. Of course, this analysis is much more difficult to apply more widely to individual beings whose purpose for existing is less clear cut. In doing so, it seems, we need to understand the life-form and what, generally, is good for it. Ultimately, what really matters in this Aristotelian account, is that individuals can live a fulfilling and flourishing life on their own terms. If we want individual beings to have a good life that is appropriate to them, then what matters is that they be able to achieve that good life. The capabilities that are valuable, therefore, in Nussbaum's view are the ones that enable individuals to flourish on their own terms.

Nussbaum initially develops her theory in relation to human beings alone. And, even within the human species, there is a high degree of variation and diversity. The capabilities approach attempts to specify what is common to humans flourishing at a high level of abstraction, that allows for a recognition both of the commonality of people as well as their diversity. Thus, on a basic level, the capabilities approach recognises that in order to flourish as a human being, it is important to be healthy and have adequate nutrition. This is a common functioning that all humans need to live a good life. Yet, this recognition does not preclude us from understanding that, in India, people regard rice as central to enabling them to flourish, whereas in South Africa, the staple is maize meal. Whilst we differ in the specifics of what makes our lives flourish – which largely depends on individual taste and choice – there is a common objective capability for all human beings to be adequately nourished. Thus, each capability for Nussbaum is *multiply realisable*.

---

24  This example is drawn from Williams 1987 *The Standard of Living* at 98.

Thinking in this way, Nussbaum thinks that, despite our diversity, we can achieve a large measure of agreement by human beings on what constitutes the objective common capabilities that are necessary for human flourishing. Since these factors are objectively common between humans, there is no ground for discrimination on grounds such as race, sex, or sexual orientation. The theory would go further in its universality to recognise that people are entitled to have their capabilities developed irrespective of nationality. Foreigners and citizens alike have similar capabilities in that every individual, universally, has the capacity to flourish. Nussbaum thinks that both domestic and international institutions need to be developed around this goal of achieving a minimum level of capabilities for every person – irrespective of nationality – equally. That does not automatically mean that a country with many refugees or foreigners must bear the sole burden of achieving their capabilities. Other countries have duties in her view to contribute towards ensuring an adequate capability set for all individuals.[25]

In South Africa (and many other parts of the world), there has been an outbreak recently of strong sentiments against foreigners which, at times, have erupted into violent and discriminatory behaviour. Such attitudes and behaviours would impede the ability of foreign individuals in South Africa to flourish and so be condemned by Nussbaum's approach. She would go further though and require South Africa, for instance, to adopt an approach that would help enable the capabilities of foreigners living therein to be realised. As such, Nussbaum's view would strongly require, for instance, that everyone be provided with healthcare services who has made South Africa their home.

Nussbaum's account allows her also to go beyond the human species and recognise that other sentient creatures are also capable of living good lives by their own standards and achieving a state of flourishing. Once again, the specific manner in which we can flourish differs with diverse forms of life. Thus, elephants receive great joy from having the capability to play in the mud, and dolphins only flourish with the capability to swim in large expanses of oceans. Human beings, on the other hand, can only flourish if given the capability to build houses in which they can form families and not be exposed to the elements.

Whilst there are differences between various species, Nussbaum also thinks it is possible to form a cross-species list of valuable functionings and capabilities that are common to all at a higher level of abstraction. In relation to the above examples, we all need to be able to have an environment to exercise the capacities that make our lives worth living. Clearly, the nature of that environment differs from elephants to dolphins to human beings. The full list of cross-species capabilities for Nussbaum involves being alive, being healthy, having one's bodily integrity respected, being able have an outlet for mental and psychological stimulation; being able to express one's emotions; being able to achieve one's goals; being able to form attachments with other animals; being able to live in a co-operative and interdependent way with other species; being able to play; and having some control over the environment and habitat in which one lives.

### 8.4.3    Dignity in the capabilities approach

Since a range of creatures have the ability to flourish, Nussbaum does not think value is confined to the human species. Indeed, she challenges the account provided by Kant that rationality is all that matters is deciding who has value. For Nussbaum, human beings are not disembodied rational agents but rather individuals that join together different dimensions of their existence. These include most prominently a bodily component (she

---

25   Nussbaum 2006 at 319–321.

refers to this as animality), a mental component (involving rationality) and a social component (sociability). The capabilities approach regards all as important to human flourishing and, as such, all as sources of value or dignity.

This approach opens the space to recognise that there is value or dignity in many varied and diverse creatures, all of which deserve respect. The human way of being and flourishing is only one way of being. Nussbaum's approach thus recognises that other forms of life have different ways of being. Just like human beings have different cultures, all of which are deserving of respect, so too, Nussbaum would claim that animals have different ways of being to humans. Different animals also combine in their own way the physical, the mental and the social. The capabilities approach thus would attribute value to all creatures who are capable of flourishing.

Nussbaum recognises that there is an overlap between her view and Singer's account described above that focuses on sentience as a precondition for our attributing moral value to a being. The overlap arises from the fact that the capacity to be an experiencing subject (being able to experience pleasure and pain) is in the real world a precondition for being an individual who is capable of flourishing. How then does her view differ from Singer and the sentience account discussed above?

Views that focus on sentience essentially tend to regard only one feature of individuals as being of moral importance, namely, the capacity to experience pleasure and pain. One of the features of the capabilities approach is its recognition that there are multiple sources of value in the lives of individuals with the capacity to flourish. These sources of value are not simply reducible to experiencing pleasure and pain. Thus, the ability to move around freely or to form social relationships is valuable in itself and is not reducible to the good or bad experiences that flow from them. An example can help us clarify the difference.

Let us consider the life of an elephant in a zoo. Elephants in the natural world will roam over large areas freely eating and foraging across these environments and being stimulated both by threats and pleasures (such as playing in the mud) that arise. In zoos, elephants are in a confined environment and only have a small space in which to move around and limited opportunities to forage. They also have limited opportunities for stimulation compared to their natural environment. Now, there are some zoos in the world that claim to treat their animals well. They do not violently assault them, provide them with adequate food and water, and even attempt to provide them with some mental stimulation. Elephants in such zoos may accustom themselves to their lives and not experience particularly severe pains (though they may well be bored). If we only recognise value as resting in sentience, we might think that those kinds of zoos are not too bad for elephants, as they do not suffer major forms of pain (like an elephant would in a circus, for instance). A capabilities view, however, will recognise that part of what is good for an elephant is to have opportunities to move around across large distances, to forage freely, and play in the mud when they can spontaneously do so. Even if they do not feel pain directly, there is something not fully realised in the life of an elephant in captive circumstances, something wasted. The capabilities approach can capture the fact that zoo life is not ideal for elephants and involves a denial of freedom even if the animals are not in pain. In fact, some empirical evidence seems to provide some support for the capabilities view. African elephants in zoos tend on average to live only 17 years whereas those in the wild live up to 56 years, which suggests there is something very problematic about keeping these animals in zoos.[26]

---

26  Mott, M 'Wild elephants live longer than their zoo counterparts' *National Geographic News* (December 11, 2008), available at http://news.nationalgeographic.com/news/2008/12/081211-zoo-elephants.html (accessed 3 March 2017).

### 8.4.4   How does the capabilities approach deal with conflicts between capabilities and individuals?

The capabilities approach is a recent approach that attempts to grapple with a number of important global challenges. It connects well with the foundations of fundamental rights and provides a method of assessing the quality of individual lives. As we saw, one advantage claimed for the approach is that it does not reduce the good of beings to one dimension such as the ability to experience pleasure and pain but includes multiple capabilities, each being of value. These capabilities are all components of the good life for individuals and give expression to what it means to flourish as a particular individual.

Whilst this more complex vision of the good (or the quality of life) for individuals may appeal to many, it also creates new problems. If we have one dimension in which to assess value, then it becomes much easier to address conflicts within an individual's life or between individuals. For instance, if I have to decide between going to a music concert or getting drunk, I need to think about what would provide me with the maximum amount of pleasure (though, as we saw in Chapter 6, this is a more complex judgement than one may initially think it is). If we have multiple dimensions of value that are not reducible to one another, how does one deal with conflicts or trade-offs between them? Thus, imagine that an artist has to decide whether to take up a creative opportunity which would involve being outside South Africa on the day of national elections far from any foreign consulate and thus rendering her unable to vote. Her opportunity to develop her capabilities for 'senses, imagination and thought' conflicts with her capability to participate effectively in the political community and make choices that govern her life. How are we to determine whether the budding artist should take up this opportunity? If these two capabilities cannot be compared, then the approach creates conflict without any possibility of resolution.

A similar problem would arise where we have conflicts between the capabilities of one person and the capabilities of another. Let us imagine a hunter who wishes to exercise his capability to shoot a large elephant for entertainment and a trophy on his wall. That vision of the world conflicts with the capabilities of the elephant to live to the end of its normal life span and to be free from violent assault. If the capabilities of one individual cannot be compared to the capabilities of another individual, it is hard to see how we can resolve conflicts like this. Such conflicts also, of course, can arise within the human species too (think of the related conflict between this hunter's capability and that of the animal rights activists seeking to exercise their capability to live with concern for and in relation to animals, plants and the world of nature).

Ultimately, there has to be some standard which is overarching and that enables us to resolve such conflicts which arise all the time and which both individual choice mechanisms and social policy must be able to resolve. It might well be that the capability theory has the resources to provide that standard. As we saw, the key criterion would focus on the flourishing of individuals. Within a particular individual, the question would be, what course of action (going to a concert or drinking) would better enhance the functioning and good life of the individual? That question may not be easy to answer, but at least it provides a standard of comparison. In relation to conflicts between individuals, we would need to ask what would enable each individual to flourish as far as possible and preserve as much space for each to achieve their goals? Hunting would seem to be an activity that could not be justified on such a view as it would involve wiping out one individual's capabilities completely. The degree of importance of each capability to individual flourishing and the potential to find less harmful ways of realising an individual capability (such as, for instance, finding alternatives to hunting which do not involve harm to any creatures and that provide a similar sensation of enjoyment to the hunter) would all play a role in deciding on the course of action for individuals and a society. It thus seems that, whilst we may recognise that there are multiple components to the good life for individuals, there is still a need for one dimension to be developed that allows for comparability and social choice.

A further difficulty that arises with the multiple dimensions recognised by the capabilities approach also involves questions of how we deal with trade-offs between individuals where this necessarily occurs. Consider, for instance, a hypothetical case where we may only have a small amount of a particular medicine that can be given to a chimpanzee or a small bird which have both been injured. Nussbaum's theory seems to recognise that both are capable of flourishing and are to be recognised as having an incomparable worth or dignity. The theory would also recognise that the chimpanzee is generally capable of exercising much more complex forms of capabilities than the bird. Nussbaum's theory does not clearly provide an answer of what to do in situations of conflict between these components of her theory. At times, she suggests that individuals with more complex capabilities should be given priority; yet, it is not clear why simply having a larger number of capabilities or capabilities of greater complexity automatically entitles one to priority. For, on Nussbaum's view, all who have the capacity to flourish have an incomparable worth and the value of capabilities is measured by the degree to which they enable individuals to do that which enables particular life forms to flourish. How then can we say one life form's capabilities are more valuable than those of other life forms?

It is useful to contrast Nussbaum's theory in this regard to the two other theories we have studied thus far. Kant's views would clearly be able to account for why rationality is important and thus would accord priority to those who are rational agents (which would generally only focus on human beings). It would also struggle with the conflict between animals in an example such as this. If the chimpanzee could be said to be a rational agent in some respects (which may well be the case if we take a wider view of rationality), then Kant's view could account for giving it priority over the bird. Singer's utilitarian view, on the other hand, would seek to provide equal consideration to all sentient creatures and attempt to create the state of affairs that would lead to the greatest overall amount of pleasure or pain. Since chimpanzees may be capable of higher levels of satisfaction and pleasure than a bird, they could likely be given priority as a result of doing so, and in a case of conflict, that approach would maximise the amount of overall happiness.

### 8.4.5 Is the capabilities approach workable?

One further critique of the capabilities view comes from those – like John Rawls – who believe that resources remain an important way of measuring the quality of life and making comparisons between individuals. Rawls does not challenge the view that resources are not valuable in themselves. He recognises that they are really means to achieve our ends. At the same time, he claims that a theory of justice must have a dimension of publicity. It must be able to identify sources of information that are public which can make claims of injustice verifiable and easily accessible to everyone. Capabilities, Rawls argues, are extremely difficult to measure or assess in a public way. They involve acquiring large amounts of information which is often very difficult to obtain. The idea, whilst well-motivated, is unworkable in that it is extremely difficult to determine for purposes of forming laws or policy what individuals do or are in a position to do with resources. Resources, on the other hand, provide a much clearer and public metric of what state individuals are in.

Consider, the following two social policies: Policy A focuses on providing individuals with a social grant (say R1 600/month) to ensure they have the resources to acquire adequate food. This policy involves simply providing a set amount of resources to people and determining whether individuals have received those grants. Policy B focuses on ensuring that every individual has the capability to be adequately nourished. This involves not simply providing resources but checking that individuals' nutritional requirements are met. Given the variation between individuals, such a policy would seem to require testing of every individual who needs social assistance and tailoring the amount of resources provided to each person according to their individual needs. Whilst Policy B seems desirable in many ways, across a population where there are millions of poor individuals, it seems unworkable. Capabilities theorists would persist in pressing the importance of recognising individual functionings that can be achieved and the need for social policy to take account of this diversity. Those following a Rawlsian approach would object to a focus on capabilities where the information sources are much more difficult, if not impossible to determine.

In some cases, those following Rawls would also point out that the achievement of certain capabilities cannot be attained by the state and is subject to factors which only lie within an individual's subjective control. It seems hard for the state to guarantee, for instance, one of Nussbaum's capabilities that involves 'an ability to have attachments to things and people outside ourselves'. The state can only try and ensure the social environment is created and the resources provided to enable individuals to achieve these capabilities. Yet, such attachments would seem to rest upon the psychological functioning of individuals, the environment in which they were brought up and much else. This critique does not diminish the importance of capabilities but suggests, once again, that a focus on resources and the objectively determinable conditions for the achievement of capabilities are better grounds for the determination of social policy.

## 8.5    African thought and the primacy of relationships

Below are three selections from important African thinkers that deal with questions concerning the scope of moral concern. They focus particularly on the place of the natural environment and animals in African thought. The first source is from the famous speech by the former president of South Africa, Thabo Mbeki, on the passing of the final Constitution in 1996, titled 'I am an African'. The second text is by Professor Chibvongodze from the University of Kwazulu-Natal, who examines literature and philosophical writings to produce an account of the foundations of African ethics and its relationship with those beyond the human species. The final text is by Professor Magobe Ramose, a Professor of Philosophy who has held positions in Belgium, the University of Venda and the University of South Africa. He outlines an understanding of *ubuntu* that also has implications for the relationship of humans with the environment around them.

| PRIMARY TEXTS | **Text 5 Thabo Mbeki: Being an African and the environment** |
|---|---|
| | I am an African. |
| | I owe my being to the hills and the valleys, the mountains and the glades, the rivers, the deserts, the trees, the flowers, the seas and the ever-changing seasons that define the face of our native land. |

My body has frozen in our frosts and in our latter-day snows. It has thawed in the warmth of our sunshine and melted in the heat of the midday sun. The crack and the rumble of the summer thunders, lashed by startling lightning, have been a cause both of trembling and of hope.

The fragrances of nature have been as pleasant to us as the sight of the wild blooms of the citizens of the veld.

The dramatic shapes of the Drakensberg, the soil-coloured waters of the Lekoa, iGqili noThukela, and the sands of the Kgalagadi, have all been panels of the set on the natural stage on which we act out the foolish deeds of the theatre of our day.

At times, and in fear, I have wondered whether I should concede equal citizenship of our country to the leopard and the lion, the elephant and the springbok, the hyena, the black mamba and the pestilential mosquito.

A human presence among all these, a feature on the face of our native land thus defined, I know that none dare challenge me when I say – I am an African![27]

## Text 6  DT Chibvongodze: *Ubuntu* is not only about the human

When the great novelist Chinua Achebe died in March of 2013, his death was likened to that of a fallen *iroko* tree. This association of the writer and the *iroko* tree seem to mirror an interconnectedness of African life and existence with nature. Conversely, the writings of Chinua Achebe immensely contributed his humanness to his fellow Africans and his literature. He was able to forge strong human relations among his countrymen. Interestingly, he did not only lend his existence or being only to his human counterparts but also to the environment and wildlife that surrounded him. In his magnum opus, 'Things Fall Apart' there is a passage where the character Okonkwo likens his humanness of humility and hard work to that of a "... lizard that jumped from the high *iroko* tree to the ground" (Achebe 1995) and fended itself. By characterising Okonkwo as a lizard, Achebe reveals how African ontology is informed by the natural wildlife and the environment.

Similarly, in his captivating "I am an African" speech delivered in May of 1996, Thabo Mbeki attributes his being, 'Africanness' and existence to the natural environment (Mbeki 2015). In this soul searching speech, he recites, "I owe my being to the hills and the valleys, the mountains and the glades, the rivers, the deserts, the trees, the flowers, the seas and the everchanging seasons that define the face of our native land". He further considers his existence and nationhood as equal to that of wildlife that populates his native land. This is captured in these candid words: "At times, and in fear, I have wondered whether I should concede equal citizenship of our country to the leopard and the lion, the elephant and the springbok, the hyena, the black mamba and the pestilential mosquito" (Mbeki 2015). Mawere adds on Mbeki's argument, reiterating that the pre-colonial methods of conserving the environment were based on the religious belief that humans and the environment are an inseparable entity (Mawere 2012). These

27   Mbeki 1996 'I Am An African'.

assertions find their roots in the writings of John Mbiti who argues that the natural environment (plants, animals and rivers) forms an important element of African religious ontology and identity (Mbiti 1969). Mbiti provides practical insights of how the humanity and existence of Africans is intertwined with that of plants, animals and rivers. For instance, he gives an example of the Akamba and the Zulu people that hold that cattle, sheep, goats and men come from the same spot and are equal before the Supreme Being. While the Herero people of Namibia regard cattle as sacred and originating from the same 'tree of life' as men.[28]

## Text 7  MB Ramose: Ecology through *Ubuntu*

Humanness regards being, or the universe, as a complex wholeness involving the multi-layered and incessant interaction of all entities. This condition of permanent, multi-directional movement of entities is not by definition chaos. On the contrary, it is both the source and the manifestation of the intrinsic order of the universe. Herein lies the ecosophical dimension of the indigenous African concept of *Ubuntu*.

The principle of wholeness applies also to the relation between human beings and physical or objective nature. To care for one another, therefore, implies caring for physical nature as well. Without such care, the interdependence between human beings and physical nature would be undermined. Moreover, human beings are indeed (part and parcel) of physical nature even though they might be a priviliged part of that. Accordingly, caring for one another is the fulfilment of the natural duty to care for physical nature as well ... The concept of harmony in African thought is comprehensive in the sense that it conceives of balance in terms of the totality of the relations that can be maintained between human beings amongst themselves as well as between human beings and physical nature ... the quest for harmony is then the striving to maintain a comprehensive but specific relational condition among organisms and entities. It is ... thus the constant strife to strike, and then maintain, a balance between human beings and physical nature.[29]

## Questions

1. When you read the famous and poetic 'I am an African' speech by the former president of South Africa, Thabo Mbeki, what picture does he paint of a particularly African relationship to the environment?
2. What is the specific relation he suggests to the animal world?
3. According to Chibvongodze, what is the underlying basis upon which animals and the environment are approached in African philosophy?
4. What evidence does Chibvongodze provide for his claim?
5. According to Ramose, in what way can the notion of *ubuntu* be extended to provide an ethic governing the human relationship with animals and the environment?
6. What is the basis for moral consideration according to Ramose and how is it distinctive from other approaches that have been studied in this chapter?
7. What is the relationship between the individual and the whole in Ramose's view?

---

28  Chibvongodze 2016 *Journal of Human Ecology* at 157–158.
29  Ramose 2009 *African Ethics: An Anthology of Comparative and Applied Ethics* at 309.

## 8.5.1 African identity and the environment

Thabo Mbeki chose to use the passing of South Africa's final Constitution as an opportunity to reflect on the nature of African identity. In the opening section of his speech (from which this extract is drawn), he situates individual human beings within a beautiful environment. Indeed, the very existence or being of the individual is seen as owing a debt to the external world which nurtures him or her. In a sense, this is similar to the understanding of community in African thought which we examined in Chapter 6. The individual does not emerge from the womb fully formed; rather it is the community that nurtures and enables an individual to grow. It is for this reason we cannot claim as individuals to be an island, but are fundamentally connected to our communities and owe duties to them. A similar point can be made about the environment. Individuals need a space in which to grow and flourish and are nurtured by their surroundings. In a similar vein, the individual cannot then come and destroy the world around them but must owe an obligation to maintain that environment to nurture further individuals.

The natural environment is also the space in which humans experience the full gamut of emotions. As Mbeki describes it, it is often the source of awe and wonder. It is also the backdrop against which our lives unfold. Mbeki also recognises that there is a distinction between the inanimate parts of the environment and those that involve living beings that have a life force of their own. Indeed, in relation to such creatures, Mbeki recognises that we share a space with them and he considers the possibility that we need to confer 'equal citizenship' upon them. This comment is significant; indeed, in Mbeki's conception, the animals are as much part of the environment as human beings and could be understood to have claims too to it. Indeed, the notion of citizenship suggests a common connection both with one another and claims to be respected as part of a holistic community that inhabits the environment. It is interesting to note that Mbeki wrote these words almost fifteen years before a detailed philosophical defence was mounted for recognising animals as citizens in a recent book called *Zoopolis*.[30]

Mbeki's view of Africanness is also notable for its humility. Humans are not the primary entities that exist in the natural world, who simply exploit it and rule over it for their own ends. They are not the supreme apex of being; instead, they are simply one presence amongst many other diverse creatures and features of the environment. Humans are deeply interconnected with the rest of the natural world, and this powerful interrelationship with it is partially definitive of what it is to be an African.

Chibvongodze builds upon these ideas and draws from both literary and philosophical sources to paint a picture of what an African approach to the environment looks like. In analysing Mbeki's speech, and drawing on further sources, he affirms the view that, in African thought, the identity of individuals is deeply interconnected with the environment. These ideas are drawn, he argues, from religion which saw the human being and the world around them as inseparable and flowing from the common source of God. The origins and source are all the same and, indeed, the far-reaching idea is expressed of the equality between other creatures, and the human being.

Chibvongodze also analyses features of African culture, which provide an understanding of the relationship between humans and the environment around them. He starts by examining some passages from the writings of the great Nigerian novelist, Chinua Achebe, in which the character and fate of human beings is analogised to features of the natural environment such as a lizard jumping off a large hardwood tree – known as the '*iroko*'. The

---

30  Kymlicka & Donaldson 2011 *Zoopolis: A Political Theory of Animal Rights.*

*iroko* is impressive in its height and grandeur and can also live for up to 500 years. The contrast with the small lizard is striking. Human beings may pretend they are grand *iroko* trees yet are actually humble beings, dwarfed by the grandeur of the rest of nature. Interestingly, Achebe was regarded so highly that his death was seen to be akin to the felling of an *iroko* tree. The use of these idioms, Chibvongodze argues, provides strong evidence of a deep interconnection between the human and the natural world in African thought.

In his article from which this extract comes, he also indicates the importance of the names given to particular clans and tribes which define their very identity. In many parts of Africa, clans are given the names of wild animals which 'stimulates a sense of affinity between people and wild animals'.[31] Similarly, African societies often utilise proverbs to a similar effect. For instance, the Ndebele and Shona proverb '*inkomo kayisengwa ngokwhelisa*' (do not continuously milk a cow until there is nothing to milk), suggests a number of important ethical messages. Clearly, it shows that self-interested behaviour can actually backfire; yet, it also provides messages relating to animal cruelty and sustainability. Animal cruelty could well be indicated by the proverb where over-milking eventually destroys the animals in question; it also could refer to the calf who is deprived of its mother's milk in modern factory farming and therefore may not grow to produce more milk. Sustainability is indicated by the fact that, if you over-use and over-consume, there will be nothing left. Chibvongodze sees this proverb as indicating that '[t]he compassion that is given to both cow and the calf leads to the realization that *Ubuntu* is not only extended to humans but further to animals'.[32]

Both Mbeki and Chibvongodze suggest an ethic of responsibility to the environment which is rooted in an African view of reality that sees the human as essentially interconnected with the world around them. This understanding connects with deep features of what it is to be an African. Taking these features of reality and identity, what ethical world view do they suggest? Magobe Ramose provides one articulation of what these understandings lead to.

### 8.5.2   *Ubuntu* and the environment

As we saw in Chapter 6, the notion of *ubuntu* places great emphasis on the relationships that exist amongst individual human beings. A person really only becomes fully realised through their relationship with others and thus treating someone else badly affects one's own sense of being in the world. Value on this view is not a particular quality of individuals – such as sentience or rationality – but is located in the relationships between individuals.

This understanding, Ramose argues, however, is not confined to relationships amongst humans themselves. Rather, the ethics derived from *ubuntu* can embrace the relationships between human beings, other animals and the environment more generally. Ramose roots African ethics in an account of reality which is conceived of as involving two important components: the first is the sense that everything that is in the world is continuously in motion and not at rest; and the second is that everything that exists is in a state of interaction with everything else. The world is thus conceived of as a dynamic space of perpetual change and connection between diverse things.

Ramose attempts to provide an ethics that is well-suited to this view of reality. Since everything is interacting with everything else, we cannot simply separate the human from other dimensions. Indeed, the first component of his view is what we may term a form of 'holism'. Human beings are just one part of a greater whole. The African view he articulates

---

31   Chibvongodze 2016 *Journal of Human Ecology* at 159.
32   Chibvongodze 2016 at 158.

thus rests on a distinction between 'humanism' – which places humans at the centre of everything – and humanness, which does not prioritise the human self but recognises the human being as connected to other human beings and features of the natural world. This interaction between beings and entities highlights the second dimension in Ramose's ethic, namely, that it is relational in nature. In other words, value lies in the space between entities (and not in individuals themselves), the relationship between all the things that are existing. Indeed, Ramose states that 'the dignity and importance of the individual human being can best be understood in terms of relations with other human beings as well as relations with physical nature'.[33]

The relational and holistic components of Ramose's vision are linked and the ethical requirements placed upon us are two-fold. First, given that everything is interconnected and our well-being is dependent on the existence of other beings and things, we are required to care for other human beings and the physical world around us. Indeed, Ramose sees humans as part of nature and thus caring for one another is in fact part of a wider duty to care for nature. Indeed, caring for others, in a sense, is also caring for ourselves. Second, we are required to live in harmony with the natural world, seeing ourselves as one part of a totality which is interdependent. There is a need, in so doing, to create a balance between humans and the natural world around us. Indeed, Ramose speaks about seeking to maintain a 'specific relational condition' among organisms and entities which seems to be a form of balance.

### 8.5.3    Which relationships have value?

Challenges to Ramose's view can be broken down into those that relate to the holistic dimensions and those that engage the relational components (though we saw that the two elements of his theory are interconnected). The 'holistic' components of his view involve an extensive concern not only for sentient creatures – he seems to provide no particular consideration for those with sentience – but all features of the environment including plants and inanimate components, such as rivers and mountains. In this respect, his view bears a striking similarity to the ecocentric views (which were briefly discussed above in relation to Singer's view) and would be subject to similar objections raised there of trying to give a deeper account of the relation between part and whole and avoiding environmental fascism in favour of the whole. Indeed, it is not entirely clear what Ramose means by 'balance' between humans and the rest of physical nature and how this is to be judged. For the purposes of the whole, is it permissible to allow some humans to die? Would it be permissible to kill individual animals? The relationship between the whole and the parts that make up the whole thus clearly requires more specification as does the notion of what 'balance' entails. Indeed, this view could potentially be developed in an attractive way for lawyers in drawing on the notion of proportionality when there is a conflict between individuals (animals and humans, for instance) and provide an attempt to recast their relationships in a different way.[34]

The approach Ramose articulates is also distinct from the other views discussed in this chapter by focusing on relationships as the locus of value or dignity. Value thus lies in the quality of the relationships between individuals rather than the individuals themselves. There is of course a philosophical puzzle here: relationships seem to exist between two or

---

33   Ramose 2009 at 312. An alternative view, articulated by Metz, holds that value does lie in individuals but not in virtue of a characteristic like rationality or sentience. Instead, it is our capacity to enter into relationships that is central, see Metz 2010 *Theoria*.

34   Bilchitz 2012 *Southern African Public Law* at 19–27.

more entities, and it is hard to see how there could be a relationship without the existence of these entities. If this is so, do we not have to recognise some value in these entities in order for a relationship to have value? Indeed, let us imagine that we have two blocks of wood sitting next to each other. There is a physical relation between them, but why would we conceive of the relationship between them as having any ethical component at all? Ethics seems to require not simply physical relations but also a capacity by individuals to enter into relationships with others. Let us now imagine a human being and a block of wood. There is of course again a physical relationship between the two but is the relation automatically ethical again? Since the wood lacks a capacity for entering into a relationship with human beings, it is hard to see what ethical value lies in the relationship between the two. On the other hand, let us imagine a human being and a dog. Here, there is potential for a relationship to form which includes a moral dimension. And the same is true of course for two human beings. It is unclear that we can read off an account of ethics from a conception of reality as involving forces between entities. Ethics seems to enter into the picture only when there is a relation between two entities that have the capacity to enter into a relationship with one another.[35] The key location of value then on this view would be in the capacities of individuals to form relationships (rather than in the relationships themselves). That capacity for relationships, however, does not seem to exist between entities that lack the ability to experience the world. It thus seems, once again, that there may be an overlap between this account and those that regard sentience as the ground of value. There seems to be a need for individuals to have a certain quality – sentience – in order for relationships between them to be possible and to have value.

### 8.5.4    Who is excluded from a relational ethic?

The accounts provided by Mbeki, Chibvongodze and Ramose all tend to be quite extensive in the relationships they include as being valuable. They see relationships, as we saw, as extending beyond the human species as far as including the whole environment. Yet, it must be pointed out that ethics which involve a relational dimension have been articulated in much more exclusionary ways. Indeed, the philosopher Menkiti, for instance, sees the notion of personhood as something which is not automatic but towards which one must strive. Individual identity, for him, is formed within the context of a community and learning its social norms. An individual only becomes a full person worthy of respect within the context of learning to understand and obey the social rules of the community. The individual thus has strong duties to the community, duties which may place major limits on his or ability to express him or herself.[36]

Thus, philosophers in this school of thought often place emphasis on relationships as being of value only if they conform to community norms and rules. Thus, we can imagine, for instance, two individuals who enter into a same-sex relationship which appears to go against existing understandings of a community's rules. Given this violation, the community may itself not recognise the relationship between these persons and adopt an attitude of hostility towards them. Indeed, restrictive relational ethics may well exclude individuals who violate social norms, from the ambit of moral concern. This renders them open to the charge that such systems fail adequately to accommodate difference between individuals and, if adopted on a wider scale (as has occurred in some African countries), would result in repressive behaviour on the part of the state.

---

35   Metz 2010 at 61.
36   Menkiti 1984 *African Philosophy: An Introduction* at 172–173.

Relational ethics also has to answer the question as to which forms of relationship count? As we saw, there is the extensive view of Ramose that relationships with the whole of physical nature count and we questioned if this is plausible. However, again, there is a more restrictive version of such systems which sees the only relationships as worthy of moral concern as emanating from relationships between people with whom individuals identify and relate. Indeed, much African thought emerged from the context of small scale societies where the concern was about the preservation of that particular group and individuals therein. It makes sense that the quality of relationships in that group was of central importance, but what about those without that group?

This question has relevance to the issue of the treatment of foreigners that was raised in the introduction. The modern state provides certain benefits and imposes certain obligations upon citizens who have full voting rights to participate in the governance of a political community. What then are our obligations to those who lie outside the system? The extensive relational ethic outlined by Ramose would include everyone within our community and is attractive in this sense. It would draw its inspiration, perhaps, from ethical practices in African societies where traditions of hospitality, for instance, extended beyond one's own village to visitors from other villages. It would enable us to treat the individual tourist who has a sudden heart attack in the public health system. However, it does not clearly provide us with a basis upon which to differentiate between the obligations to citizens and foreigners of various types. Intuitively, it seems that those with closer ties to the community, for instance, deserve stronger social benefits.

A more restrictive relational ethic might be able to account for some of our intuitions in this area. The closer our connection with someone, and the more they contribute to the community through tax, for instance, the more benefits they deserve. Thus, a permanent resident could be entitled to a pension (as the Constitutional Court held in the *Khosa* case)[37] whilst a temporary resident or tourist would not. Those with whom we have closer relationships would have more claims on us than those with whom we have less intense relationships. The difficulty here then is the converse one: to provide a basis for more universal duties which arise in relation to those with whom we lack those relationships. How could such a view, for instance, defend a duty to treat a tourist – with whom individuals in the society lack any specific relationship – who had a sudden heart attack and lacked medical insurance? There seems to be a need, on the one hand, to broaden our understanding of our obligations to include all those who are in a relation of need and vulnerability with us; at the same time, we need to recognise on such an approach that we have stronger and more extensive obligations to those with whom we have closer relationships.

A restrictive relational ethic would, in a similar vein, also perhaps suggest we have stronger obligations towards animals with whom we have closer relationships, such as dogs and cats (for instance). This may well seem plausible though, again, the difficulty for such a view would be accounting for more universal duties we owe generally to animals with whom we have limited relationships (such as those that roam freely). Perhaps such an ethic, however, could be highly persuasive if it is able to capture accurately the fact that our duties differ depending on our relationships with differing creatures. Thus, on the one hand, in relation to the domestic animals – who depend on us completely – we will have both negative obligations not to treat them cruelly but also provide them with their basic needs (such as food, and shelter) and a nurturing environment in which they can live out their potential.

---

37  *Khosa and Others v Minister of Social Development and Others, Mahlaule and Others v Minister of Social Development and Others* 2004 (6) SA 505 (CC).

On the other hand, we may only have negative obligations to avoid harming the environment in which wild animals live and many less duties to intervene, given that our relationships with them are much looser.[38]

It thus seems that relational ethics has its limitations, but also identifies many important issues which other philosophical systems leave out. How far do our relationships extend? Which forms of relationship place which forms of obligations upon us? These are interesting and important questions that the African thinkers we have studied raise and there are thus opportunities for further development of this line of thought.

## 8.6   Conclusion

This chapter has focused on the question of who is included within a theory of justice and thus who can claim rights and to whom we owe duties. We have seen four answers to this question:

1. Kant's account focuses on the capacity to be a rational agent as the ground for being considered as having value.
2. Singer's account focuses on sentience – the ability to experience pleasure or pain – as the ground for being considered as having value.
3. Sen and Nussbaum's account focuses on the capabilities of individuals – what they are able to do and be in the course of a flourishing life – as the ground of value.
4. Mbeki, Chibvongodze and Ramose focus on the relationships between individuals as the central ground of value.

The discussion has provided deeper insights as to the moral theories involved and has focused particularly on the question as to who is excluded from the domain of justice by each theory. In the beginning of this chapter, we considered some of the horrific effects that have resulted from not considering individuals as being of value and thus deserving of decent treatment. All the moral theories discussed would of course condemn slavery, the Holocaust and apartheid. The interesting question is how they do in relation to the twin issues of foreigners and other animals. We summarise the results in the table below though it fails adequately to capture the nuances of each view:

| Philosopher | Foreigners | Animals |
|---|---|---|
| Kant | Included | Excluded (only a source of indirect duties) |
| Singer | Included (strong impartial view) | Included |
| Sen and Nussbaum | Included | Included |
| Mbeki, Chibvongodze and Ramose | Included (degree of impartiality varies) | Included as part of wider environmental ethic |

As we saw, whilst foreigners are clearly deserving of moral consideration in all the theories – which would condemn strong outbreaks of xenophobia that has occurred in South Africa – there are further questions concerning whether we owe foreigners equal duties to those we owe to citizens. The African relational ethics we studied perhaps best provides us with

---

38   Indeed, recently, a compelling account has been provided by Kymlicka and Donaldson, 2011, concerning how our duties are affected by the relationships we form with animals.

some rational basis for distinguishing the kinds of duties we owe in this area in relation to whether we have closer or more distant relationships with these individuals.

In relation to animals, apart from Kant's view, we saw that all the theories included them as a direct subject of moral concern. It would not be justifiable simply to ignore the interests of animals. That would in itself have significant implications for the modern treatment of animals which often disregards their interests completely. Indeed, practices in modern factory farms which involve confining pigs in solitary confinement with the inability to move around or chickens in cages smaller than the size of A4 pages, would seem to lack any justifiability on these views. Yet, the implications of the moral views we studied would differ for certain of the practices of humans in relation to animals, such as the permissibility of keeping them in zoos. They would also differ on the extent to which each individual animal has an equal rights claim or whether their interests must be regarded in a wider way in relation to the whole environment. The African views we saw, interestingly, might again condition the kinds of duties we owe to animals through considering the nature of our interactions and relationships with them.

These views are all important to consider in developing a response to one of the key moral challenges facing South Africa and the African continent more generally: how to approach the rich diversity of human and non-human individuals that inhabit the continent.

## POINTS TO CONSIDER

1. Who is excluded from Kant's theory as having dignity?
2. Are Kant's reasons for these exclusions convincing?
3. Does Singer's account of sentience provide the best basis upon which to draw the line between those to whom we may owe moral obligations and those to whom we do not?
4. What are the differences between the capabilities approach and other approaches to justice and rights that we have studied?
5. Should the complexity of the capabilities of a creature matter when deciding on their moral value or the duties we owe to them?
6. Is there a common ethical understanding between all three writers on African ethics in these texts?
7. What dimensions of our duties to others do African views highlight that are not taken account of in other theories you have studied?
8. Can African views adequately account for our obligations to foreigners and non-human animals?

# Chapter 9

# How do we rectify past injustices?

## 9.1 Introduction

Some societies have had to reckon with large-scale past injustices. On this continent, South Africa and Rwanda stand out, each having confronted respectively the horrors of apartheid and genocide. Elsewhere, the United States and Germany have also had to deal with racism and the Holocaust respectively. How should these and other states right the wrongs of the past?

One way is to punish perpetrators of previous injustices. However, although perpetrators may be criminally liable and so merit punishment, the issue of whether and how much the state should punish offenders is the focus of Chapter 10. Instead, the focus of this chapter is on civil wrongs, that is, the violation by another of a person and/or their property. Insofar as past injustices constitute wrongdoing towards neighbours, community members, fellow citizens and so on, as opposed to the state, and so lead to a breakdown in civil relations, they may be regarded as civil wrongs. More clearly, then, this chapter is primarily concerned with civil liabilities, or otherwise who should pay damages for, or take steps to make amends, rather than whom the state should punish for it.

In many post-conflict nations, rectification is a constitutional imperative or an act of legislation. For example, in Rwanda, the National Unity and Reconciliation Commission, the country's own truth and reconciliation commission, came into effect by an act of the Rwandan Transitional National Assembly and was recognised as an organ of state set up to 'organize national public debates aimed at promoting reconciliation, foster tolerance and a culture of peace and human rights ...'[1] Similarly, the Constitution of South Africa makes provisions for the rectifying of past injustices, which subsequently led to the enactment by parliament of the Promotion of National Unity and Reconciliation Act.[2]

To effectively reckon with a difficult past, however, involves specifying what norms states should adopt to right previous wrongs. In this chapter, we shall examine four distinct sets of norms. The first concerns beneficiaries. Whom should the state compensate? Should descendants of those who were wronged be compensated as well? The second is about strategies, including considerations of best means. How should the state rectify? Should the state right wrongs by preferring victims of previous wrongs in employment decisions or should the state instead compensate them financially? Should the state simply return ill-gotten goods, for example land, to victims or should it seek to do more or something different? The third concerns the extent of rectification, that is, how far the state should go. Should it infringe on individual rights in the process of righting past wrongs or impose compensatory burdens on persons, including younger persons, who may have not actually wronged anyone? The last set of norms relates to justification. Why seek to rectify at all? What is the appropriate rationale for rectificatory justice? Should it be purely retrospective, concerned just with restoring some past state prior to the wrong, or should it instead look to the future benefits of amends? Moreover, should it seek to incorporate both rationales or otherwise aim to restore damaged relationships and reconcile offenders and victims?

The answers to these questions are not always evident. In responding to them, the chapter examines competing perspectives. We begin with Judith Thomson's case for compensation for victims of past injustice (section 9.2). Some of the challenges regarding who ought to be compensated and whom the state might compel to compensate, or perhaps to bear some of the liability for compensation, will be highlighted. The focus on Thomson's view will permit us also to highlight difficulties regarding the best means of compensation and some of the likely disadvantages of a purely retrospective rationale for rectification. Keeping in mind these difficulties, we will consider an alternative approach that looks to the future instead and on the wider social benefits of rectification (section 9.3). Our focus will be on Vincent Maphai's defense of affirmative action and preferential hiring in the South African context. At the heart of Maphai's defense is the question of whether or not the rights of some may be justifiably set aside in the pursuit of some social good, in this case compensatory justice. We will probe his supposition that a rationale for rectification that looks to future benefits does not entail correlative disadvantages at all to some.

These two rationales for rectification will figure prominently in the discussion of Thaddeus Metz's *ubuntu* moral theory in the context of land redistribution and restitution

---

1   Truth Commission: Rwanda 99, supra note 108.
2   34 of 1995, section 3(1).

in South Africa (section 9.3). As we shall see, one of the key elements of the *ubuntu* moral theory is what seeks to combine them, that is, to compensate victims in a way that realises these wider social benefits, including especially that former victims and beneficiaries of compensation are made better off. We will then assess whether land restitution to previously dispossessed persons should depend on whether they (and perhaps everyone in society) are made better-off. As well, we shall consider whether the aim of compensating victims of past wrongdoing and of realising wider social benefits, including making victims better off, are compatible at all. In this regard, we shall assess the merit or otherwise of Lungisile Ntsebeza's contention that section 25 of the South African Constitution entails incompatible clauses that ostensibly ultimately undermine the imperative to expropriate land for the purpose of restitution. Finally, the chapter contemplates the possibility that rectification should aim to reconcile victims and offenders and thus repair relationships that have been damaged because of the past wrong (section 9.5) rather than merely compensate in the sense of returning ill-gotten goods or realising wider social benefits. We shall rely on Emily Mawhinney's account of restorative justice in the context of Rwanda's transition from a genocidal past.

## 9.2    Historical injustice, culpability and compensation

**PRIMARY TEXTS**

**Text 1  Judith Thomson on preferential hiring and compensation**[3]

American philosopher, Judith Jarvis Thomson (1929), is well known for advancing a rights-based moral philosophy. She was visiting Professor at both the University of California at Berkeley Law School and at Yale Law School and is currently a Laurence S. Rockefeller Professor of Philosophy at the Massachusetts Institute of Technology (MIT).

> ... We should turn to those debts which are incurred by one who wrongs another. It is here we find what seems to me the most powerful argument for the conclusion that the preferential hiring of blacks and women is not unjust. ... It may be granted that if we have wronged A, we owe him something: we should make amends, we should compensate him for the wrong done him. It may even be granted that if we have wronged A, we must make amends, that justice requires it, and that a failure to make amends is not merely callousness, but injustice.
>
> But (a) are the young blacks and women who are amongst the current applicants for university jobs amongst the blacks and women who were wronged? ... Is it proper, much less required, that the black or woman be given preference over a white male who grew up in poverty, and has to make his own way and earn his encouragements? Again, (b), did we, the current members of the community, wrong any blacks or women? Lots of people once did; but then isn't it for them to do the compensating? That is, if they're still alive. ... And (c) what if the white male applicant for the job has never in any degree wronged any blacks or women? If so, he doesn't owe any debts to them, so why should he make amends to them?
>
> These objections seem to me quite wrong-headed. Obviously the situation for blacks and women is better than it was a hundred and fifty, fifty, twenty-five years ago. But it is absurd to suppose that the young blacks and women now of an age

---

3    Thomson 1973 *Philosophy and Public Affairs* at 380–384.

to apply for jobs have not been wronged. Large-scale, blatant, overt wrongs have presumably disappeared; but it is only within the last twenty-five years (perhaps the last ten years in the case of women) that it has become at all widely agreed in this country that blacks and women must be recognized as having, not merely this or that particular right normally recognized as belonging to white males, but all of the rights and respect which go with full membership in the community. Even young blacks and women have lived through down-grading for being black or female: they have not merely not been given that very equal chance at the benefits generated by what the community owns which is so firmly insisted on for white males, they have not until lately even been felt to have a right to it. And even those were not themselves down-graded for being black or female have suffered the consequences of the down-grading of other blacks and women: lack of self-confidence, and lack of self-respect. For where a community accepts that a person's being black, or being a woman, are right and proper grounds for denying that person full membership in the community, it can hardly be supposed that any but the most extraordinarily independent black or woman will escape self-doubt.

... Lastly, it should be stressed that to opt for such a policy is not to make the young white male applicants themselves make amends for any wrongs done to blacks and women. Under such a policy, no one is asked to give up a job which is already his; the job for which the white male competes isn't his, but is the community's, and it is the hiring officer who gives it to the black or woman in the community's name. Of course the white male is asked to give up his equal chance at the job. But that is not something he pays to the black or woman by way of making amends; it is something the community takes away from him in order that it may make amends. Still, the community does impose a burden on him: it is able to make amends for its wrongs only by taking something away from him, something which, after all, we are supposing he has a right to. And why should he pay the cost of the community's amends-making?

If there were some appropriate way in which the community could make amends to its blacks and women, some way which did not require depriving anyone of anything he has a right to, then that would be the best course of action for it to take. Or if there were anyway some way in which the costs could be shared by everyone, and not imposed entirely on the young white male job applicants, then that would be, if not best, then anyway better than opting for a policy of preferential hiring. But in fact the nature of the wrongs done is such as to make jobs the best and most suitable form of compensation. What blacks and women were denied was full membership in the community; and nothing can more appropriately make amends for that wrong than precisely what will make them feel they now finally have it. And that means jobs. Financial compensation (the cost of which could be shared equally) slips through the fingers; having a job, and discovering you do it well, yield – perhaps better than anything else – that very self-respect which blacks and women have had to do without.

But of course choosing this way of making amends means that the costs are imposed on the young white male applicants who are turned away. And so it should be noticed that it is not entirely inappropriate that those applicants should pay the costs. No doubt few, if any, have themselves, individually, done any wrongs to blacks and women. But they have profited from the wrongs the community did. Many may actually have been direct beneficiaries of policies which excluded or down-graded blacks and women – perhaps in school admissions, perhaps in access to financial aid, perhaps elsewhere; and even those who did not directly benefit in this way had, at any rate, the advantage in the competition which comes of confidence in one's full membership, and of one's rights being recognized as a matter of course.

**Questions**
1. How does Thomson characterise the idea of compensation?
2. In Thomson's view, who ought to be compensated? Are young black people and women who have not been directly wronged also due compensation?
3. Who, according to Thomson, has the duty to compensate and why?
4. Why, according to Thomson, is it not entirely inappropriate for the young white male, who may not have wronged black people and women, to bear the cost of compensation?
5. How, according to Thomson, should we compensate? Why does she insist that financial compensation is not adequate?

### 9.2.1   The principle of compensation

Suppose that Ayanda stole Minnie's bicycle and that losing the bicycle impacted significantly in some determinate way on Minnie. Perhaps she had an unhappy teenage life as a result. Most people would agree that as the wronged party it would not be unreasonable for Minnie to demand that Ayanda, the bicycle thief, makes amends, perhaps by offering an apology, and returning the financial equivalent of the bicycle or even the actual bicycle, if possible. Whatever form the response takes, it seems reasonable that Ayanda should take steps to rectify the wrong. In the selection above, Judith Thomson aims essentially to capture the common-sense intuition that the Ayanda–Minnie case seems to evince namely, that where one party has wronged another, there is a reasonable expectation that the offending party take steps to compensate for the wrong done. Roughly, then, the principle is that, 'if person A has wronged person B, then person A ought to compensate person B for that wrong'.[4]

The principle of compensation is applicable in interpersonal relations, as the Ayanda–Minnie case illustrates. But it is also applicable to relations between groups. As is well known, legislated discrimination in South Africa under apartheid was a grave injustice to the majority black population (see Chapter 3) and, in general, women have been the target of widespread and often socially endorsed forms of oppression under patriarchal structures. The injustice sometimes involved the denial of basic liberties and at other times degrading treatments that negatively impacted the dignity and self-worth of members of these groups. And although these historical wrongs were often suffered individually, they essentially targeted groups, in particular black people and women, each as a group. A careful reading of Thomson, then, suggests that black people and women, each as a group, are owed a debt of compensation, since as a matter of historical fact they have been wronged.

---

4   Thomson 1973 at 380.

### 9.2.2 The rightful beneficiary of compensation

A valid claim for compensation involves, in part, clarity regarding who should receive compensation, since compensating someone other than the wronged party would be unjust. It seems pretty clear on the compensation principle that *many* black people and women, in particular those who were wronged, should be compensated. It is unclear, however, whether *all* black people and *all* women are entitled to compensation, specifically, whether the current generation of young black people and women are also rightful beneficiaries. For example, consider the so-called born-frees, specifically the black and women contingent of this generation, born after the defeat of official apartheid and into a presumably non-racial, democratic South Africa. Should they also be compensated seeing that the relevant injustice is past?

Thomson's selection contains useful resources for navigating this intricate question and ultimately for deciding who the rightful beneficiaries of compensation might be. She distinguishes two specific claims:

a)  That the situations of black people and women have significantly improved relative to what it was in the past.
b)  That the current generation of young black people and women have not been wronged at all.

According to Thomson, it is erroneous to suppose that a) significant improvements in the conditions of black people and women entails that b) young black people and women have not been wronged at all in ways that have caused harm. The error arises in assuming that improvements in unjust conditions guarantees the complete elimination of the injustice. For Thomson, the assumption is misleading. Not only are the changes recent, their consequences are still far-reaching.

We can deduce two reasons why Thomson thinks it is false that young black people and women have not been wronged at all. First, as we already noted, the relevant historical injustices were not towards individuals as such, but were directed at black people and women each as a group. For example, legislated racism in apartheid South Africa was not simply injustice towards one black individual, for example Nelson Mandela; instead it was towards black people as a whole. So, to the extent that historical injustices were towards groups (black people and women), each group member, including young black people and women, is a victim in virtue of group membership. Second, Thomson indicates that the relevant historical injustices are self-perpetuating, in that although they were done in the past, they are able to yield further disadvantages for members of these groups. For example, one might think that the so-called 'black tax' exemplifies the self-perpetuating nature of historical injustice. Once excluded from the benefits of decent jobs, equal pay, education and so on, older generations of black people and women pass on group-based disadvantages to younger black people and women, who often have to shoulder arduous financial responsibilities on behalf of their forebears. Thomson lists negative consequences as self-doubt, lack of confidence and lack of self-respect passed on to younger members of historically oppressed groups. As such, they are also wronged in ways that have made them worse off.

### 9.2.3 Corporate and personal liability

A valid claim of compensation requires not just determining whom should be compensated but also who is liable to compensate. Again, the issue is not always clear-cut. If black people and women, including the current generation, are entitled to compensation, it would seem that the duty to compensate falls squarely on white men, since they are neither black nor women. But should *all* white men compensate? Specifically, should the young white male, who presumably has not wronged black people and women, be liable to compensate?

Thomson's first point is that the duty to compensate does not fall to the young white male; he is neither asked to give up a job he already has nor is he stripped of one. Instead the community as a whole owes compensation to black people and women, and the hiring officer acts on behalf of society when preferring them in hiring decisions. This is because for Thomson historical injustices towards black people and women are best understood in corporate, rather than individual, terms. That is, they are not reducible to (isolated and sporadic) individual acts, but are the collective acts of a community insofar as they were widespread; as was the case in Rwandan genocide; systemic, institutionalised and legislated, as was the case in apartheid South Africa. They were 'the corporate acts of a nation that imposed or tolerated ... apartheid ... and disenfranchisement'.[5] As such, a group might be liable for compensation even though its members are not personally liable. For example, Pope Francis recently apologised on behalf of the Roman Catholic Church for its role in the Rwandan genocide, although he is not personally responsible for the wrongs that were done. So, to treat a society as corporately liable for compensating black people and women is not to say that the young white male is personally liable.

Yet, the community's corporate liability to compensate imposes some burden on the young white male insofar as the community discharging that duty entails that his right to equal consideration is set aside. Why, then, should the young white male bear the burden of compensation? In response Thomson points out that although he may not have personally wronged black people and women, the young white male nevertheless has benefitted from previous wrong, including the confidence and elevated self-worth he now enjoys and that gives him the edge in the competition to access public goods. In comparison, consider that although one did not plan, implement or directly participate in a heist, one may still be personally liable to the extent that one benefits from the proceeds of the heist. Similarly, for Thomson, since the young white male has benefitted from historical injustice, it is false that he should not bear any burdens for previous wrongs done by others to black people and women. As such, he ought to bear some of the costs of compensation to black people and women.

### 9.2.4   Procedures and best means

Perhaps there are other means of compensating black people and women that would not be too costly to the young white male. Financial compensation, for example, which might entail imposing an appropriate tax or levy on the relevant parties, and distributing the proceeds accordingly, would not involve setting aside his right to equal consideration in competing for educational and employment opportunities.

Thomson offers two distinct but related reasons why preferential hiring, and not financial compensation, is the most appropriate means to compensate black people and women. Both are linked to her key idea that historical injustice robbed black people and women of their self-respect. By self-respect Thomson seems to have in mind a sense of esteem for oneself based on a recognition that one is a bearer of all the rights and privileges that comes with the recognition that one is a full member of a community. More clearly, she argues that because historical injustice essentially deprived black people and women of fundamental rights and privileges, and since full membership in a community entails enjoyment of these, it follows that they were ultimately denied self-respect.

The first reason then is that because financial compensation is unlikely to restore the self-respect of black people and women, it is not the best form of compensation. The second is that being in possession of a job and doing it well is more likely to restore self-respect for black people and women, and so preference in employment decisions is the best means to

---

5   Fullinwider 2000 *Report from the Institute for Philosophy and Public Policy* at 2.

compensate them. There are two ways we can make sense of this supposed link between having and doing a job well, on the one hand, and self-respect, on the other. First, having a job is necessary to obtain a wage, which is further necessary to acquire the basic necessities of life. Being able to do this for oneself gives one a sense of independence, which, at least a significant degree of it, is vital to self-respect in many cultures. Second, it seems that being able to do a job well might provide one with a sense of fulfilment and meaning, which, again, is an important element in improving one's self-respect.

### 9.2.5    Benefits, culpability and the morality of best means

In summary, Thomson's defense of preferential hiring of black people and women rests on four basic premises:

1.  Black people and women, each as a group, have been wronged and so ought to be compensated.
2.  The community as a whole ought to compensate black people and women.
3.  In order to compensate, the community justifiably overrides the right of the young white male to equal opportunity, since he has benefitted from previous wrong.
4.  The best means of compensating black people and women involves infringing the right of the white male to equal consideration.[6]

Premises 1 and 2 seem fairly uncontroversial, but not so are 3 and 4. With regards to 3, why should benefitting from a wrong straightaway make one liable for compensation? Suppose that the construction company my neighbour paid to repair my neighbour's driveway misunderstood the instruction and instead repaired my driveway.[7] Sure, I have benefitted from a wrong done to my neighbour by the construction company (that is, my driveway is in a better condition), but am I liable to compensate my neighbour for this wrong? The question is not whether I should be *kind* towards my neighbour, which I can do *if I so wish*. Instead, it is whether compensation is something my neighbour can rightfully claim from me or that I *owe* my neighbour. If I do not owe compensation to my neighbour because the benefit is *involuntary*, so too the young white male, who is an involuntary, as opposed to wilful, beneficiary of historical injustice.[8] Moreover, in suggesting that the white male applicant should compensate, by virtue of benefitting from historical injustice, Thomson seems to be incorrectly applying the principle of compensation, which requires that the offending party, and not the (involuntary) beneficiary, should compensate.

Moreover, perhaps, in relation to 4, the best means of compensation is not the morally right one. To see this, suppose you stole my rare rifle – there are only two of them in existence and your brother owns the other. You have been ordered by the state to return the stolen rifle, but it is destroyed by fire before you are able to. No amount of money can compensate for my precious rifle. So, you steal your brother's rifle – the only one now in existence – in order to compensate me.[9] But although this is the best means to compensate me, it is an immoral means; I am neither entitled to your brother's rifle, nor are you justified in stealing it. Similarly, it seems 'the community is paying in stolen coin, just as you would be were you to expropriate your brother's rifle to compensate me'.[10] In other words, even if preferring black people and women in employment may be the best means to compensate, it may not be the morally right means especially as it appears to rob the white male of a basic right.

---

6   Adapted from Fullinwider 1975 *Social Theory and Practice* at 309.
7   Fullinwider 1975 at 317.
8   Fullinwider 1975 at 317.
9   Fullinwider 1975 at 315.
10   Fullinwider 1975 at 315.

These objections might lead one to wonder whether there are ways of rectifying previous wrongs that are not costly to some, particularly the young white male, or do not involve employing presumably immoral means. In the next section, we examine a rectificatory rationale that purports to avoid these worries.

## 9.3    Rectification, consequentialism and individual rights

**PRIMARY TEXTS**

**Text 2 Vincent Maphai on affirmative action, preferential hiring and black advancement[11]**

Vincent Maphai (1952) was born in Pretoria, South Africa. He was Professor Extraordinaire at the University of South Africa in the Department of Political Science. He held fellowships at Harvard and Stanford and was later Professor and Head of the Department of Political Science at the University of the Western Cape. The following selection from his 1989 piece provides an alternative rationale for rectification.

> ... Affirmative action policies may be conceived of in an essentially forward-looking way as a means of furthering black or minority advancement. This, in essence, need not involve correlative disadvantages for whites or any previously advantaged group. ... The focus ... is black advancement, which is considered necessary, both for the dignity of blacks and the good of society as a whole. Although the model takes the past into account, it is nevertheless future-oriented.
>
> A major challenge facing the country is to enable blacks to take leadership positions in important sectors of community life, including the business and education institutions. Leadership is not a type of skill acquired in a lecture theatre. It is obtained through life experience. Heavy technical qualifications as such are not sufficient for leadership. Often they do play an important supportive role. If leadership is gained through experience, then it is necessary that entry points are opened early so that blacks may turn their mistakes into growth points. This in turn requires support and patience from white management. After all, people who have been excluded from the water for so long should not be expected to start swimming flawlessly immediately after the first plunge.
>
> Black advancement is also important for the broader society. South Africa cannot afford a growing black population which has no stake in some key educational and economic institutions. Otherwise those institutions will inevitably be undermined as blacks increasingly feel alienated from them. In short, the presence of capable blacks in key positions will not only benefit blacks but society as a whole, including whites. If the economy is undermined, then whites too will suffer. This concern is not motivated by a sense of benevolence, but rather that of addressing a social need.
>
> Preferential treatment may also have a social impact on numerous other fronts. Firstly, it might engender desirable psychological changes within the black community, by creating useful and respectable role models ... It is noteworthy that in general, blacks perform better and more comfortably in areas where they

---

11   Maphai 1989 *Social Dynamics* at 9, 10–12, 13–15, 16–17.

encounter sufficient and successful role models. Secondly, blacks need doctors, lawyers and other professionals with whom they can communicate with ease and who are readily available. ... So, this constitutes yet another reason why there should be black professionals. ... affirmative action might facilitate integration at work and at universities, and in so doing break new ground for a future non-racial society. It may rapture [sic] the white cocoon and in the process sensitize the white community. A more compelling argument is that affirmative action is required to minimize inequalities. If sheer technical qualification were the sole criterion, mainly whites would gain, and the inequality gap would then widen even further. Blacks would miss out on those opportunities that would have gained them the experience necessary for further advancement.

... Two comments should be made at this stage. Firstly, it should be noted that whether or not affirmative action actually results in these consequences is a purely empirical issue, which depends largely on the intention of its architects as well as the manner in which the programme is managed ... Secondly, strictly speaking, the foregoing arguments do not constitute conclusive arguments for affirmative action – certainly not when the distinction between fair equality of opportunity and affirmative action is borne in mind. These arguments merely underline the need for greater representation of the underprivileged in important positions. They do not necessarily prescribe the affirmative action route. Where possible, such representation could be achieved through a normal fair equality of opportunity programme.

... If apartheid is morally wrong because it is based on the 'irrelevant', criterion of skin colour, then is affirmative action not also morally reprehensible for precisely the same reason? For some the most objectionable feature of affirmative action is precisely this. They reject any kind of racial discrimination precisely because it discriminates on the basis of an irrelevant issue – race. Affirmative action would thus be morally wrong for precisely the same reason as racial discrimination, because it is based on the morally irrelevant criterion of race. ... This leads to a possible objection. Affirmative action and racial discrimination must be on a par. ... After all if racist clients or supporters prefer whites to blacks, then a candidate should qualify largely through whiteness. In both cases, colour and nothing else is the deciding factor.

A moment's reflection though, should demonstrate that this comparison is misleading. While it is true that colour is the common factor, the picture alters when the intentions behind affirmative action and racial discrimination are taken into account ... Affirmative action makes no claim as to the racial or gender superiority of blacks and women. What is at issue is simply that at this stage having a black or female would be more helpful than having a white male.

... Another criticism is that affirmative action is treated as a means which is justified by the end. Worse still, individual rights, like the white person's right to work, are sacrificed for a dubious social good. ... There is a genuine cause for concern that 'social good' can be a convenient tool for trampling on individual rights. ... Yet, this is exactly what the consequentialist argument employed above seems to be prescribing. It claims that society as a whole will benefit if some individuals (white/male job seekers) are discriminated against. Is social utility then, an acceptable ground for violating individual rights? ... One approach is to question the claim that there are any rights at all at issue. It is questionable whether people, black or white, are entitled to the jobs of their choice, or to automatic admission to universities. There is something suspect about a moral system which defends people's rights to whatever they would like to have. ... What people are entitled to, is the right not to be discriminated against because they are held in contempt. For example, there would be nothing wrong with a bursary scheme that caters only for women. However, something is amiss when a scheme excludes only Indians or Moslems ... based upon a contemptuous attitude towards their race and religion.

This confusion is partly the result of the conflation of distinct, though related concepts – affirmative action and equal opportunity. While people have a right to equal opportunity they cannot demand, as a matter of right, discrimination in their favour. ... In fact, the language of 'entitlement' is inappropriate here. Blacks cannot demand affirmative action as a matter of right. ... Similarly, white opposition to affirmative action cannot validly be grounded on the belief that it violates their rights. In fact, as far as affirmative action is concerned no rights are at issue at all.

**Questions**

1. What does Maphai mean by a 'consequentialist argument' in support of affirmative action? In his view, what are the anticipated benefits of such a policy?
2. Are race and gender morally relevant bases for exhibiting partiality towards others?
3. In Maphai's view, does the fact that affirmative action fails to yield the anticipated benefits mean that it lacks justification?
4. Is affirmative action reverse discrimination? Does Maphai think that we can reasonably distinguish between the policy of apartheid and a policy of affirmative action?
5. According to Maphai, why is the 'language of entitlements' or 'rights' not relevant in justifying affirmative action?

## 9.3.1   Rectification and social utility

In Chapter 6, we considered consequentialism in some detail. In this approach to morality, the right action is the one that produces the best consequences overall for all concerned. The text by Maphai attempts to ground rectification in consequentialist logic. According to Maphai, the primary aim of affirmative action and preferential hiring policies is 'black advancement', which, in turn, will yield overall positive consequences for society as a whole. He illustrates this by pointing out that black advancement, in the form of greater representation and integration of black people in key institutions, will prevent the undermining, that is, weakening and decline, of these institutions and ultimately prevent the collapse of the economy. This is because black people and women would not feel alienated from, but instead have a stake in, the survival and efficiency of key public institutions. A sense of alienation, however, might lead to a weakening of these institutions. For example, widespread protests and a sheer lack of public support by excluded black people and women are likely to diminish the efficiency of key institutions, which may significantly harm the economy. Black people and women advancement is thus likely to prevent economic collapse.

For Maphai, the enumerated benefits are ultimately in the overall interest of everyone in society, white and black, men and women. So, for example, to the extent affirmative action and preferential hiring will increase the pool of 'respectable and useful role models' for younger black people and women, and thus contribute to black advancement, it might lead to reduced inequalities and contribute towards a non-racial South Africa. Once again, the justification for affirmative action and preferential hiring policies does not depend on considerations of what black people and women deserve or have a right to, or what specifically they were robbed of in the past, but instead on the positive future consequences they are likely to yield for everyone.

As such, Maphai's justification of affirmative action and preferential hiring is forward-looking, in that it focuses on their anticipated future benefits. For him, one of the advantages of a forward-looking, consequentialist approach is that it does not involve disadvantages for white people, in particular the young white male. This is intended as a direct criticism of an approach like Thomson's, which is essentially backward-looking, in that it focuses on whether or not preferential treatment can adequately compensate for some past injustice, rather than its future consequences.[12] Maphai thinks that because it gives short shrift to future considerations, a backward-looking rationale for affirmative action and preferential hiring is more likely to justify disadvantages to some in order to adequately compensate for past wrongs.

We shall return shortly to consider whether Maphai is right that a forward-looking, consequentialist rationale for affirmative action and preferential hiring really excludes disadvantages to some, specifically the young white male. In the meantime, however, there are two other issues worth paying close attention to in the text.

### 9.3.2 Justification, effectiveness and reverse discrimination

One difficulty for Maphai's approach is that if some policy of rectification is justified because of its likely future benefits then it would seem to lack justification if it fails to realise those benefits. Suppose, for example, that rather than black advancement, affirmative action and preferential hiring policies resulted in manipulative practices, like fronting and tokenism, which involves the appointing and/or promoting of unqualified and inexperienced persons from historically deprived groups to senior positions in management with the intention of being seen as compliant with those policies, while concealing the fact that they are merely window dressing. If so, then it would seem that these policies fail to realise the envisaged wider benefits and so lack justification.

In response, Maphai argues that some policy might be justified even if it turns out to be ineffective. In other words, there is a distinction between justification and effectiveness. Whereas the latter is largely empirical, depending in part on whether the policies have been implemented well (for example, whether adequate monitoring systems are in place) or what the intentions of those who seek to implement them are (for example, they might seek to benefit themselves), the former is theoretical, involving specifying the conditions *if* when satisfied makes the practice justified. Although the implementation of these policies may sometimes be messy, Maphai is making a theoretical point that they may be justified notwithstanding the practical problems of implementation.[13] Analogously, a set of democratic principles might be justified even if they are badly implemented by a generally weak state.

Crucially, Maphai also considers the possibility that affirmative action and preferential policies are comparable with apartheid policies, in that both set of policies make 'race' rather

---

12   See Chapter 10 for more on this distinction.
13   See also Hull 2015 *Philosophia* at 127.

than 'technical' qualification, the basis for deciding who ought to be employed, and as such, involve a morally objectionable form of discrimination.

In response, he demonstrates how the forward-looking, consequentialist rationale for affirmative action and preferential hiring ensures a neat distinction between them and apartheid policies. First, he points out that 'race' and 'gender' can sometimes be justified bases for selection *given certain conditions.* For example, the choice of Idris Elba over Brad Pitt, say for the role of Nelson Mandela in a film about his life, is ultimately based on race.[14] Although Brad Pitt is an able actor, technical qualification is not the appropriate criteria for selection. Instead, the consideration is authenticity in relation to the identity and experience of the actual person. For Maphai, just as some special reasons as considerations about authenticity can sometimes justify race- and gender-based selection, so too the envisioned utility of affirmative action and preferential hiring. Second, he argues that the justification for race-based preference in affirmative action and preferential hiring policies, differs in intent from the justification for it under a system of apartheid. Under apartheid, preference is based on the supposed superiority of white people over black people (similar considerations apply to patriarchy in which gender-based preference is based on the supposed superiority of men), whereas affirmative action and preferential hiring policies are based on a recognition that 'at this stage having a black or female would be more helpful ...'.[15] In other words, it is not just the fact of being black or female, or a degrading attitude towards white people or men, that justifies affirmative action and preferential hiring policies but instead their future wider benefits for society.

### 9.3.3   Social utility and individual rights

We are yet to consider the most significant aspect of Maphai's forward-looking, consequentialist justification of affirmative action and preferential hiring namely, his claim it 'need not involve correlative disadvantages for whites or any previously advantaged group'.[16] As we saw, Thomson's backward-looking justification entailed seemingly unavoidable cost to the young white male. Does Maphai edge Thomson in this regard?

It seems not. Consequentialist justifications are typically troubled by hard cases in which realising the anticipated future benefits might involve significant costs to some. To see this, suppose that torturing a group of 50 inmates in some prison would lead to key information regarding the whereabouts and subsequent deactivation of a time bomb set to detonate in the next hour. Suppose further that one of the inmates is in possession of that information and that if the bomb were to detonate, as many as 2 000 civilians would die, including mostly children. If we decide on the basis of the likely wider benefits of torture (that is, saving lives) we are likely going to endorse torturing the 50, which essentially means 'correlative disadvantages' to 49 innocent inmates.

So, it is not immediately obvious that focusing on the likely future benefits of affirmative action and preferential hiring policies will guarantee that there are no 'correlative disadvantages' to the young white male. If the goal is *black* advancement, then these policies are on the face of it not likely to advance the young white male and might actually involve overriding his right to equal consideration. So, Maphai owes us some explanation of why focusing on the future wider benefits of affirmative action and preferential hiring need not entail 'correlative disadvantages' to the young white male. His explanation involves denying that there are any rights at stake at all. Black people have no *right* to affirmative action and

---

14   Maphai 1989 at 13.
15   Maphai 1989 at 15.
16   Maphai 1989 at 9.

preferential hiring because no one has a right to demand discrimination in their favour, and nor does the young white male. These policies are justified only because of their likely benefits, and not because of the rights of black people or in spite of the rights of white people. And, as we saw, these benefits are for all concerned, including the young white male. As such, the relevant policies cannot be reasonably opposed on the basis of young white male's rights seeing that they benefit him as well.

But why interpret the case as one in which there are no rights at stake at all rather than one in which the wider social benefits of affirmative action and preferential hiring are weighty enough to override the rights of young white males to equal opportunity? This latter option is not obviously unreasonable and seems consistent with a justification of affirmative action and preferential hiring on the basis of their wider social benefits.[17] However, Maphai thinks otherwise. For him, there is something wrong about deliberately overriding the rights of people for the sake of some social good. Perhaps, he is correct; but this is precisely the implication of his consequentialist defense of these policies, supposing we are willing to admit that there are rights involved.

It seems, then, that backward- and forward-looking rectificatory strategies may sometimes involve costs for some of the parties concerned. Even so, each one has its own advantages. Perhaps, then, the most effective strategy should seek as much as possible to balance the imperatives of reckoning with the past by way of compensating the victims and of minimising associated costs by keeping in focus the wider social benefits of rectification. In the following section, we explore the prospect that an *ubuntu* moral theory might do so.

## 9.4  *Ubuntu*, rectification and the land question

| PRIMARY TEXTS | **Text 3 Thaddeus Metz's *ubuntu* as a moral theory and human rights in South Africa[18]** |
|---|---|
| | Thaddeus Metz was Professor of Philosophy at the University of the Witwatersrand and is currently a Distinguished Research Professor at the University of Johannesburg. He has published many scholarly papers in value theory and in moral, political and legal philosophy. Metz is well known for his widely acclaimed *ubuntu* moral theory. |
| | When Nguni speakers state '*Umuntu ngumuntu ngabantu*', and when Sotho-Tswana speakers say '*Motho ke motho ka batho babang*', they are not merely making an empirical claim that our survival or well-being are causally dependent on others, which is about all a plain reading in English would admit. They are rather in the first instance tersely capturing a normative account of what we ought to most value in life ... So, the assertion that 'a person is a person' is a call to develop one's (moral) personhood, a prescription to acquire *ubuntu* or *botho*, to exhibit humanness. ... The claim that one can obtain *ubuntu* 'through other persons' means, to be more explicit, by way of communal relationships with others. ... Communal relationship with others, of the sort that confers *ubuntu* on one, is well construed as the combination of identity and solidarity. ... My suggestion about how to orient oneself toward friendly or communal relationships, in order to act rightly and exhibit *ubuntu*, is that one ought to prize or honour such relationships.[19] |

17  See Hull 2015.
18  Metz 2011 *African Human Rights Law Journal* at 537, 538, 539, 551–554.
19  Metz 2011 at 536, 537, 538, 539.

... The favoured moral theory is that actions are right, or confer *ubuntu* (humanness) on a person, insofar as they prize communal relationships, ones in which people identify with each other, or share a way of life, and exhibit solidarity toward one another, or care about each other's quality of life. Such a principle has a Southern African pedigree, provides a new and attractive account of morality, which is grounded on the value of friendship ... [20]

... As is well known, at the end of apartheid in 1994, nearly 90 per cent of land in South Africa had been forcibly expropriated into the hands of white people who constituted about 10 per cent of the population, and the new Constitution makes provision to compensate those who have been dispossessed by way of land reform (or comparable redress). It is also well known that little land has been transferred back to the black majority ... Less well known is that, according to a recent statement by the African National Congress, 90 per cent of the land that has been returned to black hands has not been productive, with the government threatening to repossess such land if its current owners do not use it to farm.

... In regard to these conditions, I have not infrequently encountered two antipodal responses to the land question, which responses share a common assumption that the *ubuntu*-based moral theory entails is false. ... Not surprisingly, the two competing approaches to land reform tend to correlate with race, making the issue black and white. On the white side, I sometimes hear it argued that whites owe no restitution to South African black people since the latter's standard of living would have been worse had whites not taken control of the country. Whites sometimes point out that in the African country where they reigned the longest, the quality of life is the best. ... On the black side, I sometimes hear Southern Africans argue that their standard of living would have been higher had whites not settled, exported all the minerals and kept the profits for themselves, and that, in any event, the right thing for black people to do, or for the state to do on their behalf, is immediately to take the land and give it back to those who originally owned it or who would have inherited it from those who did. ... The most important moral consideration, from this perspective, is restoring an original state. ... I ignore the empirical claims made by the two sides, and instead demonstrate that they both share a questionable moral premise. The premise is this: The appropriate way to distribute land today is a function of what would have happened in the absence of contact between whites and blacks. [21]

... In light of a requirement to respect human dignity *qua* capacity for communal relationships, there are two deep problems with the shared premise that the right way to distribute land today is fixed by counterfactual claims about what would have happened without white and black interaction. One problem is that it is solely a 'backward-looking' principle, directing us to base a present distribution solely on facts about the past, and does not take into account the likely consequences of a policy, where such 'forward-looking' or future considerations are morally important. A second problem is that it is the wrong backward looking

20   Metz 2011 at 559.
21   Metz 2011 at 551, 552.

principle to invoke. On the latter, one cannot reasonably deny that facts about the past are *pro tanto* relevant to determining justice in the present. It is hard to doubt that if you steal my bicycle and give it to a third party, that party does not rightfully own the bicycle and has strong moral reason to give it back to me, or to my descendants to whom I would have bequeathed it. However, the appropriate benchmark for ascertaining compensation is not a function of what would have happened had whites sailed on past the Cape, but rather what would have happened had whites fulfilled their moral obligations to blacks upon arriving there. To treat people as capable of the special good of communal relationship ... includes exhibiting solidarity toward them ...

However, it is a further mistake to suppose that only backward-looking considerations are relevant to determining a just distribution of land at the present time. Above I maintained that respect for people's capacity for friendliness can permit unfriendliness in response to unfriendliness, but most clearly when and only when responding in that way will prevent or make up for harm done to victims of the initial unfriendliness. In the present context, that means that an unfriendly action by the state toward whites, such as expropriation of land they currently hold, is justified only if it is likely to help those harmed by the land being held by whites, that is, dispossessed blacks. ... in order to run farms and keep the economy stable, blacks given agricultural land need substantial financing and training. Now, the present government has not been able to provide these well to the small number of blacks who have been given land so far, explaining the 90 per cent failure rate ... Hence, the state is not morally required to confiscate white-held land en masse, and is probably forbidden from doing so. ... Whites do owe blacks land, and so they, and the state that wrongfully gave the land to whites in the past, must transfer it in a way that is likely to benefit blacks.[22]

**Questions**
1. How does Metz characterise the *ubuntu* moral theory?
2. Does Metz's *ubuntu* theory entail that compensation towards black people is justified? If so, why?
3. Why does Metz think it is a mistake to focus on only backward-looking considerations when distributing land?
4. In what way does Metz's *ubuntu* theory seek to capture forward- and backward-looking considerations on rectification?
5. According to Metz, what precisely should the state do regarding land redistribution?

## 9.4.1 A brief historical context

In the text, Metz alludes to a rather wicked history of legislated land dispossession in South Africa that saw lands owned by the majority black population unjustly transferred to the white minority. Two key pieces of legislation crystalised that process of dispossession.[23] The first is the Natives Land Act[24] of 1913. It essentially barred indigenous Africans, that is,

---

22  Metz 2011 at 553–554.
23  See Chapter 3 for a detailed description of the apartheid system.
24  27 of 1913.

members of racial or ethnic groups native to Africa, from buying and hiring about 93% of South African land. This effectively confined African ownership of land to 7% of South African land. The Act also instituted the Native Land Commission (otherwise, the Beaumont Commission) tasked with the responsibility of determining which portion of South African land should belong to white people and which should belong to black people. The second is the Native Trust and Land Act[25] of 1936. Although it brought about a negligible increase in black ownership of land from 7% to 13,5%, like its predecessor, it also prohibited black people from buying and hiring land apportioned to white people. Because both legislations precluded land transactions between black people and white people, it effectively eliminated the prospect of black ownership of land increasing over time.

Moreover, these legislative acts ultimately led to impoverishment for the majority black population. Without land they were stripped of their primary source of livelihood and were effectively forced into servitude in that they had to work for white farmers to secure their livelihood. It is worth adding that there were notable protestations against these statutes, including in particular, a publication of 'Wrong Policy' in the newspaper, *Ilanga Lase Natal*, by John L. Dube, who at the time was president of the South African Native National Congress, criticising the Act. Protest marches were organised separately by John Dube, Saul Msane and Advocate Mangena, among others, and by Mahatma Gandhi – to no avail. It is crucial, then, to see the current demand for compensation in light not only of the wrongness of legislated dispossession of land, but also of unsuccessful activism to correct the injustice at the time.

### 9.4.2  *Ubuntu* moral principle and land redistribution

In the principle of compensation we considered earlier, it seems that black people who were previously dispossessed of land, including their descendants, ought to be compensated for land. Suppose that financial compensation would not suffice, then perhaps the state ought to redistribute lands for the purpose of restitution. The key question is: how should the state pursue the programme of land restitution? For Metz, the *ubuntu* moral theory offers some clue. To see this, however, we need to understand the theory.

A moral theory should, amongst other things, account for right actions. That is, it should plausibly explain what all right actions have in common and what distinguishes them from bad ones. So, for example, it should tell us why keeping a promise is good and why not doing so is bad. An *ubuntu* moral theory attempts to do just that by appealing to some idea of the good, as encapsulated in the notion of *ubuntu*, prominent in the belief systems of many sub-Saharan African cultures. For Metz, the oft used maxim, 'a person is a person through other persons', is believed to entail the insight at the heart of the notion of *ubuntu* that certain kinds of relationships, in particular harmonious, as opposed to discordant, relationships are constitutive of the good. He cites South African Archbishop, Desmond Tutu, approvingly:

> Harmony, friendliness, community are great goods. Social harmony is for us the *summum bonum* – the greatest good. Anything that subverts or undermines this sought-after good is to be avoided like the plague.[26]

Further, for Metz, the idea of harmony entails identity and solidarity. To identify with someone, in his view, is to think of him or her in terms of a 'we', belonging to one's group,

---

25   18 of 1936.
26   Tutu 1999 *No Future without Forgiveness* at 35.

in the sense of regarding him or her as sharing the same goals and co-ordinating together to realise those goals. A shared identity between two people means that they both regard each other in this way. Members of a family, church and so on, identify with one another in this sense.[27] To be in solidarity with another is to exhibit goodwill towards them. This includes wanting to benefit and help them. It is not the same as identifying with others, in that one might consider another as part of a 'we' but fail to wish them good. For example, an employee might be part of a firm and identify with it, but not necessarily have goodwill towards it.[28] Metz's *ubuntu* moral theory takes both identity and goodwill as constitutive of harmony. Thus, what all good actions have in common is that they honour harmony, or prize it very highly, where this roughly involves seeking to develop relationships of identity and goodwill towards others in a way that honours and respects rights. In practice, slavery, breaking of promises, lying and so on, are bad because they fail to promote shared identity and goodwill among people in ways that respect and honour their rights.

How ought we then to rectify unjust land dispossession in an *ubuntu* way, that is, in a way that honours harmony? We have seen two distinct strategies. In the first, emerging from our discussion of Thomson's selection, rectification involves compensating for the past wrong in order to as far as possible restore the original state. In this case, that would mean returning land to dispossessed black people or to their descendants. In the second, in Maphai's selection, the primary consideration is oriented to the future, specifically the wider benefits, or otherwise utility, for society. In this case, any just redistribution of land must take into consideration its wider benefits, including land productivity and economic efficiency. As Metz contemplates it, the *ubuntu* moral theory is able to combine these two supposedly distinct insights regarding compensation and utility. After warning against reducing the debate on rectification to a matter purely of the absence of any relationship between races, that is, of what would have happened had white people and black people not come into contact, Metz goes on to discuss the implication of his *ubuntu* moral theory.

According to Metz, the *ubuntu* moral theory entails that some wrong was done in the past since the legislated dispossession of land was an act that failed to honour harmony, in that it lacked identity and goodwill towards black people and did not honour their capacity for harmonious relationship. As such, the *ubuntu* moral theory entails that land be returned to those who were previously dispossessed. In addition, for Metz, the *ubuntu* moral theory entails that future considerations are also morally important. The relevant future consideration is that the transfer of lands to black people should bring about benefit and not harm to them. That is, land redistribution for the purpose of restitution should make black people better off, rather than leave them worse off than they would be without it. For Metz, this means ensuring the productivity of land and overall economic efficiency. As such, the *ubuntu* moral theory entails that the state should train and finance black people who stand to be compensated by land.[29] Moreover, he adds that since land restitution must be accompanied by adequate training and financing of black people, the state is not justified in expropriating land from all whites at once, especially where this might negatively impact on productivity and economic efficiency, precisely for the sake of black people who should live better lives as a result of compensatory policies.

---

27  Metz 2007 *The Journal of Political Philosophy* at 335.
28  Metz 2007 at 336.
29  Metz 2011 at 553.

### 9.4.3 Utility and compensatory justice

By highlighting the importance of keeping in view these future considerations when compensating for past wrongs, Metz's *ubuntu* theory is able to find some balance between the backward- and forward-looking rationales for rectification. Roughly, the state should compensate only if doing so will realise wider social benefits, including land productivity and economic efficiency, but where victims of past injustice are the ones to enjoy the benefits. In doing so, however, it seems to yield the implication that rectification by way of compensation for victims of previous wrongs depends in part on whether and to what extent it would benefit previous victims, or otherwise yield greater economic efficiency.

But why should rectification for victims for past wrongs depend on whether and to what extent it makes them better off, or realises some benefit at all? Perhaps, the restitution of land is independent of any benefits to previous victims or prospective wider social benefits of land redistribution. A modification of Metz's own 'bicycle' example can help us illuminate this point.[30] Suppose that an intruder breaks into my property, steals my Ferrari and then gets caught. Suppose further that, being a careless driver, if I were to have my Ferrari back I might pose a threat to myself and to other motorists. Now, it seems that it would be unjust to retain my Ferrari until such a time that it is established that I no longer pose any threat to others and myself. Similarly, it seems unjust towards black people to delay restitution until some wider social benefit of land redistribution, which, for Metz, is to 'run farms and keep the economy stable' and 'to help those harmed by the land being held by whites, that is, dispossessed blacks', is likely.[31] Although these benefits appear to be subsequent to restitution, Metz's *ubuntu* theory seems to suggest that realising them is a prerequisite for restitution. And so he proposes that land restitution should be done gradually and in view of these wider social benefits to those who were wrongfully harmed.

The preceding point highlights the risk of delaying compensation, that is, land restitution, when it is done in view of making the beneficiaries of compensation better off or realising wider social benefits (that is, productivity and economic efficiency). The risk seems to come in attempting to fulfil two seemingly incompatible aims: returning lands to previously dispossessed persons and seeking to realise these social benefits to them. There is no guarantee at all that pursuing the latter will accomplish the former. Whereas restitution constitutes returning victims to a condition they would have been in in the absence of the wrong, the anticipated social benefits might not be forthcoming to them. Metz, of course, insists that *victims* must be expected to benefit, but that they are not likely to benefit with a Zimbabwe-style land reform, which presumably did not take seriously the likely consequences of redistributing land *en masse*. What the Ferrari example gestures towards is merely the risk that seeking to realise social benefits might not give victims what they are justly owed or might slow down the process of compensating victims of unjust land dispossession.

Lungisile Ntsebeza has made a similar point, arguing that the South African Constitution exemplifies a similar tension, in that it seeks to balance two incompatible imperatives, namely, the expropriation of land for compensation and the protection of private ownership of property, and thereby delays the realisation of the former. For Ntsebeza, whereas expropriating land for the purpose of restitution is in the interest of victims, or their descendants, the protection of the right to property is in the interest of offenders, or their descendants. Let us briefly examine Ntsebeza's proposition.

---

30   Metz 2011 at 553.
31   Metz 2011 at 553.

PRIMARY
TEXTS

**Text 4  Lungisile Ntsebeza's 'Land redistribution in South Africa: The property clause revisited'** [32]

Lungisile Ntsebeza is a Professor at the University of Cape Town. He is the National Research Foundation (NRF) Research Chair in Land Reform and Democracy in South Africa. He has published extensively on the land question. We have extracted the following text from his co-edited (with Ruth Hall) book, *The Land Question in South Africa: The Challenge of Transformation and Redistribution* (2007).

Various reasons have been offered in attempts to explain the slow delivery in land reform. The bone of contention in current debates, it seems, is the interpretation of Section 25 of the Constitution.[33] ... The main argument ... is that the provisions of Section 25 in the Constitution are contradictory in the sense that the Constitution protects existing property rights, while at the same time making a commitment to redistributing land to the dispossessed majority. The two objectives, the argument goes, cannot be achieved at the same time simply because the bulk of land outside the former bantustans is under private ownership and consequently safeguarded by the Constitution. In this regard, a declaration that land will be made available to Africans is rendered void for the simple reason that whites privately own most land.[34]

... In the first instance, the government has itself shown great reluctance to invoke the expropriation clause. ... Second, even if the government were to pursue the issue of expropriation, there is still the question of compensation and how the price is determined. In this regard, the Gildenhuys formula could be a guide. We have seen that, according to the judge, the price of land should be determined by the market. Although the Gildenhuys formula takes into account the critical issue of subsidies, which should be deducted from the market price, the fact that compensation is based on the market price almost makes it impossible for the government to budget for land reform for the simple reason that the role of the state in determining the price is very limited.[35]

... It is intriguing that the history of how colonialists acquired land in the first instance is not receiving prominence in the determination of compensation. In so far as reference is made to history, the suggestion is that this refers to the history of land acquisition by the affected landowner. Yet, there is the history of colonial conquest and land dispossession that lies at the heart of the land question in South Africa. It is hard to imagine how any process of land redistribution that downplays this history can hope to gain legitimacy, in particular in the eyes of those who were robbed of their land. Closely linked to this is that the naked exploitation of African labour which was central to the success of white commercial farming in South Africa is, interestingly, not considered to be one of the crucial factors that must to be taken into account when the amount of compensation is calculated. Lastly, some commentators and activists have attributed the seeming reluctance to expropriate land to a lack of political will on

32  Ntsebeza 2007 *The Land Question in South Africa: The Challenge of Transformation and Redistribution* at 119, 120–121.
33  Ntsebeza 2007 at 119.
34  Ntsebeza 2007 at 120–121.
35  Ntsebeza 2007 at 122–123.

the part of the government. We have seen that, according to Hall, the 'immediate challenge' is not a legal but a political one. It is not clear what Hall means by the issue not being 'legal'.

I would argue that the issue of compensation, even if the Gildenhuys formula is used, can end up in law courts if white farmers decide to contest the compensation amount. Nothing stops them from doing that. There are implications if the matter goes to court. First, legal processes can be frustratingly protracted. For example, if the owner does not accept a compensation offer, she or he has, in terms of Section 14(1) of the Expropriation Act, up to eight months to make an application to a court. The process can drag on after this. In addition, legal processes are very expensive. Both these factors are discouraging. Even though a legal contestation would involve rich farmers and the state, it is poor, landless Africans who end up suffering either through delays and/or in instances where court decisions favour white farmers. It is also worth bearing in mind that in a court case involving the state, it is in the end the taxpayers' money that is involved. I argue that the entrenchment of the property clause in the Constitution, in particular Section 25(1), puts farmers in a very strong position in situations where they contest expropriation and the determination of price.[36]

**Questions**
1. What is Ntsebeza's central argument? Can you identify all of the reasons he gives in that argument?
2. How, according to Ntsebeza, does the constitutional right to private ownership of property impact land restitution?
3. What consideration, in Ntsebeza's view, is 'not receiving prominence' in the debate on the expropriation of land for compensation?
4. In what way does the market determining the price of expropriated land impact the process of land restitution?
5. Why does Ntsebeza insist that the challenge of land redistribution is a legal and not a political one?

## 9.4.4   Land expropriation and the property clause

The main argument by Ntsebeza is that the constitutional provision to expropriate land for the purpose of compensation is at odds with the constitutional right to private ownership of property. The key relevant clauses in section 25 of the Constitution that he mostly relies on are:

(1)   **No one may be deprived of property except in terms of law of general application, and no law may permit arbitrary deprivation of property.**

(2)   **Property may be expropriated only in terms of law of general application –**
    (*a*)  **for a public purpose or in the public interest; and**
    (*b*)  **subject to compensation, the amount of which and the time and manner of payment of which have either been agreed to by those affected or decided or approved by a court.**

---

36  Ntsebeza 2007 at 124.

(3)  The amount of the compensation and the time and manner of payment must
     be just and equitable, reflecting an equitable balance between the public
     interest and the interests of those affected, having regard to all relevant
     circumstances, including –
     (*a*)  the current use of the property;
     (*b*)  the history of the acquisition and use of the property;
     (*c*)  the market value of the property;
     (*d*)  the extent of direct state investment and subsidy in the acquisition and
            beneficial capital improvement of the property; and
     (*e*)  the purpose of the expropriation.

Whereas subsection 2 permits the state to expropriate land for the purpose of compensating
those who were historically dispossessed of land, subsections 1 and 3 allow current owners
of land to both determine the price they wish to sell the land for and to contest the
expropriation of land by the state. For Ntsebeza, this makes land restitution unlikely and
explains the slow pace of land reform in South Africa.

In support of this position, he puts forward four different considerations. First, he says,
the state is reluctant to invoke the expropriation clause. Second, even if it did, expropriation
would still be unlikely given that the state ought to pay current owners of land a price
determined by the market. In making this last point, Ntsebeza refers to the Gildenhuys
formula, proposed by Judge Antonie Gildenhuys, for determining the price of land based on
the criteria outlined in subsection 3 of section 25 of the Constitution, focusing especially on
subsections 3(*c*) and 3(*d*) as outlined above. It essentially entails that where the state is to
expropriate land it must pay current land owners an amount that is the equivalent of the
current market value of the property, less the present value of past subsidies.[37]
Notwithstanding the precision that comes with the Gildenhuys formula, Ntsebeza insists
that land reform is unlikely since the state is unable to budget for it given that its role in
determining the price of land 'is very limited'. Third, Ntsebeza adds that the criteria for
deciding whether and how to distribute land and in particular to compensate current land
owners leaves out completely the fact that current land owners have come to possess land
unjustly by way of conquest. He is not clear on how incorporating this fact might impact land
restitution, but Ntsebeza seems to be gesturing to the possibility that it might give the state
greater control in determining how and what to pay current land owners, which is then likely
to speed up the process of land restitution. His final consideration relates to the delays and
huge legal costs involved when current land owners exercise their property rights to contest
expropriation. Again, this is likely to slow down the process of land restitution.

It is worth asking, however, whether Ntsebeza's interpretation of the provisions of the
Constitution, regarding the expropriation powers of the state and property rights of current
(white) owners of land, as incompatible is plausible. After all, subsections 6, 7 and 8 of
section 25 of the Constitution explicitly allow for land restitution to redress the historical
land dispossession of black people. Subsection 8 provides that the state should not be
impeded by other provisions, including presumably subsection 1, which protects the
property rights of citizens and upon which much of Ntsebeza's argument rests. Perhaps,
then, there is really no tension between the aims of land restitution and of protecting the
property rights of citizens. If so, then ultimately the real challenge, as Ruth Hall has argued,
is not legal, in the sense that there are incompatible constitutional imperatives, but instead

---

37  Ntsebeza 2007 at 122.

political insofar as the state has failed to demonstrate the requisite political will to expropriate land for the purpose of redress.[38]

So, too, perhaps, is the intuition that Metz's *ubuntu* moral theory sought to capture: that is, implementing land restitution in a way that keeps in focus other wider social benefits, including especially productivity and economic efficiency, may not be as objectionable as initially thought. Just as there is no necessary contradiction in the constitutional imperatives to expropriate land for the purpose of redistribution, while as much as possible honouring the property rights of current land owners, so too there may be no necessary contradiction in implementing land restitution in a way that ensures agricultural productivity and economic stability, mainly with an eye towards improving the lives of victims of historical injustice. After all, strategies of rectification that honour the right to compensation of previously disadvantaged persons but fail to provide social benefits to them, including economic and political stability, 'may prove superficial' ultimately.[39]

One reason why one might find this thought attractive is that in seeking to compensate, while keeping in focus the wider future benefits, we are likely to also reconcile the victim and offender since not only are victims compensated, but also they and their offenders together may be ushered into a post-conflict, future society beneficial to all parties. Perhaps, it is ultimately this thought that underlies Metz's *ubuntu* moral theory. If so, it is worth reflecting then on the possibility that rectification should go beyond merely compensating victims by returning goods that were unjustly taken from them and/or realising wider social benefits. In particular, that it should aim to reconcile victims and offenders and repair relationships that have been damaged because of the past wrong.

In the final section, we briefly consider Emily Mawhinney's account of restorative justice in relation to Rwanda's transition from a genocidal past.

## 9.5   Rectification and restorative justice in Rwanda

**PRIMARY TEXTS**

**Text 5  Emily Mawhinney on restorative justice in post-genocide Rwanda**[40]

Emily Mawhinney is a Doctor of Law and an attorney at the United States Department of Homeland Security. The selection below is from her recent article, *Restoring Justice: Lessons from Truth and Reconciliation in South Africa and Rwanda*.

> What is it about civil conflict that makes it so difficult to resolve with conventional conflict resolution means? At the heart of the ethnic, religious, ideological or political motives guiding intrastate conflict lays interpersonal conflict between neighbors. … Practices of restorative justice are better able to resolve the interpersonal conflicts that characterize intrastate conflict because they involve and empower the parties who are in conflict. For example, a truth and reconciliation commission (TRC) can give victims, offenders, and the local community a greater sense of ownership over their own conflict resolution process by promoting forgiveness and creating a forum for truth telling.[41]

---

38   Hall 2004 *Ten Years of Democracy in Southern Africa* at 7.
39   Hall 2007 *The Land Question in South Africa: The Challenge of Transformation and Redistribution* at 92.
40   Mawhinney 2015 *Journal of Public Law and Policy* at 22, 23–25 & 42.
41   Mawhinney 2015 at 22.

Restorative justice offers an alternative framework in which the owners of the conflict themselves, the offenders, victims, and communities are empowered to resolve their own conflict. In other words, restorative justice involves the direct participation of the affected parties in the process of resolving the conflict. ... At the core of restorative justice is a dialogical triad between victim, offender, and the community, all of whom 'own' the conflict. As part of a restorative process offenders are encouraged to accept accountability for the harm they caused (as well as its repair), show remorse, and offer an apology; victims are encouraged to overcome their resentment and offer forgiveness. The community may include the family members of the offender, and family members of the victim, both of whom play an important, though amorphous role in the restorative justice process.[42]

... Restorative justice can therefore be characterized as a process rooted in dialogue between the parties involved in a conflict, and their community. Through dialogue, both the victim and the offender are given a voice to express their views and emotions, and together with the community, establish a shared understanding of the harm the offense has done and the values it violated. Some scholars suggest that justice is restored when the offender takes responsibility for his actions by expressing a sincere apology to the victim and the community, and the victim offers forgiveness to the offender. More generally, justice may be restored when the social equilibrium that was damaged by the offense is restored through social action. The goal of restorative justice is thus to bring together the estranged victim, offender, and community and restore the original trust among those parties. ... The philosophy of restoring justice through dialogue is an integral component of any truth and reconciliation commission.[43]... proponents of restorative justice argue that the practice of truth and reconciliation can be more effective in helping parties transition toward peaceful resolution of conflict. This was certainly the ideal goal of the Rwandan NURC ...[44]

**Questions**

1. How does Mawhinney characterise restorative justice?
2. According to Mawhinney, who are the agents of restorative justice?
3. What, in her view, are the proper aims of restorative strategies for rectifying past injustices?

## 9.5.1   Genocide, Gacaca courts and reconciliation

Many people are familiar with the film, *Hotel Rwanda*, which, amongst other things, explores the violent repercussions of ethnic chauvinism in Rwanda and the genocide that eventually followed in 1994. The actual events were gruesome indeed. Although something of a truce had been previously brokered by 1993, between the Tutsi-led Rwandan Patriotic Front (RPF) and Hutu-led Rwandan government, in what is popularly known as the Arusha Accords, the subsequent assassination in 1994 of the then president of Rwanda, Juvénal Habyarimana, perceived by the Hutus as perpetrated by the Tutsis, led to the slaughter of an estimated

---

42   Mawhinney 2015 at 23–24.
43   Mawhinney 2015 at 24–25.
44   Mawhinney 2015 at 42.

800 000 or more people. Most of these were Tutsis, but moderate Hutus who were seen as sympathetic to a power-sharing government involving both groups, as well as members of the Batwa group, were also murdered in the genocide that lasted about 100 days. It ended after the RPF, led by the Rwanda's current president, Paul Kagame, seized control of the country.

The immediate challenge for the new government was to reckon with that horrific past. It did so through three different instruments: the International Criminal Tribunal for Rwanda and the Rwandan national court systems, both of which pursued criminal prosecutions of perpetrators of the genocide, and the Gacaca (pronounced Gachacha) courts, which were integral to the Rwandan National Unity and Reconciliation Commission (NURC). The Gacaca court system is believed to be an extension of a traditional approach to conflict resolution in which members of the community sat together to deliberate and settle conflicts. (Gacaca refers to the act of sitting down and discussing a matter.) These courts presented the platform for the perpetrators and victims of the genocide to confront the horrors of genocide with a view to uncovering truth, reconciling all concerned parties.

In the text, Mawhinney argues that the aim of this process is restorative justice. She characterises it as 'a dialogical triad'. This means that the process involved three separate parties, the victims, offenders and the entire community, who engaged through dialogue in a truth-seeking endeavour to understand the nature, causes and effects of the harm, including the values it violated, and to repair the relationships that had been damaged. Along the way, face-to-face encounters become possible; perpetrators offer apology and seek forgiveness, which victims and the community in turn offer. For our present purposes, it is worth highlighting that Mawhinney reiterates an important advantage of the restorative justice processes, namely, that it affords the concerned parties agency and ownership of the conflict resolution process. As such, restorative justice strategies, including especially truth and reconciliation commissions, offer something more than the previous rectificatory processes we have examined. So, rather than forcing responsible parties to compensate victims or undertaking rectificatory processes by itself, the state might instead provide the platform for them to take ownership of the conflict and its resolution. The case of post-genocide Rwanda is a powerful reminder of how society might reckon with past wrongs by adopting norms that aim at reconciliation and the healing of civic relationships rather than merely returning something to them or ensuring wider social benefits.

However, the point here is not to suggest that the restorative justice processes of truth and reconciliation commissions are without difficulties. Naturally, there were several challenges, in the case of the NURC, including, for example, the lack of public support and questions regarding its neutrality following suspicions that the government appointed officials leading the commission were not impartial.[45] But, as we saw above, specifically in relation to Maphai's forward-looking justification of affirmative action and preferential hiring, there is a reasonable distinction to be made between whether some strategy is justified and whether it is effective. Perhaps, then, the implementation of the truth and reconciliation commission in Rwanda was a lot messier than in other places (for example, in South Africa, on which see Chapter 10) and less effective for that matter, but this should not undermine its underlying rationale to reconcile victims, offenders and the community.

---

45   Mawhinney 2015 at 43.

## 9.6 Conclusion

The overarching aim of this chapter has been to examine the norms post-conflict states may adopt in reckoning with an ugly past, with a view to making amends for previous wrongs. One fundamental principle around which the discussion focused is the principle of compensation: the idea that one who has wronged another ought to make amends for the wrong.

As we have seen, the principle is not as simple as it might seem initially. We have raised questions regarding who ought to receive compensation. Are descendants of those who were wronged in the past also entitled to compensation and, if so, why? We have also considered the question of who is liable to compensate. Perhaps, ultimately it is the state who has to compel previous offenders to make amends. But even this is not as simple as it might seem. What about the descendants of previous offenders? Should they be liable as well, or perhaps bear some of the costs associated with compensation?

In addition, we wondered about strategies and best means when implementing the principle of compensation. Why compensate with jobs seeing that this apparently entails overriding the rights of some to equal opportunity? Perhaps, financial compensation would suffice. Should the state simply just return ill-gotten goods to its previous owners, or should it in addition consider whether doing so would benefit those people or bring about greater social utility? Why undertake land restitution if it might impact negatively on productivity and economic efficiency, thereby potentially harming the victims themselves? Does consideration of productivity and efficiency not slow down the process of land restitution? Should we not just give back lands to those who were unjustly deprived of them? In relation to the land question, we also probed the proposition that the Constitution might be a stumbling block in the quest for land restitution. But are the relevant constitutional clauses really in conflict? Lastly, we explored different ways of justifying rectification. Should it depend on only past considerations, or are future considerations also relevant? Otherwise, is the most appropriate rationale for it to reconcile the parties involved and restore broken relationships?

These key questions related to the principle of compensation and alternative perspectives on them have been central to the chapter.

### POINTS TO CONSIDER

1. Judith Thomson argues that those who have benefitted from past injustices ought to make amends as well to victims. Do you think she gets this right? Is a compensatory principle like 'those who have benefitted from a wrong ought to pay for the wrong', plausible?

2. Is Vincent Maphai right that consideration of the overall positive consequences of affirmative action and preferential hiring policies in favour of young black people and women does not justify setting aside the rights of some people? Is it ever justified to override a person's right in order to promote some social good?

3. Is Thad Metz right that the state should not redistribute land *en masse* but should instead do so only if it is likely to benefit previously dispossessed persons? Even if it is desirable that lands are economically productive, should land restitution depend on this? Is the Ferrari example a useful analogy? If so, does it successfully show why land restitution must precede any consideration of the benefits of land redistribution to previously dispossessed persons?

4. Emily Mawhinney gives an account of restorative justice as envisioned in truth and reconciliation commissions. Do you think that an approach to rectification that aims to discover the truth about the past, reconcile victims and perpetrators, and restore relationships between them would suffice for a society seeking to reckon with an unjust past?

# Chapter 10

# Why punish the guilty?

*Thaddeus Metz*

## 10.1 Introduction

Whereas the previous chapter addressed civil liability – who the state may force to compensate others for wrongful harm, the present one takes up criminal liability – who the state may punish for having broken a just law or otherwise done wrong. This chapter considers not how to compensate victims, but rather how much to punish offenders, if at all.

Suppose that a man has been unreasonably jealous, flown into a rage and beaten up his girlfriend. What should happen to him? We suppose that, in the first instance, he ought to be fairly tried by an impartial third party such as the state. Our question is: if he were then found guilty of assault and battery, what, if anything, should the state do to him beyond making him pay some kind of reparation to his victim?

It is not obvious that the state would be morally justified in punishing him. After all, the crime has already been done, and punishing the offender would not in itself compensate the victim in substantial ways. Indeed, sometimes punishing an offender, say, by imprisoning him or her, would make it more difficult for the offender to pay restitution to his or her victim. If a criminal justice system should above all seek to help victims, it does not appear as though it would inflict a penalty on offenders and would instead use scarce resources to enable victims to heal from the ways that crimes have harmed them.

This chapter centrally addresses the questions of whether punishment is morally justified and if so, why. In addition, it considers answers to questions such as how much (quantity) punishment is justified for a particular offence and which types (quality) of penalties are appropriate, with a large focus on the death penalty.

A theory of why a court ought to punish people for breaking the law sometimes has implications for the issue of which statutes would be just for a legislature to adopt. For example, if the point of punishment were merely to prevent harm to others, then truly victimless behaviours, such as taking drugs in the privacy of one's empty home, should not be against the law. However, this chapter does not highlight these kinds of connections, and instead aims to focus strictly on when to punish someone, how much, and in what way.

In addition, although philosophers debate whether innocent people may sometimes justifiably be punished as well as what counts as 'innocence', this chapter will presume that only the guilty, suitably filled out, are *prima facie* apt for punishment. What is it about legal guilt, for example having violated a just law against assault and battery, that might render one liable for punishment of some kind and to some extent? This chapter seeks to answer these kinds of questions by appealing to philosophical moral ideals, which may or may not be reflected in a country's constitution and other laws.

It begins by considering two major justifications of punishment that have been salient in the Western philosophical tradition (section 10.2). Then, it considers a challenge to the view that the state is routinely justified in punishing offenders (section 10.3). Drawing on indigenous African ideals of restorative justice, the chapter considers whether the state should instead aim to reconcile an offender with his or her victim and the broader society, the path that South Africa took in respect of political crimes under apartheid. Next, the last major section addresses an issue regarding the types of penalties that are morally justified, supposing that some are. It considers arguments for and against the death penalty (section 10.4), after which the chapter concludes with a brief summary (section 10.5).

## 10.2 Philosophical justifications of punishment

There are several different philosophical theories of punishment's justification, but one way to divide them up is in terms of which temporal facts are thought to render it permissible. Some theories of punishment mainly 'look forward' into the future to determine whether a given penalty would be morally right to impose now. By this approach, roughly, punishment of some kind would be right if and only if it were expected to bring about good consequences down the road. When choosing which punishment is apt, an enforcer should pick the one that would involve the least expense, pain and other costs, while producing the most desirable consequences for society in the long run, for instance protecting people's rights or improving their quality of life.

In contrast, other theories of punishment mainly 'look backward' into the past in order to ascertain whether a given penalty would now be justified. Roughly, one is to look at the nature of the crime that had been committed. If there had been a crime (that was not utterly excused, say, by reason of insanity), then a penalty of some sort would be justified, where the worse the crime was, the greater the punishment should be. Proportionality or fit between the nature of the crime and the penalty is inherent to this approach, which is often called 'retributive', a matter of 'paying back' the offender with something harmful comparable in degree (and perhaps kind) to what he or she did.

Some philosophers hold elements of both kinds of theories at the same time, which means that they have to balance facts about the past and the future in order to come to a conclusive decision about whether a particular penalty is justified. However, most philosophers are interested in ascertaining whether only one approach would be enough to make good moral sense of punishment's justification.

The South African system is not 'pure' in this way, and instead mixes elements of both philosophies. For instance, South African law tends to prescribe more than the least amount of punishment necessary for good outcomes, with appeals by the prosecution sometimes leading to greater penalties for offenders thought to fit their crimes, in the way that a retributive approach prescribes.

However, South African law also permits imposing greater penalties in cases of recidivism. Where someone performed a crime, was punished for it, and afterwards did the same crime again, he or she would in that system be likely to receive a stronger penalty the second time around. That makes perfect sense on a forward-looking rationale, for the first punishment was plainly ineffective at preventing crime, suggesting that a greater one is needed to produce that good outcome. However, it makes little or no sense by a backward-looking theory; for supposing the second crime was indeed the same as the first, then proportionality requires the same penalty, and a stiffer one the second time would be unjust.

## 10.2.1   Forward-looking theories of punishment's justification

Forward-looking theories differ amongst each other, mainly in terms of which good outcomes would justify the infliction of punishment and how the latter would be expected to bring them about. In the reading below, Jeremy Bentham, a British philosopher born in the eighteenth century, offers a utilitarian account of punishment, which is one instance of a forward-looking view.[1]

### 10.2.1.1   Expounding the utilitarian theory of punishment

According to Bentham, punishment of some kind is justified if and only if it would minimise harms and maximise benefits for society in the long run, compared to not punishing and instead doing something else. Similarly, a particular degree and type of punishment is justified if and only if it would minimise harms and maximise benefits for society in the long run compared to other sorts of punishment. By 'harms' Bentham has in mind pain and by 'benefits' he means pleasures, where these could be either physical or mental.

Bentham identifies three different ways that punishment is likely to minimise pain and to maximise pleasure in the long term taking everyone's interests into account. These days, we would speak of 'incapacitation', 'reform' and 'deterrence'. Bentham places the most emphasis on the latter, which means striking fear into the offender or other members of the society, so that they will choose not to commit a crime in the future. Although punishing someone guilty of assault and battery would not in itself provide much, if any, compensation to a victim, it could do the work of preventing more people from becoming victims of a similar crime down the road. For the utilitarian that is an important factor when deciding whether the infliction of punishment would be morally justified.

---

1   For other, more recent forward-looking theories, see Morris 1981 *American Philosophical Quarterly*; Murphy 1992 *Retribution Reconsidered*; and Montague 1995 *Punishment as Societal-Defense*.

PRIMARY

TEXTS

### Text 1 Jeremy Bentham on incapacitation, reform and deterrence[2]

Jeremy Bentham was an Enlightenment-era British moral, political and legal philosopher known for having helped to found utilitarianism, the philosophical view that morality is solely a function of the extent to which an action is useful, that is, is expected to improve the quality of life of people and animals.

[T]he prevention of offences divides itself into two branches: Particular prevention, which applies to the delinquent himself; and general prevention, which is applicable to all the members of the community without exception.

Pain and pleasure are the great springs of human action. When a man perceives or supposes pain to be the consequence of an act, he is acted upon in such a manner as tends, with a certain force, to withdraw him, as it were, from the commission of that act. If the apparent magnitude, or rather value of that pain be greater than the apparent magnitude or value of the pleasure or good he expects to be the consequence of the act, he will be absolutely prevented from performing it.

With respect to a given individual, the recurrence of an offence may be provided against in three ways:

1. By taking from him the physical power of offending.

2. By taking away the desire of offending.

3. By making him afraid of offending.

In the first case, the individual can no more commit the offence; in the second, he no longer desires to commit it; in the third, he may still wish to commit it, but he no longer dares to do it. In the first case, there is a physical incapacity; in the second, a moral reformation; in the third, there is intimidation or terror of the law.

General prevention is effected by the denunciation of punishment, and by its application, which, according to the common expression, serves for an example. The punishment suffered by the offender presents to every one an example of what he himself will have to suffer, if he is guilty of the same offence.

General prevention ought to be the chief end of punishment, as it is its real justification. If we could consider an offence which has been committed as an isolated fact, the like of which would never recur, punishment would be useless. It would be only adding one evil to another. But when we consider that an unpunished crime leaves the path of crime open, not only to the same delinquent, but also to all those who may have the same motives and opportunities for entering upon it, we perceive that the punishment inflicted on the individual becomes a source of security to all. That punishment ... is regarded not as an act of wrath or of vengeance against a guilty or unfortunate individual who has given way to mischievous inclinations, but as an indispensable sacrifice to the common safety.

---

2  Extracted from Bentham 1830 *The Rationale of Punishment.*

All punishment being in itself evil, upon the principle of utility, if it ought at all to be admitted, it ought only to be admitted in as far as it promises to exclude some greater evil.

It is plain, therefore, that in the following cases punishment ought not to be inflicted: Where it must be *inefficacious*; because it cannot act so as to prevent the mischief: Where it is *unprofitable* or too *expensive*: Where it is *needless*; because the mischief may be prevented or cease of itself without it.

Cases in which punishment must be inefficacious ... are: Where the penal provision is not established until after the act is done. Such are the cases of an *ex post facto* law, and of a sentence beyond the law. Where the penal provision, though it were conveyed to the individual's notice, could produce no effect with respect to preventing his engaging in the act prohibited; as in the cases of extreme infancy, insanity, and intoxication.

The pain produced by punishments is as it were a capital hazarded in expectation of profit. This profit is the prevention of crimes. In this operation, every thing ought to be taken into the calculation of profit and loss; and when we estimate the profit, we must subtract the loss ... We should say, then, that a punishment is *economic*, when the desired effect is produced by the employment of the least possible suffering. We should say that it is too *expensive*, when it produces more evil than good; or when it is possible to obtain the same good by means of a less punishment.

### Questions

1. What is the difference between particular and general prevention? Which one does Bentham believe is the primary justification of punishment? Why does he think so?
2. The fact that an offender would suffer from punishment counts as a moral cost, for Bentham. Do you agree? That is, is punishment wrong *to some degree* simply for causing harm to the offender, even if it is often right *on balance* because of the greater good it would do?
3. What are two situations in which punishment is unjustified, according to Bentham? Use your own examples to illustrate.

In the above reading, Bentham notes three different ways in which punishment can often be expected to benefit society in the long run, and can be justified for those reasons. Bentham considers the pain experienced by a guilty party as something bad and undesirable to some extent, but claims that it is often outweighed by the goods of the greater pains that it could prevent or the greater pleasures that it could produce.

One is the incapacitating effect of punishment, most clear in the case of imprisonment, and seemingly not very relevant in the case of a fine. Upon being jailed, an offender is physically restrained from committing another crime (at least one that would harm those outside of prison), in the case where he or she wants to do so.

A second desirable result of punishment is its ability to reform an offender's character so that he or she no longer has an interest in committing crime in the future. Sometimes the threat of punishment or its actual imposition can lead a person to change his or her desires and goals; perhaps by experiencing something of what his or her victim suffered the person is inclined to change his or her mind about which choices to make.

A third respect in which punishment can be expected to make society better off, according to Bentham, is its deterrent function, with punishment 'making him afraid of offending'. According to Bentham, deterrence in respect of the society at large, and not particularly the offender, is what usually justifies punishment. He points out that, intuitively, punishment can be justified even when an offender has become reformed and is not likely to offend again. In such a case, often the reason to punish is that the 'intimidation or terror of the law' would frighten others into obeying the law.

Bentham does not argue that if someone is guilty of having committed a crime then his or her punishment is always justified. He mentions a few major exceptions in the above extract. One sort of exception is when crimes would occur even if punishment were inflicted. Perhaps, for example, the offender is incorrigible and others in the broader society would not learn of his or her punishment and so would not be deterred if the offender were punished.

Another exception is where even if punishment would likely prevent some crimes or other harms, this good would be outweighed by the bad of punishment. In the United States, for example, it can cost upwards of $40 000 (currently ZAR560 000) on average to incarcerate an offender for a year, which cost might not be worth its benefits.

A further case in which punishment of the guilty is unjustified on utilitarian grounds is when the good resulting from punishment could be obtained without the bad of punishment and by using some other means that would involve no or less pain. If, say, therapy would be likely to reform an offender and not have any costs in terms of deterrence, then it might be justified as a replacement for punishment.

### 10.2.1.2 Evaluating the utilitarian theory of punishment

Turning away from an exposition of Bentham's theory of why, when and which punishment is morally justified and towards an evaluation of it, utilitarianism and forward-looking theories more generally provide powerful rationales for maintaining a punishment system. A punishment system costs a lot of money, and it also risks making the mistake of imposing penalties on innocent parties. What the forward-looking theorist can say is that these negatives are plausibly justified by the expected positives of having a punishment institution. Even if you ended up paying a lot in tax money to support it, and even if you were to end up getting wrongfully punished by it, the utilitarian can point out that it would have been rational for you to have supported a punishment system ahead of time; setting up such a scheme is an investment that carries risks but that also promises rewards in terms of the reduction of harm, at least on balance to most of society.

In addition, some readers will find attractive Bentham's account of when punishment is unjustified. If a particular punishment would do no good, or if it would do some good but would be outweighed by the bad, or if a non-punitive response could produce the good without the bad of any punishment, then it appears irrational or merely vengeance to insist on punishing someone.

However, others will, upon reflection, find the utilitarian rationale for punishment to be counterintuitive in some ways, particularly when it comes to the questions of whom ought to be punished by the state and to what degree.[3] Consider the latter issue first.

---

3 The following cases are taken from Metz 2004 *Jurisprudence* at 563–565.

Sometimes forward-looking theories entail that it is permissible to punish the guilty more harshly than seems right. Utilitarianism could recommend harsh penalties for trivial crimes, if a small number of the former would prevent a large number of the latter. For instance, it could prescribe the torture of taxi drivers who change lanes without indicating, if this would indeed prevent so many accidents as to outweigh the costs of gravely harming a few people and making an example of them.

When it comes to whom to punish, forward-looking theories invariably prescribe not punishing those guilty of serious crimes at all, when punishing them is not necessary to prevent other serious crimes or otherwise do some good for society, relative to a non-punitive response. Imagine that a man killed his innocent wife so that he could get the life-insurance money, and that punishing this man would not do any good, either for the man or the community. So, suppose that during the trial the man found religion and had a complete change of heart, evidenced by great remorse. If so, then reform considerations would not recommend punishment, since it would be unnecessary to promote rehabilitation. By the same token, there would be no need to incapacitate the man, since for all we can tell he will not commit the crime again. However, to many it appears absurd, as the influential eighteenth-century German philosopher Immanuel Kant contended long ago,[4] to let such a murderer go scot free in the case where any punishment would not be 'economic' (economically sound), to use Bentham's term.

At this point, Bentham might still recommend punishment on grounds of general deterrence. However, suppose now that punishing the man would not deter others from committing crime because, say, others would do their crimes regardless of whether he were punished or not. Maybe others would simply be unaware of the man's court case and so would not know one way or the other whether he had received any penalty.

In this case, not only would it do no good to punish this man, but it would in fact do only harm; it would cost a lot of money to punish him and would prevent the man from contributing to society at his job. Under these conditions, forward-looking theories would instruct a judge to acquit the man or give him a suspended sentence. Or if the conditions were such that the man would be reformed and crime would be deterred upon imposition of, say, a few months in jail, a small fine or some community service, then the forward-looking theories would all prescribe such a mild penalty. Many philosophers find these to be objectionable implications.

Some might be tempted to think that they are not implausible, since the offender was, by hypothesis, rehabilitated. However, it is important to see that the current problem also arises in cases where criminals are incorrigible. If we somehow knew ahead of time that no punishment would change an offender's heart (and perhaps that some non-punitive measure would), if we further knew both that the offender would harm more guards in jail than citizens in society and that other penalties would not deter others, then a forward-looking theory could not prescribe punishment. If you think that it is precisely such a hardened criminal whom the state would have strong moral reason to punish (and should punish severely), even if it would not do any good for him or society, then you will be sympathetic to the backward-looking theories this chapter now explores.

---

4   Kant 1797/1991 *The Metaphysics of Morals* at 141–143.

## 10.2.2   Backward-looking theories of punishment's justification

The strengths of the forward-looking theories are the weaknesses of the backward-looking or retributive ones. Similarly, the weaknesses of the forward-looking theories are the strengths of the backward-looking ones.

Recall that one major advantage of the forward-looking theories is their ability to provide a powerful explanation of why a state should maintain a costly and risky punishment system. These social bads are justified when and only when there is the prospect of social goods. In contrast, it seems difficult for backward-looking theories to make sense of why a punishment system is worth the harms it creates, since they do not appeal to any of its future benefits. Instead, retributive accounts must apparently contend, for instance, that spending tens, if not hundreds, of thousands of rands to punish a given offender is justified merely in order to make the offender suffer, that is, even if it would not have a long-term benefit for him or her, the victim or society.

Recall as well the major disadvantages of the forward-looking theories, their difficulty accounting for the intuitions that it would be wrong to let a murderer go entirely unpunished (or lightly punished) and wrong to torture a taxi driver for failing to indicate when changing lanes. The natural thing to say about these cases is that these reactions do not fit the crimes. Murder should receive a comparably harmful response in the form of punishment, while failing to indicate does not merit torture, but rather something like a fine. The backward-looking theories capture these points easily, since proportionality is inherent to them. Retributive theories instruct a judge to look into the past to apprehend the nature of the crime that was committed and to order the executive branch to inflict a penalty that fits it. A judge is not to consider what the long-term effects of the penalty would be and whether they would be desirable enough to outweigh its harms.

A pressing question is precisely *why* the state ought to inflict a proportionate penalty. Some retributivists would use the language of 'desert', and suggest that the state must give a person, such as a batterer, what he deserves in the light of the choices he has made.[5] By this model, receiving a punishment is to be modelled on something like earning a failing mark for an assignment on which one performed poorly. Other retributivists would invoke the concept of fairness, contending that punishment removes the unfair advantage an offender obtained upon breaking the law.[6]

In the reading below Jean Hampton does not, however, appeal to considerations of desert or fairness. She instead argues that a proportionate penalty imposed on a batterer would express the right sort of message about his victim's intrinsic value, about what many in both South Africa and the West would call her 'dignity'. Hampton advances a neo-Kantian account of punishment. Kant argued that all persons have a dignity in virtue of their capacity for reason or autonomy (which makes them different from, and higher than, animals) and that right actions are generally those that treat people with respect, whereas wrong actions are those that are disrespectful.[7] According to Hampton, in order to avoid treating victims disrespectfully, that is, treating them as less important than they are, the state must punish their offenders.

---

5   For example, von Hirsch 1987 *Past or Future Crimes*; and Moore 1997 *Placing Blame*.

6   For example, Morris 1968 *The Monist*; and Davis 1992 *To Make the Punishment Fit the Crime*.

7   See Chapter 8 of this book as well as Kant 1785/2002 *Groundwork for the Metaphysics of Morals* at 45–49, 52–54.

PRIMARY
TEXTS

**Text 2  Jean Hampton on the expressive function of retribution**[8]

Jean Hampton was a late twentieth-century American female philosopher known for her work in political and legal philosophy. Before she died in her early 40s, she had been Professor at the esteemed University of Arizona Department of Philosophy.

Those who wrong others ... objectively demean them. They incorrectly believe or else fail to realize that others' value rules out the treatment their actions have accorded the others, and they incorrectly believe or implicitly assume that their own value is high enough to make this treatment permissible. So, implicit in their wrongdoings is a message about their value relative to that of their victims.

A retributivist's commitment to punishment is not merely a commitment to taking hubristic wrongdoers down a peg or two; it is also a commitment to asserting moral truth in the face of its denial. If I have value equal to that of my assailant, then that must be made manifest after I have been victimized. By victimizing me, the wrongdoer has declared himself elevated with respect to me, acting as a superior who is permitted to use me for his purposes. A false moral claim has been made. Moral reality has been denied. The retributivist demands that the false claim be corrected. The lord must be humbled to show that he isn't the lord of the victim. If I cause the wrongdoer to suffer in proportion to my suffering at his hands, his elevation over me is denied, and moral reality is reaffirmed.

[R]etributive punishment is the defeat of the wrongdoer at the hands of the victim (either directly or indirectly through an agent of the victim's, e.g., the state) that symbolizes the correct relative value of wrongdoer and victim. It is a symbol that is conceptually required to reaffirm a victim's equal worth in the face of a challenge to it ... How does the infliction of pain constitute such a symbol? The answer is that pain conveys defeat.

Consider that retributivists typically endorse the *lex talionis* as a punishment formula ... That formula calls for a wrongdoer to suffer something like what his victim suffered, and ... it is frequently mocked by those who point out that delivering to the criminal what he delivered to the victim can be impossible or ridiculous or both in many instances.

But the punishment formula does not seem quite so silly if it is interpreted as calling only for proportionality between crime and punishment. To inflict on a wrongdoer something comparable to what he inflicted on the victim is to master him in the way that he mastered the victim. The score is even ... If her victimization is taken as evidence of her inferiority relative to the wrongdoer, then his defeat at her hands negates that evidence.

A critic might query this analysis by worrying that even if retributive punishment is one way to achieve this end, it might not be the only way or even the best way. And if there is another way to reassert the victim's value that is as good as, or better than, the punitive method, then why shouldn't the retributivist permit or prefer that method ...?

---

8   Extracted from Hampton 1988 *Forgiveness and Mercy.*

But I contend that punishment is uniquely suited to the vindication of the victim's relative worth, so that no other method purporting to achieve vindication could be preferred to it. Suppose we gave a victim a ticker-tape parade after the crime to express our commitment to his value. Still the fact that he had been mastered by the wrongdoer would stand.

[R]etribution isn't about making a criminal better; it is about denying a false claim of relative value. The reformed and penitent murderer ....is still ... the same person who committed the murder, because he retains the agency which produced the murder (i.e., he is still an agent who chose to perform this act). Thus he is the one who implicitly claimed superiority over the victim through the crime, and he remains the one who must be levelled in order to negate the evidence of superiority provided by the crime. If he is truly penitent, he may be just as interested in seeing that claim denied as the family of the victim.

**Questions**
1. What does Hampton think is the essence of treating another person wrongly? What makes it wrong to rape, steal and the like? Can you think of any actions that seem wrong (and perhaps should be illegal), but are not captured by her explanation?
2. What is *lex talionis*? Can you provide an example in which it does appear to be either impossible or ridiculous to fulfil?
3. How does Hampton make sense of the idea that punishment ought to be comparable to the crime?

## 10.2.2.1  Expounding the expressive theory of punishment

Hampton's expressive version of retributivism is the view that state punishment is justified because it is the right way for it to disapprove of those who have degraded others upon breaking laws. One deeper reason for the state to express disapproval, for Hampton, is to affirm the superlative inherent value (dignity) of victims in the face of denigrating mistreatment by offenders. Were the state not to punish the guilty, even ones who felt bad for what they did, that would be to respond to victims as though they are unimportant, as though they do not matter.

The way that Hampton would respond to the query posed at the start of this chapter, about what the point of punishment is when it does not help victims, is that victims need more than merely *compensation* for the way they have been *harmed*. In addition, they need *recognition* for the way they have been *degraded*, something that Hampton believes only punishment can express.

Other expressivists influenced by Kant's ideas about the dignity of persons have suggested that there are additional respect-based reasons for a state to express disapproval of an offender through punishment. For instance, some maintain that doing so is the only or right way for the state to treat offenders as responsible moral agents. If a person knew that an action was wrong and against the law, if it was within his or her power to avoid performing it, and if he or she knew what the cost would be of doing so, it appears that he or she has brought the penalty on himself or herself. To acquit such an offender would be to treat him or her like an animal or a child, a being that lacks agency, by this line of argument.[9]

---

9  Morris 1968; Rachels 2003 *The Elements of Moral Philosophy* at 130–140.

The right amount of punishment, in Hampton's view, is whatever is proportionate to the seriousness of the offence. The more culpable the offender for the act, and the worse the act's immorality, the more serious the offence. And the more serious the offence, the stronger the expression of disapproval of it must be, and hence the harsher the penalty for it has to be. Thus Hampton's theory appears to ground what for many are the intuitively correct answers to the questions of how to punish a murderer or a taxi driver who has not indicated.

### 10.2.2.2    Evaluating the expressive theory of punishment

One apt concern to raise about Hampton's view is whether she can provide an adequate explanation of why only punishment of the offender would adequately express respect for the victim's value. On this score, there is the above counterexample of throwing the victim a ticker-tape parade, a type of public celebration in which streams of paper are thrown down onto people's heads from on high. Why does Hampton think that, say, a battery victim would not be adequately recognised by such a parade in the absence of punishing her offender? Is her explanation convincing?

Consider, too, an additional way of apparently humbling an offender that is not punitive. For example, why think that forcing a batterer to compensate his victim is not an adequate way for the state to 'vindicate' the victim and 'master' the offender?

Another worry about Hampton's view is what she calls the 'symbolic' value of punishment. Can symbolic considerations truly be worth the costs of punishment?[10] If one asks what the proper function of a state should be, an almost universal answer is that it ought at least to fight serious crime. This account of the state's purpose does not jibe well with backward-looking theories of legal punishment such as Hampton's; for they deny that punishment is morally justified because it promises to prevent crime. For them, crime must be fought by using only non-punitive means. If paying back offenders were to prevent actions such as theft, rape and battery, that would be welcome, but would not help to justify the imposition of punishment. To many philosophers, this is implausible; instead, a central reason to set up and maintain a punishment system is to control crime.

## 10.3    A challenge to punishment: Seeking reconciliation

Probably every state in the world punishes law-breakers, even if there are great differences amongst countries over the content of their laws. However, just because a practice is common does not make it right. Might there, upon reflection, be good moral reason to abolish or at least significantly reduce the practice of punishing people for violating the law?

### 10.3.1    South Africa's Truth and Reconciliation Commission

Some reason for thinking the state ought not punish offenders as frequently as it currently does comes from a characteristically African reflection on South Africa's Reconciliation Act,[11] which forbade the punishment of many of those guilty of human rights violations during apartheid. Specifically, this Act formed the Truth and Reconciliation Commission (TRC),[12] which was tasked with granting amnesty from criminal (and also civil) prosecution to those who confessed to apartheid-era political crimes. To obtain amnesty, offenders were required to make full disclosures about their wrongdoing, but they were not required, say, to express

---

10    For the view that no account of retribution is worth the drawbacks of punishment, see Husak 1992 *Nous*.
11    Promotion of National Unity and Reconciliation Act 34 of 1995.
12    For details about the TRC, see Truth and Reconciliation Commission of South Africa 1998.

remorse about what they had done or apologise to their victims. In addition, amnesty was not contingent on victims having forgiven offenders or consented to amnesty being granted. The decision was to be made by the TRC and solely on the basis of whether the offenders were judged to have revealed everything about their misdeeds. According to the *TRC Report*, more than 7 000 people filed for amnesty.[13]

There had been amnesties in the past for political crimes, but they had been blanket or unconditional ones. In contrast, South Africa was the first to employ conditional amnesty on a large-scale basis, forgoing punishment if and only if offenders confessed fully to their crimes. If suspected offenders did not so confess, then, by the Reconciliation Act, the state could carry out the usual punitive process against them.

Since South Africa's TRC, other countries have also adopted conditional amnesties. For example, Rwanda's Gacaca courts were set up to deal with the some 800 000 Tutsis and moderate Hutus murdered, as well as approximately 250 000 women raped, during the 100 days of ethnic conflict in 1994. Perpetrators were often given no or light sentences in exchange for the disclosure of truth, expression of remorse and willingness to compensate victims.[14]

Although South Africa's Reconciliation Act did not abolish punishment for political crimes, it did reduce the amount of punishment for them relative to what would have been available under the normal rule of law. One central rationale for this Act was that it was the most likely way to effect reconciliation between white and black peoples in South Africa, who had of course been divided in serious ways during apartheid. Neither the Reconciliation Act nor the TRC clearly define what is to be understood by the word 'reconciliation'. Presumably, though, it means not merely peace consequent to a period of serious social conflict, but also some kind of integration between former enemies in the form of democratic decision-making and harmonious relationships when it comes to education, business and other forms of day-to-day interaction.[15]

However, the appeal to reconciliation is probably not deep enough to satisfy a sceptic. What is so important about reconciliation? Why think that it is more important than the deterrence or retribution that would come with punishment? In the following reading from Desmond Tutu, he appeals to values salient in the African tradition to answer these questions.

| **PRIMARY TEXTS** | **Text 3  Desmond Tutu on *ubuntu*'s justification of restorative justice[16]** |
|---|---|
| | Desmond Tutu was Archbishop of the Anglican Church in South Africa, bestowed a Nobel Peace Prize in 1984 for his struggle against apartheid, and Chair of South Africa's Truth and Reconciliation Commission. |
| | Our country's negotiators rejected the two extremes and opted for a 'third way' [of dealing with apartheid-era political crimes–ed.], a compromise between the extreme of Nuremberg trials and blanket amnesty or national amnesia. And that third way was granting amnesty to individuals in exchange for a full disclosure relating to the crime for which amnesty was being sought. It was the carrot of |

---

13   Truth and Reconciliation Commission of South Africa 1998 *Truth and Reconciliation Commission of South Africa Report* (Vol. 1) at 12, 34.
14   United Nations Department of Public Information 2014 *The Justice and Reconciliation Process in Rwanda*.
15   For philosophically sophisticated accounts of reconciliation or related ideas informed by the African tradition, see Krog 2008 *South African Journal of Philosophy*; Ramose 2012 *Journal on African Philosophy*; and Metz 2015 *Theorizing Transitional Justice*.
16   Extracted from Tutu 1999 *No Future without Forgiveness*.

possible freedom in exchange for truth and the stick was, for those already in jail, the prospect of lengthy prison sentences and, for those still free, the probability of arrest and prosecution and imprisonment.

Was what the government intended doing through the Truth and Reconciliation Commission not going to encourage people to think that they could commit crimes knowing that they would get amnesty? Is it ever enough for perpetrators merely to apologize and be humiliated through public exposure? What about justice?

[U]ltimately this third way of amnesty was consistent with a central feature of the African *Weltanschauung*—what we know in our languages as *ubuntu*, in the Nguni group of languages, or *botho*, in the Sotho languages. What is it that constrained so many to choose to forgive rather than to demand retribution, to be so magnanimous and ready to forgive rather than wreak revenge?

*Ubuntu* ... speaks of the very essence of being human. When we want to give high praise to someone we say, '*Yu, u nobuntu*'; 'Hey, so-and-so has *ubuntu*.' Then you are generous, you are hospitable, you are friendly and caring and compassionate. You share what you have. It is to say, 'My humanity is caught up, is inextricably bound up, in yours.' We belong in a bundle of life. We say, 'A person is a person through other persons.' It is not, 'I think therefore I am.' It says rather: 'I am human because I belong. I participate, I share.' A person with *ubuntu* is open and available to others, affirming of others, does not feel threatened that others are able and good, for he or she has a proper self-assurance that comes from knowing that he or she belongs in a greater whole and is diminished when others are humiliated or diminished ...

Harmony, friendliness, community are great goods. Social harmony is for us the *summum bonum*—the greatest good. Anything that subverts, that undermines this sought-after good, is to be avoided like the plague. Anger, resentment, lust for revenge, even success through aggressive competitiveness, are corrosive of this good. To forgive is not just to be altruistic. It is the best form of self-interest. What dehumanizes you inexorably dehumanizes me ...

[P]erhaps justice fails to be done only if the concept we entertain of justice is retributive justice, whose chief goal is to be punitive, so that the wronged party is really the state, something impersonal, which has little consideration for the real victims and almost none for the perpetrator. We contend that there is another kind of justice, restorative justice, which was characteristic of traditional African jurisprudence. Here the central concern is not retribution or punishment. In the spirit of *ubuntu*, the central concern is the healing of breaches, the redressing of imbalances, the restoration of broken relationships, a seeking to rehabilitate both the victim and the perpetrator, who should be given the opportunity to be reintegrated into the community he has injured by his offense.

This is a far more personal approach, regarding the offense as something that has happened to persons and whose consequence is a rupture in relationships. Thus we would claim that justice, restorative justice, is being served when efforts are being made to work for healing, for forgiving, and for reconciliation.

**Questions**

1. In exchange for what did the Truth and Reconciliation Commission (TRC) grant amnesty from criminal and civil prosecution for apartheid-era political crimes? How might someone who also favours conditional amnesty argue that there should have been more conditions than that? What additionally should offenders have arguably done in order to be free from prosecution?
2. Try to sum up in your own words what Tutu means by *ubuntu*.
3. How does Tutu define 'restorative justice'? Why does he believe that it is more 'personal' than retributive justice?

## 10.3.2   Expounding Tutu's defence of reconciliation

Tutu makes two distinct arguments for the TRC's approach to apartheid-era political crimes.[17] One is that it purportedly follows from an *ubuntu* ethic characteristic of sub-Saharan peoples. The word 'ubuntu', and cognate terms such as 'botho' (Sotho-Tswana) and 'hunhu' (Shona), literally means humanness. In this sense, an individual can have more or less *ubuntu*, that is, can be more or less of a real human being, where the more, the better. Sometimes the word 'ubuntu' is used these days to describe a certain way of life common amongst traditional African peoples or a philosophy grounded on it. These senses of the term are derivative from the more basic, literal understanding of it as humanness; they indicate a lifestyle or worldview that is a function of a value system according to which one ought at bottom to strive to live a genuinely human way of life.

Implicit in much thought about *ubuntu* is the idea that there are human capacities that are both distinct from, and more valuable than, what else can be found in the animal, vegetable and mineral kingdoms. Specifically, human beings are capable of relating to others in a particular way that no other beings can, and when they exercise this capacity they exhibit *ubuntu*. When human beings fail to exercise this capacity, then a variety of indigenous African peoples would say of them that they are not living humanly, or are not a person, or, in serious cases, are even animals.[18]

Note that to say that someone is not being a genuine human or is a non-person is not to be taken literally, so that this individual is no longer a bearer of human rights. Instead, these are metaphorical points: the individual is not realising what is best about human nature, and so is not truly a human being in the way that a jalopy is 'not a *real* car'.[19] The phrase 'a person is a person' is, in part, a prescription to become a real person.

How does one become a real person? The rough answer is 'through other persons'. More explicitly, for Tutu what is special about human nature is our capacity for social harmony; we exhibit *ubuntu* to the extent that we are party to harmonious relationships with other people.

Tutu does not offer a precise and comprehensive definition of social harmony, but instead gives several examples of it.[20] On the one hand, he mentions generosity, hospitality

---

17   A third argument is more political, namely, that the TRC was necessary to avoid further bloodshed and to foster peace in South Africa. This kind of rationale is not as generalisable to societies that have already transitioned away from such conflict, where this chapter is concerned to address how to respond to 'everyday' crimes in them.

18   Nkulu-N'Sengha 2009 *Encyclopedia of African Religion*.

19   Gaie 2007 *The Concept of Botho and HIV/AIDS in Botswana* at 33. Recall a similar point from Chapter 3, that for some natural law theorists an unjust statute is not a *real* law.

20   This analysis of harmony in the African tradition draws on Metz 2014 *Encyclopedia of Quality of Life and Well-Being Research*. See also Mokgoro 1998 *Potchefstroom Electronic Law Journal* at 17, 22–23.

and compassion, which could be summed up as 'caring for others' quality of life'. On the other hand, he also refers to participating, being open to others and belonging, which one might call 'sharing a way of life' with others. The combination of sharing a way of life with others while caring for their quality of life is a good definition of friendship (or even a broad sense of 'love'). So, one way to understand Tutu's interpretation of *ubuntu* is to say that he believes we are more human insofar as we are friendly (or act in loving ways) towards others.

One might not be *better off* if one lived a genuinely human life, so construed, but one would seem to be a *better person* for doing so. That is, to exhibit *ubuntu* as Tutu interprets it does not necessarily mean that one will be *happy* in the sense of feel lots of pleasure or get much of what one wants (note that these are states that animals can also exhibit). That is not the sort of self-interest he has in mind. Instead, Tutu is suggesting that we live best when we develop our higher selves, that is, when we realise our social, moral nature.

If we ought above all to live harmoniously with others, then it appears that we should often strive to reconcile with those who have wronged us. An ethic of harmony does not necessarily entail pacifism.[21] After all, one is probably not valuing harmony properly if one refuses to use coercion when necessary to prevent criminals from doing serious harm to innocent people. However, if coercion of an offender were not necessary to protect innocents from harm, then it appears that an *ubuntu* ethic, as Tutu understands it, would forbid it. Such a principle well explains the aptness of conditional amnesty. Do not punish offenders if they are willing to confess their misdeeds and, presumably, are willing not to do them again (and perhaps are willing to compensate their victims).

It appears that the logic of this approach would apply not merely to countries undergoing major transitions from large-scale injustice and serious social conflict, but also to more everyday crimes. If a batterer confesses to his wrongful deed and makes it clear that he would not do it again, then, instead of punishing him, perhaps the state ought to give him a chance to make restitution to his victim.

Tutu's second argument for the TRC's approach is that seeking reconciliation, or what he calls 'restorative justice', is a more personal approach than seeking retributive justice. He argues that the 'backward-looking' focus of retributivism is inapt. It does not at all seek to do the offender any good, instead seeking merely to do him or her harm, which, in turn, also does little to benefit the victim. Tutu recommends an approach that instead seeks to repair the broken relationship between the offender and his or her victim, so that it is, in the ideal case, good for both persons.

Although this is 'forward-looking' reasoning, it is not a utilitarian justification of punishment. First, in appealing to the value of a certain kind of (harmonious) relationship, it differs from the utilitarian's focus on individual pleasure. Second, Tutu's suggestion is that, in many cases, seeking out such a relationship would mean refraining from punishing offenders, and instead seeking to rehabilitate them.

### 10.3.3   Evaluating Tutu's defence of reconciliation

Tutu presumes that reconciliation should often come instead of punishment, but a good question to pose is whether reconciliation might in fact be more likely only after punishment has been imposed. The idea here is not that justice should have been favoured over reconciliation, the common point that Tutu addresses in the extract above; the idea is instead the less frequent suggestion that reconciliation itself can often require the initial punishment of those who have done wrong. After wrongdoers have undergone some penance, then, and

---

21   See the reading by William Idowu in Chapter 3.

perhaps only then, would many victims be inclined to move on, to accept reconciliation, and perhaps even to forgive in the way Tutu recommends. Something like this view appears to have been held by many victims who testified at the TRC.[22]

The more frequent criticism of Tutu's position is that punishment is required for reasons of retribution, even if not for those of reconciliation. In the context of the TRC, Hampton would point out that the degrading treatment by human rights violators has not been countered. The message that offenders are worth more than victims objectionably still stands since offenders have not been punitively humbled.

Tutu offers one way to respond to the retributivist: invoke an *ubuntu* ethic that is *prima facie* attractive and entails the rejection of retribution. *Ubuntu* requires creating, sustaining and enriching harmonious relationships and hence seeking the good of those party to them, whereas retributivism believes that inflicting harm is right in itself, regardless of future outcomes.

However, another interesting way for Tutu to respond would be to suggest, as one South African philosopher has,[23] that the TRC was in the circumstances the best way of expressing disapproval of offenders and of standing up for victims. The retributive alternative to the TRC would have been trials, but the TRC has contended that courts would not have done nearly as well at providing information about crimes that had been committed.[24] For one, there were not enough judicial resources available to prosecute on behalf of 21 000 victims and for the nearly 38 000 violations that they reported.[25] For another, offenders would have been inclined to protect themselves in trials by withholding the truth, if not lying.[26] Perhaps the best that could have been done, when it comes to Hampton's concern to recognise the dignity of victims, was to obtain comprehensive information about the wrongs that took place and then to make public denouncements of them.

Which is to be preferred from a backward-looking standpoint, the punishment of a few established to be guilty through trials, or the merely verbal denouncement of many established to be guilty through their confessions? Hampton would suggest that the latter is utterly insufficient for failing to 'negate the evidence of superiority provided by the crime'. Would she be correct, or are there ways of rebutting (at least to some degree) an offender's attitude of superiority without punishment?

## 10.4 Types of penalties: Is the death penalty justified?

Previous sections of this chapter have addressed whether the state should punish at all, why it should, and how much it should. In contrast, this section addresses the question of which kinds of penalties are permissible. In particular, it focuses on the 'ultimate' punishment, the death penalty. It does not consider which form of execution might be justifiable, say guillotine, electric chair or hanging, but instead whether execution of any sort is morally right, even on the assumption that an offender is guilty of an extremely serious crime such as torture and murder.

---

22   Hamber et al 2000 *Psychology in Society* at 30–32, 37–39.
23   Allais 2012 *Philosophy and Public Affairs*.
24   Truth and Reconciliation Commission of South Africa 1998 (Vol. 1) at 121–123.
25   Truth and Reconciliation Commission of South Africa 1998 (Vol. 1) at 170, 173.
26   An additional factor, more political, is that it is unlikely that the apartheid government would have relinquished power if criminal trials had been forthcoming.

## 10.4.1   Arguments for the death penalty

It might seem on the face of it that the two major rationales for punishment would straightaway justify the death penalty. After all, surely the death penalty deters crime and is a fitting punishment for certain, serious crimes, one might strongly suggest. However, upon considering utilitarian and retributive rationales for capital punishment more closely, it is not obvious what they entail.

Bentham addressed the death penalty in his work, and argued that utilitarianism in fact does not support it.[27] One thing he notes is that capital punishment is not necessary to incapacitate an offender, since the state could protect the public by keeping him locked up, just as it does with those who are criminally insane. He says that:

> it is never thought necessary that madmen should be put to death. They are not put to death: they are only kept in confinement; and that confinement is found effectually to answer the purpose.

When it comes to deterrence, Bentham contends that those who commit serious crimes are quite willing to risk their lives compared to more law-abiding citizens. In addition, Bentham draws on a commonly made empirical claim that certainty and not severity is what deters. He says that from a killer's perspective:

> [T]he infliction of [death] as a punishment is an event by no means certain. It is in itself uncertain; and the passion he is supposed to be influenced by, withdrawing his attention from the chances that are in favour of its happening, makes it look still more uncertain.

That is, what scares people from committing serious crimes is much more the chance of getting caught than the harshness of the penalty if they get caught. If that psychological claim is plausible, then, since the chance of getting caught and sentenced to death is quite low (particularly in states with poorly trained detectives and prosecutors), the death penalty will not deter much, if at all.

Bentham was writing in the eighteenth and early nineteenth centuries and was not relying on scientific studies of the effects of the death penalty. Since then, however, many scientists have tried to look carefully at the deterrent effects of capital punishment. A very large majority of criminologists, close to 90% of them, currently believe that there is no evidence that the death penalty deters homicide more than life imprisonment.[28]

What else might a utilitarian be able to say in favour of capital punishment? Are there ways in which it could make society better off, if it is not necessary either to incapacitate or to deter?

Turning to retribution, the death penalty is patently proportionate to the crime of (certain kinds of) murder. It therefore appears that the retributivist is committed to thinking that the death penalty is justified. That was certainly Kant's view, when he said that if someone has committed murder, then:

> he must *die*. Here there is no substitute that will satisfy justice. There is no *similarity* between life, however wretched it may be, and death, hence no likeness between the crime and the retribution unless death is judicially carried out upon the wrongdoer … This fitting of punishment to the crime … can occur only by a judge imposing the death sentence in accordance with the strict law of retribution.[29]

---

27   See the chapter titled 'Capital Punishment Examined' in Bentham 1830.
28   Radelet & Lacock 2009 *Journal of Criminal Law and Criminology.*
29   Kant 1797/1991 at 142.

However, there are retributivists who argue, *contra* Kant, that the death penalty is not justified. Consider, for example, what Hampton says about other forms of corporal punishment:

> [H]aving an eye gouged out, having acid thrown in one's face, losing fingers, being tortured – these are treatments one would refuse to consider permissible for animals, much less humans, and which may damage people so as to cause them (at least to appear) to lose value. So the retributivist who is committed to reasserting moral truth must beware that her way of reasserting it does not implicitly deny for the criminal what it seeks to establish for the victim ... [I]f the retributivist wants to establish the relative equality of victim and offender, he does not want to treat the offender in such a way that her value as a human being is denied.[30]

Hampton does not assert that punishments must be proportionate as a basic intuition; she instead argues that fitting penalties are apt because usually they are necessary in order to counter the degradation of the victim by the offender. This underlying rationale for proportionality – to recognise the *equal* dignity of the victim and the offender – gives Hampton reason to reject many forms of corporal punishment that would express the attitude or judgement that offenders have less value than they in fact do.

Now, an analogous claim might go for the death penalty. Perhaps it, too, is inherently degrading, and so unable to perform the retributive function that Hampton advocates. Something like this is the view of the South African Constitutional Court, often expressed through the ethical lens of *ubuntu*.

## 10.4.2 Arguments against the death penalty

| PRIMARY TEXTS | **Text 4 The Constitutional Court of South Africa on the death penalty**[31] |
|---|---|

From 1993 until 1996, when South Africa's final Constitution was ratified, the Constitutional Court adjudicated in the light of the interim Constitution.[32] The selection below is taken from a case decided in 1995, in which the Court unanimously ruled the death penalty (for crimes other than treason) to be inconsistent with (especially) the right to life in the interim Constitution and the reference to *ubuntu* in its preamble. Although mention of *ubuntu* does not appear in the final Constitution, the right to life remains explicit there.

Justice Pius Langa:

> The ethos of the new culture is expressed in the much-quoted provision on National Unity and Reconciliation which forms part of the Constitution ... [I]t suggests a change in mental attitude from vengeance to an appreciation of the need for understanding, from retaliation to reparation and from victimisation to *ubuntu*. The Constitution does not define this last-mentioned concept.

> The concept is of some relevance to the values we need to uphold. It is a culture which places some emphasis on communality and on the interdependence of the members of a community. It recognises a person's status as a human being, entitled to unconditional respect, dignity, value and acceptance from the members of the community such person happens to be part of.

---

30 Hampton 1988 at 136.
31 Extracted from Constitutional Court of South Africa 1995 *The State v T Makwanyane and M Mchunu*. Case No. CCT/3/94.
32 Constitution of the Republic of South Africa Act 200 of 1993.

An outstanding feature of *ubuntu* in a community sense is the value it puts on life and human dignity. The dominant theme of the culture is that the life of another person is at least as valuable as one's own. Respect for the dignity of every person is integral to this concept. During violent conflicts and times when violent crime is rife, distraught members of society decry the loss of *ubuntu*. Thus heinous crimes are the antithesis of *ubuntu*. Treatment that is cruel, inhuman or degrading is bereft of *ubuntu*.

Justice Tholakele Madala:

[T]he death penalty rejects the possibility of rehabilitation of the convicted persons, condemning them as 'no good', once and for all, and drafting them to the death row and the gallows. One must then ask whether such rejection of rehabilitation as a possibility accords with the concept of *ubuntu*.

One of the relative theories of punishment (the so-called purposive theories) is the reformative theory, which considers punishment to be a means to an end, and not an end in itself—that end being the reformation of the criminal as a person, so that the person may, at a certain stage, become a normal law-abiding and useful member of the community once again ... And in terms of this theory of punishment and as a necessary consequence of its application, the offender has to be imprisoned for a long period for the purpose of rehabilitation. By treatment and training the offender is rehabilitated, or, at the very least, ceases to be a danger to society. This, in my view, accords fully with the concept of *ubuntu*.

'The measure of a country's greatness is its ability to retain compassion in time of crisis.' This, in my view, also accords with *ubuntu*—and calls for a balancing of the interest of society against those of the individual, for the maintenance of law and order, but not for dehumanising and degrading the individual.

Justice Yvonne Mokgoro:

As this constitution evolves to overcome the culture of gross human rights violations of the past, jurisprudence in South Africa will simultaneously develop a culture of respect for and protection of basic human rights. Central to this commitment is the need to ... recognise the right to and protection of human dignity as a right concomitant to life itself and inherent in all human beings, so that South Africans may also appreciate that 'even the vilest criminal remains a human being'. In my view, life and dignity are like two sides of the same coin. The concept of *ubuntu* embodies them both.

Although it has been argued that the currently high level of crime in the country is indicative of the breakdown of the moral fabric of society, it has not been conclusively shown that the death penalty, which is an affront to these basic values, is the best available practical form of punishment to reconstruct that moral fabric. In the second place, even if the end was desirable, that would not justify the means. The death penalty violates the essential content of the right to life ... in that it extinguishes life itself. It instrumentalizes the offender for the objectives of state policy.

Once the life of a human being is taken in the deliberate and calculated fashion that characterises the described methods of execution the world over, it constitutes the ultimate cruelty with which any living creature could ever be treated ... The state is the representative of its people and in many ways sets the standard for moral values within society. If it sanctions by law punishment for killing by killing, it sanctions vengeance by law. If it does so with a view to deterring others, it dehumanises the person and objectifies him or her as a tool for crime control. This objectification through the calculated killing of a human being, to serve state objectives, strips the offender of his or her human dignity and dehumanises.

**Questions**

1. Does the logic of Justice Madala's view also forbid sentencing anyone to life imprisonment without the possibility of parole? Why or why not?

2. Justice Mokgoro does not argue that the death penalty does not deter; she instead argues that, supposing it were an effective deterrent, it would be immoral to use the death penalty for that purpose. It would treat the offender merely 'as a tool for crime control'. Does the logic of her argument apply to other harsh penalties such as life imprisonment or hard labour?

3. How might a defender of the death penalty invoke Hampton's theory of punishment in order to respond to Justice Mokgoro's charge that it is merely 'vengeance' to permit execution as a fitting sentence for killing?

The South African Constitutional Court Justices emphasise a dimension of *ubuntu* that Tutu does not. While Tutu focuses on harmonious relationship as being characteristic of *ubuntu*, Justices Langa and Mokgoro instead highlight the respect in which it prescribes respect for human dignity. These seem like very different ideas.

Upon reflection, however, these facets of *ubuntu* might be consistent with each other, and even mutually supportive. Consider: why should one seek to share a way of life with persons and to care for their quality of life? A promising answer is that other persons have a dignity that demands such harmonious engagement. It would arguably be degrading to be indifferent to persons by remaining isolated from them or failing to help them, and even worse, of course, to subordinate others and harm them.

There are two straightforward ways that the advocate of capital punishment can respond to the Court, by arguing either that it is not necessarily degrading or that, even if it is, it is on the whole morally justified. Some retributivists (though not quite Hampton) suggest that the death penalty is not degrading, but is instead a way of showing respect for the offender as a person who made the free but unfortunately wrongful choice to commit a serious crime. Receiving a fitting penalty is a way of treating a person as though he or she is responsible for his or her terrible behaviour, while receiving a less than fitting penalty would in contrast treat the person as though he or she is not really an agent.[33]

One problem with this rationale, however, is that few murderers would like to be shown such respect. Would you feel degraded if you were guilty of a serious crime but received a disproportionately light sentence?

The other way to respond is to grant that there would be something degrading about capital punishment but to maintain that there is some, even stronger moral reason to impose

---

33   See van den Haag 1986 *Harvard Law Review*.

it anyway. On this score, it is useful to think about other situations in which it seems justifiable to kill people. For instance, it appears permissible to shoot a would-be killer in self-defence. If you were innocent and an aggressor were coming at you with a knife, it would be justifiable for you to pull out your gun and shoot him or her, if truly necessary to save your life. Shooting this aggressor seems to be 'cruel' and might even count as 'objectifying him as a tool for crime control', but is permissible on the whole anyway. One might suggest that similar remarks apply to capital punishment.

The issue now is whether killing in self-defence is analogous to executing an offender. One salient difference is that the former is not 'calculated' in the way the latter is, which appears important for Justice Mokgoro. Another is that an aggressor is someone in the process of committing a crime, whereas the offender has already committed a crime, so that killing is not necessary to save an innocent life. One might suggest that executing an offender would deter other killings, but, as was discussed above, there is only poor evidence that this is true. Furthermore, there might be an important moral difference between killing an aggressor to prevent *him or her* from killing an innocent, on the one hand, and killing an offender to prevent *others* from killing an innocent, on the other. Justice Mokgoro might plausibly argue there is objectification in the latter case, but not the former.

## 10.5   Conclusion

Returning to the case of the jealous man who wrongfully attacked and hit his girlfriend, should the state punish him? Or should it rather seek to effect reconciliation between him and his girlfriend (and her friends family, and the broader society), at least if he has confessed and will not do it again? If it should punish him, is that merely because doing so would be most likely to effect such reconciliation? Or would his punishment be justified because it would benefit society in the long run or because imposing it would be essential to counter the way he degraded his victim? If some kind of punishment were justified, how much would be? Should a court impose whatever fits the nature of his crime, or should it instead look forward to consider what the effects of a given penalty would be when it comes to offender reform and general deterrence?

As with all the other big questions posed in this book, this chapter does not seek to arrive at a final answer to the ones about punishment explored here. Instead, its aim has been to acquaint the reader with some philosophical perspectives on the justification of punishment that have been salient in the Western and African traditions, to enable the reader to obtain a critical perspective on them, and ultimately to come to a decision for himself or herself.

### POINTS TO CONSIDER

1. Suppose the man discussed in this chapter had come to feel bad about how he had harmed his girlfriend. Should the state punish him? Should it depend on what the victim wants to happen to him? Why or why not?

2. The backward-looking theorist denies that the state should try to fight crime by using punishment. How else might it try to fight crime? Could it do so effectively without using punishment?

3. Justice Madala appears to think that *ubuntu* prescribes the ends of incapacitating offenders and seeking to reform them and doing so through punishment. Tutu, in contrast, believes that *ubuntu* often means not punishing offenders at all. Which has the better interpretation of *ubuntu*, in your view? Justify your answer.

# Chapter 11

# Concluding remarks about key philosophical distinctions

DAVID BILCHITZ, THADDEUS METZ AND ORITSEGBUBEMI OYOWE

The aims of this book have been to acquaint the reader with some central questions in jurisprudence, to sketch some of the ways they have been answered in both the Western and African philosophical traditions, and to offer some critical perspectives on these views. Central questions addressed have included the following:

- What is the nature of law?
- What is the relationship between law and morality/justice?
- How should judges interpret the law?
- Is it possible for judges to be objective when they adjudicate?
- What would constitute a just distribution of property and liberty in society?
- Who is owed duties of justice or moral treatment more generally?
- Who is obligated to advance justice, say, by aiding others?
- How should wrongful harm be compensated?
- Why and when should lawbreakers be punished?

While these questions are diverse, the kinds of answers to them that this book has critically explored have exhibited some similar patterns. We conclude by highlighting six recurrent philosophical themes.

One important distinction has been between *forward-looking* accounts of morality and justice, and more *backward-looking* ones. The former views evaluate a law or policy in terms of the extent to which it is likely to produce some desirable result in the future (and are sometimes called 'consequentialist'), whereas the latter do so instead with regard to whether it respects something about the past (one form of 'deontology').

For example, in the context of distributive justice (Chapters 6 and 7), utilitarians believe that a just way of distributing wealth is determined by whatever would bring about the greatest amount of happiness in the long run. This is a forward-looking approach. Libertarians, like Robert Nozick, however, contend (roughly) that a just distribution of wealth is one that is determined by the history of transactions that led individuals to have control over certain resources (for instance, whether they held goods as a result of agreements that people freely made, perhaps long ago). This is a more backward-looking approach. For another example, in the context of criminal justice (Chapter 10), utilitarians believe that a just punishment is whatever would incapacitate, reform, or deter, that is, whatever would tend to make society best off in the future; retributivists, on the other hand, instead contend that a just punishment is one that fits the nature of the crime that has already been committed.

Although it would not be inconsistent to be a utilitarian about one dimension of justice and not another (there could be some reason to adopt a different approach), a neat philosophical package is one that invokes the same basic approach for a variety of different issues. If the consequences of a certain distribution of wealth are important for appraising which laws are made, then they are probably going to play a role in evaluating how to enforce them when they are broken. Similarly, if facts about the past, for example which choices people have voluntarily made, are relevant to distributive justice, then they are likely to be relevant to criminal justice, too. Particularly influential political and legal philosophers, such as John Stuart Mill, Ronald Dworkin and Kwame Gyekye, have been those who have reflected on a variety of forms of justice and suggested that there are a small handful of basic principles that can ground all of them.

A second salient distinction in this book has been between *individualist* accounts of morality and justice, on the one hand, and *relational* ones, on the other. An individualist approach ascribes significance to what philosophers call 'intrinsic' properties, features that are internal to a person (or animal) and that make no essential reference to anyone or anything beyond it. In contrast, a relational approach ascribes significance to 'extrinsic' properties, features of a person (or animal) that do essentially involve interactions with something else.

Recall that these distinctions arose in discussions about who is owed just or otherwise moral treatment (Chapter 8). For example, the utilitarian believes that a being matters for its own sake if it is capable of experiencing pleasure or pain, and the Kantian contends that an individual matters only if it has the capacity for rationality or autonomy. These accounts are both similar in one sense; they attribute value because of a characteristic – whether it be sentience or rationality – possessed by individuals irrespective of their relationship to anything else. These views differ, as we saw, from perspectives – many of which are drawn from African moral theory – that hold that what matters about an individual is his or her relationships with other human beings or animals (or perhaps his or her capacity to relate to them). By these views, individual characteristics alone are not enough. It is something beyond (though including) each individual that confers value.

The individualist-relational distinction was also central to reflection on who owes what to others (Chapter 7). A purely individualist approach would hold that we owe the same duties to all those with certain characteristics such as sentience or rationality; a relational approach, on the other hand, differs in recognising that the relationships we have had with others affect our duties towards them. For instance, a relational view accounts well for the widely held intuition that one owes more to one's family, friends and neighbours, even if they are not suffering as much as others who are distant strangers.

Still other places where the individualist-relational distinction was prominent was in the contexts of compensatory justice (Chapter 9) and criminal justice (Chapter 10). One view, as we saw, was that the point of compensatory justice should be to return an individual to the unharmed state he or she would have been in, in the absence of wrongful interaction. It can be described as individualist in that it focuses on improving the position of an individual who was harmed. On the other hand, there is the view that the point of compensation is to repair the broken relationship between the harmed person and the wrongdoer. This approach can clearly be seen to be relational in nature. Similarly, the view that the point of criminal justice should be to improve the quality of life of individuals (perhaps by deterrent punishment) is individualist, whereas the view that its point should be to foster reconciliation between offenders and victims is relational.

A third recurrent distinction has been between *Western* and *African* philosophies. In the introductory chapter, we raised the question of what constitutes African philosophy. We saw Peter Bodunrin challenge the idea that geographical labels are to be attributed on the basis of the origins or ethnicities of the philosophers. Someone born and reared in Africa, he suggested, can do Western philosophy, while someone who has grown up in the West can do African philosophy. Instead, it seems more likely that what makes the philosophies merit different labels concerns which perspectives are salient in them, how they emerged from their particular contexts, and how they engage with issues in these respective contexts.

Having studied the material in this book, it is useful to think about the differences that have emerged between these philosophies. Such differences emerged quickly with the discussion towards the beginning of the book about the nature of law (Chapter 2). In particular, we looked critically at influential Western positivist theories of law that focus, roughly, on formal criteria for the identification of law, such as a rule of recognition. Whether these criteria apply to African societies has provided an opportunity to reflect on whether Western and African societies share the same concept of law.

Moreover, in this book we have often characterised Western normative approaches as individualist and African ones as relational (in particular, Chapters 3, 6, 7, 8, 9 and 10). The dominant moral and political philosophies from Europe and North America over the past 200 years have been variants of utilitarianism and Kantianism (including Rawlsianism), which consider the pleasure and autonomy of others, respectively, to be of key importance when interacting with them. That is not to say that there have been literally no relational approaches in the West: one could point to what is often called the 'ethic of care'[1] (emerging from feminist theory) or the communal ethic of the young Karl Marx,[2] for instance. However, the view that what merits moral attention is something internal to an individual, such as a person or an animal, has been much more influential in this tradition.

Conversely, when it comes to the African philosophical tradition, particularly southern African thought about *ubuntu*, what stands out is the emphasis on relationship, often characterised in terms of harmony, community, cohesion or reconciliation. Again, that is not to say that there are no strains of individualism amongst philosophers from Africa; on this score one could point to the view that what matters morally about an individual is his or her degree of life-force, an imperceptible energy that has come from God. However, even philosophers who believe that vitality is of basic importance contend that harmonious or communal relationships are essential for cultivating it.[3]

A fourth major distinction running through various chapters is between *dignity* and *welfare*. Welfarists believe that what demands moral attention from an agent is his or her ability to influence people's (and animals') quality of life for better or worse. The thought is that individuals have important interests that they care about and that state officials ought to satisfy. In contrast, dignitarians contend that an agent instead should, at bottom, treat people with respect, which might not involve making them live better lives. What instead matters is the fact that a being is alive (consider the view that life is sacred) or the capacity for autonomy, where the way to show respect is to protect and honour the individual, not to give the individual pleasure and remove his or her pain.

This contrast was important in discussions of distributive justice (Chapter 6). Utilitarians are of course welfarists. They believe that just allocations of liberty and property are whatever would produce happiness and reduce misery in the long run. In contrast, John Rawls is plausibly viewed as a dignitarian. He believes that the state should allocate social primary goods, that is, generally useful resources that people can use to make a wide array of choices

1   For example, Noddings 1984 *Caring: A Feminine Approach to Ethics and Moral Education.*
2   For example, Marx 1844 *Comments on James Mill.*
3   For example, Bujo 1997 *The Ethical Dimension of Community*; Magesa 1997 *African Religion: The Moral Traditions of Abundant Life.*

for themselves. Such an approach is a way of showing respect for people's autonomy, letting them make their own decisions regardless of whether the state believes they are good ones or not.

The distinction between welfare and dignity also featured in the discussion of who can have rights (Chapter 8). There, it was considered whether animals might deserve moral treatment for their own sake either because they are capable of suffering, as per utilitarianism, or because they have a dignity in virtue of various capabilities characteristic of their species, Martha Nussbaum's approach.

Criminal justice is yet another debate where the contrast between welfare and dignity was important (Chapter 10). Recall that several South African Constitutional Court Justices have appealed to the value of human dignity to argue that the death penalty is degrading; on the other hand, some defend the death penalty by contending that it would deter serious crimes and thereby make society better off.

A fifth philosophical distinction that has featured in this book is between *subjectivity* and *objectivity,* particularly as it concerns moral thought. Recall that a subjective approach is one according to which certain truths are dependent on the mind, where an objective one is the denial of that. An objectivist holds that there are truths about morality that are independent of what any human beings happen to believe about it; it also usually goes together with the idea that at least some people know some of these truths.

This distinction first appeared in reflection on the essence of law (Chapter 3), with the natural law theorist contending that law is necessarily constituted by objective justice, by norms that are in fact just, and the positivist denying such an essential connection. The distinction reappeared when discussing how judges should interpret the law (Chapters 4 and 5). Some major theorists argue that judges need to adopt objective methods to interpreting the law, which might focus on either the 'core' meaning of a statute (as per HLA Hart) or determining the purpose thereof. Similarly, Ronald Dworkin believes that we cannot help but think that justice is not whatever a group happens to believe it to be and that judges must try to do what is right, objectively speaking. In contrast, many postmodernists, as you may recall, contend that all interpretation is subjective, so that there is no universally correct answer as to what is just and unjust. Judges, therefore, unavoidably bring their subjective experience and values to bear in interpreting the law.

Finally, a sixth major philosophical theme of *Jurisprudence in an African Context* has been between *theoretical* or general approaches to law and justice, on the one hand, and ones that are *particularist,* on the other. A large majority of the book has expounded and evaluated theories of law and of justice, that is, comprehensive accounts of how to understand law, how to distribute resources, how to punish infractions, and so on. However, there have been occasions when this sort of philosophical method has been questioned.

For example, when discussing the nature of law (Chapter 3), the possibility was raised that there is no essence to law, that there are no core features universally shared by all legal systems, and that the only way to understand law is in terms of the varying ways it has been manifested in different societies. This possibility, that each society has its own notion of law, was foreshadowed when we highlighted the view – derived in large part from African thought – that law necessarily includes the received customs of a particular people (Chapter 2). Similarly, when considering how to interpret law (Chapter 5), it was noted that postmodernists, and feminists influenced by them, tend to eschew the search for generally applicable conceptions of what would be just, instead maintaining that any justifiable beliefs about justice are going to be restricted to specific contexts such as, say, South African society or perhaps even something more narrow.

We hope that readers, having arrived at the end of the book, have come to appreciate some of the benefits of jurisprudence that we suggested in the introductory chapter. We hope that readers are now able to approach law better – whether it be in practice or in other parts of the legal profession such as the judiciary or academia – in the light of what they have learned from philosophical reflection, and that the issues covered in this book will continue to be a source of contemplation throughout the readers' legal careers. We also hope that perhaps readers will have found themselves appreciating intellectual enquiry into the nature of law and justice for its own sake.

# Bibliography

## Books

Appiah, KA. 1992. *In My Father's House: Africa in the Philosophy of Culture*. New York: Oxford University Press.

Austin, J. 1790-1859. *The Province of Jurisprudence Determined: Being the First Part of a Series of Lectures on Jurisprudence or the Philosophy of Positive Law*, 2nd edition. London: John Murray.

Bell, D. 1992. *Faces at the Bottom of the Well: The Permanence of Racism*. New York: Basic Books.

Beyleveld, D & Brownsword, R. 1986. *Law as a Moral Judgement*. London: Sweet & Maxwell.

Biko, S. 2005. *I Write What I Like*. Johannesburg: Picador Africa.

Bilchitz, D. 2017. Corporate Obligations and a Treaty on Business and Human Rights: A Constitutional Law Model? In Deva, S & Bilchitz, D (Eds). *Business and Human Rights: Context and Contours*. Cambridge: Cambridge University Press.

Bix, B. 1996. Natural Law Theory. In Patterson, D (Ed). *A Companion to Philosophy of Law and Legal Theory*, 2nd edition. Malden, MA: Blackwell Publishing Ltd.

Blackstone, W. 1765. *Commentaries on the Law of England*. Repr. Chicago: The University of Chicago Press, 1979.

Bujo, B. 1997. *The Ethical Dimension of Community*. Translated by Nganda, CN. Nairobi: Paulines Publications.

Callicott, JB. 1987. The Conceptual Foundations of the Land Ethic. In Pojman, LP & Pojman, P (Eds). 2008. *Environmental Ethics: Readings in Theory and Application*. Belmont, CA: Wadsworth Cengage.

Cohen, GA. 1995. *Self-ownership, Freedom and Equality*. Cambridge: Cambridge University Press.

Collins, RO & McDonald Burns, J. 2007. *A History of Sub-Saharan Africa*. Cambridge: Cambridge University Press.

Connell, R. 2007. *Southern Theory: The Global Dynamics of Knowledge in Social Science*. Sydney, Australia: Allen and Unwin.

Cornell, D & Muvangua, N (Eds). 2012. *Ubuntu and the Law*. New York: Fordham University Press.

Cornell, D. 1991. *Beyond Accommodation: Ethical Feminism, Deconstruction and the Law*. New York: Routledge.

Crenshaw, KW, Gotanda, N, Peller, G & Thomas, K (Eds). 1995. *Critical Race Theory: The Key Writings that Formed the Movement*. New York: The New Press.

Cross, M & Ndofirepi, A (Eds). 2017. *Knowledge and Change in African Universities*, Volume 2. Rotterdam: Sense Publishers.

Davis, M. 1992. *To Make the Punishment Fit the Crime*. Boulder, CO: Westview Press.

Derrida, J. 2002. Force of Law; The 'Mystical Foundation of Authority'. Translated by Quaintance, M. In *Acts of Religion*, Anidjar, G (Ed). New York: Routledge.

Doron, I (Ed). 2008. *Theories on Law and Ageing: The Jurisprudence of Elder Law*. Dordrecht: Springer.

Dworkin, R. 1977. *Taking Rights Seriously*. London: Duckworth.

Dworkin, R. 1986. *Law's Empire*. Cambridge, MA: Belknap Press.

Dworkin, R. 2011. *Justice for Hedgehogs*. Cambridge, MA: Harvard University Press.

Dzobo, NR. 1992. Values in a Changing Society: Man, Ancestors, and God. In Wiredu, K & Gyekye, K (Eds). *Person and Community: Ghanaian Philosophical Studies*, Volume 1. Washington, DC: Council for Research in Values and Philosophy.

Elias, TO. 1956. *The Nature of African Customary Law*. Manchester: Manchester University Press.

Finnis, J. 2011. *Natural Law and Natural Rights*, 2nd edition. Oxford: Oxford University Press.

Foucault, M. 1977. *Discipline and Punish: The Birth of the Prison*. Translated by Sheridan, A. London: Allen Lane.

Frank, J. 1930. *Law and the Modern Mind*. New York: Tudor Publishing.

Friedman, M. 1970. The Social Responsibility of Business Is to Increase Its Profits. In Beauchamp, TL, Bowie, NE, Gordon, D & Pearson, A (Eds). 2009. *Ethical Theory and Business*, 8th edition. London: Prentice Hall.

Fuller, LL. 1969. *The Morality of Law*, revised edition. New Haven, CT: Yale University Press.

Gaie, J. 2007. The Setswana Concept of Botho: Unpacking the Metaphysical and Moral Aspects. In Gaie, J & Mmolai, S (Eds). *The Concept of Botho and HIV/AIDS in Botswana*. Eldoret, Kenya: Zapf Chancery.

Gbadegesin, S. 1991. *African Philosophy: Traditional Yoruba Philosophy and Contemporary African Realities*. New York: Peter Lang.

George, RP. 1999. *In Defense of Natural Law*. New York: Oxford University Press.

Gewirth, A. 1978. *Reason and Morality*. Chicago: University of Chicago Press.

Gilligan, C. 1982. *In a Different Voice: Psychological Theory and Women's Development*. Cambridge, MA: Harvard University Press

Gray, JC. 1921. *The Nature and Sources of the Law*, 2nd edition. New York: Macmillan.

Gyekye, K. 1997. *Tradition and Modernity: Philosophical Reflections on the African Experience*. New York: Oxford University Press.

Hall, R & Ntsebeza, L. 2007. Introduction. In Ntsebeza, L & Hall, R (Eds). *The Land Question in South Africa: The Challenge of Transformation and Redistribution*. Cape Town: HSRC Press.

Hall, R. 2007. Transforming Rural South Africa? Taking Stock of Land Reform. In Ntsebeza, L & Hall, R (Eds). *The Land Question in South Africa: The Challenge of Transformation and Redistribution*. Cape Town: HSRC Press.

Hampton, J. 1988. The Retributive Idea. In Murphy, J & Hampton, J (Eds). *Forgiveness and Mercy*. New York: Cambridge University Press.

Hart, HLA. 1994. *The Concept of Law*, 2nd edition, with postscript by Raz, J & Bulloch, P (Eds). Oxford: Oxford University Press.

Hawthorn, G (Ed). 1987. *The Standard of Living*. Cambridge: Cambridge University Press.

Higgs, P, Vakalisa, CG, Mda, TV & Assie-Lumumba, NT (Eds). 2000. *African Voices in Education*. Lansdowne: Juta.

Kant, I. 1785. *Groundwork for the Metaphysics of Morals*. Translated by Wood, A. New Haven, CT: Yale University Press, 2002.

Kant, I. 1797. *The Metaphysics of Morals*. Translated by Gregor, M. New York: Cambridge University Press, 1991.

Kant, I. 1963. *Lectures on Ethics*. Translated by Infield, L. Indianapolis: Hackett Publishing.

Kant, I. 1996. *Immanuel Kant: Practical Philosophy*. Translated by Gregor, MJ. Cambridge: Cambridge University Press.

Kymlicka, W & Donaldson, S. 2011. *Zoopolis: A Political Theory of Animal Rights*. Oxford: Oxford University Press.

Leckey, R & Brooks, K (Eds). 2010. *Queer Theory: Law, Culture, Empire*. New York: Routledge.

Leiter, B. 2007. *Naturalizing Jurisprudence: Essays on American Legal Realism and Naturalism in Legal Philosophy*. Oxford: Oxford University Press.

Llewellyn, K. 1930. *The Bramble Bush: On Our Law and Its Study*. New York: Oceana Publications.

Lyotard, J-F. 1984. *The Postmodern Condition: A Report on Knowledge*. Translated by Bennington, G and Massumi, B. Manchester: Manchester University Press.

Leopold, A. 1977. *A Sand County Almanac: And Sketches Here and There*. Oxford: Oxford University Press.

Lyons, D. 1984. Rights, Welfare and Mill's Moral Theory. In Waldron, J (Ed). *Theories of Rights*. Oxford: Oxford University Press.

MacKinnon, CA. 1987. *Feminism Unmodified: Discourses on Life and Law*. Cambridge, MA: Harvard University Press.

MacKinnon, C. 1989. *Toward a Feminist Theory of the State*. Cambridge, MA: Harvard University Press.

Magesa, L. 1997. *African Religion: The Moral Traditions of Abundant Life*. Maryknoll, NY: Orbis Books.

Marais, H. 2011. *South Africa Pushed to the Limit: The Political Economy of Change.* Claremont: UCT Press.

Mbiti, JS. 1969. *African Religions and Philosophy.* London: Heinemann.

Menkiti, I. 1984. Person and Community in African Traditional Thought. In Wright, RA (Ed). *African Philosophy: An Introduction.* Washington, DC: University Press of America.

Metz, T. 2004. Legal Punishment. In Roederer, C & Moellendorf, D (Eds). *Jurisprudence.* Lansdowne: Juta and Company Ltd.

Metz, T. 2015. A Theory of National Reconciliation: Some Insights from Africa. In Corradetti, C, Eisikovits, N & Rotondi, J (Eds). *Theorizing Transitional Justice.* Surrey: Ashgate.

Metz, T. 2017. Africanising Institutional Culture. In Cross, M & Ndofirepi, A (Eds). *Knowledge and Change in African Universities*, Volume 2. Rotterdam: Sense Publishers.

Mignolo, W. 2011. *The Darker Side of Western Modernity: Global Futures, Decolonial Options.* Durham: Duke University Press.

Mill, JS. 2001. *Utilitarianism.* Indianapolis: Hackett Publishing Company.

Miller, D. 2005. Distributing Responsibilities. In Kuper, A (Ed). *Global Responsibilities: Who Must Deliver on Human Rights?* London: Routledge.

Montague, P. 1995. *Punishment as Societal-Defense.* Lanham, MD: Rowman & Littlefield.

Moore, M. 1997. *Placing Blame: A Theory of the Criminal Law.* Oxford: Oxford University Press.

Murove, MF (Ed). *African Ethics: An Anthology of Comparative and Applied Ethics.* Scottsville: University of Kwazulu-Natal Press.

Murphy, J. 1992. *Retribution Reconsidered.* Dordrecht: Kluwer Academic Publishers.

Murphy, M. 2009. *Natural Law in Jurisprudence and Politics.* New York: Cambridge University Press.

Nnaemeka, O (Ed). 1998. *Sisterhood, Feminisms, and Power: From Africa to the Diaspora.* Trenton, NJ: Africa World.

Noddings, N. 1984. *Caring: A Feminine Approach to Ethics and Moral Education.* Berkeley, CA: University of California Press.

Nozick, R. 1974. *Anarchy, State and Utopia.* Oxford: Blackwell.

Ntsebeza, L. 2007. Land Redistribution in South Africa: The Property Clause Revisited. In Ntsebeza, L & Hall, R (Eds). *The Land Question in South Africa: The Challenge of Transformation and Redistribution.* Cape Town: HSRC Press.

Nyerere, JK. 1968. *Ujamaa: Essays on Socialism.* Dar es Salaam: Oxford University Press.

Nussbaum, MC. 2006. *Frontiers of Justice: Disability, Nationality Species Membership.* Cambridge, MA: Belknap Press.

Odera Oruka, H. 1997. *Practical Philosophy.* Nairobi: East African Educational Publishers.

Odora Hoppers, CA. 2000. African Voices in Education: Retrieving the Past, Engaging the Present and Shaping the Future. In Higgs, P, Vakalisa, CG, Mda, TV & Assie-Lumumba, NT (Eds). *African Voices in Education.* Lansdowne: Juta.

O'Neill, O. 1996. *Towards Justice and Virtue: A Constructive Account of Practical Reasoning.* Cambridge: Cambridge University Press.

Pojman, LP & Pojman, P (Eds). 2008. *Environmental Ethics: Readings in Theory and Application.* Belmont, CA: Wadsworth Cengage.

Posner, R. 1990. *The Problems of Jurisprudence.* Cambridge, MA: Harvard University Press.

Pothier, D & Devlin, R (Eds). 2006. *Critical Disability Theory: Essays in Philosophy, Politics, Policy, and Law.* Vancouver: UBC Press.

Rachels, J. 2003. *The Elements of Moral Philosophy*, 4th edition. New York: McGraw-Hill.

Ramose, MB. 1999. *African Philosophy through Ubuntu.* Harare: Mond Books.

Ramose, MB. 2003. The Ethics of *Ubuntu.* In Coetzee, PH & Roux, APJ (Eds). *The African Philosophy Reader: A Text with Readings.* New York: Routledge.

Ramose, MB. 2009. Ecology through *Ubuntu*. In Murove, MF (Ed). *African Ethics: An Anthology of Comparative and Applied Ethics*. Scottsville: University of Kwazulu-Natal Press.

Rawls, J. 1999. *A Theory of Justice,* revised edition. Cambridge, MA: Belknap Press.

Rawls, J & Kelly, E (Eds). 2001. *Justice as Fairness: A Restatement*. Cambridge, MA: Belknap Press.

Raz, J. 2004. Can There Be a Theory of Law? In Golding, MP & Edmundson, WA (Eds). *The Blackwell Guide to the Philosophy of Law and Legal Theory*. Malden, MA: Blackwell.

Regan, T. 1983. *The Case for Animal Rights*. Berkeley: University of California Press.

Rhode, DL. 1989. *Justice and Gender*. Cambridge, MA: Harvard University Press.

Sen, A. 1992. *Inequality Re-Examined*. Cambridge, MA: Harvard University Press.

Sen, A. 2010. *The Idea of Justice*. London: Penguin Books.

Singer, P. 1975. *Animal Liberation: A New Ethics for Our Treatment of Animals*. New York: Harper Collins.

Singer, P. 1995. *Animal Liberation*, 2nd edition. London: Pimlico.

Singer, P. 2004. Ethics beyond Species and beyond Instincts: A Response to Richard Posner. In Sunstein, C & Nussbaum, M (Eds). *Animal Rights: Current Debates and New Directions*. Oxford: Oxford University Press.

Smart, JJC & Williams, B. 1973. *Utilitarianism: For and Against*. Cambridge: Cambridge University Press.

Strauss, L & Cropsey, J (Eds). 1987. *History of Political Philosophy*, 3rd edition. Chicago: The University of Chicago Press.

Sunstein, CR & Nussbaum, M (Eds). 2004. *Animal Rights: Current Debates and New Directions*. Oxford: Oxford University Press.

Taylor, P. 1981. Biocentric Egalitarianism. In Pojman, LP & Pojman, P (Eds). 2008. *Environmental Ethics: Readings in Theory and Application*. Belmont, CA: Wadsworth Cengage.

Towa, Marcien. 1971. *Essai sur la problematique philosphique dans l'Afrique actuelle*. Yaounde: CLE.

Tutu, D. 1999. *No Future without Forgiveness*. New York: Random House.

Unger, RM. 1986. *The Critical Legal Studies Movement*. Cambridge, MA: Harvard University Press.

Von Hirsch, A. 1987. *Past or Future Crimes: Deservedness and Dangerousness in the Sentencing of Criminals*. New Brunswick, NJ: Rutgers University Press.

Waldron, J (Ed). 1984. *Theories of Rights*. Oxford: Oxford University Press.

Wamala, E. 2004. Government by Consensus: An Analysis of a Traditional Form of Democracy. In Wiredu, K (Ed). *A Companion to African Philosophy*. Malden, MA: Blackwell Publishing Ltd.

Wettstein, F. 2009. *Multinational Corporations and Global Justice*. Stanford: Stanford University Press.

Williams, B. 1987. Interests and Capabilities. In Hawthorn, G (Ed). *The Standard of Living*. Cambridge: Cambridge University Press.

Williams, P. 1992. *The Alchemy of Race and Rights*. Cambridge, MA: Harvard University Press.

Wiredu, K. 1997. Democracy and Consensus in African Traditional Politics: A Plea for a Non-Party Polity. In Eze, EC (Ed). *Postcolonial African Philosophy: A Critical Reader*. Cambridge, MA: Blackwell Publishers.

Wiredu, Kwasi. 1980. *Philosophy and an African Culture*. Cambridge: Cambridge University Press.

Wiredu, Kwasi. 1996. *Cultural Universals and Particulars: An African Perspective*. Bloomington: Indiana University Press.

Wittgenstein, L. 1953. *Philosophical Investigations*. Translated by Anscombe, GEM. Oxford: Basil Blackwell.

Wolff, J. 1991. *Robert Nozick: Property, Justice and the Minimal State*. Stanford: Stanford University Press.

Wright, RA (Ed). 1984. *African Philosophy: An Introduction*, 3rd edition. Lanham: University Press of America.

## Encyclopedias

Metz, T. 2014. *Ubuntu*: The Good Life. In Michalos, A (Ed). *Encyclopedia of Quality of Life and Well-Being Research*. Dordrecht: Springer.

Nkulu-N'Sengha, M. 2009. *Bumuntu*. In Asante, M & Mazama, A (Eds). *Encyclopedia of African Religion*. Los Angeles: Sage.

## Journal articles

Akintayo, A. 2012. The Pliability of Legal Texts under a Transformative Constitution in Perspective. *Southern African Public Law* 27(2):639.

Allais, L. 2012. Restorative Justice, Retributive Justice, and the South African Truth and Reconciliation Commission. *Philosophy and Public Affairs* 39:331.

Bell, D. 1995. Who's Afraid of Critical Race Theory? *University of Illinois Law Review* 39(4):893.

Bilchitz, D. 2007. Book Review: Understanding Jurisprudence. *South African Law Journal* 124(4):900.

Bilchitz, D. 2009. Moving beyond Arbitrariness: The Legal Personhood and Dignity of Non-Human Animals. *South African Journal on Human Rights* 25(1):38.

Bilchitz, D. 2010. Do Corporations Have Positive Fundamental Rights Obligations? *Theoria: A Journal of Social and Political Theory* 57(125):1.

Bilchitz, D. 2012. When Is Animal Suffering Necessary? *Southern African Public Law* 27(1):3.

Bodunrin, PO. 1981. The Question of African Philosophy. *Philosophy* 56(216):161.

Bonilla, D. 2013. Legal Clinics in the Global North and South: Between Equality and Subordination – an Essay. *Yale Human Rights and Development Law Journal* 16(2):1.

Brink, D. 1988. Legal Theory, Legal Interpretation, and Judicial Review. *Philosophy and Public Affairs* 17(2):105.

Cahn, NR. 1991–1992. Looseness of Legal Language: The Reasonable Woman Standard in Theory and in Practice. *Cornell Law Review* 77:1398.

Chibvongodze, D. 2016. *Ubuntu* is Not Only about the Human! An Analysis of the Role of African Philosophy and Ethics in Environment Management. *Journal of Human Ecology* 57(2):157.

Cornell, D & Van Marle, K. 2005. Exploring *Ubuntu*: Tentative Reflections. *African Human Rights Law Journal* 5(2):195.

Davis, D. 1996. The Twist of Language and the Two Fagans: Please Sir, May I have Some More Literalism. *South African Journal on Human Rights* 12:504.

Davis, D. 1997. Of Closure, the Death of Ideology and Academic Sand Castles: A Reply to Dr Fagan. *South African Journal on Human Rights* 13(1):178.

Davis, DM. 2012. How Many Positivist Legal Philosophers Can Be Made to Dance on the Head of a Pin: A Reply to Professor Fagan. *South African Law Journal* 129(1):59.

Delgado, R & Stefancic, J. 1993. Critical Race Theory: An Annotated Bibliography. *Virginia Law Review* 79(2):461.

Doron, I & Meenan, H. 2012. Time for Geriatric Jurisprudence. *Gerontology* 58(3):193.

Dryden, AJ. 2001. Overcoming the Inadequacies of Animal Cruelty Statutes and the Property-Based View of Animals. *Idaho Law Review* 38:177.

Dugard, J. 1986-1987. The Jurisprudential Foundation of the Apartheid Legal Order. *The Philosophical Forum* 18:115.

Dworkin, R. 2004. Keynote Address. *Acta Juridica* 1:1.

Fagan, A. 1995. In Defence of the Obvious – Ordinary Meaning and the Identification of Constitutional Rules. *South African Journal on Human Rights* 11(4):545.

Fagan, A. 2010. The Secondary Role of the Spirit, Purport and Objects of the Bill of Rights in the Common Law's Development. *South African Law Journal* 127(4):611.

Fagan, E. 1996. The Longest Erratum Note in History: *S v Mhlungu and Others*. *South African Journal on Human Rights* 12(1):79.

Fagan, E. 1997. The Ordinary Meaning of Language – A Response to Professor Davis. *South African Journal on Human Rights* 13(1):174.

Fish, S. 1982. Working on the Chain Gang: Interpretation in Law and Literature. *Texas Law Review* 60(3):551.

Freeman, AD. 1978. Legitimizing Racial Discrimination through Antidiscrimination Law: A Critical Review of Supreme Court Doctrine. *Minnesota Law Review* 62(6):1049.

Fuller, LL. 1958. Positivism and Fidelity to Law – A Reply to Professor Hart. *Harvard Law Review* 71(4):630.

Fullinwider, RK. 1975. Preferential Hiring and Compensation. *Social Theory and Practice* 3(3):307.

Goodin, RE. 2016. Duties of Charity, Duties of Justice. *Political Studies* 65(2):268.

Hamber, B, Nageng, D & O'Malley, G. 2000. 'Telling It Like It Is....' Understanding the Truth and Reconciliation Commission from the Perspective of Survivors. *Psychology in Society* 26:18.

Hart, HLA. 1958. Positivism and the Separation of Law and Morals. *Harvard Law Review* 71(4):593.

Hull, G. 2015. Affirmative Action and the Choice of Amends. *Philosophia* 43(1):113.

Husak, DN. 1992. Why Punish the Deserving? *Nous* 26(4):447.

Idowu, W. 2006. African Jurisprudence and the Reconciliation Theory of Law. *Cambrian Law Review*. 37:1.

Jobodwana, ZN. 2000. Customary Courts and Human Rights: Comparative African Perspectives. *Southern African Public Law* 15(1):27.

Kelsen, H. 1941. The Pure Theory of Law and Analytical Jurisprudence. *Harvard Law Review* 55(1):44.

Kennedy, D. 1982. Legal Education and the Reproduction of Hierarchy. *Journal of Legal Education* 32(4):591.

King Jr, ML. 1963. The Negro Is Your Brother. *The Atlantic Monthly* 212 (August):78.

Klare, KE. 1998. Legal Culture and Transformative Constitutionalism. *South African Journal on Human Rights* 14(1):146.

Kretzmann, N. 1988. Lex Iniusta Non Est Lex: Laws on Trial in Aquinas' Court of Conscience. *American Journal of Jurisprudence* 33:99.

Krog, A. 2008. 'This Thing Called Reconciliation....'; Forgiveness as Part of an Interconnectedness-towards-Wholeness. *South African Journal of Philosophy* 27(4):353.

Lacroix, CA. 1998. Another Weapon for Combatting Family Violence: Prevention of Animal Abuse. *Animal Law* 4:1.

Langa, P. 2006. Transformative Constitutionalism. *Stellenbosch Law Review* 17(3):351.

Lenta, P. 2001. Just Gaming? The Case for Postmodernism in South African Legal Theory. *South African Journal on Human Rights* 17(2):173.

Lockwood, R. 1999. Animal Cruelty and Violence against Humans: Making the Connection. *Animal Law* 5:81.

Madlingozi, T. 2008. The Constitutional Court, Court Watchers and the Commons: A Reply to Professor Michelman on Constitutional Dialogue 'Interpretive Charity' and the Citizenry as Sangomas. *Constitutional Court Review* 1:63, available at http://journals.co.za/content/conrev/1/1/EJC28129

Maphai, VT. 1989. Affirmative Action in South Africa – A Genuine Option? *Social Dynamics* 15(2):1.

Matolino, B. 2015. Universalism and African Philosophy. *South African Journal of Philosophy* 34(4):433.

Mawhinney, EB. 2015. Restoring Justice: Lessons from Truth and Reconciliation in South Africa and Rwanda. *Journal of Public Law and Policy* 36(2):21.

Meekosha, H. 2011. Decolonising Disability: Thinking and Acting Globally. *Disability and Society* 26(6):667.

Metz, T. 2007. Towards an African Moral Theory. *The Journal of Political Philosophy* 15(3):321.

Metz, T. 2010. For the Sake of the Friendship: Relationality and Relationship as Grounds of Beneficence. *Theoria* 57(125):54.

Metz, T. 2011. *Ubuntu* as a Moral Theory and Human Rights in South Africa. *African Human Rights Law Journal* 11(2):532.

Mnyongani, F. 2012. The Status of Animals in African Cosmology: A Non-legal Perspective. *Southern African Public Law* 27(1):88–102.

Modiri, JM. 2012. Towards a '(Post-)Apartheid' Critical Race Jurisprudence: Divining Our Racial Themes. *Southern African Public Law* 27(1):232.

Modiri, JM. 2013. Race as/and the Trace of the Ghost: Jurisprudential Escapism, Horizontal Anxiety and the Right to Be Racist in *BOE Trust Limited*. *Potchefstroom Electronic Law Journal* 16(5):582.

Moerane, MTK. 2003. The Meaning of Transformation of the Judiciary in the New South African Context. *South African Law Journal* 120(4):708.

Mokgoro, JY. 1998. *Ubuntu* and the Law in South Africa. *Potchefstroom Electronic Law Journal* 1(1):1.

Mokgoro, Y. 2010. Judicial Appointments. *Advocate* 23 (December):43.

Morris, H. 1968. Persons and Punishment. *The Monist* 52(4):475.

Morris, H. 1981. A Paternalistic Theory of Punishment. *American Philosophical Quarterly* 18(4):263.

Moseneke, D. 2002. The Fourth Bram Fischer Memorial Lecture: Transformative Adjudication. *South African Journal on Human Rights* 18(3):309.

Mureinik, E. 1994. A Bridge to Where: Introducing the Interim Bill of Rights. *South African Journal on Human Rights* 10(1):31.

Nussbaum, M. 2003. Capabilities as Fundamental Entitlements: Sen and Social Justice. *Feminist Economics* 92(2–3):33.

Nwakeze, PC. 1987. A Critique of Olufemi Taiwo's Criticism of 'Legal Positivism and African Legal Tradition'. *International Philosophical Quarterly* 27(1):101.

Odora Hoppers, C. 2001. Indigenous Knowledge Systems and Academic Institutions in South Africa. *Perspectives in Education* 19(1):73.

Okafor, FU. 1984. Legal Positivism and the African Legal Tradition. *International Philosophical Quarterly* 24(2):157.

Okafor, FU. 1988. A Philosophic Reflection on African Native Laws. *Journal of Value Inquiry* 22(1):39.

O'Neill, O. 2001. Agents of Justice. *Metaphilosophy* 32 (1/2):180.

Osha, S (Ed). 2006. African Feminisms. *Quest: An African Journal of Philosophy* 20(1–2):5.

Oyowe, OA. 2013. Individual and Community in Contemporary African Moral-Political Philosophy. *Philosophia Africana* 15(2):117.

Oyowe, OA. 2014. An African Conception of Human Rights? Comments on the Challenges of Relativism. *Human Rights Review* 15(3):329.

Pogge, TW. 2001. Priorities of Global Justice. *Metaphilosophy* 32(1–2):6.

Radelet, M & Lacock, T. 2009. Do Executions Lower Homicide Rates? The Views of Leading Criminologists. *Journal of Criminal Law and Criminology* 99(2):489.

Raghuram, P & Madge, C. 2006. Towards a Method for Postcolonial Development Geography? Possibilities and Challenges. *Singapore Journal of Tropical Geography* 27(3): 270.

Ramose, MB. 2001. An African Perspective on Justice and Race. *Polylog*, available at: https://them.polylog.org/3/frm-en.htm

Ramose, MB. 2012. Reconciliation and Reconfiliation in South Africa. *Journal on African Philosophy* 5:20.

Roux, T. 2009. Transformative Constitutionalism and the Best Interpretation of the South African Constitution: A Distinction Without a Difference. *Stellenbosch Law Review* 20(2):258.

Singer, P. 1972. Famine, Affluence, and Morality. *Philosophy and Public Affairs* 1(3):229.

Taiwo, O. 1985. Legal Positivism and the African Legal Tradition: A Reply. *International Philosophical Quarterly* 25(2):197.

Thomson, JJ. 1973. Preferential Hiring. *Philosophy and Public Affairs* 2(4):364.

Tushnet, M. 1984. Critical Legal Studies and Constitutional Law: An Essay in Deconstruction. *Stanford Law Review* 36(112):623.

Ulriksen, MS & Plagerson, S. 2014. Social Protection: Rethinking Rights and Duties. *World Development* 64:755.

Valdes, F. 1995. Afterword & Prologue: Queer Legal Theory. *California Law Review* 83(1):344.

Van den Haag, E. 1986. The Ultimate Punishment: A Defence. *Harvard Law Review* 99(7):1662.

Van Marle, K. 2003. 'The Capabilities Approach', 'The Imaginary Domain', and 'Asymmetrical Reciprocity': Feminist Perspectives on Equality and Justice. *Feminist Legal Studies* 11:255.

Walker, LEA. 1992. Battered Women Syndrome and Self-Defence. *Notre Dame Journal of Law, Ethics & Public Policy* 6(2):321.

West, R. 1988. Jurisprudence and Gender. *University of Chicago Law Review* 55(1):1.

Williams, JC. 1989. Deconstructing Gender. *Michigan Law Review* 87(4):797.

Wiredu, K. 2009. An Oral Philosophy of Personhood: Comments on Philosophy and Orality. *Research in African Literatures* 40:8.

## Reports

Fullinwider, RK. 2000. The Case for Reparations. *Report from the Institute for Philosophy and Public Policy* 20(2/3):1–8.

## Conferences

Hall, R. 2004. Restitution and the Politics of Land Reform: Stepping Outside the Box. Paper Presented at a Conference on *Ten Years of Democracy in Southern Africa*. Queens University, Kingston, 2–5 May.

## Internet sources

Africa Hunger and Poverty Facts, available at http://www.worldhunger.org/africa-hunger-and-poverty-facts/

ALL4WOMEN. 2014. Herceptin: Hopeful New Breast Cancer Treatment, available at https://www.all4women.co.za/176637/health/herceptin-hopeful-new-breast-cancer-treatment

Aristotle. 350 BCE. *Nicomachean Ethics*, available at http://classics.mit.edu/Aristotle/nicomachaen.html

Bentham, J. 1830. *The Rationale of Punishment*. London: Robert Heward, available at http://www.archive.org/stream/therationaleofpu00bentuoft/therationaleofpu00bentuoft_djvu.txt

Boddy-Evans, A. 2017. Apartheid Quotes – Bantu Education, available at https://www.thoughtco.com/apartheid-quotes-bantu-education-43436

BorgenProject. 2015. Poverty in Africa Facts, available at http://borgenproject.org/10-quick-facts-about-poverty-in-africa/

Coleman, M. (Ed). 1998. *A Crime against Humanity: Analysing the Repression of the Apartheid State*, available at http://v1.sahistory.org.za/pages/library-resources/onlinebooks/crime-humanity/crime-index.htm

Constitutional Court of South Africa. 1995. *The State v T Makwanyane and M Mchunu*. Case No. CCT/3/94, available at http://www.saflii.org/

Corbyn, Z. 2011. Hungry Judges Dispense Rough Justice. *Nature* 11 April, available at http://www.nature.com/news/2011/110411/full/news.2011.227.html

Gates, HL Jnr. 2014. How Many Slaves Landed in the US? (1 June), available at http://www.theroot.com/how-many-slaves-landed-in-the-us-1790873989

General Assembly of the United Nations. 1973. International Convention on the Suppression and Punishment of the Crime of Apartheid, available at https://treaties.un.org/doc/publication/unts/volume%201015/volume-1015-i-14861-english.pdf

Holmes Jr, OW. 1897. The Path of the Law. *Harvard Law Review* 10:457, available at http://www.gutenberg.org/files/2373/2373-h/2373-h.htm

Hosking, DL. 2008. Critical Disability Theory. Paper presented at the 4th Biennial Disability Studies Conference, Lancaster University, UK. 2–4 September, available at http://www.lancaster.ac.uk/fass/events/disabilityconference_archive/2008/papers/hosking2008.pdf

International Criminal Court. 1998. Rome Statute, available at http://legal.un.org/icc/statute/99_corr/cstatute.htm

Judicial Service Commission. 2010. Summary of the Criteria Used by the Judicial Service Commission when Considering Candidates for Judicial Appointments, *Politicsweb* 16 September, available at http://www.politicsweb.co.za/documents/new-guidelines-for-selection-judges--jsc

Mandela, N. 2006. *Ubuntu* told by Nelson Mandela, available at https://www.youtube.com/watch?v=HED4h00xPPA

Mariotti, M. 2009. Labor Markets during Apartheid in South Africa. *Working Papers in Economics & Econometrics*, No. 503, available at https://www.cbe.anu.edu.au/researchpapers/econ/wp503.pdf

Marx, K. 1843. *On the Jewish Question*, available at https://www.marxists.org/archive/marx/works/1844/jewish-question/

Marx, K. 1844. *Comments on James Mill*, available at https://www.marxists.org/archive/marx/works/1844/james-mill/

Mbeki, T. 1996. 'I Am an African', available at http://www.soweto.co.za/html/i_iamafrican.htm

Mill, JS. 1863. *Utilitarianism*, available at https://www.utilitarianism.com/mill5.htm

Mott, M. 2008. Wild Elephants Live Longer Than Their Zoo Counterparts. *National Geographic* (11 December), available at http://news.nationalgeographic.com/news/2008/12/081211-zoo-elephants.html

Oladosu, J. 2001. Choosing a Legal Theory on Moral Grounds: An African Case for Legal Positivism. *West Africa Review* 2(2), available at http://westafricareview.com

Promotion of National Unity and Reconciliation Act 34, 1995, available at http://www.justice.gov.za/legislation/acts/1995-034.pdf

*S v Makwanyane and Another* (CCT3/94) [1995] ZACC 3; 1995 (6) BCLR 665; 1995 (3) SA 391; [1996] 2 CHRLD 164; 1995 (2) SACR 1 (6 June 1995), available at http://www.saflii.org/za/cases/ZACC/1995/3.html

Truth and Reconciliation Commission of South Africa. 1998. *Truth and Reconciliation Commission of South Africa Report, Volumes 1-7*, available at http://www.justice.gov.za/trc/report/index.htm

United Nations Department of Public Information. 2014. *The Justice and Reconciliation Process in Rwanda*, available at http://www.un.org/en/preventgenocide/rwanda/about/bgjustice.shtml

United Nations. 1948. *The Universal Declaration on Human Rights*, available at http://www.un.org/en/universal-declaration-human-rights/

United States Institute of Peace. Truth Commission: Rwanda Law No. 03/99, available at https://www.usip.org/publications/1999/03/truth-commission-rwanda-99

Voyages. 2013. The Trans-Atlantic Slave Trade Database, available at http://www.slavevoyages.org/assessment/estimates

# Table of cases

# Table of legislation

# Index